Translation of

Orheyev
be-vinyana u-be-hurbara
[Orheyev Alive and Destroyed]

Memorial Book of the Jewish Community of Orhei, Moldova

Originally in Hebrew
Edited by Y. Spivak
Published in Tel Aviv, 1959

Published by JewishGen

An Affiliate of the Museum of Jewish
A Living Memorial to the Holocaust
New York

Orhevev be-vinyana u-be-hurbara

Orheyev Alive and Destroyed

Memorial Book of the Jewish Community of Orhei, Moldova

Copyright © 2012 by JewishGen, Inc.
All rights reserved.
First Printing: March 2012, Adar 5772
Second Printing: March 2019, Adar II 2019

Editors: Terry Lasky
Layout: Terry Lasky and Joel Alpert
Image Editor: Jan R. Fine
Cover Design: Jan R. Fine
Publicity: Sandra Hirschhorn

Published by JewishGen, Inc.
An Affiliate of the Museum of Jewish Heritage
A Living Memorial to the Holocaust
36 Battery Place, New York, NY 10280

"JewishGen, Inc. is not responsible for inaccuracies or omissions in the original work and makes no representations regarding the accuracy of this translation. Digital images of the original book's contents can be seen online at the New York Public Library Web site."

The mission of the JewishGen organization is to produce a translation of the original work and we cannot verify the accuracy of statements or alter facts cited.

Printed in the United States of America by Lightning Source, Inc.

Library of Congress Control Number (LCCN): 2012932383
ISBN: 978-0-9764759-6-5 (hard cover: 530 pages, alk. paper)

Cover photographs: Illustrations from the original Yiddish book

JewishGen and the Yizkor Books In Print Project

This book has been published by the **Yizkor Books in Print Project,** as part of the **Yizkor Book Project** of **JewishGen, Inc**.

JewishGen, Inc. is a non-profit organization founded in 1987 as a resource for Jewish genealogy. Its website [www.jewishgen.org] serves as an international clearinghouse and resource center to assist individuals who are researching the history of their Jewish families and the places where they lived. JewishGen provides databases, facilitates discussion groups, and coordinates projects relating to Jewish genealogy and the history of the Jewish people. In 2003, JewishGen became an affiliate of the **Museum of Jewish Heritage - A Living Memorial to the Holocaust** in New York.

The **JewishGen Yizkor Book Project** was organized to make more widely known the existence of Yizkor (Memorial) Books written by survivors and former residents of various Jewish communities throughout the world. Later, volunteers connected to the different destroyed communities began cooperating to have these books translated from the original language—usually Hebrew or Yiddish— into English, thus enabling a wider audience to have access to the valuable information contained within them. As each chapter of these books was translated, it was posted on the JewishGen website and made available to the general public.

The **Yizkor Books in Print Project** began in 2011 as an initiative to print and publish Yizkor Books that had been fully translated, so that hard copies would be available for purchase by the descendants of these communities and also by scholars, universities, synagogues, libraries, and museums.

These Yizkor books have been produced almost entirely through the volunteer effort of researchers from around the world, assisted by donations from private individuals. The books are printed and sold at near cost, so as to make them as affordable as possible. Our goal is to make this important genre of Jewish literature and history available in English in book form, so that people can have the personal histories of their ancestral towns on their bookshelves for themselves and for their children and grandchildren.

Lance Ackerfeld, Yizkor Book Project Manager

Joel Alpert, Yizkor Book in Print Project Coordinator

Title Page of Original Hebrew Edition

א ו ר ה י ו ב

בבנינה ובחורבנה

בעריכת

יצחק ספיבק   מרדכי רוטקוב   מרדכי פרנק

הוציא לאור ועד יוצאי אורהיוב

ציור השער ע"י יוחנן סימון

סיון תשי"ט   יוני 1959

"הדפוס החדש" בע"מ, תל-אביב

Translation of the Title Page of Original Hebrew Edition

Orheyev Alive and Destroyed

Edited by

Yitzchak Spivak
Mordechai Rotkov
Mordechai Frank

Published by the
Association of Orheyev Descendants

Sivan Tashyat   June 1959

"Hadpus Hahadash" Limited Tel-Aviv

Preface for the Translation

This book about Orgeyev evolved from my interest in finding out about my family's history in Europe.

In 1988 I began to research the maternal side of my family history. My grandmother had lived with me all of my life until she passed away in 1966. My mother had kept the few possessions of my grandmother – picture postcards sent over from her relatives in Russia between 1900 and 1930, which fascinated me. My two eldest aunts had actually been born in Russia – Orgeyev, Bessarabia to be exact. I didn't know how long my grandparents had lived there, but I knew that we still had relatives there in 1929 – from one of the postcards.

By about 2000 I had a figured out most of my family tree and had even contacted extended family members in Moldova, Romania and Israel. But, I still knew very little about the town of Orgeyev. Through my association with JewishGen, the main Internet web site dealing with Jewish genealogy, I learned that there was a Memorial (Yizkor) book about the town, written in a both Hebrew and Yiddish. I am not able to easily translate Hebrew, and do not know any Yiddish, but I am good enough to pick out words, phrases and names in Hebrew. I decided that I would translate the Table of Contents in the hope of finding the name of one of my relatives. Once I completed that task I realized that there were a very large number of pictures of groups of people with their names in the captions. So I began to translate the Table of Figures and the captions on all of the pictures – with the help of a few people that had agreed to help me.

After completing the translation of the Table of Contents, the Table of Figures and the Figure Captions, I realized just how much the stories in this book could tell me about life in Orgeyev and about what happened during the Holocaust. It no longer mattered to me whether or not any of the people in the book were my relatives because what happened to these people and what their lives were like had to be pretty much the same as my ancestors. I became possessed with finding out what this book had to tell me. I solicited volunteers and also organized a fundraising campaign to hire a professional translator. The rest is history as the entire book has now been translated and is now being published. I learned more from this experience and from the chapters of this book than I could have ever imagined. It brought the story of my ancestors to life, gave me even a greater appreciation of what it meant to be a Jew in Russia and what my ancestors went through in order to give me the life that I now have. My hope is that the readers of this book will also gain this appreciation of the lives of their ancestors from this town.

Terry Lasky, Orhei Yizkor Book Translation Project
Coordinator
January 28, 2012

Acknowledgements for the Translation

The translation of this Yizkor book was a labor of love for a small number of people but required the support of a much larger group to make it a reality.

The most important contributor, in the mind of the project coordinator, was Marsha Kayser. She donated an enormous amount of her time translating large sections of the book, including all of the Yiddish chapters. She also kept the project coordinator on the straight and narrow path by ensuring that his work was carefully checked and critiqued. Enough can not be said about her support of this project.

Boaz Nadler and Tamar Rachevsky Milner also donated a significant amount of time in translating portions of this book. In addition Rachel Weitz, Marsha Kayser's Yiddish teacher, supported and helped Marsha with all of the Yiddish translations.

The majority of the rest of the book was translated by Jerrold Landau – in fact he translated the majority of the book. Although he was paid for his services he charged much less than any other translator while delivering a superior product. If he had charged a much higher rate this book might not have been completed. I also have to acknowledge all of the people who contributed the money that was used to hire Jerrold. There are too many to name and some wish to be anonymous, but you all know who you are.

Finally, a lot of thanks go to the JewishGen staff that is often forgotten since they work behind the scenes. They obtained the necessary approvals, set up the donation mechanism and did all of the uploading of the final product.

All of this support left me with the easier tasks: coordinating the project, scanning and cropping of over 200 pictures, translating the picture captions, translating the table of contents, translating the table of figures, translating numerous listing of names throughout the book, constructing the surname index, validating the translation, insuring the standardization of the formatting and the names, and soliciting the contributions. This list looks very extensive but was small in comparison to some of the other contributions listed above.

Terry Lasky, Orhei Yizkor Book Translation Project Coordinator

TABLE OF CONTENTS IN THIS BOOK

Translated By Boaz Nadler, Marsha Kayser and Terry Lasky

Part IV - The Holocaust

Part V - In Summary

Chapter A1

Notes From the Project Coordinator

One of the more important aspects of a Yizkor book translation is to allow the readers to find information about their relatives. This requires that the names in the book are transliterated in such a way as to yield the names that readers are expecting. This is a fairly difficult task because of the way that the Hebrew names are specified and other anomalies within this book.

1) Vowels are not specified within the Hebrew portions of this book;

2) Many Hebrew consonants (e.g. feh/peh beit/veit, etc.) are not distinguishable from one another because the distinguishing characteristics are not specified;

3) The same person listed in the Table of Contents, in a chapter, in the List of Figures and in a Figure Caption will often have their surname spelled several different ways;

4) If five different people were to transliterate the same surname there would probably be at least four different spellings.

This project coordinator felt that it was important to establish some guidelines and transliteration methods that were, at least, consistent and explainable. The first decision was to determine what the "end product" of the transliteration should be. Should the names reflect the period and location, should they be "modernized", or should they be "westernized". The following thoughts yielded a final answer:

1) These people all lived under the Russian/Romanian influence and most of them died there;

2) Modernization of names would, at best, be very risky since there is nothing to indicate how names were modernized;

3) Westernization would be unfair to all of the people reading this book that are from Israel, South America and other countries besides North America;

Orheyev Alive and Destroyed

4) It is important in genealogy to understand family names as they changed over time.

It was, therefore, decided that the names should reflect the period and location in which these people lived. The consequence of this is that you will find Yosef not Joseph, Yitzchak not Isaac, Goldshteyn not Goldstein, Veitzman not Weitzman and other such differences. The methods used for transliteration were slightly different for Given names and Surnames, and are described below.

Given Names: In order to establish a consistent method it was decided that a published source (that had both the Hebrew and transliterated equivalent) should be used as a basis. Several sources were investigated and it was decided that "The Complete Dictionary of English and Hebrew First Names" by Alfred J. Kolatch (1984) best met the criteria previously discussed. It proved to be a good source since over 80% of the Hebrew spellings in this Yizkor book were found in Kolatch's book. The other 20% were generated by using the techniques that are discussed in the Surname discussion that follows.

Surnames: Surnames were much more difficult because there was no single source that would satisfy the needs. A transliteration table was generated after examining many sources and transliterated names. The table reflected differences if a Hebrew letter was at the beginning of a name, in the middle or at the end because it's location often had a major effect. There were always exceptions to every rule and there were in this situation. As indicated above, the same surname was often spelled several different ways and in these cases the most "complete" Hebrew spelling (e.g. that which specified the most complete set of letters) was used and the others were made to agree.

The following is the transliteration table that was used. The Hebrew letter is specified followed by the Latin characters used if it was at the beginning, in the middle or at the end of a name.

alef   a/e/o/u, a/e/o/u, a/e/o/u
beit(veit)   b, b, b/v
gimel   g, g, g
dalet(daleth)   d, d, d
heh   h, h, a/e (a if female, e if male)
vav   v, v/o/u, v/o/u
zayin   z, z, z

het	ch, ch, ch
tet	t, t, t
yod	y, i/y, i/y
kaf(khaf)	k, ch, k
lamed	l, l, l
mem	m, m, m
nun	n, n, n
samekh	s, s, s
ayin	a/e, a/e, a/e
peh(feh)	f/p, f/p, f/p
tzadi	z, tz, tz
qof(kof)	k, k, k
resh	r, r, r
shin(sin)	sh, sh, sh
thav(tav)	t, t, t

Some of the primary exceptions were the following letter combinations:

tet-shin	ch
zayin-shin	zh
tzadi-'	ch
tzadi-qof-yod	sky
zayin -'	zh
vav-vav	v

Finally, it was decided to standardize on -ovitz as an ending instead of -ovich, no matter which was specified.

When the table and exceptions were applied against all of the given names in the book over 95% of them agreed with the transliteration found in Kolatch's book. For the surnames the hard part was deciding where to place vowels, what ayin should be, whether vav was a v or an o/u and determining whether the feh/peh should be an F or an P. In order to aid in this dilemma three sources were used to determine the possible spellings, the pronunciation and the possible placement of vowels.

1) Jewishgen Family Finder (using the Daitch-Mokotoff soundex)

2) "Jewish Names in the Russian Empire", by Alexander Beider

3) The transliterated 1906-07 Bessarabia Duma Lists

The transliterated Bessarabia Duma lists were specifically from the town of Orgeyev and were also part of the basis of Beider's book. These two sources were from Russian transliteration, so it was important to use their concepts and not their actual spellings.

The result of all of this is really twofold. First, when searching for a surname the following should be taken into consideration (if you were using the Daitch-Mokotoff system it would be done for you):

1) Also check Z and CH if your surname begins with TZ, TS, KH or CH;

2) Also check SH and Z if your surname begins with S;

3) If it begins with P or F then check both;

4) Remember that a vav can be a V or an O/U (within a name only), so check for alternate spellings within a name;

5) Vowels are very questionable since they are "arbitrary" so expect possible differences in the vowels and their placement.

Secondly, there are many names (especially in the figure captions) that have only initials instead of given names. This only causes a problem if the initial is a feh/peh or an alef (ayin was never found as an initial or it would have also been a problem). In those cases the value was put in brackets (unless the same person was found with a given name elsewhere in the book). You will, therefore, sometimes find "[alef]." or "[feh]." to indicate that the actual initial is not known.

Even after all of this was done sometimes the same surname ended up being spelled different ways. The project coordinator tried to keep this from happening but with 6 or 7 different translators some slipped through during the validation and formatting step.

Terry Lasky
Project Coordinator

Chapter A2

Index of Surnames

This index is not part of the Yikzor book, it was constructed by the project coordinator to help in locating information about specific surnames. If you haven't read the "Notes from the Project Coordinator" you should read it first - it gives an explanation of the transliteration of the names in this book and some hints for locating family names.

The following list indicates in which chapter(s) the surname is located. If the number is preceded by an "F" it is a Figure number rather than a chapter number.

Chapter A3

LIST OF FIGURES

Chapter 1

Prologue

by The Editorial Board

Translated by Boaz Nadler

… and in opening this book, with the editorial work finished and the book sent to be printed, before we "bless on our accomplishment," it is worthwhile to pause a minute and review the way this book has come into being.

Since the first convention in Hadera (in 1951), a couple of years have gone by -- years of groping and searching, of disappointments and accomplishments. In the end, we were able to overcome the obstacles and to present to the community of Orheyev descendants the material shaped and collected into the most suitable form.

Our goal was to present the image of our beloved city in its glory and in its ruins. We wanted this book to serve as a mirror, through which the lives of our ancestors and of our brothers and sisters -- lives that follow a traditional path as in any typical Jewish village in the Diaspora -- will all become transparent.

To this end, in interviews with many people from Orheyev, we encouraged them to speak or write about as many details as possible, especially those that added detail to the description of life in the Jewish community.

We also met with the Holocaust survivors, those that made it to the shore of our homeland, from whom we know of the terrible fate that came to most Jews in Orheyev under the hands of the enemy.

It is worthwhile to note that most of the material is the product of ordinary people for whom writing is not their profession, people who do not consider themselves as "writers of the society." Each and every one of them poured out his thoughts, as they were kept and remembered in their hearts.

The simplicity, the good will, and above all, the eternal truth -- these are the characteristic features of all those people that helped us in this task.

May all of them be blessed!

We would also like to thank all of our friends and colleagues who have responded to our challenge, and have contributed their time and money to make this book come true.

The Editorial Board: Yitzchak Spivak, Mordechai Rotkov, Mordechai Frank
1958, a decade in Israel.

Chapter 2

Excerpts from the Writers

Bessarabia and its uniqueness

Translated by Boaz Nadler

Some of the most distinguished Israeli writers (S. Ben-Zion, Doctor Zvi Vasilavsky and A. Epstein) have written about the unique characteristics of the people of Jewish Bessarabia. Through their excerpts, a faithful image of the lives of our own town people is reflected, and many details about the lives of our ancestors from 50 years ago are made clear through their picturesque descriptions.

Excerpts by Abraham Epstein

Bessarabia – a plain land filled with sunlight, fields and vineyards, its land fertilized and fresh, and its people well built and powerful, all crops of the land. A lively energy is found in them; even the Jews show the signature of the place: strong and muscular, and in fact good Jews, observant ones. Their image is as those Bessarabian nuts, whose outer shell is strong, while their inside is soft and tender…

(From "Bessarabia writers")

Doctor Zvi Vasilavsky

Small and tiny was the Jewish tribe that placed its tent, a nomadic Jewish tent, in the wide fields of Bessarabia. Poor and negligible was this tribe among the great Jewish tribes that lived in the dry lands of Vohlin, Podolia and new Russia and that were densely populated and carried an ancient history. Minute was also its part in the Jewish culture of the Diaspora of the last generations: A few sad melodies, a gypsy Moldovian-Vohlin Jewish mixture, bringing tears to your eyes and softening your heart with the sunset on a Saturday evening, and bringing a unique flavor in the prayers during the days between Rosh Hashana and Yom-Kippur – this is the only gift to the nomadic Jewish temple, that Jewish Bessarabia brought with it. Simple Jews lived there. Their food – mamaliga, and their drink – Bessarabian wine. Their food more than an egg, while their religiousness, less than an olive. Only the reflecting light of the Podilic Hasidim, is shining their light from the black land to the blue sky. Their life table is full, but their spiritual table, poor and miserable. If a Jew from Lita would come by, only lightly knowledgeable in the Bible and the Mishnah – he would be considered a scholar, a Rabbi. In contrast, many of the Jews are farmers, workers of the land, muscular and strong. In their love for the land, they were not blessed with being overly pampered, but were closer to the origins of life and the world.

Excerpts by S. Ben-Zion

"A typical town in Bessarabia of those times…. The streets – dust and trash in the hot summer days, and deep mud in the rainy days. But around the town and beyond it – large fields, green from one horizon to the other, and beyond them – mountains with vineyards and groves and herds of sheep and cattle…the town satiated with all the surrounding goods distinguishes itself from most Moldavian villages and other towns and cities…"

"The Jews from Teleneshty are simple people. A Jew that knows books and a chapter of the Mishnah (Jewish oral laws) is a rare vision. Even more scarce is a person who speaks Russian; and one who knows how to sign his name in Russian was regarded as a scholar in Israel and around the Moldavians. The "Haskala" – (Jewish enlightenment and education movement), this name was still heard there in those days… The Hasidic (pious) Jews were of the simple type. Small "Hasidic Rabbis", wearing "Kutshmas", which are not known or notable in Poland, would visit the town from time to time – bringing happiness and joy to Teleneshty. Most belonged to the group of the Hasidic Rabbi from Rashkobi, also a simple Jew, satisfied with prayers and reading chapters from the Mishnah. Among the Hasidim were also educated ones, from Telne, Sadgora, and also from Habad. These were "fine Jews", and most of them were called by the names of their town of origin, which means that they were not natives of Teleneshty. The teachers in the town were mostly all from Poland….The town Jews are lovers of wine -- and the wine is poured generously -- and nuts and "Pastrusa" (dried and spicy meat) and other things; they eat and drink and enjoy themselves ….."

S. Ben Zion, one of the notable writers of the previous generation (Born in Teleneshty, and in this description gives a clear view of a typical Bessarabian town life, in the Orheyev county), gives a faithful description of his home town, Teleneshty, and its Jews, in the previous century.

Chapter 3

My Homeland

by Y. Spivak

Translated by Boaz Nadler

I wouldn't be wrong if I said that Orheyev, the name of our town, is almost never mentioned in any book, and if by chance its name is mentioned it is incidentally so, in conjunction with a different principal subject. This is not the case for the other cities and towns of the Bessarabia region. I shall not talk about Kishinev, the capital of the region, which has been mentioned in newspapers and books before, during and after the pogroms of 1903, nor about the small towns and villages whose size and population is comparable to that of Orheyev (Kalarash, Teleneshty, Soroki, Beltsy) and whose names were mentioned here and there. Rather I shall talk about Orheyev, which unfortunately, is not mentioned anywhere.

Our town did not serve as the birthplace for a known artist, nor has it left any legacy, neither in words, lyrics, nor paintings. This envy broke my heart, and I've said to myself, can we put up with the fact that in place of Orheyev there will only be left an empty void, and its name will never be mentioned again… and if we, the last generation, who saw with our own eyes the terrible destruction of our town do not fill this empty vacuum, then who will do it?

But the world will not shed a tear if Orheyev will remain without reminiscence. Thousands of communities have lost their names with no reminiscence. However, we, the last generation of Orheyev descendants, our hearts will die in pain if the memory of Orheyev, our home town, will be totally lost.

Thus, a few words of farewell in view of its ruins.

Our hometown is precious to us anytime its memories come into our hearts. In it we were born and educated, in it our own unique character was formed and through it we walked until we came to Israel. This Orheyev was not a legend but a living reality, and now it seems to us like a dark shadow.

"Gdoley Torah" did not come to live within your boundaries; known writers did not straddle your streets. The simple ordinary people, they are the ones who lived within you. And amongst these, we shall always remember the youth, the young generation whom I have had the pleasure to encounter when I stumbled upon Orheyev in the twenties. There I found outstanding youth groups, who left the comfort of their parents' homes, and lived in basements and attics, solely to be able to continue a Zionist education and achieve self-realization. These are the ones whom, with sweat and hard work, have padded the new way to their followers. These young people, whose numbers attained hundreds, whom by coming to Israel have become stronger and fortified and have taken up important positions in our community.

Every time I recall the memory of my dearest friends who have not been able to come to Israel, but rather died in the Holocaust, and recall that Orheyev has been totally destroyed and its presence deleted from the face of the earth, I say to myself: these pages will serve as a soul to our town, and a living memory for all the sacred and innocent people who were exterminated there.

Figure 1 - My town, a general view from the Ibanus

Part I - History of the Town and the Community

Chapter 4

The Bessarabian Region at the End of the 19th Century Demographical Lines

Translated by Rachel Weitz & Marsha Kayser

This region is located between the Prut River on the west and the Dniester River on the east. It borders Austria on the northwest, the Black Sea on the southeast, and the Danube on the south.

The way the administration partitioned the region, Bessarabia was divided into eight regions. At the head of every region was the capital city and its "daughters," its villages and its farms: Akkerman, Bendery, Izmail, Orheyev, Soroki, Beltsy, and Khotin. Four more cities that were not in this jurisdiction: Bolgrad, Kiliya, Kagul, & Reni.

In 1812, this region was annexed to Russia, and that same year Kishinev was declared the capital city in the district of Bessarabia.

The Russian government found Jewish inhabitants who had lived here for a very long time, and it subjected them to the same taxes as the other inhabitants. But subsequently an order was issued which prohibited Jews and gypsies from holding government positions in this region.

In 1839 another edict was issued to evacuate the Jews who lived close to the border and to relocate them a distance of 50 kilometers from these borders. In 1842 the Jews were forbidden to purchase, from the estate owners, land that was cultivated by the local inhabitants. However, the Jews from Russia received permission to come to Bessarabia and settle with no restrictions.

The inhabitants of Bessarabia by religion and nationality: Moldavians 47.6%, Malorussians 19.6% (ed. note: Little Russians), Jews 11.8%, Velikorussians 8% (ed. note: Great Russians), Bulgarians 5%, remainder of the peoples and the tribes 8%.

The percentage of the inhabitants of the cities and towns: Jews 37.4 %, Velikorussians 24.4%, Malorussians 15.7%, Moldavians 14.2%. The rest vary.

The Jewish population in Bessarabia (according to the census of 1897) reached 228,528: 112,662 men, 115,866 women. The Jews made up 37.4% of the population in the cities; in the districts outside the cities and the towns Jews were 7.2% of the population. In 1838 some settlements in Bessarabia grew from villages to towns, and the number of Jews increased.

Occupations of the Jews of Bessarabia: Of the 112,000 men, half supported themselves and their families. Of 115,000 women, 10% were financially independent and the rest were dependent upon their families. Typically every provider supported an average of 2.5 dependents.

The men were mainly tradesmen such as tailors, shoemakers, smiths and milliners, and the rest worked in the small manufacturing industries required in every city and rural municipality. Also 9% were engaged in the grain trade, 8% in the wood and lumber businesses, and 11% in other trades. The women were mainly engaged in sewing, housework, and as helpers in retail stores.

In this region there were also a few factories. Of 377 factories, 106 (28%) were owned by the Jews, and compared to other factories, those owned by the Jews were inferior. While every factory of a non-Jew in South Russia was mechanized and had 314 workers on average, a similar Jewish factory had only 21 workers.

The Jewish Settlements (and in "Colonies") in Bessarabia

Town	# of families	# of people	land size (in desaytins*)
Dombrovani	219	1,132	1,179
Lublin	68	411	234
Vertyuzhany	74	397	390
Dumbrovitsa	120	716	436
Bricheva	158	820	289
Markuleshty	158	820	504

*(ed. note: 1 desaytin = 2.7 acres)

The Agriculture of the Jews of Bessarabia

Bessarabia is considered one of the few districts within the boundaries of the Settlement in which the participation of the Jews in agriculture was considerable. According to the census of 1897, there were Jews employed in agriculture in the districts of Soroki, Orgieev, and Bieltsy, actually over 16,000 Jews in agriculture, equivalent to 4% of the non-Jewish population in the district, or 7.2% of Jews involved in agriculture. Farming: There were more than 4,000 Jews who worked in farming, 1000 on the tobacco plantations, and the rest in different branches of agriculture.

They became involved in the tobacco plantations in the 1860's, by 1899 most of those engaged in tobacco plantations were Jews, and the size of the land was about 1,500 desaytins: the most famous places among the tobacco plantations were Kremenchuk, Horganshty, Chinisheutsy, Selishte, among others.

Literacy Rates

Religion	men	women
Provuslav *	66% male	66.7% women
Catholics	51% male	47% women
Jews	49% men	24% women
Others	16% men	4% women

(*Russian Orthodox Christians)

(this information according to Ruska Evreiskaia entsiklopediia – ed. note: Russian Jewish Encyclopedia) Volume 4 from 1910 edition
Y. Ben-Asher

Chapter 5

Orheyev and its Jewish Settlement in Ancient Times

By M. Beyt David (Davidson)

Translated by Rachel Weitz and Marsha Kayser

An Historiographical Description

The harsh topography of Orheyev enclosed the city on three sides. To the south below the city, the Reat River flowed between Orheyev and the suburb of "Sloboda", which was connected to the city by a wooden bridge: this was on the road to Kishinev. Between east and west it was hemmed in between the mythological mountain "Ivanus" and the "Shes" (steppe), a wide valley of streams, and therefore it didn't leave Orheyev much room to develop and expand its borders except in a northerly direction; indeed, the city streets and alleys are narrow because of the squeeze, but the few main streets are over 2.5 kilometers beginning from the head of the Triangle Bridge in the south to the steppe in the north, which was on the way to the town of Rezina on the shores of the Dniester River.

Figure 2 - "Sloboda" on the Reat

Unfortunately, the city of Orheyev was not discussed extensively in history books, and this leaves knowledge of her antiquity vague and the history of the Jews in this place unclear, with no way to investigate further.

Figure 3 - The valley near the Ibanus

Taking Testimony for Liberating an "Agunah"

We find proof for the existence of Jews in Orheyev in the 16th century in the ancient rabbinical literature of the Maharam, may he rest in peace, from Lublin. In this literature there exists a document of taking testimony for releasing an "agunah," (ed. note: a woman who cannot remarry, either because her husband will not give her a divorce, or because his death cannot be verified) and this is an especially valuable historical document for us because it sheds light not only on the existence of Jews here but also provides evidence of the dangers in the lives of the Jews who lived at that time in Bessarabia and the Moldovan steppe in general and in the city of Orheyev in particular. Because of its importance we will present it as is.

"Reb Israel, son of Shloyme (Shlomo), testified: 'I was here in Orheyev and I asked about the dead… so several non-Jews here said that they had been drowned, and several said they were killed in the wood, and after that a few non-Jews also said that they died violently… One of the gentiles wore the head scarf of the Jew Nisen and I immediately recognized it…'

Menachem, son of Reb Avrum, testified: 'I was in Orheyev and I also saw the head scarf.'

Reb Shimon testified again: 'A gentile came to me in Soroki and told me: I was also in the place where they assaulted the Jews… I saw how they tied them and led them with their money and …and they answered me, the "Burok" from Orheyev ordered me to bring the Jews with their money to him'…"

Even though the date of the incident is missing here, it is known that it happened in the year 1613, and this kind of testimony passed from Bessarabia of those days through the Bet Din (ed. note: Court of Jewish law) in the city of Bar Padolin to the Bet Din of Lublin. Taking into account the rough roads and hardship of transportation in those days, we can imagine the special value of this document which survived all through the generations, from which we also learn about the relationship between the local gentile residents and the Jews, because the gentile in Soroki does not hesitate to tell Shimen the Jew (called the Reb) what he witnessed in Orheyev…

And in addition to this incident, something that happened every day, every political upheaval or economic crisis naturally resulted in the Jews being its first victims - those Jews living here thanks to the "privileges" accorded them to fulfill the political or economic needs of the time or because of "privileges" for which the Jews paid a lot of money.

On top of that, the Jews experienced quite a few incidents of blood libel here. The Moldovian historians tell of nine incidents of blood libel in Moldova, and one of them occurred in the time of the Moldovian prince Michei Rokovitz, in order to extort money from the Jewish population that was under his dominion. He staged a blood libel in the district of Orgieev in the village of Onitskan, according to which a Christian child was found who was murdered by the Jews for religious purposes. News of this blood libel created outrage in the rest of the world, and thanks to the sage ("chucham") Bashi in Kushta, the Ottoman empire interfered and sent a special messenger to Iasi. After many attempts the Jews were released from prison, and the sword of death was lifted from their heads.

The lack of assurances for people's safety here, as in all Moldovian principalities, for the very long period of 400 years, frequently forced the residents in general and the Jews in particular to flee across the Prut River and to wherever the wind would carry them. This caused the population to decline year by year, and when the Russians won Bessarabia from the Turks in 1812, all of Bessarabia was in ruins.

The First Census

In the year 1816-17, the first census was conducted. However, the results of this census were so faulty that there is no point and no possibility of relying on them, even though we will mention the data from this census: 318 townships and villages found then in the district of Orgieev were divided into 12 districts. In District #1 were the villages Bravitsa, Samashkany, and others with 33 Jewish families, merchants, and shopkeepers. In District #2, among other towns, was the township Rezina and its surroundings, 78 families, and altogether 111 shopkeepers and merchants. In District #12 was Teleneshti and its surroundings, 234 Jewish farms altogether with 345 families. There are no data about the other districts of this census. We know about the existence of the community of Kalarash from the (1818) ledger of the chevrah kadisha (ed. note: burial society). Also not mentioned are many more small settlements which, despite their size, had public institutions for religious life and education, such as synagogues, in which many Jewish families found a home. The town of Orheyev itself appeared in the census with 219 men and 19 women in the general population, but the Jews and Armenians were not mentioned.

In the time of transition when Bessarabia changed from Turkish rule to Russian rule, we see a big drop in the Jewish population in Orheyev and in the district. The statistics for 1798 registered 450 shopkeeper taxpayers, and by following this estimate, the total number reached 4000 people. Then in the first census after the conquest in 1817, they found 345 families in general in several places in the district; there were no numbers for Jews in Orheyev. Panic from the war seems to have caused the Jews to flee to Romania and to other places, and the Jewish settlements dwindled. We see a radical change in the growth of the Jewish population at the end of the 19th century.

According to the census conducted among the Jews in 1847, to determine the number of young men eligible for the draft, there were 1,960 people in Orheyev and altogether 4,403 Jews (men 2,217, women 2,186).

According to the census conducted in 1897, the number in the entire district was 213,000, among them 26,699 Jews according to the following distribution:

Town	General Population	Jews
Orheyev	12,336	7,144
Kriulyany	2,056	338
Olishkany	2,943	341
Rezina	3,652	3,182
Samashkany	700	79
Teleneshti*	4,379	3,876
Tuzara-Kalarash	5,153	4,592
Other Settlements	181,781	7,147

*A written report from August 19, 1941 by the head of the battalion of the gendarmerie in Khotin stated the property found in the township of Teleneshti according to Colonel Mnekutza as follows: 692 houses, 11 grain mills, 5 oil factories, a factory for processing wool, 5 furnaces, 1934 hectares agricultural land, 73 hectares pasture, 595 hectares vines (see M. Karp, volume 2, pg 143.)

From these numbers we learn that the Jewish population of Orheyev grew tremendously in the second half of the 19th century. While after the conquest of Bessarabia in the 1820's, the number of Jews in Orheyev was 345 families or approximately 1,400 people, at the end of the century their number in the entire district was approximately 26,699 and in Orheyev itself 7,144 people (3,476 men and 3,668 women).

The Jewish Population According to Demographic Research

It is worthwhile to introduce the statistical data regarding the manner of growth of the Jewish population in our city that Dr. Moyshe Shlissel, a resident of our city (native of Mashkovtsy, the district of Orgieev) published at the time. Relying on the registration books of the rabbinate that the appointed Rabbi Yosef Ben Yoel Pagis gave him, Dr. Shlissel surveyed a period of 50 years from 1877-1926. The survey encompasses three life events: A) birth, B) mortality, and C) marriage age.

A) Birth: In the survey period (1877-1926) there were 14,125 Jewish children born in Orheyev. Of those, 7,926 were boys and 6,499 were girls (55% boys, 45% girls).

B) Mortality: During this time 8,264 Jews died in our city, among them 2,111 children up to 1 year old (25% of Jewish deaths), 2,016 children 1-10 years old (24%). On average, for every year, there were 165 deceased. The smallest number of deceased was in 1881 (78 people) and in 1892 the biggest number of deceased (271).

C) Marriage age: In the period mentioned (1877-1926) 3,827 Jewish weddings were conducted, 78 per year. Of those, there were 2,889 Jewish weddings that were registered for the first time and 938 Jewish weddings registered for the second or third time, which makes 75.5% registered once, 24.5% registered two or three times.

The Distribution of Marriage According to Age and Gender

Years	Average Age of Groom	Average Age of Bride
1877-1886	23	19
1887-1896	25	20
1897-1906	25	24
1907-1916	25	23
1917-1926	26	24

Dr. Shlissel and his demographic research conclude: this count of the population is indeed a drop in the ocean compared to what needs to be done in coming generations regarding improvements in the process of physical maturation and in the health of the Jews in Bessarabia in general and in particular in our city. This adds another layer to the research of the demography of our people in the Diaspora. (Bessarabia AZ"E pamphlet 13-14)

Indeed, Dr. Shlissel unknowingly performed a considerable service when he presented the data that brought reliable testimony to the development of the demographical record of our community. Of course it did not occur to him that a day will come when this one layer (one brick) will testify about a community that existed and is no more…and for that may his name be for a blessing.

The Character of the Historical City

What was the face of the city of Orheyev during the time of transition from Turkish rule to the rule of the conquering Russians? When Orheyev was taken over by the Russians in 1812, it was a small provincial township that did not have more than 3 or 4 narrow streets about 1 km in length, beginning at the bridge and ending at the Mark Shul (the synagogue of the market). There were a few winding alleys and very meager huts covered with reeds and straw on both sides of those alleys. In the rainy season the entire village would drown in a sea of muck and mire which would make traveling there, as in all of Bessarabia, extremely difficult. In most cases it was possible to travel the muddy roads with oxen and horses. In the summer months when the mud would dry, sand and dust would fill the air to such a degree that it was suffocating.

Thanks to the gorgeous view of the area, the fertile land with thick woods, orchards, limestone quarries, and all the features that are needed for economic development, it is no wonder that Jews were drawn here and, for practical purposes, settled here and dealt in commerce and industry to earn their livelihoods. In 1834, twenty-two years after the conquest, Orheyev was declared the capital of the district. Every Sunday farmers would stream in to the market (bazaar) from the entire area, bringing their produce and grain and their farm animals to be sold in the "Sinoyah" Square next to the Church of the "Holy Nicolai."

The Jews also made a living from trading the goods of the villages with merchants of different crafts like shoemaking, carpentry, metalworking (smithies), and so on. Indeed, the Jewish settlement at the time of the Russian occupation was very small but its growth began to accelerate year by year. We do not have well-based information about the make-up of the Jewish settlement from those days. We do not know which groups first came after the initial early settlement or where they came from, but it is known that besides the economic conditions that we mentioned, an increase in the settlement here was also caused by political factors (denying the civil rights of the Jews in the time of Ekaterina, the deportation of Jews from the villages, and the decree of the canton) and also the special rights the Russian government promised to the settlers who would come to the Bessarabian district to farm. Therefore many Jews who were interested in farming and raising cattle were the ones who were attracted to the area. In the summertime when the sheep gave birth, they would sell the lambs for slaughter and the skins to merchants, and the quality of the sheepskins and the lambs was so well recognized that it was known at the big fairs held in Birmlinitz and in Balta in the Ukraine. In Orheyev the merchants bought these skins wholesale to sell them abroad. Others also would make a living from the wood trades. This line of agriculture branched off to a few secondary industries that gave a serious push to the economic development of this region.

Tens of families in Orheyev made a living from the industry of hats and furs for local consumption and for marketing at the annual fairs. Another important branch of agriculture was the production of cheese from sheep's milk. The cheese ("brinza") would be purchased by the farmers and city folks, and they would eat it with great relish along with the "national dish" of "mamaliga" (ed. note: a yellow cornmeal polenta) which was so loved by the Bessarabian population; the dairy industry also went far beyond the borders of Bessarabia.

There were also tenant farmers working on large estates who would grow grain for local settlements and for export. Well known at this time in Orheyev was the estate owner Leyb Reznik who had come here from Poland as a young man (in those days the government discharged, from military service and taxes, those Jews who settled in Bessarabia). Reznik at first made his living from a small shop and after accumulating some money began to cultivate some land. In time he purchased more land and developed a big farm. Although he was very successful in the grain market, he kept the shop. In a very short time his small shop became a large store selling a variety of goods and was well known in the entire region. After his death he left a lot of property, a big estate with thousands of hectares and many houses. We have to mention here that, despite his wealth, his name does not appear among the donors who gave for our city's public needs. The only enterprise he established while alive was the synagogue named after him.

Among other estate owners in a later period (from the 1890's to World War I) we should mention the families Averbukh-Barsutsky, Rozen, and Motl Reznik (the son of Leyb Reznik). In the later years more farms with different crops such as tobacco came into being as a means of livelihood. They also grew sunflowers for oil for the locals and for export, cultivated vineyards for wine, and grew orchards (apples, pears, plums, cherries, apricots, and nuts) that employed hundreds of people. In addition many families made their living from businesses that branched off from agriculture, and they reached respectable economic status.

The period from the 1820's to the 1870's was marked by accelerated economic development. The Jews were permitted to live in the villages, purchase land under their own names, and were exempted from taxes and military service. Despite that, we cannot report satisfactory achievements for small businesses that had little income, for craftsmen and peddlers, and for many who barely made their living for lack of financial resources and who used their entire income to pay the interest on borrowed money. The big competition was against them, their work was exhausting, especially so for craftsmen with endless work hours and with the decline of their income due to the competition. The low social status of the craftsmen at this time also depressed them, as they were isolated in their own professional circles.

It became worse from the eighties on, which was a period of restrictions implemented by the emergency law of Russia - the Christian citizens expelled the Jews from commerce and cruelly made the terms of every negotiation a harsh burden. The government oppressed the Jews with heavy taxes that led to a drop in all types of commerce. The mandatory draft law uprooted the young from their families (for a period of four years) and also uprooted whole families from their homes because they were denied citizenship and were deported from the villages. All of this paralyzed the activities of the Jewish settlements here.

Regarding the deportations from the villages, "Segev" (ed. note: The Sublime or The Great) Shmuel Gershon Baru writes in "Hamelitz" (The Advocate) Number 177, July 27 1887:

"Yesterday fourteen Jewish families were brought here from the village of Kobylka which is nearby. All of them are people who lived in the village for many years, before the famous May Laws were published, and their meager livelihood trading with the local peasants was strained. Also among the expelled were a few craftsmen and one old man who had lived in this village for thirty years and who had also had land and a vineyard. All of this happened to them due to the fault of the local clerk who had not registered them in the Jewish List kept for the people who lived in the villages a few years before. All the efforts of these miserable people at the district government offices, and also the testimony of the peasants of the village that they had lived there more than 10 years, did not help them. Many of them are planning to bring a complaint before the ministers and the legislators who sit in Peterburg. But what can those unfortunate people do before their case will be clarified? Where will they find their livelihood in our city where seventy-seven people will be crowded in the one available branch of business? And there will be too much competition which will collapse the trade, leading to their complete bankruptcy. On top of that there will not be enough craft work, which will lead to a lack of a means of support"...

The Community at the End of the 19th Century

Unfortunately, as with the rest of the city, there is not any written or printed document reflecting the public's conception of the Jewish community at its beginning, and it is a fact that the community of Orheyev was backward in this regard compared to its siblings, the villages of Teleneshti and Tuzara-Kalarash which are in the same district. During the same time they already had important institutions for meeting public needs, the existence of which were documented and left for future generations. For example it is known that information recorded in "Pinkas" (ed. note: the community ledger) in Teleneshti in the year 1794 was used for research material for the reactionary historian E. Povolski, in his research for "The Economics of the Companies and Associations in Moldova." There is also more evidence that we know about, which is a compliment to Teleneshti where, holding an office, the famous gifted rabbi Reb Israel from Teleneshti, may he rest in peace, and the astute rabbi Reb Shloyme (Shlomo) Flahom, may he rest in peace, etc… In the "ledger" already written in the year 1804 for the society for learning Mishnah (ed. note: the early interpretative analysis of Talmudic law) in the community of Tuzara-Kalarash, the person who recorded the columns for this society copied the most important things about the image of community and left a record of its existence.

It's not the same with Orheyev, there is only one legend about the first rabbi Reb Nakhumtshe, may he rest in peace. The rabbi once complained to the community that his salary was not enough for the survival of his family and he asked for a raise. Trying to be humorous, they answered him jokingly: Our dear rabbi, it is well known that our forefather Jacob crossed the Jordan with his cane …and as long as our rabbi holds his cane may he, please his highness, go from house to house and ask for his salary from the "homeowners."

Even though this is only a legend, there is no doubt that, as in any legend, there is some truth in it; we can learn from it how wretched the economic situation was and also about the makeup of the society that was composed of a mix of immigrants from different districts - people did not know each other and as a result, institutions and organizations to benefit the community's welfare suffered because the immigrants did not realize their importance and the dire lack of these public services.

It is worth mentioning that all the foundations that symbolize the public image of every Jewish community existed in Orheyev since its beginning from the Russian occupation until the holocaust. Also we should trust the story which the elderly from our city related - that the big synagogue on the Reat River, where the city began and from which it expanded, was already in existence in the first half of the 18th century. The "Hadmur" Rabbi Chanoch Zilberfarb related according to the elderly Reb Zelikel, may he rest in peace, that according to tradition, the "Ba'al Shem Tov" (ed. note: "the owner of the good name," a title of esteem, from the name of the founder of Hasidism) visited here, and he immersed himself in the mikvah (ed. note: ritual bath) which was next to this synagogue. The elderly among us still remember this big synagogue where the wall leaned on a stone support with walls below the ground for at least one meter, and the structure of the building was extremely old, which was evidence of its antiquity.

Figure 4 - The large synagogue

The synagogue second in importance to this central synagogue on the Reat was called "The Kloiz" (ed. note: a small synagogue) and was also as old as the central synagogue. It contained about 200 seats in addition to a side room that was used during ordinary days for "minyan", and on Shabbos simple Jews would gather here and Reb Zelikel, the old shoykhet (ed. note: a ritual slaughterer of kosher meat), or Reb Alter Menashes would teach and discuss with them the week's Torah reading portion.

As the settlement grew and developed, due to lack of space, more and more houses of prayer began to be added, for example "Bet Homidrash", the synagogue of the Talna Hasids where not only the Hasids but also the educated townspeople would pray. In this synagogue there was a concentration of people who were the first to become active in service to the community in the first "Hibat Zion" organization (Fond of Zion), and in the period of political Zionism it was also a meeting place for the young Zionist members.

At the end of the previous century more synagogues were added, among them the Chabad Synagogue, the Synagogue of the Caretakers ("Hashamashim"), the Synagogue of the Market ("The Shuk Synagogue"), the Tailors' Synagogue, "The Yeshiva", the Boineh Shul (named after the neighborhood with the municipal slaughterhouse), the "Kafestra" Synagogue named for the stall of the leather workers who made harnesses ("kafestra"): at this time the wealthy resident Reb Henikh Tabachnik, may he rest in peace, donated a plot of land and on it was built the "Shoemakers" Synagogue, so we had synagogues for all levels of society - people of Bet Homidrash, and Hasids, craftsmen, people involved in civic affairs – and despite diverse social classes and other distinctions that existed in this community, public affairs were not affected, and people treated each other with fondness and respect.

This is how we see the city of Orheyev, its gradual development as a community, and its cultural and economic institutions, a community which after the time of the legendary rabbi was led by other famous rabbis and judges, for example Rabbi Moyshe Chayim Elkin, who excelled as a modest and learned person. He led his community for 30 years and died in the year 1902, and after him came his son Rabbi Avrum Yosef Elkin who was educated by his father in Torah, was taught to be a "mentsh" (fine person), and was also highly respected by the community. He wrote a book in his own hand about the Six Hundred Thirteen Mitzvot (ed. note: religious commandments), which survived and garnered the approval of the geniuses of the generation. Another tsadik (ed. note: Hasidic rabbi or pious man) who came to live in our city, the "Hadmur" Rabbi Chanoch Dov Zilberfarb, became very popular in the community, especially among the workers and the simple Jews. Highly respected, he lived in our city for a few years until he was fortunate when he got older to make aliyah with his family to Israel and settled in Tel Aviv.

The "shokhtim" (ed. note: plural of shoykhet) had an important role in our community, even though for practical reasons they sometimes had to do secular work that did not fit their religious position, but some of them excelled in helping their community and in loyal and devoted activities for the community's welfare. Here we have to mention the respected name of Reb Zelikel, "Shoykhet ve bodek" (ed. note: shoykhet specialist certified to inspect the animal for defects after slaughter in order to insure that it is kosher), in his position of moyel (circumciser) specialist who was fortunate "to make a bris" (perform circumcisions) for three generations and was a kosher Jew with a good and pleasant manner, so much so that we must point it out. There was also "Shoykhet ve bodet" Reb Moyshe, son of Rabbi Binyumin Yonovich, who became known by the name Rabbi "Moyshe the Shoykhet," and who for a long time headed the religious program for progressive education. When a need for higher education in religious studies was felt, they established a yeshiva for gifted young men who also wanted to study the Gemara (ed. note: the commentary of the Talmud) and interpretation of Rashi (ed. note: a commentary named for the 11th century Talmudic scholar Rashi) and other editions. Even though not exactly like the yeshivas in Lithuania, a great effort was made to have the learning here concentrated on Talmud and the writings of rabbinical authorities.

To complete the public image of Orheyev in the 1880's we have to include the writings of the famous traveler Ephraim Reinard in 1877:

"Orheyev - a small city in a valley, her houses built of wood, with about 4,000 inhabitants and about 1/3 of them Jews. Most of them "in the dark," believing in the nonsense of the Hasidim but are practical people who are engaged in craft work and commerce and live a peaceful life, but the sparks of the enlightenment have started to penetrate the hearts of the young, the elite of the city, those who can understand Hebrew and Russian. They try as hard as possible to get educated in this village and also to attract their friends to learn, so there is hope that soon the new generations will benefit from the knowledge of their brethren in villages close by."

And indeed after a relatively short time the hope of the traveler Reinard became true and not only did the new generation become more knowledgeable from its brothers in the villages but in a very short time the public life here changed almost in every way - the cultural, the social, the economic.

As the Jewish settlement grew and developed, the needs of the public as a community became more relevant. Differences in the settlement took shape, and people were more enthusiastic about volunteering in the community and public life, devoting their lives to public service and making a strong commitment. The institutions that existed here were improved and as needs developed, new institutions were established which we will discuss in upcoming chapters.

Chapter 6

Communal Institutions

by M. Rotkov

Translated by Jerrold Landau

In this article, it is not my intention to present a full survey of the struggles, victories and setbacks that the communal workers and institutions experienced during the time of the existence of the community.

The sources that I came across are very poor. I had to select them from the archives, leaf through the pages of the Hamelitz, Hatzefira and other newspapers, and speak with elders who still are with us – efforts that required a great deal of time and an indescribable amount of effort.

Despite my efforts, I did not succeed in recording all of the details that were fit to be recorded. Some are not described completely, and there were important activists whose names and activities have been removed. I consciously skipped over disagreements in communal life, whether the cause was political or personal, despite the fact that it is possible to assume that each person was in his own camp and believed in the purity of his motives and the righteousness of his struggle, which was only for the benefit of the public.

My prayer is that the reader will find the material presented interesting, and will gain an idea of the prominence of the community and its institutions – whose ways were not fenced with roses – and that my words will explain what is obscure, and that there will be a salvation of some memory of our destroyed community. This will be my reward.

A. Medical and Social Assistance

Medical assistance for the sick was the chief concern of the community. The following articles that we have found in the newspapers from those days testify to this.

In "Hamelitz", 5726 (1866), Issue 33, we read about the native of our town Yosef Rabinovitz:

"The terrible illness cholera, that brings pestilence and death in its wake, came also to our town. It affected a neighborhood of the houses of the poor. They were the first to be affected.

"Goodhearted people from our community arose and decided to put a stop to it. These include Reb Shlomo Volovsky, Reb Baruch Nisenboim, Reb Menashe Feinsilver, Reb Leib Rozenfeld, and finally Reb Avraham Davidovitz. They did not rest day and night. They gathered money from all generous people, and helped the doctors distribute medicine to those who were sick at home and in the hospital.

"It is worthwhile to praise the wonderful doctor, Dr. Waltuch, a dear man, who took it upon himself to visit the ill in the hospital and at home without any payment – until he himself became ill."

From here it is clear that already at that time, almost a century ago, there was a hospital.

To our dismay, we did not find any other information about communal matters in our city in general and about the hospital in particular, until about 20 years later, in an article that was published in "Hamelitz" on June 8, 1887. The writer "Segev" tells us the following: "The house that was built in the yard of the hospital on the accounts of the generous philanthropist Mr. Zelig Klister, for which he paid about 3,000 rubles, has four large rooms, and is separated into two sections, one for men and one for women. Great benefit will come from it. Instead of 12 beds, there will now be 24. Now the doctor can examine the sick people in the old house, and not in the room of the beds. The office and pharmacy will be there as well. Dr Shachnovitz, who is well loved by the community, has been invited to be the director. (He came to our city from Lithuania in 1865.)"

Fifty Years of the Hospital

For fifty years (from 1866 until 1914), that passed in a characteristic manner, a group of people were active, some of whom were mentioned above. With honor and awe, we bring to our memory the doctors Dr. Waltuch, the first in the hospital, followed by Dr. Shachnovitz and Dr. Yitzchak Rabinovitz, who served for a period as directors of the hospital. (The latter moved to Kishinev in 1898). This era ends with the passing of the elder Dr. Shachnovitz in 1903, and the entry of new powers, doctors and activists. Dr. Kohan is remembered. He served a number of years until he moved to Odessa. At that time (1904) Dr. Nirenberg came to us from Kishinev. (He had returned from the Russo-Japanese war). He earned the appreciation of the community. Zaikovitz and his two children Eliusha and Yesha served as medics (feldschers), who assisted the doctors in the hospital.

The merciful nurses were faithful assistants to the doctors. These included the young woman Raisel the daughter of Reb Moshe Lezer Sharf, Reveka Grigoriovana Rabinovitz, Ina Kornblit-Yagolnitzer, and Chaika the daughter of Chayim Davidovitz. All of these served with purity and awe for their task.

At the end of the first decade of the 20th century, a new hospital building was erected in the north of the city, at the edge of Bessarabkaya Street. It was headed by Dr. Warshavsky, who was assisted by nurses.

The period of time between the outbreak of the First World War (1914) until the end of the 1920s was a time of difficult national and social revolutions, which strongly influenced life. Despite the many efforts expended by the communal workers, they did not succeed in providing sufficient medical assistance to the poor residents of the city.

A Bright Period for the Hospital

In the years 1928/1929, a new communal council was chosen. The concern for the hospital was given over to Yaakov Volovsky chairman, Liuba Gluzgold, David Marinyansky treasurer, Meir Goldberg, Yisrael Hirsh Soroker, and Shabtai Shapira. These were men of great energy and vision who were inspired to help their fellowman. An unexpected source of income came their way. At that time, the surgeon Dr. Lashko (a Christian) served in the regional hospital. He excelled as a surgical expert. On account of a debate that broke out between him and the director of the region hospital Dr. Montianu, Dr. Lashko decided to leave his post, and turned to the supervisors of the Jewish hospital with the recommendation that he be allowed to tend to the ill in one of the rooms of the hospital. In return for this use, he would give over 20% of his salary for each operation, over and above the hospital fees that the sick person paid to the management. The offer was accepted, and beneficial results were seen already at the beginning of the time Dr. Lashko worked there. Large sums from sick people of means streamed into the empty coffers of the institution. It was necessary to erect another, larger building that would befit the new work conditions.

A New Building for the Surgical Division

The idea was fine, but how would it be realized?

To the credit of the aforementioned hospital committee, we should point out that their efforts and abilities to bring in large groups of the residents of the city and region to work to this endeavor, and their personal dedication to every member of the committee, stood well for them, and they succeeded in raising more money than was expected. The members Meir Goldberg of blessed memory and Yaakov Volovsky did important work. They left their affairs and went out to the villages of Kipercheny, Biyeshty, Tsareni, Kapreshty, and others. They raised large sums. A general campaign was conducted among the residents of the city, who responded generously. Several rooms were sold to the pharmacist and communal worker Mr. Rubinstein, Yaakov Volovsky and others who expressed their desire to perpetuate the names of their beloved.

This era (1931-1939) can be considered as the brightest of the 75 years of existence (1866-1939) of the medical assistance institution in our city.

The set of obstacles and disruptions in the existence of the hospital is very long. A large number of the communal workers continued the constant struggle with great dedication and without getting tired. Of the previous era (until 1929), we recall the pharmacist Avraham Rubinstein, Aharon Gluzgold and his son Liuba, Leib Ziserman, David Marinyansky, David Brandeis, Shual Dyukman (the watchmaker), Motel Chulsky, Shabtai Shapira and others.

However the great merit fell to the hands of Volovsky and his friends. They brought the hospital to great medical heights, and it became a splendid hospital. The name of the hospital became famous in the region and outside of its borders. Many, both Jews and Christians, were assisted, and benefit from the faithful service of the staff of doctors as well as the administrative staff. It is worthwhile to mention here the name of the director of the institution Mendel Beyder, a man upright in his ways, faithful to his task, and appreciated by all with whom he came in contact. He perished in the Holocaust along with his entire family.

The activists worked for many years, and gave of the best of their time and energy for the benefit of this dear enterprise. However, to our despair, the destructive sword of Hitler and his comrades, may their names be blotted out, fell upon the enterprise and its patients together. The only survivor of the group of activists mentioned above whom escaped and arrived in the Land was Meir Goldberg and his family. However, to our dismay, this dear man perished from our midst. He died in the winter of 1954 from a malignant disease. Our hearts mourn for those who are no longer. May they always be remembered for good.

The Old Age Home in Orheyev

The second most important philanthropic organization, aside from the hospital, and whose initial development was tied to the hospital, was the old age home.

In "Hamelitz" number 83 from July 30, 1886, David Leib Fikhman writes:

"Mr. Zelik Klister, who wished to do a good thing in memory of his three daughters who perished one after another in their youth, donated 2,000 rubles to the building of an institution for the poor elderly.

Figure 5A - Old Age Home (Women)

Seated from right to left: 1. M. Reznik 2. [feh]. Vurgaft 3. [alef]. Moshkovitz 4. [ayin]. Zislis 5. L. Lidid 6. [alef]. Rapoport 7. L. Kruglyak 8. [feh]. Mazlover
Standing: 1. S. Adesser 2. R. Pasechnik 3. [feh]. Katz 4. S. Frimis 5. S. Goldenberg 6. B. Goldenshteyn 7. S. Moshkovitz 8. N. Timentzer 9. S. Shames

"Today, many honorable people of the city - including the physician of the region, and one of the justices of the peace in our city who are kindly disposed to the Jewish people, Dr. Rabinovitz the doctor of the hospital, and many of the residents - have gathered together to lay the cornerstone and to bless Mr. Klister for his act of great generosity to the elderly and poor in our city, who until this point wandered through the streets as shadows, without finding a place to rest.

"Dr. Rabinovitz and others explained to the community the good that would come from such a place."

Figure 5B - Old Age Home (Men)

Seated from right to left: 1. Bursuker 2. Gorodishtyan 3. [alef]. Slepoy 4. [feh]. Chaimovitz 5. C. M. Stiklyar 6. M. Gutman 7. Kislyuk 8. D. D. Taran 9. [alef]. Gelman **Standing:** 1. Y. Yavsker 2. M. Moshkovitz 3. Kaner 4. M. Beker 5. [alef]. Kogan 6. L. M. Shoyvelenke 7. Y. D. Goldenberg

Mirel the Shindern (From the story of Batya Duchovny)

Mirel the Shindern maintained a unique enterprise, which excelled and served as a faithful source of income for the institution.

This woman of our town had a sensitive heart. She knew how to dance a "Poilish". The community loved this dance. Mirel danced enthusiastically and warmly. She volunteered to dance this dance at weddings. She enthusiastically included the in-laws, who, with good spirits, emptied their pockets to the benefit of the coffers of the institution.

A different group of women whose hearts were concerned about the situation of the abandoned elderly, also dedicated themselves to assisting the old age home.

Mrs. Shachnovitz the wife of the doctor, Mrs. Alte Rozenfeld (the wife of Reb Hirsh the grain merchant) and Mrs. Brandeis the wife of David took upon themselves the responsibility of strengthening and broadening the capabilities of the institution. Through their efforts rooms and beds were added, a well was dug in the courtyard of the hospital, and the scope of activities was broadened. The circle of families who donated meals and food provisions was expanded. Thus, they succeeded in strengthening the institution until the outbreak of the First World War in 1914. At that time, a decline began. The difficult economic situation had a bad effect on the institution, and the efforts to preserve what was were for naught.

New Faces to Assist the Institution

This situation continued until 1920. That year, a meeting of residents was convened for the purpose of improving the situation of the institution. The meeting selected several additional members for the committee, headed by Batya the wife of David Duchovny. She was a middle-aged woman full of energy and initiative. She introduced radical changes in the leadership of the institution. Her motto was: to solicit donors and volunteers to the extent possible, to improve the building, to obtain provisions, and to oversee the maintenance of the building, and the sanitary and health conditions of the institution. A special prayer room was set up, donated by the chairwoman, Mrs. Batya Duchovny (6,400 Lei). The "Liadabnik" (ice well) in the yard was repaired, which raised funds from the sale of ice. Mrs. Duchovny also set up income funds that turned into a constant source of income, such as the "Golden Book" (1928), support from the city council and community, and new regular donors. She reinstituted the old custom of collecting "meals" and donations for food provisions. Finally, she set up contact with the Landsmanschafts in the United States and South America, many of whose members collected donations from Orheyev natives in America for the support of the institution. Avraham Hecht left in his will a third of the income of his house for the benefit of the institution. Yosef Duchovny and his wife Sara (a member of the committee) took it upon themselves to prepare a Torah Scroll for the institution at its fiftieth anniversary. It is worthwhile to praise Mrs. Shprintza Fleshler, the director of the kitchen, who gave her best to increase the pleasure of the residents of the institution.

The Chevra Kadisha (Burial Society)

We do not know when the Chevra Kadisha began to operate in Orheyev, and what were the principles of its founding. In the old cemetery, on the slope to the valley, to the left, old graves are scattered and monuments stick up from the ground. Only with difficulty is it possible to make out the letters on the monuments. There is the "ohel" (burial canopy) of the rabbi of Orheyev, which testifies to its ancientness. In this era (1910-1918) the cemetery was neglected. There was a small and narrow immersion room, and the fence was broken, without anyone concerning themselves about its repair. With the selection of the well-known communal worker Moshe Kalmanovitz as the head of the Chevra Kadisha, a fundamental change in the proceedings of the organization took place. From them, burial fees were collected from the family of the deceased, corresponding to their economic status. Grants were obtained from the city council and the authorities, and the income grew.

Figure 6 - Old Age Home

With time, significant sums were collected. These served to strengthen the hospital, as well as for other communal matters. A house was put up with a large 'tahara' room (ed. note: for the ritual washing of the dead body before placing it in the coffin) and a mikva of water, as well as a waiting room for the community and sextons. The area was enlarged and a stone fence was put up around the cemetery. We remember the dedication of those who occupied themselves with matters of burial. Reb Itzikel (the matchmaker), his son Akiva Simes, and finally Reb Shmuel Roitman. We recall as well the activists who were chosen by the community, Moshe Kalmanovitz, David Mimis, Mordechai Man, Yisrael Hirsh Soroker, Motel Chulsky and others, who did a great deal to strengthen the cemetery in a fitting manner.

In the latter period (1945-1955), the elderly Reb Ben-Zion Chaimovitz did a great deal for the cemetery, including the fixing of the fence, until he made aliya to the Land in 1955.

According to him, the sign on the fence still exists, upon which the names of the activists who erected the new fence in the 1920s are engraved.

Assistance for the Poor

Another important social institution was the "Ezrat Aniyim" (Assistance to the Poor). Shabtai Rabinovitz headed this institution for a long time, despite his own meager means. He toiled to provide assistance to the needy with a righteous desire.

With the change of the protocols of the running of communal matters in the 1920s, a new committee was appointed, headed by the communal worker Itzik David Cheriyan (Chait). From then on, there was order in the distribution of support. The person in need would present a request to the committee, who would then determine for what purpose the requestor intends to use the loan. At times, they would offer advice. This policy guaranteed to some degree that the recipient of aid would use it in a constructive fashion. The Ezrat Aniyim society received support from the city council, from the meat tax, and primarily from Maos Chittin (ed. note: charity given for distribution to the poor before Passover).

Maos Chittin

The collection of Maos Chittin took place in every Jewish community. For many years, the activists of Ezrat Aniyim in our city would visit the residents of the city between Purim and Passover to solicit donations in order to provide matzos for the poor of the city. The new committee of Ezrat Aniyim decided to levy a tax for this purpose. Rather than making the rounds to the doors of the residents and being dependent on donations of the citizens, they came to an agreement with the owners of the matzo bakeries, who were obligated not to sell matzos without an authorization from the Maos Chittin committee. However, this policy did not yield satisfactory results, for it was difficult to follow after every matzo purchaser. In order to prevent unwanted occurrences, it was decided that the baking of matzos should be in the hands of the community.

The administrators of the community invested a great deal of energy and effort in order to remove the baking of matzos from the veteran bakers. Then, Ezrat Aniyim took the baking of matzos upon itself, and thereby succeeded in collecting the tax, in accordance with the economic status of every individual. This policy led to a great increase in income, and the committee was able to broaden its support of the needy. The most active in this endeavor was the member of the evaluation committee, the communal worker Yisrael Hirsh Soroker of blessed memory. This man worked day and night in the matzo warehouse, and requested Maos Chittin from everyone who came through. Many answered his request in a generous fashion. From that time, the communal workers were able to provide the necessities of the Passover holiday to those in need.

The Community and the Ukrainian Committee

Social, health and cultural institutions existed and functioned for many years under the direction of representatives who were elected solely by the synagogue attendees, without the participation of the populist masses of the community and without communal auditing. Indeed, various activists dedicated their best efforts to serve the communities, but they were unable to get satisfactory results. An organized, concerted and directed effort was needed in order to supervise the use of communal funds.

In 1917, with the breakup of Czarism in Russia, the problems of organizing national life in an autonomous fashion arose – in a democratic fashion with due seriousness.

Through the urging of Zionist activists - Yosef the son of Yoel Pagis, the Rabbi Mitaam, Moshe Kalmanovitz, Yitzchak Shapirin, Moshe Hoichman, Simcha Kestlicher, Dr. Berkovitz, Yehudah Yagolnitzer, Avraham Lipshin, Akiva Simes, David Duchovny, Leib Ziserman, Moshe Chalyk, as well as the activists from the left leaning circles Moshe Ravich, Yitzchak Sherman and others, joined by circles of workers and small scale merchants such as David Muchnik, Moshe Shochet, Zelik Kleiner, David Belfer – a provisional committee was established that took upon itself the responsibility of preparing a charter that would set out appropriate conditions of operation for each institution, and would require them to give an accounting of their activities. Dr. Nirenberg of blessed memory, a man acceptable to the community, headed this committee. Rabbi Y. Pagis and Dr. Berkovitz were chosen as assistants. They rented a six room dwelling in the house of Hirshel Mashkautsan on Torgovia Street, and collected all of the ledgers of the institutions. They hired Gedalya Chokla as bookkeeper and Nissel Pagis as secretary. However, before the community managed to centralize all communal matters, the terrible tragedy took place to the Ukrainian Jews, and massive streams of refugees came into Bessarabia.

Our city, which was close to the Dniester, served as a refuge and point of transit for the refugees. The provisional communal council turned overnight into a committee to aid the refugees, and the vital communal matters were pushed to the side.

The Ukranian Committee

With the increase of the stream of refugees in 1920 in Kishinev as well, a Ukrainian committee was organized that was supported by the Joint (Distribution Committee). There were many problems: a) immediate accommodation for families, that is a place to sleep and minimal financial support; b) obtaining transit passage from the leaders of the Romanian army; c) making contact with the families of the refugees in America; d) obtaining a permit from the government for those who wish to remain in Bessarabia. At one time, there was the need for judicial and economic care, social assistance, and dealing with all types of problems that arose from this care. A branch of the Ukrainian committee was organized in Orheyev as well, which indeed was the same communal council with its members, and other volunteers who worked on behalf of the refugees in all necessary areas. The unforgettable effort and dedication of Moshe Kalmanovitz and his wife Leah should be noted.

Figure 7 - Torgovia Street (the market district)

Young and old were assisted by them. Among the others, it is appropriate to note Leibel Kleiner, an active member of Tzeirei Zion and Leib Stolyar, who would trick the guards of the bridge with the pretext that he was accompanying the refugee, who was a worker who was assisting him, and that they were going to work in Sloboda. Thus, he succeeded in bringing dozens of refugees to the route to Kishinev, and saving them from the talons of the Sigurnata (Security Police).

Indeed, the spontaneous response of the Jewish population in Bessarabia in general, and of the residents of our city in particular, to assist their unfortunate brethren who fled from the evil in Ukraine was epic and glorious. On the other hand, the communal activists were detained for 3-4 years from doing anything for the local needy. The economic situation was generally bad, and the communal council had to concern themselves with social issues. Aliza Shpilberg-Chokla tells about this era:

"In May 1925, my father Gedalya, who served as the accounting director of the communal council for many years, died. The communal council hired me as a cashier. I began working in January 1926. Nissel the son of Yoel Pagis and Miryam Beznos (today Rabinovitz who lives in Herzliya) worked in the office.

"Since the communal council renewed its activities in 1924, it succeeded in uniting all of the civic institutions that were dependent on the Jewish community, and it obtained a provisional permit from the Romanian government to authorize the communal charter. The united institutions worked under this charter for several years without disturbance.

"This organizational situation brought a serious change in income, because of the levying of taxes, the increased distribution from the city council, and the meat tax. Several amendments to the communal charter were added, such as the maintaining of organized accounting, communal audits, etc."

Aliza adds: "With appreciation, I recall the significant help that we communal workers provided to the communal leaders in their difficult task of supporting those who suffered from ill fortune. We attempted to provide them with the necessary information as quickly as possible. To those who lost their livelihoods, we would discretely deliver assistance to their homes, and thereby prevent any dishonor to them…"

The New Council in its Political Struggle

With the change of the central authorities, national political problems came to the fore that required astuteness and judicial knowledge in order to protect the national matters of communal life. To this end, the council invited three lawyers to the secretariat of the council: Yosef Shaiovitz, Siuma Pisarevsky and Tuviya Kohan. They designed a charter for the community and obtained appropriate permits as judicial experts. The government directed the community to transfer the educational and cultural institutions, the Talmud Torah, the Yeshiva and the library to the government educational network – which implied the closing of these institutions in the event of failure to fulfill this command. Indeed, these institutions were closed for a certain period. The leadership of the Talmud Torah was forced to join the network due to economic considerations, appoint a principal, and a Christian teacher to teach the Romanian language. The directors of the Yeshiva, thanks to the strong intervention of the communal secretary Y. Shaiovitz, received permission to maintain the Yeshiva under the condition that it would also be included in the public network, and teach religious studies in the afternoons. The students had the right to continue in Gymnasium without examinations. All of the teachers and directors were allowed to be Jews.

The Outbreak of the Storm (1938-1939)

We can get some idea of the economic and political situation of the Jewish community of Orheyev at the outbreak of the storm, from the letters that were received in the summer of 1938 from Itzel Fasir and Yechiel Leyderberg (to the writer of these lines).

Fasir writes: "Our economic situation is very depressed. However, the decree to prove our rights of citizenship is even harsher. From the time of the conquest of Bessarabia, many of the residents of Orheyev who were registered as being born in Transnistria and were not able to locate their birth certificates, which had never been requested of them, as well as the refugees from Ukraine who remained in Bessarabia, are indeed able to obtain certificates for the payment of a significant sum of money. However, most of those who are lacking the certificates are from among the poor."

In order to ease the obtaining of citizenship, the communal council set up a judicial office that helps those who turn to it with advice and guidance. This is the committee that has been described in the Yiddish newspaper Unzer Tzeit that is published in Kishinev (8 Adar I, 5698, February 7, 1939).

The Orheyev Jewish Community

(this announcement was found in the archives by Mrs. Fania Rosenthal, the sister of the poet Zalman.]

Announcement

Permit us to announce to the entire Jewish population of the city of Orheyev and the villages of the region that the Orheyev Jewish Community has founded a judicial office that will give specific information regarding any questions about rights of citizenship.

All Jews are requested to come to the office, where they will receive the necessary information.

The office hours are from 9 a.m. to 1 p.m., and from 4 p.m. to 9 p.m.

The Jewish Community of Orheyev

"… The political situation is also depressed. Permission is not given for a gathering unless it is to be conducted in the Romanian language. This decree prevents the majority of the community that does not understand Romanian from being able to participate in meetings. Therefore, the communal institutions have been hard hit. The Tarbut School, which does not have the legally required labor department, stands to be closed by the government unless a way is found to unite the school with the ORT trade school. Even under this circumstance, we will have to overcome many serious obstacles.

"The government decision to revoke the independence of the Jewish credit cooperatives and to include them in the Romanian cooperative network is also frightening. The roots of the cooperative movement in the economic and social realms of Jewish communal life for its 40 years of existence are known. The directors of the "Farband" and its head Yosef the son of Yisrael Pagis (the lawyer) are fighting with all of their talents to prevent this decree, however, without positive results. Imagine for yourself how great the destructive influence will be on the loan funds in their place, and also for us. How knows what is to come?"

From the letter of Leyderberg (July 1939) (Avraham Malovatsky supplied the letter to the editors.)

"… The political tension continues to increase. An army draft was proclaimed up to the age of 50. Daily, masses are sent to the regiments. The population is perplexed and confused, and nobody knows what tomorrow will bring… The selling of matzos was limited because so many Jews had been drafted to the army. This negatively affected the allocations of the communal council. On the other hand, the stress upon many families whose husbands had been drafted, and to whom the community was not able to offer assistance, increased. Even with this difficult situation, the "oppositionists" did not desist from spying on the communal council. Luck was in their favor. The central Liberal government fell, and the Taranists (ed. note: Peasants' Party) came to power. One of their comrades was appointed as head of the branch, and thereby their status in the community took hold. The previous council, headed by Yaakov Volovsky, was fired. In the meantime, the suffering of those who required help grew, without anyone coming to the rescue."

Figure 8 - Board of the Labor Bank (1920)

Seated from right to left: 1. D. Belfer 2. A. Shander 3. Y. Milshteyn 4. C. Veksler 5. [alef]. Rybukovsky
Standing: 1. Yaakov … (tinsmith) 2. C. Vaksman 3. S. Huberman 4. B. T. Keyser 5. N. Sapozhnik 6. M. Farber 7. H. Shinman

Indeed, the clouds that darkened your skies, oh community of Orheyev, grew even before the hand of the enemy overtook you. Your activists struggled greatly for your existence for many dozens of years. However, the storm destroyed and uprooted. The holy community fell, Orheyev and its natives perished and were destroyed by strangers…

May their memory be kept with us forever.

Figure 9 - City Council (1924-1929)

Seated from right to left: 1. Lawyer Moshe Ravich 2. Rivka Levinson 3. ... 4. ... 10. ...
Standing: 1. ... 2. ... 3. M. Roitkov 4. ... 5. Y. Faser 6. ... 7. M. Goichman 8. M. Frant 9.
D. Trostnitsky 10. Yehudah Yagolnitzer 11. Avraham Lipshin

B. Educational and Cultural Institutions

75 Years of the Existence of the Talmud Torah (1866-1940)

It is a known principle, from that time and always, that the first concern of our Jewish brethren is the education of their children. The lone settler in a remote village would invite a "melamed" to teach his children "Yiddishkeit" (Judaism). Similarly, in every town, groups of parents who had the economic means would hire a melamed for their children. However, nobody concerned themselves with the children of the poor, and on occasion, they were left out of the study of Torah, or they would have to satisfy themselves with merely learning how to read and write.

Such were the educational conditions in our city as well 75 years ago.

At that time, a group of activists arose to rectify the educational situation, concerning themselves primarily with the children of the poor.

Yosef Rabinovitz writes the following in "Hamelitz" of March, 1866: "In our town, a source of salvation was opened for the children of the poor. That is the Talmud Torah, the likes of which there never was before in Orheyev or in any other of the cities of Bessarabia. However, luck was not satisfied with the "Good" that fell to the lot of our children in the Talmud

Torah. A curse was awaiting them that turned into a blessing. Within a few months of the opening of the Talmud Torah, the building went up in flames, and the children that remained were not able to study Torah. However the hands of the activists did not weaken. Within a brief period of time, they fixed up a house of seven large rooms, filled with lights. 112 children studied Torah there from seven teachers who carried out the holy task. Many families who have the means also send their children to this school…"

The Study of the Russian Language

"Mr. Savitch was the representative of the government. He was a Christian with a liberal outlook, the regional supervisor, the overseer of the regional schools, and a wise and beloved man. He took it upon himself to supervise the studies and to concern himself with all matter relating to the Talmud Torah and it success. He believed in the vital importance of ensuring that the students would become proficient in reading and writing of the language of the land, accompanying by a deep understanding of the spirit of the Jewish community that is concerned about the preservation of its religion and customs. In order to remove any suspicion from himself lest his intention was to bring the Jewish students under the wings of Christianity, he advised the supervisors to agree to send the children aged 10 and above for two hours of "Prichodskvaya" (elementary school) and to the regional school every day in order to study Russian language. One of their teachers would accompany them, sit in the class, and ensure that the Jews sat with their heads covered, and not intermingle, Heaven forbid, with the children of the other religion." The writer adds, "... when the supervisors and the parents of the students saw that Mr. Savitch had only good intentions, they agreed to his recommendations. Thirty students of the Talmud Torah would attend the Prichodskvaya, accompanied by their teachers.

In those days, it was a daring act for the parents and the supervisors to send Jewish children to a Christian school. Therefore, according to the words of the writer: "There were many fanatics in our city that complained and groaned bitterly about the fate of these children. They became angry at the supervisors, and were prepared to destroy the Talmud Torah to its foundations." On the other hand, we find an important assessment in Hamelitz about the aforementioned step of the parents and the teachers by the editor "Erez", as follows: "... Hear this our brethren in the cities of Poland and Bessarabia, and take a lesson, this matter will only succeed with a willing soul and good intellect!" It seems that there were very few Jewish communities where public education for the children of the poor stood at the forefront of the thoughts of the communal activists in the way that it did in Orheyev.

To our distress, we were not able to find any other information about communal life in Orheyev in the newspapers, and the era of 1866-1887 is closed to us. Apparently, after Y. Rabinovitz left the city, another writer did not arise for about 20 years. This was the writer Shegav.

A New Building for the Talmud Torah

We read the following in Hamelitz number 135 from 1887:

"… the command already came to the civic council to remove 6,000 silver rubles from the Korovka (meat tax) to build an eight room building. The laying of the cornerstone will take place in a few days."

"After the government officials ensure with seven eyes (ed. note: check closely to ensure that the edict was being followed) that there would be no melamed without a teaching permit, and the few who had permits could not have more than ten students in one class, the tuition fees rose to a point that most of the community could not afford them. Therefore, many more parents wished to enroll their children in the Talmud Torah. They were not successful, for the building was too small to contain the 120 students who had studied there the previous year. Approximately 50 students were not accepted, and everyone's eyes were waiting for the day when the new building would be built, and there would be room for more than 200 students.

"The group of activists, headed by Reb Alter Feinsilver, the faithful and dedicated activist in matters of education, invested much effort in convincing the residents of our city of the urgent necessity of erecting a large building that would be able to accommodate all of the children of the city who are knocking at its doors. Despite the obstacles that the obscurantists put in his way, and despite the fact that they succeeded in pushing him aside from the leadership of the Talmud Torah, Reb Alter did not rest until he succeeded at what he set out to do. The city merited to celebrate the laying of the cornerstone for a building that it can take pride in."

The first principal Mr. Weiland had to be fired after years of dedication to this holy task of education on account of the opposition of the Orthodox. After him came the principal Stachik, who also had to leave his post. Then, the well-known Maskil Yosef Rabinovitz was invited to direct the institution. He also did not last long, and Weiland was returned once again. However, he was once again forced to leave his post after his opponents did not keep their promise of giving him a free hand in the style of teaching.

At the end of the 19th century, the veteran teacher Mr. Krips became the principal of the school and served for close to a decade. A few of his students who are with us still recall the "strong hand" with which he used to conduct himself toward the students.

At the end of the first decades of the 1900s, Krips left the school on account of old age. His place was taken by the young teacher who had recently arrived in our city, Yitzchak Sherman. A new era in the life of the institution began with him. He was blessed with ability, and he was very cultured. He invited the finest young pedagogues in our city, and he raised the institution to a level fitting of its name. The curriculum was set by the entire teaching staff, and was befitting of a four-year government public school curriculum. In addition to the general studies, there was a Hebrew lesson for three hours a week, as well as lessons in Yiddish, and Jewish history in the Yiddish language. Despite the fact that the curriculum was very heavy, the teachers were loved by the students, and the students felt connected to the school.

Figure 10 - Yitzchak Sherman

In the era between the end of the 19th century and the days of the Russian Revolution in 1917, the following Zionist teachers taught: Reb Mendel Naychin, Michael Groyser, Yosef the son of Yoel Pagis, and Ze'ev (Velvel) Shaposhnik-Shafin; and the following members of the Yiddish Socialist Bund Party: Amalya Branover, Fania Isakovna Rabinovitz, her husband, Piatr Abramovitz, Eida Gelbrukh, and others. This teaching staff, under the direction of the intelligent and communally conscious Yitzchak Sherman, succeeded in finding common ground in their work despite their difference of opinion with respect to the language battle that was taking place in the Jewish street. The principal similarly succeeded in improving the budgetary situation, and one can consider the achievements of this era to be among the most important in the existence of the institution.

Figure 11 - Talmud Torah (1917) – Study Room

Seated from right to left: 1. ... 2. ... 3. Michael Groyser 4. Yitzchak Sherman (headmaster) 5. Mendel Naychin
Standing: 1. ... 2. ... 3. Velvel Shaposhnik 4. Leah Fisher 5. Fania Rabinovitz 6. Simone Rabinovitz

The Curse of Romanization

In the first years of the Romanian rule of Bessarabia, the minorities, including the Jewish population, benefited from the political achievements of the Russian Revolution. The Jews achieved the possibility of autonomous governance of the Jewish schools of Bessarabia. A supervisory office was established in 1917, and Messrs. Shlomo Halels and Yitzchak Sherman were appointed as the supervisors in Bessarabia. Within a few years, the conquering authorities realized that autonomous education could serve as a means against the Russification that pervaded on the Jewish street. Very quickly, however, the reactionary government police began to stray from its liberal attitude toward the minorities, and evil decrees impinged upon and restricted the national rights. The governing office was closed after a brief period, and at the end of the 1930s, the Talmud Torah was ordered to appoint a Romanian principal and to shorten the hours of Hebrew studies.

Throughout 75 years, this important popular institution overcame all of the tribulations of the times, struggled valiantly for its existence, and imparted elementary education to thousands of students from among the poor. Within the walls of the Talmud Torah the children breathed comfortably, and benefited from full light and clear air, that was not found in the homes of their parents.

Everything was destroyed and passed from the world during the Holocaust.

The concern of the activists in our town for the education of the children of the workers and the poor was accompanied by the concern of finding them a trade. Already during the 1880s, an institution for the study of trades was set up alongside the Talmud Torah. Thus writes the teacher Baruch Shalom Naychin (in Hamelitz number 166 from 1885): "In recognition of the wedding of our king, may his honor be exalted, the directors of the Talmud Torah have decided to build a large building in the courtyard of the Talmud Torah to teach crafts and trades to the students. The building was already built and plans were already laid to obtain a permit from the council, and on the first day of the year 1886 it started to function". The community also had the desire to teach trades to the children since the small-scale business, peddling and other "airy forms of livelihood" did not sustain those that practiced them. After two years of the existence of the trade classes along side the Talmud Torah, the teacher Mendel Naychin writes the following in Hamelitz number 200, year 1887: "We can realize how precious are crafts and trades now in the eyes of our Jewish brethren from the fact that half of the youth who studied trades in school are children of the householders and well-off." To our dismay, the above lines do not state the number of youths who studied trades, whether they obtained work after they completed school, and whether the trade school lasted for a long time. In our era, from the beginning of the 20th century until the 1920s, we did not hear anything about the existence of a trade school until the establishment of the ORT School.

The ORT Trade School

After the First World War, the organization that spread trades among the Jewish Population, ORT, increased its efforts in Bessarabia. In 1923, two divisions for the study of trades were established in the Talmud Torah building. On account of the lack of fitting conditions, we cannot point to important achievements during the first period. The development grew stronger with the transfer of the trades division to a building that was obtained from the Workers' Loan Society in order to establish a trade school with the participation of ORT.

This is how it happened:

Our community of workers knew better than any other community about the vital need for an institution in which its children would obtain general education and simultaneously be educated in a trade – so that the youths would not go through the seven levels of hell of studying a trade as an apprentice to a craftsman. The matter of setting up a fitting institution occupied the Workers' Loan Society for years already, and they even set up a fund for this purpose. However, larger sums were needed in order to bring this to fruition.

Figure 12 - ORT Technical High School

The Donation from Y. A. Milshteyn
The Representative of the Joint (Distribution Committee)

At their annual meeting in 1924, the advisory committee of the fund proposed the establishment of a trade school. At that same meeting, our friend Yitzchak Milshteyn, who also represented the Joint to the ORT organization, participated from the Joint. His opinion was that the community of workers itself would not be able to bear the yoke of the budget needed for the school, and he proposed that the local ORT committee be taken as a partner. With combined forces, they should search for a fitting location, and thereby improve the work conditions of the institution.

Figure 13 - ORT Graduating Class of 1924

Seated from right to left: 1. ... 2. Freiberg 3. Noyman 4. Averbukh
Standing: 1. ... 2. ... 3. Chuvis 4. Laufer 5. ... 6. Strol 7. headmaster L. Rozenfeld 8. ... 9. ...
10. Clara Osipovna 11. M. Lemberg 12. Bozinyan 13. Rechevsky 14. ...

That year, an agreement was reached between the loan society and the ORT committee to join forces. Y. Milshteyn secured a donation from the Joint of the sum of 150,000 Lei in order to purchase a building, as well as 70,000 Lei to improve the building and make it fitting for the needs of a proper school.

The Struggle for its Existence

Despite the fact that the housing conditions and furnishings were arranged appropriately, the other problems were not solved so simply. There was a great difference between the restricted curriculum that existed in the Talmud Torah, and that which the directors of the ORT School proposed. At a time when the Talmud Torah was forced to dedicate most of the school hours to theoretical studies, and the study of trades was a subordinate matter, the desire of all of the activists and teachers of the ORT School was to instill in all of the students general knowledge that would serve them well in obtaining and earning their livelihood through a trade. The school committee attempted to secure a fitting principal and teachers, people with higher education, who would agree to work in depressed conditions with a limited budget. We should positively mention the dedication of the workers of the school, who carried out their work faithfully despite the low salary, and educated dozens of young men and women in Torah and trades.

There were many debates among the members of the committee with respect to the cultural and national-political direction that would be imparted to the students. The head of the committee, M. Ravich, who was a veteran Yiddishist, and the first principal of the school Marek Solomonovitz Rapoport did not agree to include Hebrew studies. On the other hand, a portion of the members of the committee saw the need to ensure that the school graduates were comfortable in Hebrew, so as to enable their aliya to the Land. After Rapoport left, the school was directed by Avraham Daskel, and finally by Leibel Rozenfeld, a chemist and the native of our town. Then, the Zionists had the upper hand.

Indeed, many who were educated by the ORT School made aliya to the Land and fit in very well. Without doubt, knowing something about the language significantly eased their absorption.

From the words of Sima Taran-Karabelnik, a student of the school during the years 1923-1924:

"… I will never forget that fortunate day when we were informed of the opening of a sewing department for girls and a carpentry department for boys by the ORT organization.

"Most of the students of the school were from among the poor. The hours of study in the walls of the Talmud Torah were the only hours of light and joy during our childhood, in contrast to the conditions that we found at home when we returned from the Talmud Torah. A dark room, cold, hunger, and depressed conditions that faced Mother and Father were our lot during the hours that we spent at home. When the time came to finish the course of studies in the Talmud Torah, the question of what next faced the boy or girls. To our good fortune, the trade division opened up.

"I remember the degree of love and enthusiasm with which we dedicated ourselves to our studies, both theoretical and technical. The teachers as well were imbued with their dedication and their interest in new teaching methodologies. (The teaching day was divided into 2 hours for theoretical studies and 6 hours of trade studies.) They dedicated their time to the various efforts of the school. An exhibition of our work was arranged at the end of the teaching year. How much effort did they dedicate to the success of this event.

"The purpose of the exhibitions was threefold: a) to publicize the achievements of the students; b) to encourage the students to excel at their work; c) to earn some income from the sale of products, a portion of which would be used to support the students. Of course, this event was very important to the students, and this promoted the success of the exhibition in no small way. How happy was I when I received my first paycheck, 30% of the proceeds of the sale of my products.

"The activists of the ORT school served in their roles for many years, despite the fact that there were many financial difficulties as well as disruptions due to the lack of teachers. Nevertheless, the students succeeded in attaining a significant professional level in three years of studies. Some of the graduates of the sewing division transferred to the old trade school in Kishinev that was directed by Mrs. Babitz in order to complete their studies. There too, they excelled in their professional knowledge and their cultural level. The following were the members of the committee throughout the years of existence of the ORT school in partnership with the Workers' Loan Society:

"Dr. Shlissel, as chairman, who served for about 3 years until he moved to Kishinev; M. Ravich, Yitzchak Fasir (vice-chairmen), Yonah Shamban, David Belfer, and others.

"Principals: as has been stated, Rapoport, Solomon, Markovitz, Avraham Daskal, Leib Rozenfeld, N. Davidovitz.

"The teachers (male): the aforementioned plus A. Malovatsky, Ada Rechevsky and Pinchas Zadonaisky.

"The sewing teachers (female): Klara Osipovna (of Kishinev), Bilah Grigoriavna and Chana Leifer.

"The carpentry directors: Chayim Ben Baruch (Yefim Borisovitz) of Kishinev, Yonah Shamban and others."

The Laying of a Nationalistic Educational Foundation in our City

A group of parents who were activists in Tzeirei Zion (Young Zion), who were not satisfied with the local educational situation, did what they could to lay the foundation for nationalistic education.

Various communal activists preferred the various communal aid organizations and abandoned the needs of nationalistic education. The two popular schools in the city, the Yeshiva and the Talmud Torah, were not appropriate for our spirit from a nationalist Zionist perspective. The Yeshiva was influenced by the Orthodox activists, whereas in the Talmud Torah, the ideas of the Yiddishists took the fore. Those who desired a progressive nationalistic education in the Hebrew language were forced to take up the yoke of founding their own school, fitting for the spirit of the Zionist movement. The activists of the towns of Bessarabia, headed by the "Cultural Center" in Kishinev, who founded schools in the Hebrew language, served as an example.

These educational institutions proved their viability and served as a shield against the spread of Romanization in Bessarabia.

The Birthpangs of the Kindergarten

In order to change the educational situation in our city, in 1924, a group of parents made efforts to establish a kindergarten for their children that would serve as the basis for the establishment of a Tarbut School. To this end, the promoters turned to the heads of the Zionist movement in the city and requested organizational help and communal protection. However, their thoughts were that there was no hope in obtaining financial support from the community, and the chances of maintaining the kindergarten on the accounts of the parents alone were very slim. Therefore, they were not prepared to help, and this "enterprise" was doomed from the outset.

Figure 14 - Child Care Founders 1924

Seated from right to left: 1. L. Rozenfeld 2. B. Duchovny 3. Y. Naychin 4. Volovsky
Standing: 1. M. Rotkov 2. R. Davidovitz 3. Y. Galperin 4. G. Shneurson (kindergarten teacher) 5. Y. Roitman

Disappointed from the negative response of the community to our issue, we turned to the Cultural Center in Kishinev to assist us with guidance and in establishing the kindergarten. The center sent Mr. Shvartz of blessed memory to us, a gifted teacher and activist in the Center (he was a former resident of our city), in order to take care of the matter. Mrs. Shvartz strengthened our hand, and we immediately decided to open up the registration of children. A committee was selected (in 1914) consisting of M. Rotkov, Leibel Volovsky, Batya Duchovny, Yaakov Galperin, Gerisha Rozenfeld, Roza Shapira, and Yaakov Roitman. The members of the committee visited the homes of the parents and registered 25 children. It seemed that the dream had turned into reality. Behold, the kindergarten arose to existence! Only now did the difficulties become apparent: the problem of appropriate premises, equipment, a piano, and unforeseen expenditures. These problems were sufficient to affect the activists and bring them to despair. Furthermore, there was the problem of the lack of experienced kindergarten teachers. This problem stood with all its strength, since we were in need of a person of exceptional organizational ability who would be able to withstand the difficulties that already stood before our eyes and ones that were liable to become exposed as time went on. After lengthy negotiations, the Center provided us, with the recommendation of Mr. Y. Alterman the principal of the seminary for kindergarten teachers in Kishinev, Bluma Shneurson of Bendery, Bessarabia. She was a talented young woman, full of energy, and a graduate of the seminary. She was a kindergarten teacher who was appropriate for the local conditions. (Today she is a kindergarten teacher in Petach Tikva.)

Already at the time of the first discussion with Mrs. Shneurson about the equipment of the kindergarten, it became clear that the tuition fees of the parents must be increased in order to assure the existence of the institution throughout the year. We also overcame that, and on Cheshvan 8, 1924, the first Hebrew speaking kindergarten was opened in Orheyev.

Throughout the first 3-4 months of its existence, the kindergarten won the appreciation of our community. Echoes of the Hebrew language spoken by the children to their families attracted the hearts of the community. Many locals as well as people from outside the city, who were affected by the achievements of the kindergarten teacher in her work, visited the kindergarten. It is appropriate to note the tremendous performance of the students of the kindergarten at the public Purim festivities. The larger community saw the proficiency of the children in the Hebrew language, which became a spoken language to them, and appreciated the value of the achievements of the kindergarten. Indeed, we successfully concluded the first year and prepared to maintain the kindergarten for the second school year.

We again faced budgetary difficulties at the beginning of the second year, which endangered the existence of the kindergarten. A significant number of parents, to whom the tuition fees were a heavy burden, were forced to forego their good desire to give their children a Hebrew education, and removed their children from the kindergarten. The budget was affected greatly by this. The activists of the institution had no choice other than to restrict the expenditures to a minimum. On the other hand, a large portion of the committee opposed the maintaining of the kindergarten on a tight budget, for fear that this would have a bad influence upon the studies and bring uncertainty to the future of Hebrew education in the city at a time when there was no communal support. The few that were "crazy about the issue" claimed that since this was a first degree matter of national life tied functionally to the Zionist movement, the heads of the community who also included communal activists would be forced to take into consideration the existence of the kindergarten, and they would finally help out the enterprise. After difficulties and deliberations, it was decided to maintain the kindergarten for the second year on a restricted budget.

The writer of these lines did not easily accept the unpleasant task of informing Mrs. Shneurson that she must forgo a significant amount of her salary, which was otherwise liable to impinge upon the restricted budget. Nevertheless, Mrs. Shneurson responded in the affirmative with the recognition that without a sacrifice on her part, the committee would not be able to sustain the kindergarten in which she invested her best efforts. The kindergarten opened, and we also overcame all difficulties and ended with a limited loss. Thus, we attained the objective. The children of the kindergarten served as the basis for a Hebrew school patterned after the schools conducted by Tarbut.

When the children of the kindergarten transferred to the school, the question again arose if we would be able to sustain the kindergarten, since we now had to concern ourselves with the existence of the school. On the other hand, some of the members of the committee saw the need to maintain the kindergarten into the future in order to prepare a reserve of students for grade 1 every year. However, this time, we did not have the means to enroll more than a few children whose parents were able to bear the expenses of the kindergarten. Once again, there was the need for additional cutbacks. Under such conditions, there was no possibility of maintaining a kindergarten teacher from outside the city, whose living expenses were large. Mrs. Yehudit Naychin of blessed memory, who worked as an assistant to Mrs. Shneurson, came to our aid. Yehudit the daughter of the teacher Mendel Naychin had pedagogical expertise and refined personal character traits. She was of a noble spirit, a dedicated Zionist activist, and she agreed to work in the kindergarten despite the financial difficulties that affected us. It is fitting to point out that her agreement was decisive in the maintenance of the kindergarten, which opened and operated for a third year despite the fact that the number of children was small and the budget was extremely restricted. The Hebrew kindergarten in Orheyev was closed at the end of the third year.

The Tarbut School

It is natural that the group of parents who bore the yoke of the existence of the kindergarten, worked a second time and with greater energy to set up the

Hebrew elementary school. Indeed, before the second year of the kindergarten ended, we already entered into negotiations with the Tarbut Center in Kishinev in order to obtain a permit from the Romanian government to open a first grade.

After the center obtained a permit for us, we approached the task with double energy. First, we requested once again that the communal council include us in the network of educational institutions, for guidance, supervision and communal budgets. This time as well, as was with the case of the founding of the kindergarten, the writer of these lines had to struggle greatly with the Yiddishist Mr. Yitzchak Sherman of the communal council on the one side, and on the other side the following representatives of the religious stream: Messrs. Moshe Yonovitz, David Muchnik, Zelik Kleiner and Yosef Duchovny. However, through the strength of our attainments with the kindergarten, we earned the support of the heads of the community. At a meeting of the communal council that was dedicated to our matter, it was decided to affiliate us with the community. This decision encouraged us further. From now on, we would be under the assured and official communal protection.

Nevertheless, we knew that we would not be helped greatly from a budgetary perspective, for the needs of the community always exceeded its financial capabilities. However, we felt a certain security in our activities.

It was a great achievement for us that the community set aside a room in the Talmud Torah building, and we were freed from a concern over premises. Then, we had two problems to solve: the problems of a certified teacher and the problem of the budget. One was tied with the other.

D. Mozhelyan was educated by and a frequenter of the household of the distinguished teacher Reb Mendel Naychin, one of the activists of Tzeirei Zion, who was faithful and dedicated to national renaissance. We placed all of our hopes in him that he would succeed in establishing the new enterprise on a firm base and raising it to the level of an institution worthy of its name. Indeed, we were not disappointed. We overcame the difficulties of the first year, and from then on, we added a new class and new teachers year by year. In the second year, Mr. Shneur Geynichovitz became a teacher. He was one of the forces and activists in the "Bnei Yisrael" organization, a wonderful teacher and counselor (today the principal of a school in Israel for more than 20 years). In the third year, Avraham Rechulsky joined the teaching staff. He was a young man with a progressive religious outlook, and was enthusiastically dedicated to national education (presently, he has worked in Kupat Cholim for many years). That year, a music class was instituted. Sarah Fleshler, a teacher in the government Gymnasium for girls, was invited for that task. She was a talented young woman from an impoverished family who succeeded in completing the course of studies in the Gymansium in Orheyev, and who got a job as the secretary of the Gymnasium. With the anti-Semitic atmosphere that pervaded in the Romanian community, it was a significant achievement for a Jewish educator to be appointed to such a responsible position. Rechulsky left the school in the fourth year, and Binyamin Yonovitz (the son of Moshe) and Chaya Naychin joined as teachers. She was the daughter of Baruch Shalom Naychin who was also an activist in Bnai Yisrael. She was the only girl of our town who left university studies and joined a Hachsharah Kibbutz. She did not shy away from any difficult work, and she cut down trees along with the boys during the cold winter months.

Figure 15 - David Mozhelyan

At the beginning of the fifth year of studies, Mozhelyan left the city, and the parent committee invited Moshe Fisher and his wife Rachel, who returned to our city from the university, as principal and teacher. They continued along with Geynichovitz, B. Yonovitz and the student Zadonaisky (the son-in-law of Yosef the son of Yoel Pagis) to continue the level that was forged by those who came before.

Two Years of the Hebrew Gymnasium

As is known, the course of studies in public school was four years. Those children who completed the four grades faced the question: what next?

Some of the parents who did not have the means transferred their children to the Romanian Gymnasium. However, most of the parents decided to open a class with the curriculum of a government Gymnasium. This was a bold step on the part of those parents, for the conditions of maintaining a public school were very different than those needed to maintain a high school. However, the anti-Semitic conditions that pervaded in the government schools on the one side, and the educational achievements of the students and pleasant atmosphere in the Hebrew school on the other side, justified the bold step of the parents. At that time (1930) Yechiel the son of David Duchovny, who had completed his studies in the University of Vienna, returned to the city. He was a second generation Zionist. He took upon himself the directorship of the first grade of the Gymnasium, with the goal of establishing the rest of the grades. The second teacher was the young woman Klara the daughter of Ben-Zion Chaimovitz, who was also a native our city.

Figure 16 - The Girl's Gymnasium

Thirty students, who graduated from the school, studied in the first class, and continued on to the second year.

It is appropriate to note that the achievements of the students in their studies influenced the community positively, and especially influenced the parents. Mothers who were far-removed from communal activism dedicated themselves with heart and soul, and took the financial responsibility toward the teachers and strengthening of the class upon themselves. The following stand out from among the parents that worked on behalf of the gymnasium: Mrs. Vaynshteyn the wife of the textile merchant Avraham Vaynshteyn, Zalmina Bogoslavsky (today a resident of Kiryat Motzkin), Batya Duchovny, Moshe Chalyk as communal representative, and others.

Figure 17 - School of Culture, 4th Grade

Seated from right to left: 1. B. Yonovitz 2. S. Geynichovitz 3. M. Fisher 4. R. Markovetsky 5. L. Nairner

Much goodwill and energy was dedicated by the principals, the teachers and the parents, during the two years of the existence of the two gymnasium classes. The children were examined by teachers of the government gymnasium, and not one child failed. The level of studies did not fall beneath that of a government institution. Even the relationship with the communal council was positive. Nevertheless, the parents had to forego their will to provide a Hebrew education to their children on account of the economic situation that was worsening with each passing day. It was clear that there was no future to the young institution, and with great anguish to those who cared for it, the gymnasium closed in 1932.

The Longevity of the Tarbut School

The fate of the public Tarbut School was not the same as that of the gymnasium. Both on account of its popularity and its vitality, the school took root over its first five years, and became an organic part of the educational network of the community. Those communal representatives, Messrs Yonovitz, Muchnik and Kleiner, who were negative at first, now agreed to support its existence by provided support from the communal budget. Rooms in the courtyard of the Talmud Torah were donated and set up for the needs of the school. The physical conditions improved. The positive relationship with the community and particularly the appropriate educational level strengthened the hand of the activists. Some of the founders of the school stood with us even when their children finished the course of studies, and gave of their energy until the destruction of the city and all that was precious in it.

From among the workers of the school, it is appropriate to point out the cleaning lady, the widow Sara Perlov (the mother of Matityahu, her husband fell in the First World War). This woman, whose entire salary from this institution barely supplied enough money to feed her only child, cared for the children of the school with motherly dedication, ensured that the children would not be cold during the winter, and made sure that they would finish their meals.

Bitter and difficult was the struggle of the group of parents to whom the matter of nationalistic Hebrew education was dear. This was unusual work. Money and blood were invested until finally an institution was established in which hundreds of boys and girls from among the working class were educated in the purity of the Hebrew language and with love of the nation. Even those who continued their education in government educational institutions were fortified with the national spirit that the Tarbut School imparted to them. In that era (the 1920s), Romanization was on the ascendancy, and assimilation consumed the best part of the Jewish community. These hundreds of youth were a shield in the face of the stream of assimilation, and they also played an honorable role at the appropriate time in the various streams of the Zionist movement.

Many of the students of the school made aliya to the land and participated in the building of the Land. (One of them, Menachem Rotkov of blessed memory, fell in the War of Independence).

An expression of the deep national consciousness and appreciation for its supporters by the active parents is evident from the following letter.

"From the Parent Committee of the Tarbut School in Orheyev, A letter Presented to the teacher Shneur Geynichovitz, Nissan, 5692 (April 2, 1932), on the occasion of his aliya to the Land

Dear Friend!

You took a very responsible task upon yourself to be a teacher in the Hebrew school. You took upon yourself the duty of educating the children to be among the builders of the future of our nation and our Land. The way is not paved with roses. It is full of obstacles and stumbling blocks from outside and within. Education in our city was damaged and in decline, and you were called to fix it. You approached your work with great faith, and your spirit was exposed with your first steps. You won the hearts of the students, and awakened in them a love for you and your teachings. You planted a love of their studies and of Hebrew education into their hearts, and prepared them to be among the builders of the national future of our nation.

Great were the obstacles that stood in the path. You overcame them. With the faith and trust that beat in your soul, you brought the goal closer.

Now, after five years of hard work, you are leaving our school as a victor. Your goal was attained. The school is imbued with your spirit, and it will continue along its path with this spirit. Even though your departure from us is difficult for us and our children, we are comforted by the fact that when you come to arrive at the desired land, you will find a field of activity for your tireless energy; for even there, in the land of national redemption, you will have many fans.

Our dear friend, please accept our recognition and appreciation. We take leave of you at this time with great anguish. We promise you that you and your blessed work in our institution will remain etched deeply in our hearts for a long time.

Signed by the members of the parents' committee: Moshe Chalyk, Shimon Sirkovitz, Mordechai Rotkov, Sh. Malis, Fishel Aberman, Ina Volovsky, Avraham Libertov, Yehudah Leib Rapoport, Shmerel Beker, David Belfer, Baruch Kerdik, A. Belocherkovsky, David Muchnik, Mania Sharf"

Written and presented by the master of ceremonies M. Rotkov.

Chapter 7

The Struggle for A Jewish Party

(For the 1929 parliamentary elections)

by Avraham Malovatsky

Translated by Jerrold Landau

With the founding of the "Jewish Party" (Partidul Evreiesc) in Romania, a branch was also founded in our city. Avraham Lipshin was chosen as chairman. He was a man of great energy and initiative, a dedicated nationalist who knew how to foster respectful relationships with the local authorities. Aside from this, he was not afraid of strongly criticizing the persecution and terror of the heads of the government. He related with scorn and hatred to those Jews who ingratiated themselves to the landowners. His appearances at public gatherings were always greeted with enthusiasm, for he was a popular and gifted speaker in juicy Yiddish. He, along with Dr. Nachum Berkovitz, Yosef the son of Yoel Pagis, Efrayim the son of Yisrael Pagis and Eidel Yagolnitzer conducted a wide range of activity in the entire Orheyev region for the benefit of the slate of the Jewish Party. The Romanian authorities persecuted and oppressed the opposition parties, whether on the right or the left, and it is no wonder that they fought against the young Jewish Party to the point of destruction.

The authorities in our city were well aware of the Jewish organizational power, and when the time of the elections approached, they employed barbaric tactics to prevent the appearance of our party's list in the region.

One event is etched in my memory that typifies the battles of the authorities during the time of the parliamentary elections in Romania, and the struggle of the local Jewish Party.

At that time, I worked as the official secretary in the notary office of Simcha Shechtman (one of the two Jewish notaries in all of Bessarabia). Among the many clients of our office were most of the political parties, whose official electoral lists were registered permanently with us.

The days of the election approached, and all of the parties in our town were able to arrange and present their lists of candidates to the chairman of the electoral committee. Our party suffered greatly from the lack of financial means, and it struggled hard to designate appropriate candidates for its list. Two days before the deadline for the submission of lists, Avraham Lipshin appeared in our office with a number of Jewish voters to sign the list in accordance with the law. After the signatures of the candidates were authorized by the notary, they were given to the Jewish lawyer A. Nayman in order to present to the electoral committee. The lawyer arrived at the regional courthouse toward evening. He entered the hallway, and at the moment that he approached the room of the chairman of the electoral committee, forces of the secret police attacked him. Despite his loud shouts, the door of the chairman of the electoral committee did not open. The list of the Jewish party was forcibly removed from the hands of the lawyer and torn to shreds.

The news of the destruction of the list spread immediately through the city. The Jewish delegates were perplexed, and their anger was kindled. The chairman of the Jewish Party, Avraham Lipshin, did not despair, and he immediately began to arrange a new list. The local authorities that had been victorious in the first round decided to win the second round as well. Detectives and policemen stood around the three notary offices and did not allow the Jews to enter the door of the offices. They almost lost any hope of delivering a new list to the electoral committee.

I was afraid the entire time about the fate of our list. Therefore, I produced two additional copies of the Jewish list, and kept them as a reserve, without telling anyone. Now the time came to bring out the copies in order to renew the list and present it to the electoral committee.

I returned to the office at night, took out the copies, arranged all of the formalities from scratch, and ran with the lists to the house of the notary so he could sign it. He very willingly signed the papers and returned them to me.

I wanted to run to Lipshin, but I was afraid that the detectives and police might be surrounding his house. Therefore, I set out for the house of Simcha Kestlicher, a candidate of the Jewish list. I gave him the list, and asked him to get in touch with Lipshin.

The next morning, Lipshin appeared in our office. There were dozens of Jews surrounding the office, and the police were obstructing their entry to the office. Lipshin turned to the police and strongly demanded them to disband and not prevent the Jews from entering and signing the list. In the meantime, the gathering of Jews increased, and the police was forced to enlist additional forces to control the crowd.

The struggle lasted until 11:00 a.m. At that time, the police chief arrived and ordered the police to break the siege on the office, for the list of the Jewish Party had already been presented in full to the electoral committee by a Christian lawyer (a member of the opposition party).

Only then did it become clear that the gathering of Jews around our office was a smart ploy by Lipshin in order to divert the attention of the authorities away from the room of the chairman of the electoral committee, by encouraging a concentration of the police forces in a different location. This would allow the lawyer to enter the room of the electoral committee. The authorization of the party in Orheyev was received with great joy not only by the Jewish community, but also by the other competing parties who were struggling with all their might against the terror of the "Liberal" government.

The election campaign passed, and the stubborn struggle produced positive results. The list obtained a significant number of votes in the Orheyev region. Four representatives of the Jewish Party were elected: the lawyer M. Landau, Mesha Vaysman, Sami Zinger, and Fisher. They knew how to defend national matters with national pride.

Figure 18 - Bessarabskaya Street

Part II - The Youth and National Resurrection

Chapter 8

The Beginning of Chibat Zion

by M. R.

Translated by Jerrold Landau

The First Delegates from the Region of Orheyev

Orheyev had the merit of having three residents of its region among the first and most prominent of the group of activists that founded and established the Chibat Zion movement in Bessarabia and across its borders. One of them, Yosef Rabinovitz, a native of Orheyev, was selected by the Chovevei Zion chapter in Kishinev, which was headed by Dr. Labontin, Dr. Slutsky and others, as a delegate to the Land of Israel in order to see the conditions in the Land from close up.

The second one, whose honor preceded him in his Zionist activities, was Meir Dizengof, who was the mayor of Tel Aviv. He was a native of the village of Akimovichy in the region of Orheyev. Dizengof was the first representative to the Chovevei Tzion convention in Drozagnik (June 16, 1887). He was chosen by the heads of the movement in Kishinev. He excelled in his presentation and personality.

The third, Nachum Roitman, was born in a village near Teleneshty in the Orheyev region. He was also a distinguished personality, and a very active Zionist. He played an important role in the Chovevei Zion movement in Bessarabia during the 1890s.

At the time that Dr. Cohen Bornstein organized the "postal department" in Kishinev, N. Roitman was one of the two secretaries, and the prime composer of the circulars and letters, which served as the theoretical basis for the doctrine of Zionism.

After the death of Engineer Gotlieb the delegate of the Keren Kayemet LeYisrael (Jewish National Fund), N. Roitman was invited to stand at the head of the Keren Kayemet. From them, the masses of the people drew near to this activity and made their donations in a generous fashion.

These were the prominent sons, men of vision and deed who, with their personal talents, stood above the others of their generation in the region of Orheyev and all of Bessarabia, and earned an honorable place in the Zionist movement for them, even though their place was missing in Orheyev itself. Nevertheless, with their great influence in the movement, it is without doubt appropriate to specially note them in the history of the city and its activists.

The Chovevei Zion Movement in Orheyev

In their "Hamelitz" writings, Baruch Shalom Naychin and Avraham Borsutsky testify that on Sunday, the first day of Chanuka of the year 1896, the tenth anniversary of the founding of the Chovevei Zion movement in our city will be celebrated.

From here, it is clear that the Chovevei Zion organization was founded in 1886; however we are lacking any information on the activities of the organization until 1890. In its ledgers of 1902, the Odessa committee includes a list of donors to the committee of "Supporters of the Jewish Settlers in the Land of Israel" from the three years of 1890-1892. It includes 24 donors who donated 3 rubles or more in 1890, and 28 donors in 1891, over and above the approximately 70 donors who donated up to one ruble annually during those two years.

The activities of the organization paused in 1892. In Hamelitz number 229 of the year 1896, the following is written about the reason for the pause: "In our city, the Chovevei Zion organization stands out. A fine future has been foretold for it as well. Unfortunately, however, the plate turned over, and the number of members is dwindling from day to day. The reason is that several people resolved in their hearts to leave their country and to make aliya to the Holy Land with the hope that they will fill all of their wants there, and that they will find all good there. They did heed the warnings that are printed in the newspapers on a daily basis that those who do not have sufficient money to purchase land and to support themselves in the first years after their arrival should not plan to make aliya, for the Zionist action committee in Jaffa is not able to help them, etc. After these impetuous people came to the Land and saw that their hope had been shattered, they complained to the members of the active committee that they were men of iniquity, etc... Many of these disappointed people returned to their homes, which had a bad influence upon the people of our city. They became impediments and slandered the Land, brazenly stating: 'If a Zionist preacher appears in our city again, we will rise up against him and pass judgement upon him...' For this reason, the members of this organization in our city became weakened, and the strength of the movement dwindled drastically."

The situation of the movement improved greatly after about two years. The number of members doubled, and the donations for the benefit of the settlements increased. However, disturbances never ceased from the Orthodox sector.

In Hamelitz number 223 from 1894, we read among other things: "In this year, the idea of the settlement of the Land of Israel spread out significantly... The people brought many donations for the benefit of the settlement, and the number of members doubled. More than 50 rubles were collected from the collection plates of the Eve of Yom Kippur. The profit from the etrogim that were brought by the members from Jaffa also went to the benefit of the settlement. However, this angered the opponents of the organization, and they searched for pretexts to disturb the work of the activists. They poured disgrace and wrath upon the members in our town, and vented their wrath upon the etrogim, stating that the etrogim from Corfu (Italy) were kosher without doubt, and the etrogim from the Land of Israel were grafted, so it was forbidden to recite a blessing upon them. These instigators gathered the townsfolk each evening and disseminated their slander about the movement. One of their members even permitted himself to defame the prominent rabbis who forbade the etrogim of Corfu, claiming that they were clean-shaven and complete apikorsim (heretics)."

With all this, after a year, the fortunes of the organization in the city once again were on the rise. B. Sh. Naychin writes about this briefly in Hamelitz number 80 from the year 1895, as follows:

"Thanks to the official from our town, Mr. Borsutsky, and to all of those who helped him at all times, our city collected more than 700 silver rubles for the support of the settlement in the Land of Israel, despite the anger of the zealots who opposed this mighty effort and placed obstacles along the path to impede the actualization of this idea in the community."

The Ten Year Celebration of the Chovevei Zion Organization in Orheyev

Many were the obstacles and detractors that impeded the activities of the movement in those days... However, the movement gave rise to people of spirit who made the national cause into the highest goal of their lives. A group of dedicated activists arose in our city who dedicated themselves to the success of the Zionist ideal with all their hearts. These were Avraham Borsutsky the head of the organization; Moshe Ravich (lawyer); Aharon Fikhman (wealthy merchant); Shmuel Lipshin (merchant); Sender Pagis (merchant); Reb Alter Menashe's (merchant); and Fania, the wife of A. Borsutsky. (Aside from Alter

Menashe's, all of them participated in the Zionist conventions in Odessa.) The group of activists struggled strongly against all of the obstacles and brought the Chovevei Zion organization in our city to the conclusion of a period of ten years of activity.

We read about the celebration of the first decade of the existence of the organization in Hamelitz number 263 from the year 1896 (B. Sh. Naychin):

"The preparations of the Chovevei Zion organization in our city went on for approximately one month. Their facial expressions expressed their feelings, for the joy in their hearts continued to grow. They were preparing for the great festivity – that of the decade since the day that the youth of our city united their hearts into one organization bearing the name of Chovevei Zion. The day designated for celebrating the decade of Chovevei Zion is the first night of Chanukah, the holiday of the Maccabees. On the first night of the Festival of Lights, all of those invited, the members of Chovevei Zion of our city, gathered together, with signs of joy and gladness radiating from their faces for they merited to reach this great festivity. How many adventures did the idea of the love of our land go through during those ten years! This holy idea suffered greatly from the hands of its detractors and obstructers who came from our midst. It persevered and was strengthened, and will send its fruits throughout the entire Jewish Diaspora.

"Chovevei Zion of our city gathered at 6 p.m., and the honorable Mr. Alter Feinsilver opened the gathering with a few words. Then, a memorial was made to the soul of our Gaon Rabbi Yitzchak Elchanan Spector of blessed memory and the soul of the lover of Zion Dr. Pinsker of blessed memory. Then the official of our town, Avraham Borsutsky, arose and described to the gathering all of the efforts for the idea of love of Zion, and the events that took place with regard to it. Later, the preacher from Zion Mr. Lantzman, who had been invited to our city for this event, delivered his address on the occasion of this celebration. Then, the tables were set, and those gathered partook of treats and drank wine from our Holy Land, the fruits of the sweat of our farmers who are developing the fields of our Land. Letters of blessing and telegrams arrived from Rabbi Shmuel Mohilever may he live long, Professor Bielkovsky of the Odessa committee, the chairman Mr. Grinberg, and others.

"My pen is too short to describe the spiritual pleasure and joy that was felt by each and every one of us. The attendees returned home glad and joyful."

Chapter 9

The Beginnings of the Tzeirei Zion
(Young Zion) Movement

by A. Y. Golani[1]

Translated by Jerrold Landau

Figure 19 - Youth of Zion

I moved to Orheyev in the year 5668, a city in which the people were of a high cultural level. There, there was an important Zionist movement headed by people of the intelligentsia including Avraham Borsutsky. The veteran Zionists were the Zionists of the shekel or Zionists of the shares (of the Settlement Treasury). Aside from the shekel and the shares, they had no involvement with the movement. The majority of the sons and daughters of these Zionists leaned toward the Russian Liberation movement, and only the Borsutsky family (Avraham and his wife Fania) raised high the banner of Zionism. The youth gathered around them. I also joined this group, and with time I became involved in the activity. Along with the other members, we developed wide-ranging Zionist activities. We convened gatherings in synagogues and private halls. We arranged reading evenings in the Hebrew language, and we busied ourselves with the spreading of the Hebrew language among the youth. There was a broad Socialist movement there. The Bund also struck roots among the workers in the various places of work. A war of words was waged between them and us. Since I myself was a worker, my words were heeded and accepted by the workers. Our gatherings were clandestine. Since the authorities persecuted every liberation movement in Russia, we would gather on winter nights in basements. In the summer, we would find secret places on the crests of Mount Ivanus. It once happened that the police conducted a search in my house. I was imprisoned in the home of the governor of the city for one day. From that time, my status rose in the eyes of our opponents.

Figure 20 - A. Y. Golani

In those days, news reached us about Tzeirei Zion chapters that sprouted up in various places of our region. Ferment began among our members as well. We saw the need to split off from the veterans, and we searched for a basis for Zionist activity among the masses. The Tzeirei Zion movement began to crystallize in Kishinev with the efforts of Yosef Shprintzak, who came from Warsaw to live in Kishinev.

Avraham and Fania Borsutsky indeed belonged to the General Zionists, but they searched out the possibility of practical activity in the circles of the veterans and did not find their desire. They opened up their homes to our group of youths. The path of Tzeirei Zion was not clear and set. Each city and town had its own style, different than that of its fellows. At that time, it issued a

proclamation in Orheyev with the following motto: "With blood and fire Judea
fell, and with blood and fire Judea shall arise". This was to impart a
revolutionary style into the young movement, patterned after the other youth
movements. That year (5665), the war between Tzeirei Zion and the members
of Ogdana grew stronger, according to the testimony of Freiburg. Famous
propagandists such as Dr. Mosenzan appeared in southern Russia. He passed
through Bessarabia in a victory journey. When he passed through Orheyev, his
strongest detractors were silenced. The influence of his words upon the masses
was deep. At that time, the star of Chayim Grinberg, a native of the city of
Kalarash, was rising. Our movement began to spread out and broaden. It took
on the distinctive appearance of a movement of workers, close in spirit and
form to the Russian S. R. movement. Then, Tzeirei Zion of Orheyev took
council and decided to utilize their own power for publicity in the towns and
settlements of our region. Among those who took on this task were Yosef the
son of Yoel Pagis, Yosef the son of Yisrael Pagis, and the writer of these lines.
During these travels, I came to the town of Dubossary on the banks of the
Dneister and settled there for two years…

Figure 21 - Yosef Shprintzak in Orheyev

[1] During the time of his wandering, A. Y. Golani of blessed memory came to Orheyev and
spent approximately two years there. He was one of the important activists in the Tzeirei
Zion movement, and his influence was deeply felt. He made aliya to the Land in the year
5665 and was one of the first teachers. Golani died in the year 5714 / 1954 in Ramat Gan
and was buried in the settlement of Nahalal, of which he was one of the founders.

Chapter 10

In Our Group

by A. Malovatsky

Translated by Jerrold Landau

In 1919, the stream of Jewish refugees from Ukraine to Bessarabia increased. For many of them, our city was a temporary stopover on their way to the Land of Israel. For the most part, these were chalutzim (pioneers) from Ukraine who prepared themselves for aliya while they were still in their places of residence.

Figure 22 - Youth of Zion

Seated from right to left: 1. [feh]. Rotkov 2. Y. Dyukman 3. N. Davidovitz 4. L. Kleiner 5. Y. Shander
Standing: 1. Y. Kohan 2. B. Klepner 3. Y. Shvartz 4. L. Fisher 5. M. Rotkov 6. D. Dyukman 7. H. Barinboym

As a first step to assist and put up these refugees, the Zionist of our city established a Beit Chalutzim (House of Pioneers) in the yard of the well-known Zionist activist Gershon Weinstock of blessed memory. He set aside a wing for this in his spacious home. The pioneers sustained themselves by the fruits of their labor for the entire time that they were in the city. They strongly opposed the offers of the communal institutions to come to their aid with financial support. The youths did not reject any physical labor. Daily, it was possible to see them going from house to house armed with saws and axes, asking the local Jews to hire them for the chopping of trees. Many of the pioneers had a high level of intelligence. Their contribution to the culture, the education and the consolidating of the pioneering movement in our city was recognizable. The local youth would willingly visit the Pioneering House. The direct contact between them and the pioneers did much to strengthen the connection. A revolution took place in the hearts of our townsfolk.

At that time, a group of youths organized themselves through the efforts of Tzeirei Zion and leased a large plot of land in the region of Orheyev in order to prepare themselves for aliya to the Land. It is appropriate to point out the member Leibel Kleiner, one of the most dedicated and active people in the Zionist movement from his early youth. He put the best of his abilities into the organizing of this group. He himself also participated in the Hachshara (Zionist preparation). However, only a portion of the group succeeded in making aliya in 1920 as the first pioneers. These included Moshe Roitman of blessed memory (murdered in Haifa in the disturbances of 1929), and, may they live, Yaakov the son of Shaul Dyukman (Bar Shaul) Yitzchak Rapoport, Zeev Davidovitz, Yosef Shinder, his parents, and others.

The Hechalutz movement that spread out throughout Bessarabia struck roots in our city as well, and the number of youths who prepared themselves for aliya grew every year. In 1923 we were witness to the aliya of the Bnei Yisrael group from our city.

Our members of Tzeirei Zion were the first to become involved in every activity for the benefit of the Hechalutz movement. The Hechalutz center in Kishinev began a large scale activity for the training of chalutzim and transferring them to the Land, even though there were no sources of money that were sufficient to sustain the activities. From time to time, they would turn to the chapters in the cities of the field for help. I remember that the center declared a "Hechalutz Week" in Bessarabia, and then we began a large-scale activity in our city. We enlisted activists from all of the streams to publicize the aims of Hechalutz and to collect money. The activists of the Zionist movement volunteered to speak in the synagogues during the Sabbath services and our city was in the first row with respect to donations for Hechalutz Week.

The depression of 1926/1927 that affected the Land caused the return of some of our townsfolk, filled with disappointment and complaints. There were those who slandered the Land. The sworn opponents of Zionist seized this opportunity, and greatly castigated the Zionist movement. Even the General Zionists acted helplessly. Despite all this, the circle of Tzeirei Zion activists in the city was undaunted, and stood its guard. Even though the authorities forbade us from meeting, we overcame the difficulties and conducted clandestine activities. We conducted weekly meetings in the home of a different member each week in order not to arouse the attention of the secret police. The active members conducted discussions on issues of the day, and joined with the members of the ranks in the study of the annals of the workers' movement and the history of Zionism. The weekly publication of Tzeirei Zion in Bessarabia, "Erd un Arbiet", was distributed by us to the local Jews.

The members of Tzeirei Zion took an active role for the Keren Kayemet LeYisrael (Jewish National Fund). They conducted the "Purim Players" activities in the city for the benefit of the fund. For that purpose, we prepared a brief play about the life of the Jews in the Diaspora and in the Land. When Purim came, the players visited the houses of the wealthy people where many guests would participate in the Purim feast, and performed their play. This way, they succeeded in collecting significant sums for the benefit of the Keren Kayemet LeYisrael.

Figure 23 - Activists of the Jewish Fund

At that time, Chayim Shorer, a member of Hapoel Hatzair, came to Bessarabia to direct the collection for the benefit of the Workers' Fund of the Land of Israel (Kapai). When he came to our city, we gathered to take council in the home of Eidel Yagolnitzer of blessed memory, one of the General Zionists whose spirit was close to the Tzeirei Zion and who dedicated a great amount of his time and energy to it. We called a meeting, but to our great dismay, only very few answered our call. Shorer described to those gathered about the great depression that was taking lace in the Land, and the difficult conditions that pervaded in the settlement, especially among the community of workers. When he finished, the registration of pledges began. However, only one person, Dr. Nirenberg, not a Zionist but a faithful Jew who was dedicated to national causes, donated a significant sum.

In 1928, the first kernel of Poale Zion was formed in our city by the members Yisrael Weisman, the brothers Shlomo and Tovia Bozinyan, Baruch Lemberg and others. The members of Tzeirei Zion assisted the young initiators greatly, and dedicated much cultural and education activity to the members of the kernel.

Figure 24 - The Aliya of Eidel Yagolnitzer

The local authorities persecuted all Zionist activities, even those conducted with the permission of the central government. I recall one incident that is worthy of note. The director of the Keren Hayesod division in Bessarabia at that time, Yitzchak Berger of blessed memory, arrived in our city to open the annual campaign for that fund. He was armed with a permit from the central government in Kishinev. Based on it, the local authorities would issue a permit to conduct a lecture and a public gathering. A large gathering was arranged in the large kloiz, and that speaker portrayed to the gathering the worsening situation of Jews in the Diaspora, and the "tragedy" (tzaar) that is too great to bear. He called upon our community to generate to the funds for the settlement and development of the Land, etc. Here I should point out the importance of the pushka (charity box) of the Keren Kayemet LeYisrael. The detective who was present interpreted the words "tzaar" and "pushka" in their Russian meaning, that is to say: that the speaker was calling upon the gathering to revolution with the assistance of cannons (pushki in Russian). Based on this he issued a statement to the local authorities, which was transferred to the military authorities in Kishinev. Of course, Mr. Berger was brought to court. He was only exonerated after great intercession and efforts that lasted for a protracted period.

With the rise of the National Charanists (the National Farmer's Party of Romania) to government, a change for the better occurred in the political situation in Romania. The movement spread wide and opened a Zionist hall. On account of that, it was possible to conduct wide branched activity among the youth. Within a short period of time, hundreds of youths who left the study benches were attracted, and dedicated themselves to the movement. These included working youths. Counselors arose from among the youth, who were dedicated to the movement with heart and soul. They educated the members to strive for personal actualization.

The visit of the member Meir Grabovsky was also an event that left a great impression. He came to us in 1933 in order to organize the members of the workers movement in advance of the elections for the 18th congress. By chance, he became entangled with our secret police. The situation was as follows: after we verified the time of the arrival of our guest with the Tzeirei Zion center in Kishinev, we waited for him at the designated time. However, by chance, the car arrived early, and we were not there in time to greet him. When we arrived at the station, he had stumbled into a member of the Sigurnata secret police. The name Grabovsky which is a decidedly Russian name, the black shirt he was wearing, and his lack of knowledge of the Romanian language aroused the suspicion of the detective, who transferred the guest to the Sigurnata. When I found out about this, I hurried to Eidel Yagolnitzer of blessed memory, and we both went to clarify the reason for the arrest. Yagolnitzer, who knew the director of the secret police very well, entered straight into his office. After giving him an appropriate bribe, he freed the guest.

M. G. stated that the Revisionists disrupted his appearances in most places that he visited. He asked if there might be disruptions by them in our city as well. We calmed him with the fact that the Revisionists in our city were only a small group, and they certainly would not be brazen enough to endanger themselves, so they would not disrupt. Finally, Grabovsky appeared before a large gathering who listened to him quietly and with great interest. There is no doubt that his lecture earned a significant number of votes for the Workers' Movement list.

Figure 25 - Youth of Zion

Below right to left: 1. Y. Leyderberg 2. S. Fromberg
In the middle: 1. B. Yonovitz 2. Ester Duchovny 3. A. Malovatsky
4. G. Yonovitz 5. Shaiovitz
Standing: 1. ... 2. Y. Rapoport 3. Derubitsky

The agronomist Feigin of blessed memory, who worked among the Jewish farmers in Bessarabia as a counselor from the ORT organization, would often visit our city. Even though he was busy, he would give of his time for discussions with the members and lectures about life in the kibbutz, the group, the workers settlements and the Moshava.

An important Zionist activity, which led many of the community of workers to found a chapter of Haoved (The Worker) in our community, sprung up in the wake of the visit of the emissary from the Land of Israel Geler (who was killed in 1937 in the Galilee). His purpose was to prepare professionals over the age of 35 who were needed by the Mandatory Government for aliya, and to provide them with the aliya permits. Tzeirei Zion did a great deal for preparing members of Haoved for aliya, and many indeed registered for aliya and made aliya to the Land.

In 1934, a chapter of Buslia opened up in our city through the efforts of Tzeirei Zion. After some time (around 1935) the Hachshara group of Buslia was established. The yoke of strengthening it and leading it was placed completely upon the workers and responsible people of Tzeirei Zion. The members of the various Buslia chapters in Bessarabia turned to our Hachshara group. At first, the pioneers worked at wood chopping, with the desire to find jobs that were more lucrative and stable. However, the state of labor in the marketplace was depressed, and it was hard to find work. The group dwindled greatly and was in danger of folding. Then, we found a way out of our crisis. We turned to David Dizengof of blessed memory (a relative of Meir Dizengof of blessed memory) who owned a factory for bricks and tiles, and we asked him to employ pioneers, even though the work was difficult and there was a question if the young people would be able to persevere with it. Despite this, he agreed to hire some of the pioneers for work as an experiment. He became convinced of their serious attitude to work, and he continued to obtain workers from among the pioneers. In the end, more than 50 members of the group worked in this factory, and thereby, its existence was assured for an extended period.

In 1935, Yosef Shprintzak visited Bessarabia. He was known to Bessarabian Jewry already from his successful work in Kishinev prior to his aliya to the Land. His appearances in public gatherings and participation in conventions left a deep impression upon the masses. Shprintzak appeared at a large gathering in the movie theater, which was too small to hold all the attendees. After this meeting, a party was arranged in honor of the guests, in which members of all of the streams of the movement in our city participated.

It was felt that black clouds were approaching and covered the skies of the Jewish street already a long time prior to the outbreak of the world war. However, who would have thought that the end would come so rapidly…

Figure 26 - Yosef Shprintzak in Orheyev

Figure 27 - Roof tile factory of D. Dizner (Dizengof)

Workers: Pioneers from the "Hehalutz&148; branch in Orheyev.
Sitting in the middle: A. Malovatsky

"The Children of Israel" - "Bnei Yisrael"

Chapter 11

The Social and National Background

by M. Frank

Translated by Jerrold Landau

The era of "The Children of Israel" was a romantic and very interesting episode in the life of the Jewish youth of Orheyev. This energetic youth, full of energy and youthful enthusiasm, aroused itself and found itself on a path that was not a path. It was determined decisively that the way of Jewish life in the Diaspora was lost for it completely. Before the eyes of this youth that struggled greatly with searching for its path and believed in its ability to forge a new path, stood one focal point – the liberation of the Jewish nation and the ingathering of the nation in its ancient homeland with the foundations of equality, justice, labor and creativity.

In the Wake of the First World War

The era was that of the end of the First World War. Humanity as a whole was weary, bleeding, and licking its wounds. The Jews gave their appropriate "donation of blood" to the war that was foreign to them since they were "citizens of the entire world", and of course "faithful" to their native lands. They fought in the opposing camps and unknowingly spilled the blood of their brethren. When the war ended and Russia began its great revolution, the masses of workers and farmers in the vast expanse of Russia breathed easier, for they saw the revolution as a ray of light and hope for a better future. At that time, a terrible wave of bloody pogroms began for Russian Jewry.

The ruling class, who did not wish to come to terms with the revolution and the new conditions that were created, stood at the head of the counter revolutionary movement, gathering around them many dark and criminal forces. Thus was forged the covenant of hatred between every "black force in the Russian community."

The enemies of the revolution began a civil war with the intention of overturning the revolution and returning the government to their hands. As an intermediate stage on the path to their goal, they began murdering Jews and pillaging their property. Pillaging bands passed through Ukraine and throughout the expanse of Russia. Many gangs became incited under the leadership of the generals Petliura, Denikin, Wrangels and others as they pillaged, raped, burned and murdered Jews. When the revolutionary forces fought against the many gangs and against the intervention at that time, Romania invaded Bessarabia in response to the request of the Bessarabian reactionaries, and conquered it.

Brotherly Assistance to the Refugees from Ukraine

With the conquest of Bessarabia by the Romanians (1918), our Jewish community was cut off from the large Jewish community of Russia. The only connection that remained was the large stream of refugees from the sword of the gangs on the eastern side of the bank of the Dniester.

Naked and lacking everything, weary and emaciated from hunger, Jewish refugees arrived in Orheyev and were received with open arms. They found a warm corner in every Jewish home. All of the communal institutions, synagogues and private homes were filled to the brim with refugees. People neglected their occupations and livelihoods, and dedicated themselves willingly to the care of the refugees. Gershon Weinstock, Leibel Kleiner, Moshe Kalmanovitz, Leib Stolyar and others served as a fine personal example to us youth, for making their nights as days in order to assist the unfortunate people.

The myriads of refugees had no possibility of establishing themselves in Bessarabia, and they desired to emigrate abroad, including to the Land of Israel among other places.

The Balfour Declaration and its Influence upon the Youth

At that time, the Land was freed from the Turkish yoke and the German conquest. Jewish battalions (made up of volunteers from every corner of the earth) marched at the head of the liberation army, alongside the British troops that were lead by General Allenby. The Balfour Declaration was proclaimed immediately after this, and Lord Herbert Samuel was appointed as the first High Commissioner of Judea. These events had a deep influence on the Jews of the Diaspora, including of course upon us, the youth of Orheyev.

The Zionist movement began to turn to practicality. We imagined the "Redeeming Messiah" in the form of youths strong in body and spirit, pioneers who were prepared for work, with weapons in their hands – forging with their sweat the path of the nation, and leading it. In the eyes of our spirit, we beheld the downtrodden and persecuted Jew suddenly straightening out his form, feeling for the first time that he too had the right to exist upon the earth, that he also had an ancient, desolate homeland, and that he wished to grace its earth. The joyous news excited the Jewish consciousness, broke down barriers on the

Jewish street, and also reached the ears of the gentiles. Our Christian neighbors began to relate to us with more honor.

In the Jewish home, the day to day worries were pushed aside into a corner, as they made room for serious, revolutionary thoughts. With trembling in the heart, they began to whisper about the practical possibility of aliya to the Land of Israel.

The Awakening of the Youth to Zionist Activity

We were then youths of the age of 13-15, and we absorbed the overwhelming odor of blood that was left by the war. With our own eyes we witnessed Jewish communities burnt by the fire of the disturbers. We followed behind the caravans of refugees, tormented by agony and despair, with their eyes begging for assistance. Then vistas were exposed from the east.

Filled with enthusiasm and enchanted with the splendor of the revolution, we were simultaneously pining for the dream of the revival of the Jewish nation. We girded ourselves for the national liberation. We became stormy from the depth of the idea. Many difficulties fluttered before our eyes, and we had to solve them. We joined the revolution with all our hearts. However, we did not see in it the solution to all of the problems that arose and tormented us. Could a revolution in one country bring an answer to our national problems? Could it guarantee our nation the possibility to live in a nationalist-socialist economic community? Would we not fall victim to any change or movement in the social forces of the world?

At first, the blue and white flag fluttered next to the flag of the Red Revolution, but the bearers of the flag tread upon ground that was not of their homeland. As opposed to their Russian comrades who felt the soil of their expansive homeland, this was lacking for us. We were only able to feel for our ancient homeland, a Land that must be built up and established anew. However, how would this homeland arise? What would be the economic, national and social basis for its existence?

Figure 28 - Dreaming of the "homeland"

Sitting from right to left: 1. Davidovitz 2. B. Naychin 3. N. Suslensky (one of the pioneers to Israel) 4. B. Chuvis 5. L. Veitzman 6. M. Rabinovitz 7. … Z. Davidovitz and L. Veitzman hoping for a dream come true

The Zionist Movement and the First Pioneers in our Town

In those days, a Zionist movement existed in Orheyev that was not particularly variegated with respect to political differences. For all intents and purposes, there were two factions: the General Zionists and Tzeirei Zion (Young Zion). Even though there were no essential differences between them, the "cream of the crop" of the Jewish community of the city belonged to the General Zionists (headed by Ben-Zion Furer, Dr. Berkovitz, Nissel Duchovny, Yosef Pagis, Chalyk, David Duchovny, Leib Stolyar, Kestlicher, Shapirin, the Weinshenker brothers, Yehudah Yagolnitzer, and others). Young people still mainly belonged to Tzeirei Zion, some of them students and some of them practitioners of the free trades. They were headed by Mordechai Rotkov, Berel Klepner, Leibel Kleiner, Davidovitz, Leah Fisher, Yehudit Naychin, Guralnik, Dora Dyukman, Marosia Averbukh and others.

These, like those, would gather on occasion for meetings, festivities and various celebrations. They would speak at length about the vision of the return to Zion. The political situation of both of those factions did not obligate their members to practical outcomes - that is to say, to actualization. Indeed, some people arose who rebelled against "parlor room" Zionism and made aliya to the land. Among them were Ben-Zion Ford of blessed memory, Nissel Duchovny, Avraham Daskal, Berel Lupatner, Yaakov Dyukman, Yitzchak Rapoport, Roitman of blessed memory, Yosef Kohen, Shinder and others. However, this was a transient episode, without continuity. The youth movements did not yet exist in the city, with the exception of Maccabee (led by Yasha and Matba Sherman, Menashe Eydelman, Moshe Feinman and others).

The Organized "Bnei Yisrael"

We, a small number of youths who were students of the gymnasiums, were not organized into any movement. We gathered together to chart our future course. The participants in this meeting included Niunia Suslensky, Yisrael Shamban, Chaya Naychin, Shneur Geynichovitz, Mordechai Frank, Dov Snitkovsky, Hershel Dikler, Yechiel Duchovny and others. The goal, to "clarify our path in life," was directed to the future of each one of us as it was intertwined and connected with the future of the rest of the members, at one with the lot of the nation. The best of the youth of Orheyev joined us (Avrahamel Bronshteyn, Ganya Zimmerman, Herzl Dyukman of blessed memory, Liuba Muntzer, Rivka Ziserman, David Shrayberman, Yaakov Chalyk and others). We became a serious factor in the Jewish street. The attractive force of our faction was great, and many people joined us. We organized into groups in order to facilitate intensive activity. The group of "wise people" stood at the head. They directed and led the cultural and educational activities of all the groups. We conducted our work in a clandestine fashion for two reasons: a) the Romanian government, and b) the parents.

Most of the parents were not pleased with our numerous meetings that were fraught with the risk of arrest. They did not understand our goals and wished to see us continue along their path of life – obviously in an improved fashion. They wished that we would continue our studies, complete university, and become established in life. In truth, we felt that our studies were important, but we felt that the value of the studies was intertwined with our desire for a new life in the homeland. In our hearts we tied our lot with that unknown Land that stood in desolation for thousands of years as it was awaiting its children to return to its borders.

Figure 29 - Bnei Israel, first group

Seated from right to left: 1. N. Suslensky 2. C. Naychin 3. Y. Shamban (Ben-Shem)
Standing: 1. M. Frank 2. Y. Duchovny 3. S. Geynichovitz 4. [alef]. Bronshteyn 5. G. Zimerman

We grew from a small number of people to a large number of groups, composed of people from various classes and ages. We had not yet clarified our political stand, but we knew that we must toil and study a great deal, and research deeply so that we would able to set and establish in a clearer fashion those things that would lead to the desired goal.

We were not connected to any organization or youth group for a simple reason – such did not exist. With our own flesh we witnessed the reality that was developing, and we made deductions from it.

"The Nation of Israel Lives" - "The Nation of Israel – an Eternal Nation"

This was the motto that we established for ourselves. From here also came the name "Bnei Yisrael". We established the Hebrew language as absolutely obligatory upon all the members of Bnei Yisrael. We greeted each other with the word "Shalom". At first it was strange to hear the new ring of the unknown language. Few of us knew Hebrew. However, we quickly became comfortable with the language. We chatted in it with pride, even though at times we botched it to the point of laughter.

The topics with which we dealt were sociology, national economics, Bible, history, literature and Hebrew. We paid special attention to the topic of sociology. We studied "Drouin" for many months (the lecturer was Niunia Suslensky). Aside from Drouin, we read "Wells". We delved into Bible and other sources so that we could find some connection to that topic. In this manner of study and research, we wished to deduce all of the economic and spiritual factors that influence the character and makeup of man – which direct his soul and his way of thinking. The goal was to educate a person anew to delve into the fundamental bases, to distance from a bad source, with the aim of forging the most ideal character of the sublime person. In explanation, the person of healthy mind and body, who lives and sustains himself from his work, the person whose entire essence is to create the conditions of a life of happiness on earth, for himself and his fellow and to all humans. To prevent war and bloodshed among nations.

"Bnei-Yisrael" – and the Land of Israel

Through this lens of peace and brotherhood on earth, we also saw Israel building its desolate land and turning it into a fruitful garden, ingathering its scattered children from the corners of the earth.

We began to prepare ourselves to meet these goals. We imposed upon ourselves the duty to realize our goals practically, and to serve as a personal example for others. Our path was strewn with obstacles: the home, the family, the street, and also the government – everyone was against us. Indeed, there was a national awakening, and there were Zionist activities – but not to the point of actualization. Many saw us as dreamers of dreams, and waited for time to pass, the illusions to dissipate, and our return to being good children. Our parents did not want to hear about our plans that were related to the abandonment of our studies, leaving our homes, and aliya to the Land of Israel. We, devoid of any experience in life, dependent on our parents' table, with a warm family atmosphere, did not know the taste of toil, and had never tasted the taste of lack. The lot fell with these conditions: A decision was made by the Bnei Yisrael organization that demanded personal actualization from every one of its members – pioneering preparation (hachshara), activity for the Keren Kayemet LeYisrael (Jewish National Fund), and finally of course, also aliya to the Land. Our knowledge of the Land was scanty. With boundless joy, we would listen to anyone who came to tell us about the Land. I recall how happy I was when I was invited to Dyukman's home to hear about the Land from comrade Yitzchak Spivak, who had come to visit Orheyev. We heard about the far-off Land, its desolation for thousands of years and its lack of cultivation. It was a Land whose few residents suffered from malaria. Its soil was covered with bogs, and it was thirsty for water to water the soul of man and beast. It was a Land awaiting pioneers who would come and turn the malarial swamps into fruitful ground.

We knew that were facing difficult conditions – the task of a pioneer who would go ahead of the camp, forging the path for the many that would follow.

This was a task that demanded physical strength and strength of spirit, an iron will and strong abilities. We took upon ourselves many activities for the Keren Kayemet LeYisrael in all of its forms, except for the one of practical value – the financial area. We regarded this work as one of the most important means of explaining our path to all strata of the people. The distribution and emptying of blue boxes, the sending of greetings for festivals and joyous occasions, registration for the Golden Book, the planting of trees, the bands for memorial days and brochures for the Sabbath – these and the like were the vehicles for this holy task.

Figure 30 - Bnei Israel

Seated from right to left: 1. Y. Shamban 2. C. Dyukman 3. D. Snitkovsky -- Sinai
Standing: 1. D. Frank 2. R. Katz 3. Y. Zeylik 4. C. Katz 5. H. Dikler

During that time, I filled the task of secretary for the Keren Kayemet in Orheyev. I remember those Fridays, about two hours before candle lighting, when the young group of Bnei Yisrael, children of the ages of 9-11, pure and pleasant, would be enlisted for work for the Keren Kayemet LeYisrael. They would receive the boxes and brochures for the Sabbath with great devotion and boundless dedication. Filled with enthusiasm, they would visit all the houses and distribute the letter that explained the activities of the Keren Kayemet in Hebrew and Yiddish. I felt that at that time, this was the most effective means for instilling the Zionist idea in every Jewish home.

One of the announcements of a concert of the Bnei Yisrael choir under the direction of P. Ziserov during the days of Chanuka 5684, December 1924.

28 Kislev 5685

In the Shoemaker's Synagogue of Orheyev
A Chanuka Celebration with the choir of
BNEI YISRAEL
Under the direction of the director
Pinchas Ziserov

First Section

A) Hanoten Teshua Lamelachim
(Performed by the entire choir with the participation of Aberkanter)

B) Lighting of Chanuka Candles
(performed by the entire choir with the participation of Aberkanter)

Hanerot Halalu (performed by the choir)

C) Vaani Tefilati (choir)

D) Birfoach Resahim (choir)

Second Section

A) Amnan Ken (choir)

B) Mizmor Ledavid (choir)

C) Betzeit Yisrael march (choir)

Direction.

Printed by Gelbruch Malkevitz - Orheyev.p

Aside from our work in the Keren Kayemet LeYisrael, we also worked in the realm of Hebrew cultural activities. At that time, we were engaged in a fierce battle with the Culture League and the Yiddishists. That war was about the abandonment of the soul of the youth, and we prevailed. We had the upper hand! We took the civic library into our hands, thanks to the great dedication of several members who worked to develop the library. This library quickly turned into a cultural institution and a gathering place for the youth and the Jewish population in general.

Figure 31 - Aliyah of friends to Israel

Aside from the library, we worked for the development of other cultural branches: a drama group of the Bnei Yisrael organization directed by Arkadi Loshakov. The leadership of the circle was given over to comrade Yechiel Duchovny. We immediately began to search for an appropriate repertoire. After many debates, the group of wise people decided to begin preparations for the play "Going and Coming" by Sholem Asch. The plan failed, however. On the other hand, we were very successful in establishing the Bnei Yisrael choir under the faithful directorship of the late Pinchas Ziserov. We took him in from circles that were strange to us, but he dedicated himself to the idea with all his soul. He invested much toil and energy into the choir, and raised it to a high standard. The members of the choir were boys and girls from all strata of the community of Orheyev. Through meetings and choir rehearsals, the group became united into one will for the actualization of its goal – instilling of Hebrew song from the Land of Israel to the wider circles of the Jewish community of Orheyev, and raising it to a significant artistic level. We had fine and serious forces in the choir. From among the girls, there was Chava Dyukman and Chana Katz, who are with us here, Rivka Katz of blessed memory, Brona Bronson, Fleshler, Bozinyan, and others. From among the boys there were Moshe Fisher (today in the Land), Mozlin of blessed memory, N. Suslensky, and others. We also had one gentile with us, the assistant of the priest. He helped us greatly and participated in all of the concerts and appearances of the choir.

Figure 32 - Choir of "Bnei Israel" under the direction of P. Ziserov

Seated below from right to left: 1. Fleshler 2. … 3. C. Fleshler 4. Katzap 5. Vaksman 6. Bozinyan
In the middle: 1. Vaksman 2. D. Kleiner 3. Shor 4. P. Ziserov 5. N. Suslensky 6. L. Veitzman 7. C. Dyukman
Standing above: 1. … 2. … 3. D. Shrayberman 4. … 5. C. Katz 6. Mordkovitz 7. D. Zimerman 8. R. Katz

I cannot move on from that era without telling about an unforgettable episode in the annals of the choir. This took place on the birthday of Pinchas Ziserov of blessed memory. We presented him with a parchment scroll with the writing of a scribe, written by Matityahu Gleybman of blessed memory. Its inscription was as follows: The perpetuation of the founder of the choir and its director in the Golden Book of the Keren Kayemet LeYisrael. How happy was the man. His face beamed with joy at this festive occasion. With the assistance of the choir, we succeeded in consolidating the cultural life of the city. We organized parties and celebrations that were always very successful.

Bnei Yisrael as Pioneers and on Hachshara

One of the most splendid chapters of the annals of Bnei Yisrael was the era of pioneering, the time when we children of the householders abandoned our school benches in the universities, exchanged our linen clothes for heavy work clothes, took up the work implements in our hands, and turned into workers – primarily unemployed workers. The main task was to search for work, and this was mainly devoid of success. The reasons for lack of work were many and varied, but one result was hunger. Hunger in the winter, in the freezing, in a poor dwelling. Our straits grew with the knowledge that there were only a number of steps to traverse, only one road to be crossed, numbered steps, and everything would change from top to bottom. For the home of Mother and Father, a warm home of plenty, would receive you with open arms. Nevertheless, our members did not choose this easy route, and they stubbornly and persistently continued on the new path that they had chosen, with all of the consequences and results of this tortuous path – an educational movement – pioneering – aliya to the Land – becoming rooted there.

Today one thing is clear, our toil was not in vain. We established groups of pioneers in Orheyev who made aliya to the Land under the banner of Bnei Yisrael. The vast majority took root in the land of the homeland, in the village and city. Everyone in his own corner continued to work, maintaining his connection to the crucible that forged him, remaining faithful to the educational line that is the Workers' Movement of the Land of Israel.

Chapter 12

From Thought Into Action

by D. Sinai

Translated by Jerrold Landau

In 1917, the year of the Russian Revolution, the Jewish population in Orheyev began to organize and forge a new way of life for communal life in the city. The representatives of the Zionist organization came to us and awakened the hearts of the Jews of the towns to the Zionist vision.

Figure 33 - Youth of "Bnei Israel" studying

Seated from right to left: 1. [feh]. Groisman 2. H. Dyukman
Standing: 1. D. Ostrovsky 2. D. Snitkovsky 3. C. Vaynshtok 4. Y. Dyukman

In 1918, the year of the Balfour Declaration, we were youths, and we penetrated into the circle of activities in Orheyev. We visited the meetings and listened to Zionist publicity. Our awakening was comprehensive.

In 1919-1920, with the stream of refugees that arrived to our city, many of the best activists of the Zionist movement arrived in our city, leading to a change in the thinking of our youth. The news of what was taking place in the

Land rekindled the desire for Zionism and aliya to the Land of Israel in the hearts of the youth.

How jealous were we of the chalutzim when we saw them with their axes and saws over their shoulders, on their way to chop trees or to shovel the snow after a storm during the harsh winter days. This appearance aroused in us, a small group of gymnasium students, a feeling of a need for a revolt against the order of our lives. We gathered together for discussions about the future. We engrossed ourselves in the pages of Zionist literature. The desire was great for the writings of Ahad HaAm. We absorbed his words about the founding of a national homeland – a spiritual center for the Jewish nation, and for preparations for labor, for actualization, for the building of the homeland. We wished to be like the sons of Moses.

We did not find our place among the veterans of that time in Tzeirei Zion. We said that we must forge our own path. We debated extensively about our role in the education of youth, and in consolidating the idea of independence.

We organized small groups for the tasks of publicity and preparation. We saw a lone goal before us – aliya to the Land. We entered into negotiations with the Hechalutz center regarding matters of hachshara, but the path was long to actual pioneering hachshara. We felt that we must create a Zionist atmosphere in the city not only through reading books on Zionism, but also through deeds. We organized flag days for every holiday and festival. We penetrated into the Maccabee sporting organization. We organized a choir and a drama group. We slowly conquered the Jewish street for Zionism and its desires, as we moved over to actual deeds. During the major vacation in 1923 the first group of Bnei Yisrael was organized, who left the house of their parents and ascended the mountain to Rozen's agricultural farm. This was the beginning of our preparation for agricultural work and life in a commune. The first days were difficult, as we stood in a row with "gentile" youths with a spade in the hand – as they doubled their efforts out of suspicion that we wished to impede their work. However, we withstood it and held our stand. How lovely were those days and nights in the field! We were tired after a hard day of work, but filled with the joy of creativity and desire for life. We sat for entire nights and dealt with issues relating to our aliya to the Land. Our hachshara had an influence also on the studying youth who were far from Zionism. Discussions and day to day communal life between the different groups won over the hearts for us. For example, how great were the emotions and joy on the day that the Hebrew University of Jerusalem opened. That day was a day of celebration for the students of the gymnasium. The eyes sparkled from joy and in the hearts there was a prayer that we merit to join those who actualize.

In 1925 – Mordechai Frank, a member of our group, made aliya. He was the first representative who tied Bnei Yisrael to the land. We had to work to expand the circle and to prepare the best of the comrades for actual Hachshara. Then a number of students got up and left their studies, despite the opposition of their parents, and went to Hechalutz for Hachshara. In our first steps, we ran into difficult problems such as: a place to live, work, livelihood. The conditions were difficult, and a difficult internal war was waged inside of us.

Figure 34 - "Bnei Israel" kibbutz members departing for training

With the Hechalutz center, we dealt with the direction of a chalutz (pioneer). We members of Bnei Yisrael felt that a chalutz should prepare himself for a literal life of labor, and for the creation of a cultural community. Our motto was: a person of healthy body and spirit. Indeed, we know how to create this with our own powers, but we were not able to do that which we wished. We left Kishinev, far from the city and its problems.

Figure 35 - Pioneers of "Bnei Israel"
1. [feh]. Lederman 2. S. Bronshteyn

We arrived at the large vineyard where we had to work in agriculture. Suddenly, a physical weakness overtook our members. The Bnei Yisrael group became organized in Hechalutz and returned to Orheyev.

We succeeded in attracting a number of members from outside our city who joined us. This was a great source of joy to us. We began to set ourselves up in a rented house in a yard of the Auerbach house. We went out to seek work, particularly in the chopping of trees. We even signed an agreement with the communal council for 3,000 pods of wood. We set out for work. Our parents did not make peace with the fact that we gymnasium graduates had left our studies and turned into woodcutters and water drawers. However we did this with purity of heart, and did not see this as reason for pride or boasting of might. Slowly but surely we penetrated into the yards of the Jews of the towns, and we conducted the work. We also turned to the gymnasium principal Vasilia Vasilovitz with a request for work. We asked to cut wood for him. However, he did not agree – he refused to give over this degrading work to us, his students.

Figure 36 - First branch of "Bnei Israel", 1925-26

Below from right to left: 1. S.Bronshteyn 2. M. Zigberman 3. S. Kleinman
In the middle: 1. Sharf 2. ... 3. Sinai 4. ... 5. T. Averbukh 6. B. Hentin 7. [feh]. Katzovman
Above: 1. L. Kuchuk 2. Y. Ben-Shem 3. C. Naychin 4. [feh]. Etlis 5. Ab. Garber 6. L. Munder

We took upon ourselves the hardest of labors at the time of the baking of matzos. Our male youths worked with the machines and our female youths worked with the dough. Even though the conditions of existence were difficult and the work exhausted our strength, we still managed to create a warm corner in the Hechalutz chapter, which attracted all classes of the youth of the town. How pleasant were the evenings in the chapter, when we gathered together for discussion, deliberation, song and dance. We organized a group of "Friends of Hechalutz" for our friends who did not go in our path. The connection between us was strong. I remember one Passover night when we all gathered together, the friends and supporters of the chapter with the delegates of the Hechalutz center, for a party, and we felt like one family. We attempted to draw the youth near with our cultural work within the chapter and outside of it. We created a unique social and cultural reality.

Then came the call from Mordechai from the Land regarding the need to send a number of members in order to establish the organization in the Land of Israel. Chava Dyukman and later Yisrael Ben-Shem made aliya at that time. In due course, Snitkovsky and Shmuel Sharf made aliya to the Land (the latter did not become adjusted and returned).

Figure 37 - Baking of Matzos
Yaakov Yudel Beznos training pioneers in the baking of Matzos

In June 1926, a small group gathered in Haifa: Frank, Yisrael Ben-Shem, Chava Dyukman, Sharf and other members who were not from our city but who joined us in the land. We lived in a hut in the German Colony. The Histadrut organization directed us to the road to Nahalel. One day during the afternoon, we took our belongings, boarded a wagon hitched to a pair of mules and left Haifa to an unknown destination, filled with enthusiasm and a sublime state of spirit.

We arrived to the area of Nahalel around noon. We did not know where we were. The wagon driver showed us the exact place where we were to set up the camp of three tents. We were sent to work on the road. The labor was difficult and backbreaking, but it was performed with creative joy. We set up camp after the work. We moved it after the completion of each kilometer of the road. We slowly became acclimatize to the Land, and felt the spirit of Bnei Yisrael in the Land through all of our labor. The connection with the Diaspora continued, and many waited for the day when they could join us. However, the crisis of lack of work that pervaded at that time in the Land led to the closing of the doors of the Land and a break in aliya. We, a small group of chalutzim, faced the difficult problem of physical sustenance. The desire for independent creativity obligated us to think about additional means. We set up a point, a bunk and tents, in the region of Nahalel. Even though the living conditions were very difficult, and the lack of work was tormenting us, our spirits did not fall and the joy in our camp was great. Girls from the agricultural school as well as workers would come almost every night, and we would dance endlessly.

Figure 38 - Pioneers of "Bnei Israel" in the homeland

From right to left: 1. C. Dyukman -- Sinai 2. Shmuel Sharf 3. Dov Snitkovsky -- Sinai 4. Yisrael Ben-Shem -- Shamban 5. Mordechai Frank

The break in aliya continued and gnawed at our hearts. The question was, until when? It hung in the air like a nightmare.

When the situation improved slightly with the news of the renewal of aliya, M. Frank left for the Diaspora in order to organize groups of members for actualization.

He returned along with a group from the town. The joy in our camp was great, and the people of Nahalel joined in our rejoicing. Avigdor Garber, Bilah Hentin, Shlomo Bronshteyn, Penina Chalyk, Tovia Averbukh of blessed memory, Leibel Kuchuk and Fania Nairner arrived. The reinforcement was strong enough. We gathered strength and energy, and set out to the breadths.

The group became organized, and we decided to establish an auxiliary farm. In the interim, the connection with the Diaspora strengthened, and Miryam Beznos along with others made aliya. Chalutzim from Bessarabia arrived among the first of the Fifth Aliya. The heads of Gordonia – Moshe and Naomi Zinger (today in Massada) and others arrived. The debates about the directions of the group and its place in the kibbutz movement were endless. We did not see ourselves as different from the people of other groups, and we established a connection with "Hechaver" and an agricultural center. We searched for ways to actualize our goals without a direct connection with the existing movement.

The programmatic deliberations began with the arrival of the first ones of Gordonia. We were unable to accept upon ourselves the doctrine of Gordonia, even though we saw no difference in our approach.

We wished to be independent in our path, without being bound to ideas or doctrines, and to found the group as an agricultural unit similar to other groups, without a specific connection to Gordonia. However, the group disbanded. The members of Gordonia were forced to leave, and 2-3 other members left with them. We were not able to bring the matter to conclusion despite the efforts to strengthen the group. The disruption in aliya for several years was not conducive to the organization of the youth in Orheyev into movements such as Gordonia, Hashomer Hatzair and Poale Zion. It appeared that our members of Bnei Yisrael were also tiring, and were not able to overcome the difficulties. After the members of Gordonia left us, a kernel for a group in Hadera was founded named Massada. There were fundamental debates about its direction, whether it should be an independent group or should join to one of the existing groups. We deliberated day and night, and did not come to a clear conclusion. What took place previously again happened. The group broke apart. Some of them went to the Mishmar Hasharon group (Avigdor, Bilah, Tovia of blessed memory and others), then located in Herzliya. The rest continued to search for a path. It finally became evident that we would not be able to maintain the idea of an independent kibbutz group on our own. Therefore we decided to join one of the Kibbutzim of Hechaver, even though we agonized about the energies and means that we had invested into an independent group. We overcame our hesitation and transferred to the Gan Shmuel group (then a member of the united Kibbutzim).

Much water flowed since those days. New conditions were created, some passed and others continued. However, the path of creativity and labor, faithful to the founding principles of Bnei Yisrael with its vision and aim to actualization remained the heritage of all alumnae of Bnei Yisrael. Even though we did not merit having an independent farm, all of the ideas that we dreamed about in the Diaspora were later imparted to the youth of Orheyev. That youth followed along our path in its masses – the path of Zionist actualization.

Figure 39 - Yaakov Idil Beznos and family
On the stairs of their house, Miryam, before going to Israel

Chapter 13
The Excitement Among the Youth

by Avraham Bronshteyn

Translated by Jerrold Landau

The city was located on the banks of the Reat River. The heights of the city, with its building and huts, most of them Jewish homes, literally rose from the midst of the city. The Sobor, the building of the Pravoslavic Church, looms atop of the summit of the hill, in a large, fenced courtyard. The historians would say that the Sobor was built by Stefan the Great, the prince of Moldova who lived in the 16th century. This is possible, but the city was known many years before that era. Archeologists were able to find, in their excavations of the foundations and the heights, artifacts from the time of the Tatars and even from earlier years.

Figure 40 - On the top of the Sobor Hill and on its left the bridge

The city was built upon a hill and valley. It is surrounded by mountains on two sides, based upon rock and limestone. The wide, fruitful valley spreads out beneath the mountains. It was perhaps for this reason that many residents of the city had dreams and visions. Their heads were in the heights and their eyes looked longingly at the vast expanse that spread out before them.

Figure 41 - Branch of "Bnei Israel" in training in Serbinika (agricultural ranch)

On the slope not far from the Sobor, stood – to differentiate between holy and profane – the Great Synagogue, "Di Groise Shul". It was old, or so it appeared in contrast to the Christian church. It was about 1/3 sunken into the ground, supported by pillars. It was gloomy from the outside, but filled with light on the inside. It was decorated with floral drawings on the walls, and the view of the eastern side was jolly. Surrounding the synagogue stood the low houses of the Jews, old like it, with small windows and walls whitewashed with shiny white. A blossoming tree poked out of the yards here and there.

On the narrow streets surrounding the old synagogue, not far from the tall Sobor, the special Jewish character, the "Bessarabian" was molded and forged – just like in other places in the rich and fruitful area – the worker, living from the ground, as a toiler or tenant – or as a merchant of wheat or agricultural products. This Jewish character was for the most part not expert in the "secrets of the Torah." He was simple in his ways, accommodating to guests, with a wide heart open to all who turned to him.

When vast Russia entered the age of capitalism, railways were built, and industrial enterprises and mines sprouted up. Bessarabia took part in this economic rise. In it too, railways were built and factories were founded, primarily for the production of agricultural products.

Orheyev was far from the railway line, but the economic development reached it as well. Large flourmills were established, which sent their products afar. There were factories for oil and other smaller factories. The wine and fruit business also developed. The city widened and grew, spreading out broadly from the historical hill around the Sobor and the old synagogue. Roads and buildings, communal institutions and schools were added to it. During that era of development (approximately in the time prior to the First World War), a large hospital was built for the Jewish community of the area. A gymnasium for boys was opened in addition to the gymnasium for girls that was already in existence.

Then, a new factor arose in the city – the studying youth. At the end of the previous century, the ideal of the young generation in the city was to develop and open for themselves a store, or to emigrate abroad to do business in "a free manner" without restrictions of the "boundaries of the settlement," and to thereby lay the foundations for their private economic lives. Then the studying youth appeared and brought with them different ideals: distancing themselves from commerce, or becoming a doctor, engineer or a teacher. New mottoes appeared: to work for the "masses", to raise the level of the "people", and to give even their lives for it and for its redemption. The words were indeed vague and clouded. The influence of the powers that spread throughout the intelligentsia and progressive workers throughout the expanse of Russia was great. However this did not prevent these vague desires from being revolutionary with respect to the somnolent and frozen life of the city at that time. They excited and enthused the youth in all strata.

This was the era of the rule of the youth on the Jewish street, the rule of the excited spirit in the midst of the youth. The previous generation did not have anything new to say. Things were said particularly about the Romanian conquest and the rupturing of connections with Russian Jewry and the great Russian revolution – a rule of shameless pillage of the treasures of the region and a state police built upon the open instilling of fear and bribery. They were indeed saved from the tribulations of the pogroms and the civil war across the Dniester, but they also lost the great spiritual influence that came from there. Severed from their roots, the masses of youth in Bessarabia rose up, and had to search for the influence from their own midst and to find new content and a way of life. The agitation was great, and the tribulations of the searching for a path were difficult.

Opinions consolidated in two directions: with the nation for independent life and national revival in the homeland – Zionism; or with the agitation and great revolution that passed over wide Russia and the nations surrounding it. In fact, the two movements were influenced from each other. As is known, the Bund struggled to find Jewish autonomy and to create some sort of independent

Jewish life in the exile. From its side, Zionism was also greatly influenced by the revolution and its mottoes about social justice, a society without oppressors and the oppressed, the honor of work and labor, etc.

Figure 42 - Flour mill of L. Gluzgold

Seated from left to right: 1. Leibe Gluzgold 2. Rima Gluzgold (wife)
Standing: 1. Efrayim Daskal 2. Avraham Kupchik 3. Aizik Rozenfeld 4. Shmuel Teytelman

In our city, both streams of the Poale Zion movement had very little influence. The Bessarabian Zionist youth, who were mainly studying youth or were led mainly by them, with their class divisions that existed, was quite small. They more easily accepted the doctrine of Tzeirei Zion (Young Zion), for they saw them as more integral from the perspective of the Zionist longing and being based on the idea of individual actualization and the building of the future life in the homeland. The path of the class war, the forging furnace behind the revolution, and the strong social changes that must be traversed were seen as too "extensive" to reach to the desired goal of social justice. What was "simpler" and "quicker" than personal actualization? We will all become chalutzim (pioneers). We will establish Kibbutzim, we will live from the land in general, and manual labor in particular, and the future fine society will arise! The Bessarabian youth, even though they lived in cities and towns, were very far from being true city youth, with all the sophistication. Nature and manual labor were never strange to the youth, and it is no wonder that they followed their ideal spirit, which to us seems slightly naive from our more distant perspective. This Bessarabian youth established a movement of hundreds and thousands of pioneers who were prepared for actualization, the vast majority of whom made aliya to the Land and bestowed of their spirit to the workers movement in the Land.

Figure 43 - Gymnasium for boys, Class of 1925

Photograph taken at the reunion in 1935.
Those in Israel: Dov Sinai, Ganya Zimerman, David Shrayberman

One of these youth movements was the "movement" or "organization" of Bnei Yisrael in Orheyev and its environs. It was influenced by the doctrine of Ahad HaAm on the one hand, and the Tzeirei Zion movement of southern Russia and Bessarabia on the other hand. From Ahad HaAm it not only received its name Bnei Yisrael (patterned after Bnei Moshe), but also the idea of pioneers marching in front of the people, directing and showing the path to the masses. It inherited the idea of individual actualization that was to be expressed primarily by the pioneering path, and secondly by the use of the Hebrew Language in the day to day life of the members of the movement.

The influence of this movement in the life of the small city was indeed amazing. There were farmers in our city, but the deliberate movement of "gymnasium students" to agriculture – something like this had never happened before. There were Jewish woodchoppers in our city, albeit few, for wood chopping was for the most part performed by gentiles. However, the existence of woodchoppers from among the children of the most honorable householders in the city – there never was such a thing. The Bnei Yisrael pioneering house quickly became the sole and most important meeting place for the youth of the city. A new wind blew there. It suddenly became clear that the new ideal that was contrary to the existing reality, not to be a merchant, was progressive albeit not yet complete and sufficient. A complete person who is worthy of honor was obviously a revolutionary who overturns the norms of society – but this too was different than the norms of his life; for those who descended from the school bench straight to a life of labor and toil; who forewent with astonishing ease the conforms of life in the orderly parental home and who exchanged them for work with the spade in the field or vineyard, sleeping on uneven boards in the pioneering house and eating food that was at times insufficient…

With seven eyes the youths of the city looked at these strange boys and girls. The heart was attracted to them through hidden longings for change that could come also to their mundane, single-focussed lives.

Figure 44 - The community troupe in its performance during Purim

Seated from right to left: 1. Zaikovitz 2. R. Katz 3. [feh]. Chokla 4. A. Malovatsky 5. C. Katz 6. R. D. Frank 7. S. Rapoport
Standing: 1. Y. Dyukman 2. D. Shrayberman 3. S. Bronshteyn 4. L. Munder 5. S. Dyukman 6. H. Dyukman 7. N. Davidovitz 8. L. Kelmaner 9. S. Geynichovitz

Figure 45 - The Pioneers "Bnei Israel" in Orheyev chopping down trees

From right to left: 1. D. Sinai 2. Yisrael Ben-Shem 3. Arye Kuchuk 4. ... 5. S. Sharf 6. B. Hentin 7. ... 8. M. Zigberman 9. S. Bronshteyn

From this Bnei Yisrael group sprung out the Hechalutz and pioneering youth movements of the city – Gordonia and Hashomer Hatzair. Aliya to the Land began from them, not just of lone individuals, but of entire groups that increased with the passage of time, and that with time, influenced the movement in the Diaspora from the far reaches of the desired Land. Thanks to them, Hebrew became a living and spoken language in the mouths of the youth of the city. Love of the Land of Israel and the dream for aliya became concepts that were close to the hearts of everyone, as it had not been in any other era. These boys and girls of Hechalutz and of the youth movements were also the first to take part in any practical Zionist activity, and the forces behind all Hebrew cultural activities in the city. They worked on behalf of the Keren Kayemet, organized a choir which became known throughout the nearby region, established a theatrical troupe, took care of the communal library, etc.

In one word – they did whatever the rest of the youth did in every city throughout Romania, Poland, Galicia and other places, where Zionism brought in its wake the spiritual and cultural revival of the nation in the Diaspora.

Then the black and dark year arrived. The impure beast overpowered the nations of Europe, and cut off this youthful activity. The song in the youth groups was silenced, the joy ceased, and the enthusiastic pioneering dancing stopped. The joyous activities stopped, and were replaced by oppression and terror. Those who were not saved by fleeing eastward perished, died and were murdered – and only their memory remains in the heart like a scorched stone – without comfort...

The youths and the rest of those pining in the Diaspora, a large group who stood on the threshold of aliya and actualization, who prepared and dreamed about joining themselves to the ranks of those who made aliya – and were cut off before their time by the hands of the beasts of prey – shall be remembered forever.

Their lips that spoke Hebrew and their eyes that dreamed the dreams of Zion and Jerusalem, their hearts that beat stormily on behalf of the nation and the homeland shall be remembered forever.

Their deeds that were performed and not completed, their desires that were beckoning over the horizon but not actualized, their dreams that withered and cut off in fire, in machine guns, in strangulation, in famine and disease, through torture by strangers and crushing of the honor of mankind shall be remembered forever.

Their dreams and desires are like fire in our bones. We, those that survive, have the duty to bring them to life, to continue with them, and to actualize them.

Let them be remembered forever...

Figure 46 - Soccer team "Hadror" 1925

Figure 47 - Maccabi, Orheyev branch

Seated from right to left: 1. S. Bronshteyn 2. Y. Sherman 3. S. Sirkovitz 4. D. Volovitz 5. V. Eydelman 6. … 7. Rabinovitz
Standing right to left: 1. S. Berkovitz 2. Rapoport 3. [feh]. Reznik 4. Rabinovitz 5. B. Klepner 6. Vaynshtok 7. Y. Leyderberg 8. Y. Groyser

Figure 48 - Maccabi, Orheyev branch, 1918 (Yard of Talmud Torah)

At the top of the pyramid stands Penina Zeylik, in the center below
is Dina Sherman and on her right is Yehudit Furer

Jewish Youth Organizations

Chapter 14

Gordonia

by A. Yagolnitzer-Shemovny

Translated by Jerrold Landau

In 1927, the Gordonia group was founded by Shneur Geynichovitz and Shlomo Bronshteyn. The first to join Gordonia were the 5th and 6th grade students of the gymnasiums. Following them, the working youth joined, including those who worked in workshops and stores. The number of members reached 50-60.

Since general meetings were forbidden by law, we were forced to meet in private homes for the purpose of "conversation". The content of the conversation was general topics, history, Zionism, and the doctrine of A. D. Gordon. In addition to the discussions, there were also Hebrew lessons given by those who knew Hebrew, especially by the teacher Shneur Geynichovitz.

The first celebration that was organized to mark the founding of the chapter is still etched in my mind. It took place in Suslensky's workshop on the eve of Simchat Torah. This celebration served as a form of farewell party for Shlomo Bronshteyn on the occasion of his aliya to the Land. With the passage of time, this first Simchat Torah celebration turned into a tradition in the life of the movement. The Romanian authorities accepted the character of the Zionist movement. They recognized it and did not interfere with our work. We decided to search for a suitable headquarters for the chapter. Through the intercession of activists for whom the matter of the movement was close to their hearts, we received a room in the Yeshiva building, which served as our meeting hall.

With the opening of the hall, the members were divided into various groups: older youths of age 16-18, up-and-coming youths of the age 14-16, and scouts of the age of 12-14. Counselors were trained and arose from the chapter. Members of the older group (who knew Hebrew for the most part) directed members of the younger groups. The chapter was directed by forces from the youth (independent direction), a council of advisors, secretaries and treasurers. It sustained itself by its membership dues.

Each group met twice a week. On the Sabbath there was a general gathering of all of the groups in order to deal with a common topic. This gathering concluded with dancing.

The movement carried out its activities in a modest manner. The movement refrained from smoking, salon dances, cracking seeds, etc. There was also a set uniform (gray shirts).

Figure 49 - Gordonia branch, 1931

Each group met twice a week. On the Sabbath there was a general gathering of all of the groups in order to deal with a common topic. This gathering concluded with dancing.

The movement carried out its activities in a modest manner. The movement refrained from smoking, salon dances, cracking seeds, etc. There was also a set uniform (gray shirts).

The members kept their obligations honestly. When we received a plot of land in the yard of the ORT School, we decided to actualize the idea of the distinguished teacher A. D. Gordon. We called this plot of land "Gan Yarok" (Verdant Garden). It became the central point for the activities of our chapter. Every group tended to it and guarded it day and night according to a rotation. One could see groups of children with their counselors each evening as they were assembling in the hall of the chapter waiting for their turn. On Sabbaths, excursions were arranged to the Seleshty Forest outside the city for the purpose of drawing the youth close to nature and communal life. These excursions were an experience for both the members and the counselors. The first inter-chapter meeting, which took place in Kishinev on the occasion of the visit of Nachum Sokolov, left a great impression. At this meeting, the high organizational level of the members of Gordonia of Orheyev stood out. Our movement flourished and continued on until the day finally came when most of the Jewish students belonged to Gordonia. Members older than age 18 were required to go on hachshara for actualization, or to leave the movement. The "Keren Aliya" (aliya fund) was founded in our first year of existence.

Figure 50 - Gordonia group, 1936

Figure 51 - Gordonia
In the center Aliza Yagolnitzer-Shemovny -- on her left Avraham Rechulsky

The first hachshara group was in "Massada" (Bessarabia). With the increase of the stream of aliya to the land, several hachshara points were established in the region of Orheyev, such as the chapter of Onitskany. In Teleneshti, where Jews who owned vineyards lived, a hachshara chapter was founded in the fields of Dr. Kleiderman and Petrushka. Our members stood up to the test of the work, and were encouraged also by gentiles such as General Yanoshovich. Two hachshara chapters existed in Orheyev itself in the Talmud Torah building. The members obtained work in the brick kiln of Dizengof (from the family of Meir Dizengof). They were employed in the cutting of trees, baking of matzos for Passover, etc.

Figure 52 - Gordonia, drama band

Standing: 1. R. Daskal 2. [alef]. Vyshkautzan 3. Y. Yadovsky -- Zeevi (coordinator of the group) 4. L. Cheriyan 5. M. Gendler 6. [feh]. Belfer
Seated 2nd Row: 1. M. Lipshin 2. Y. Gondelman -- Rozenberg
Seated 3rd Row: 1. [feh]. Baudfein 2. R. Liniveker

In order to attract the community and also meet our budget, we arranged various celebrations: Bialik celebrations, whose content was lectures and recitals; celebrations of the 24th of Shvat dedicated to A. D. Gordon; we also put on performances such as Jeremiah, Shulamit, The Children of the Ghetto, and performed a parody of the community at the time of the strike of the shochtim (ritual slaughterers). The community looked approvingly upon our activities and streamed to these celebrations. Some of the performances were also brought to nearby cities. Gordonia played an active role in the Keren

Kayemet, Keren Hayesod, Chalutz Week (on Passover), and the distribution of the shekel (Zionist movement membership token) for the congress.

Gordonia also served as the instigating force in the founding the Tarbut School and the Hebrew Gymnasium. It also worked to increase the number of Hebrew readers in the civic library. The readership reached to one quarter of the number of readers. The Gordonia chapter founded groups in Rezina, Teleneshti and Chinisheutsy. Until the time of the Second World War, many of our members made aliya to the Land and settled in villages, cities and different Kibbutzim such as Massada, Chulda, Chanita, Sarid, Nirem.

Two of our dear members fell in Hadera during the disturbances of 5696 (1936): Anshel Muchnik and Yehudah Spivak.

Figure 53 - Gordonia, preparation group

Seated below from right to left: 1. S. Gisenblat 2. ... 3. M. Broytman 4. M. Machlis 5. B. Shuchman
In the middle: 1. C. Muchnik 2. M. Frank 3. Shaposhnik 4. ... 5. ...
Upper row: 1. M. Rechulsky 2. Shrayberman 3. M. Ziserman 4. R. Chaimovitz 5. ... 6. Suslensky 7. T. Muchnik 8. Grovokopatel 9. Tartakovsky

Figure 54 - Gordonia, Orheyev branch

**Figure 55 - The nest separated from their
friends after their immigration to Israel**

Figure 56 - Gordonia, 1932

Chapter 15

Hashomer Hatzair (The Young Watchman)

by Ch. Ben-Yaakov

Translated by Boaz Nadler

Figure 57 - "Hashomer Hatsair" cell, 1931

I now remember those ancient and unforgettable days more than 50 years ago, when the pioneer youth groups were founded in Orheyev. The Zionist idea conquered the hearts of the youth. But some of these "golden boys" were not attracted to the other changes that were occurring around us, and they continued to see everything from a very personal viewpoint. The most happy and ignorant, so to speak, were those young people who were able to obtain an academic degree, even under the cost of assimilation, and yet for whom the Zionist recognition struck a cord and grew strong. We were extremely impressed by the first group of pioneers from Orheyev, the group of "Bnei Israel" (Sons of Israel) that immigrated to Israel and settled near the Sharona group, where they worked on paving the road from Haifa to Nazareth.

Letters full of enthusiasm then came to Orheyev, calling us to come as well.

Shneur Genikhovitz, one of the founders of the pioneer group, rebuffed the youth for their pursuit of "life's convenience and pleasures," and called upon the Jewish youth to prepare themselves for their new lives in the future. He was the founder of the "Gordonia" branch in Orheyev. There were furious debates within the movement about the best way to fulfill the pioneering ideology. The arguments moved from the branch into the street, and entered into father's and mother's house and into the family. Due to these differences in opinion, some of us left "Gordonia" and founded the first branch of "Hashomer Hatzair" in Orheyev. Within a short period of time, we were able to draw to our group a few dozen boys and girls, high school students of various ages, and our cell grew larger day by day. We received instructional pamphlets and other material, and held vigilant discussions. These were done in the following manner: first the instructor opened the discussion with a specific subject and then a debate started. In this way, many issues and questions were clarified, and eventually summarized by the instructor.

We committed ourselves to a lifestyle of learning and education, and along this process combined with self reading, our opinions were formed. Apart from long discussions we would organize Israeli folklore nights, with dances and songs, and we made field trips to far away places as an integral part of our educational program. These trips were astounding. Besides a close encounter with the surrounding nature, this prepared us for communal life in the future. This is how we were drawn into the training in "Halutz" and later to immigrate to Israel to a life in a Kibbutz.

Our lives were filled with joy. The joy of living and of creation blended together. We were ready to face the future, and trained ourselves towards a life of manual labor in the Kibbutz.

A few remarks are appropriate about the involvement of our parents in the changes that occurred in the life of the Zionist youth of our town. Despite the differences in opinion between "fathers and sons," one can say that most of the parents eventually agreed, without much of a choice, with the new reality. They realized this out of understanding, combined with a fear that their world was falling down before their eyes. Our way led us to the land of Israel. We did not believe that the "old people" were capable of starting a new life in a new country, and indeed they stayed there to face their destiny, which led to their doom.

Chapter 16

Hashomer Hatzair

by Emuna Munder

Translated by Marsha Kayser

This is how we founded the group "Hashomer Hatzair" (The Young Watchman) in Orheyev.

It was in about 1929. During the time when the "czarists" came to power it was a little easier to breathe. One was even allowed to open various cultural institutions.

Previously, when not even a small gathering was permitted, we met secretly. What great joy there was when "on a new day," as the saying goes, there were initial announcements from two sides: 1) whoever wants could come to register in the Zionist hall, which was in the yeshiva; 2) an announcement from the Culture-League which had also opened by then. Brur was the more leftist workers' youth, and included a group who had just left "Ort," the Workers-Shul, and turned leftist. I myself, still objective, went to the Zionist hall where, although suspicious, they took me in, believing that I was sent by my friends, in order to investigate how they got such an important member as A.R. Thus were created kibbutzim (agricultural collectives in Palestine/Israel); we learned Hebrew and the older ones organized into groups. The younger, the majority educated, separated themselves from the others and established the "Gordonia" group. In the hall there remained a small group of worker friends who were also searching for something but lacked know-how. First came the friend Kh.D., an expert from the "Hashomer Hatzair" program, who suggested that we be the first organizers and lay the first stone from the organization "Hashomer Hatzair" Orheyev. Initially I was close to saying "We shall hear and we shall do" (ed. note: Biblical quote meaning to obey the commandments) because I knew that we knew too little in order to establish the right educational youth-organization (on our own.) But it so happened that those who were "leftist" were on their guard and were prepared to brainwash the entire youth, since we had taken to the work with little knowledge under difficult conditions. We sought help from friends from "Shomer Hatzair," who are today the main leaders of their kibbutzim and are activists and leaders of the country (ed. note: Israel). They would often come to help us with various conversations, lectures, and in all areas, Zionism, socialism, Jewish education. One time even friends on a mission from Eretz-Yisroel came and brought us a few observant Jews. At the beginning it was very difficult, often fights with other organizations would take place. But this only strengthened the will to make progress and advance on all fronts. It was successful - in Orheyev a cell was started that brought many settlers whose help was devoted to the construction of Eretz-Yisroel, - many of them in the kibbutzim.

And to close, I want to remember, with deep pain and pride, our friend Shaul Averbukh, may his memory be blessed, from Shomer Hatzair in Orheyev, who fell during the heroic fight to free the "Negba" Kibbutz. Those close to him and his friends will always remember, his name is sacred...

Figure 58 - "Hashomer Hatsair", group members

Below from right to left: 1. [alef]. Beznos 2. Y. Svavolsky 3. ... 4. V. Dyukman
Above: 1. S. Bogoslavsky 2. Z. Katzap 3. S. Shaposhnik (Rozenfeld) 4. Shustik 5. [alef]. Mishkis (Munder)

Figure 59 - "Hashomer Hatsair", preparation branch, 1935

Chapter 17

Poalei Zion

by B. Lemberg

Translated by Jerrold Landau

After the imposition of Romanian rule upon the population of Bessarabia (1918-1923) and the crushing of the communist fermentation, a more liberal spirit began to blow, with the desire to attract the community and to integrate it into the economic and Romanian cultural perspectives.

The Jewish citizens began to get used to their new conditions. Business relations were forged between Moldova and Harghita, and children began to be sent to Romanian schools. The youth continued their studies in universities. Communal institutions began to participate with the Jews of Romania, and at times they were helped by them with regard to government institutions and with regard to forging civilian and political relations. For some of the Jews, it seemed as if the liberal rule of Romania would continue, and the Jewish population would become rooted from both an economic and national perspective, without disturbance.

However, most of the Jewish youth, along with many other strata of the progressive Jewish population, did not believe in these delusions. They rather believed in Zionism. The movement for aliya to the Land strengthened in Bessarabia, including Orheyev. A group of studying youth called "Bnei Yisrael" was organized in 1922-1923, with the objective of preparing themselves for the building up of the Land. In its wake, Gordonia and Hashomer Hatzair organizations were founded. These movements attracted primarily the studying youth. The Jewish workers, who were also not satisfied with life in the exile, did not find their place in their youth organizations. The desire for Zionist organization in the eyes of the workers, as well as their economic, professional and social needs, stood at the head of their worries. They were also concerned that the portion of the workers would not be ignored in the distribution of aliya permits.

**Figure 60 - Members of "Poalei Zion", "Haoved" and "Dror"
Conference of Yiddish Socialist Workers Parties -- Poalei Zion,
Orheyev, 1926**

Upper Row from right to left: 1. Yaakov Kulik 2. … 3. Arye Balan 4. Likodrietz 5. Sima
Fudman 6. Avraham Portnoy 7. Shteynshlager 8. Filarsky 9. S. Chananis 10. Buka
Bozinyan
2nd Row: 1. … 2. Leah Meizler 3. … 4. … 5. Yehoshua Zamochovsky 6. D. Kopelyuk 7.
Avraham Finkelshteyn 8. Chaya Shaposhnik 9. Aharon Meizler 10. Zila Gondelman 11.
Moshe Levinson
3rd Row: 1. Yitzchak Sofer 2. Miryam Portnoy 3. Yitzchak Kupertzansky 4. Yisrael
Vaysman 5. Baruch Lemberg 6. David Munder 7. Sima Bozinyan 8. Chaya Portnoy 9. …
4th Row: 1. Yehudit Portnoy 2. Rach 3. Shteynshlager 4. Mania Bozinyan 5. Gondelman
6. Shlomo Lechtman 7. Dushker

The First Meeting of the Workers

I concluded my army service in 1925. I met with my friends Yisrael
Vaysman, David Munder, Zamochovsky, Avraham Finkelshteyn and others,
and we discussed the matter of organizing the workers of Orheyev into the
Zionist movement. Indeed, we had no knowledge of the Poalei Zion party;
however we knew that the path of the worker in the Zionist movement was
different than the paths of the existing movements with their traditional

frameworks. At this meeting, we decided to dedicate ourselves to studying the problems of the workers of the Land of Israel, and to develop the idea of the Poalei Zion party and the Hechalutz (pioneering) movement. It seemed as if the time was ripe for this. From our first steps, we already earned the recognition of many comrades who joined our publicity events in a regular fashion.

At first, the meetings were arranged in secret on account of the ban on assembly. As time went on, members of the Zionist council in our city – Pagis, Dr. Berkovitz, and Y. Yagolnitzer – obtained permits for meeting places for the organizations of the Zionist movement, at first in the Yeshiva and later in various places in the city.

We broadened our activity in the meeting places. We established contact with the Poalei Zion headquarters in Warsaw, and received publicity material from them. Similarly, we established contact with the regional secretary in Chernovits, Chayim Geler (today a member of the active committee of the Histadrut). After that, we did not stumble in searching for a way. We were assisted at all times with material and direction for our activities. The agronomist Chayim Feigin of blessed memory also helped us significantly. He had a significant role in the establishment of the Poalei Zion party in Bessarabia in general and in Orheyev in particular.

Figure 61 - Youth Group, "Poalei Zion"

The cradle of the Hechalutz (pioneers) of Poalei Zion in Romania was Orheyev. Tradesmen from among our members, including carpenters, locksmiths, drivers and tailors decided to prepare themselves for aliya to the Land.

The Hechalutz center in Kishinev was composed of representatives of Gordonia, Hashomer Hatzair and representatives of the Working Land of Israel. They were primarily concerned with strengthening the Hachsharah kibbutzim that was close to their spirit. Of course, they were not interested in nurturing a Hachsharah kibbutz that was not in accordance with their spirit. Any suggestion and request from our part to establish Hachsharah depots for Poalei Zion did not come to fruition. Therefore, we decided to set up a Hachsharah depot in Orheyev with our own initiative. We established contact with the estate owners in our region. After much toil and difficulty, we succeeded in establishing a Hachsharah depot in the vineyard of Moshe Vaynberg. Throughout the summer, we worked in the vineyard of the aforementioned, as well as in the nearby rock quarry and at various other agricultural pursuits.

When the fact of the founding of our Hachsharah depot became known, the center sent a number of pioneers with the advisor Buzia Feingold (of Lipkany, today a worker in the Port of Haifa). Members from Teleneshti and other villages in the region joined us (Malka, Yosef, and others). Our numbers reached to close to 40 men and women, and we all lived in the shed in the vineyard. We studied Hebrew and also conducted publicity discussions. In the meantime, Poalei Zion Hachsharah depots were set up in Bukovina and Ruget. Finally, a Hechalutz center for Poalei Zion was set up in Chernovits, headed by the members Yisrael Samet, Yosef Schiff, Motel Fierman, Buzia Feingold, Liuba Gukovsky (killed in Maagan Michael (ed. note: kibbutz on the coast, north of Hadera)), and the writer of these lines.

Due to reasons that could not be foreseen from the outset, the depot in Orheyev could not continue operations, and many of our members transferred to the depots in Bukovina. However, many remained who did not have the financial means to travel there. For those people, it was necessary to create Hachsharah opportunities in our region.

The agronomist Feigin directed us to Azriel Bolochnik from the village of Kriulyany. With his assistance we reached an agreement with the landowner Sheftilul to establish a Hachsharah depot on his estate. Our pioneers moved to Kriulyany, and other members from that place joined them (Yehudit Berliand, Mendel Trafzin, Chasya Krashkovitz and others). We ended up with 48 members, and we worked there until the end of the autumn.

Figure 62 - Poalei Zion

Standing from right to left: 1. Sander Filarsky 2. Pinchas Erlikh 3. Chava Polinkovsky 4. Chaya Shaposhnik (Finkelshteyn) 5. Yaakov Vaynshteyn 6. Avraham Finkelshteyn 7. Moshe Fisher 8. ... 9. Shaike Kantor 10. Y. Yochist 11. ...
2nd Row: 1. Avraham Portnoy 2. ... 3. Sima Bozinyan 4. ... 5. Rachel Legerman 6. ... 7. Nachman Shaposhnik 8. ...
3rd Row: 1. Ester Filarsky 2. Aharon Filarsky 3. Gershon Shaposhnik 4. Yehudit Portnoy 5. Zecharya Olitsky 6. Rivka Kisilov 7. Tuviya Bozinyan

On account of the proximity of the village to the Dniester, the government suspected us and investigated our "legitimacy" from time to time. A few of our members were arrested for interrogation, and were freed thanks only to the intercession of the landowner. This caused a waste of time and interruptions. We overcame all obstacles, and our turn came for aliya, but then an additional obstacle came to the fore. The aliya center in Kishinev found that the Hebrew fluency of several of our members was insufficient, so they did not authorize their aliya. All of our explanation that it was improper to require from our members, who were mainly workers, the same level of fluency as the studying youth did not succeed. Only after the aliya of our first group in 1934 did I succeed in convincing the secretariat of the Kibbutz Hameuchad to send emissaries to Bessarabia to prepare members for aliya.

The last of our members made aliya in 1939 before the outbreak of the Second World War.

Figure 63 - Poalei Zion, the pioneers

Row 1 above from right to left: 1. Arye Balan 2. Yaakov Kulik 3. … 4. Avraham Finkelshteyn 5. … 6. Yitzchak Kupertzansky 7. … 8. Mesha Grinberg 9. … 10. …
Row 2: 1. Zamochovsky 2. Gedalyahu Sandler 3. … 4. Chaya Finkelshteyn 5. Baruch Lemberg 6. Malka Lubarsky 7. Frayda Vaysman 8. Miryam Portnoy 9. Yehoshua Kantor 10. …
Row 3: 1. … 2. … 3. Rivka Katz 4. … 5. David Munder 6. … 7. Sara Lemberg 8. David Grinblat 9. Yitzchak Gondelman
Lying: Shlomo Lekhtman

Figure 64 - Poalei Zion, the pioneers

Standing from right to left: 1. Yaakov Kulik 2. Yadua Lau 3. Avraham Finkelshteyn 4. Mesha Grinberg 5. Yehoshua Zamochovsky 6. Malka Lubarsky 7. Yehoshua Kantor
Seated row 2: 1. ... 2. ... 3. Kupertzansky 4. Baruch Lemberg 5. ... 6. David Munder 7. David Grinblat 8. Sara Lemberg 9. ... 10. ... 11. ...
Row 3 below: 1. ... 2. ... 3. ... 4. ... 5. Shlomo Lechtman 6. ... 7. Chaya Finkelshteyn 8. ... 9. ... 10. ... 11. ...

Chapter 18

The Beginning of Hechalutz (the first pioneers)

by Yitzchak Rapoport

Translated by Jerrold Landau

At the time of the Romanian conquest of Bessarabia, the Zionist movement of our city showed no signs of life, for fear of the Sigurnata that suppressed all communal movements. The few members, I among them, transferred to agricultural work with Rozen, Vaynshtok and others, from where we received news on what was transpiring in the Land of Israel. Then, we organized a small group and decided to make aliya to the Land. To this end, we got in touch with the center in Kishinev, and traveled there to appear before the center. We began to concern ourselves with passports. The lawyer Shimon Goldberg assisted us in this matter. We were forced to forge signatures, since our parents objected to our aliya. Then the Ukrainian disturbances began, and many Jews fled across the Dniester to our region. The youth received the refugees and helped take care of them. Moshe Kalmanovitz headed this effort. At first, the refugees were not permitted to go to houses, and they were held in detention camps. We provided them with assistance and food. They were finally freed from the camps. We accommodated the distraught people among the residents and in synagogues. Until this day, I recall one terrifying event. A rumor spread that the gentiles murdered a family of six people as they crossed the Dniester and pillaged their property. Miraculously, a baby survived who was tossed into a well. To his good fortune, the water was frozen in that well, and the child remained alive. By chance, people heard the screams. They hurried and took the child out alive. He was brought to our city. The uncle of the child was found in the city, and thus he was saved. He arrived in the Land with his relatives. Today he is one of the dear pioneers and activists in the Land, and can be found on one of the Kibbutzim. I cannot forget the funeral of the family members. The entire city followed along, and bitter weeping and wailing were heard from all sides. From that time, we began to take more and more interest in the lives of the refugees. We obtained a house from Vaynshtok, purchased utensils, and helped them get organized. We searched for work for the younger ones, and tried to forge connections for them. We arranged lectures, and visited them often. During that time, we got in touch with the center in Kishinev in order to arrange travel certificates to the land.

After a short while, we received the news that we would shortly set out for the Land of Israel. The joy was great. We were five people from Orheyev who joined the group that was departing. I will not forget the day that I took leave of the city. It was a winter day. We rented wagons, loaded our baggage, and left. Moshe Kalmanovitz and Zionists from the city stood on the big bridge. Leib Stolyar poured water, and we took leave of them with blessings of success, and wishes to see each other in the Land.

Figure 65 - The Pioneers at the G. Vaynshtok house, 1920

We arrived in Kishinev and joined up with a larger group of pioneers. This was the sixth group of 180 people. We set out for Galati and waited for a boat that was going to Kushta. There in Galati, we were set up in the building of Beit Hechalutz until we received news about the departure. When we arrived in Kushta, we received news that we had received our certificates. Our joy was boundless, and we began to prepare for the journey with great joy. We embarked upon an Italian boat, received food from the Joint and the committee of delegates of the Land of Israel. The journey lasted for two weeks. We suffered no small amount from lack of food, but we overcame. The hope to see the Land shortly increased our strength. As we drew near and arrived in Beirut, Arabs ascended the boat and told us that there were disturbances in the Land, and many Jews were killed. They continued on and told us that we would also be slaughtered the moment we reached Haifa. We immediately gathered in the belly of the ship and declared a state of emergency. We decided not to lose spirit, and to make additional efforts to reach the Land, even if it would require sacrifice. We gathered weapons that were with us. These included scrap metal and even empty bottles, since there were almost no weapons. When we arrived in Haifa, boats of the port came to greet us with a member of the committee of delegates and the captain Dov Hoz. They told us about the disturbances and the murder of Brenner and his family, the Beit Chalutz that was destroyed, and the 38 pioneers that were murdered. They also told us that the English government, via the Jewish commissioner, forbade all immigration to the Land in order not to arouse the wrath of the Arabs, so we must sail on to an unknown destination. The news crushed us. We were dejected, without any recourse.

We sailed to Egypt. We remained in Alexandria for three days, and nobody was permitted to approach the boat. By chance I made contact with one Jew, and I asked him to inform the Zionist committee or the communal council about our situation, and to request help. Immediately, representatives of the Joint and the communal council arrived, and brought us food. The Chief Rabbi interceded with the governor, and they agreed to let us off the boat. We were brought to the well-known quarantine area in Alexandria. We suffered a bit from lack of food, but the most important thing was the freedom that we had there. We were able to arrange our baggage and wash our clothes. After a few days, the governor issued an order to send us back on a boat, but not the same boat. It was rather a small boat, filled with merchandise. We were informed that we were being returned to Kushta. We suffered greatly from hunger since there was almost no food. On the boat, we found grains of corn and onions in the storehouses, which we feasted upon. We reached Kushta after four days. We were received by the committee of delegates, and put up on the Jewish settlement of the I. C. A. (ed. note: Jewish Colonization Association). We began everything from scratch. We erected tents, set up a kitchen, and everything went properly. We organized a collective life. Some of us worked in fields as farmers, and others worked in the forests. The girls worked in the kitchen and other utilities. We received comforting news from the Land. Life there was becoming quieter. We were informed that soon an English Major would come to check that there were no communists among us. The first examination went successfully. Forty of us received aliya permits, including me and the others from my city. The joy was great. We would finally be able to achieve the awaited objective. We reached Haifa after a brief period. This time we were greeted by family members and people from Orheyev, including Moshe Roitman. We disembarked from the boat that day and we were sent to quarantine outside the city. We spent about ten days in tents. Acquaintances and relatives visited us daily, and brought us good things and Israeli newspapers. We were organized into groups when we left quarantine. Our group, including Moshe Roitman, joined the group of the Haifa port, which was headed by Berel Repetur. We received various jobs, including the unloading of heavy railway links and coal from ships. The heat was great, and bothered us no small amount. There was no water at the port. The work was grueling and tiring. We worked diligently and overcame everything. The contractors gave us large quantities of work, and we filled their demands. The Arab porters were not able to stand up to the competition, and we thereby took over the work in the port. After some time, we obtained beasts of burden. A group of wagon drivers also was transferred to us. The aliya increased, the settlement increased, and Haifa became a city with a large and organized Hebrew settlement. Moshe Roitman finally left the work in the port, and purchased a store for the sale of meat. At that time, riots again broke out in the Land (1929). Roitman fell victim during the riots at the hands of a co-professional. Thousands of people participated in his funeral, but the English would not permit us to travel to the cemetery. Only several friends, myself included, received permission, and accompanied our friend to the communal grave in Lower Haifa.

Part III – Memoirs

A: Education and Culture

Chapter 19

Memories from Over Fifty Years Ago

Yitzchak Spivak

Translated by Rachel Weitz & Marsha Kayser

These pages will start with unrelated memories from my life as best as I can remember them. Much of what happened in those days has been forgotten. I can no longer recall all of it, but parts come, not in one stream of thought, and for this reason it will skip around.

As I present parts of my life's story, I do not mean to emphasize in any way major events in the lives of my family and expose them in any way. I know that my life is not that different than the lives of others of my own age, with whom I shared so many experiences about fifty years ago. Especially because of that, I say to myself, I like to write down chapters from my life, and these chapters should reflect somewhat the lives that my peers and I shared in different stages in our lives. While we were young and innocent and still together, we spoke one language and said the same things. The way our kind was raised and developed, our kind of people is similar, and you can learn about one from the other. There is of course something unique about each person - I am not going to talk about the uniqueness but about the things that they shared - we were all poor, we all received traditional education: "kheder," yeshiva and continuation in a kloyz (ed. note: study house). Everyone was independent with no special supervision, care, or guidance from parents. Even if it was a fateful time, usually blind coincidence was the determining factor, and with no help or advice, each one paved his way in life.

And in some lines when I described memories from the life of my mother Shprintza, may she rest in heaven, the only intention was to draw an image of the typical Jewish mother in those days. Their most earnest desire was to see their son engaged in Torah and the Commandments, and their strongest wishes, even when the parents were facing the end, were that their precious son would study a chapter in Mishna to honor his parents' memory.

Days of Childhood

I am a native of Orheyev. I spent my childhood roaming her byways. There I passed the days of my youth. I never left the place until I was sixteen or seventeen, except when, as the son of a poor family that struggled to make a meager living, I went with my grandfather to nearby villages for our work. My father did not teach me, and I did not have a rabbi that would watch over me and guide me in the right direction. My father Asher, may his memory be blessed, did not have time to think about taking care of me and educating me. All his life he was consumed with earning a living, which kept him away from home as he went to nearby villages (Seleshty, Orgineshty, Trifeshty, Chinishevtsy) and the tobacco plantations in which his whole family was engaged. My mother Shprintza, may her memory be blessed, died when I was a young child, and then I moved to the house of my grandfather Yehudah Moyshe, blessed be his memory.

"I was a child alone" - those poetic words reflect what happened to me - being alone and abandoned. I did not know the feeling of a warm touch or affection, and I don't remember even one day of my childhood that was joyous. I do not remember any playful and exciting days in those my childhood days...

Occasionally, to help myself, I would try a new way in life to satisfy my soulful longing and to lift my spirits. My development was not guided and was already predetermined. There was no consistency, I zigzagged back and forth, and sometimes I turned sharply. And through pain and struggle I moved from one stage to another and there were many stages: from the yeshiva to the study house, from there to the bookstore, from the bookstore to the book bindery, from there to teaching in the "moshevah" (ed. note: town). Later on in Kalarash and from there to Kishinev, from Kishinev to pedagogic courses that were in Grodno, and from Grodno to Odessa, from Odessa to Israel on the ship Ruslan (1920).

As a child of 7 or 8, we lived on Lithuanian Street. I don't know why the street was called this. Guesses about the name made no sense. Our flat was six steps down from the street level (a "boshkeh"). The floor was made of clay. Every Friday night we would mix new clay and horse manure on the floor and spread it out in honor of the Sabbath.

Once my mother took me, handed me a bucket, and started to gather manure which she put in the bucket. On the way, I also bent to collect some manure - but she did not let me do it. "It's enough that you are carrying the bucket, it's not fit that a child who studies the Gemara should get his hands dirty."

We moved to Isser Litvak's house, which was on the same street. One day a fire started, I don't remember how, but I remember the sound of the alarm that my mother and the neighbors heard. The neighbors rushed in when they heard the screams and started to put out the fire that erupted from different corners. One came with a pail of water, another removed our belongings, all the kids were taken to nearby neighbors' houses, and when the fire was completely out, my mother started to collect her children (two sons and three girls). Hearing her call, we gathered around her.

My older sister Leia, may she rest in peace, burst out crying when she saw the messy pile next to the house. My mother asked her not to cry, silly girl, be thankful that we are all alive and healthy, and as she said that, she lifted her hands and whispered: "Thank you oh God, merciful God, for the grace that you bestowed upon me, all my infants are around me," and her face shone with joy (from God's grace.)

I remember the Shabbos before Passover ("Shabbot Hagadol") my mother lay sick, her strength had left her, and she lost consciousness and fainted. Grandma Rivka and the rest of the household cried bitterly, and the neighbors gathered. Grandma (hovering over the children): "A terrible disaster has come upon us, children, come quickly to the synagogue, only merciful God can help us." When we came to the synagogue, the prayers stopped, the ark was opened before us, Grandma started to pray to God, crying and asking him to have mercy on the young 'chicks' and that for them, please send a cure to her only daughter, the sole survivor after ten sons. When we returned home, we found the neighbors caring for my mother. Misting her face with water, they gave her "drops for weakness" (ammonia drops). She came to, opened her eyes, turned her head from one side to the other, and asked where is Itzikl. Immediately they took me to her bed. She extended her arm and took my hand and pressed it to her heart and whispered, "My dear Itzikl, promise that you will study a chapter of Mishnah for the elevation of my soul," and then immediately closed her eyes.

Figure 66 - One of the "pupils" and "psalm readers"

Every day I beseech G-d for all those people who are charitable to me, they should be well and strong and have many blessings all of the days of their lives. Moshe Leib ben Shmuel Tzvi, may he rest in peace, Kiro

In the winter following the death of my mother, may she rest in peace, I would get up early on Shabbos, before dawn, and go to the synagogue ("to the Tailors' Shul") which was close to our home, and together with the "Tehilim" (ed. note: Book of Psalms) readers, we would read chapters from "Tehilim," and at the end of every day I said Kaddish and usually I would be one of the few to say it. I began sharing this mitzvah with my younger brother Yaakov who was two years younger than me. On one of the Shabbos nights, a very difficult winter night, very stormy and dark outside, the mud in the street deep and sticky, the narrow paths where people walked during the day disappeared completely. That night I awakened and did not know the time. No clock at home. It seemed that the time to go to synagogue had arrived. I awakened my brother. At first he refused, saying, "I am very tired, it is very cold, I want to sleep some more." But when I started to appeal to him, "We could say Kaddish five times and there will be no one else but us," he was tempted, we got dressed, and we left the house. Outside, it was very dark and gloomy and the silence - terrible and horrifying. I was afraid to go close to the houses because a dog might jump on us. We walked in the middle of the road, sinking in the mud, which was freezing. My brother clung to me, and his hand was in my pocket. Clenched and holding each other, we got to the synagogue, which was closed with no light from within. We walked all around, and there was no way to go in. I told my brother: "Let's go to the study house - over there they are probably already open." We were stepping in the mud, so he clung to me again, and again in the middle of the street, we turned toward the study house. We arrived and the study house was also closed. We were standing by the door, and my brother cried, "I am very cold." I appealed to him, "Soon probably the shames (ed. note: the synagogue's caretaker or sexton) will come and open the door, the 'goy' will come and light the oven." We waited and waited and Lev the shames didn't show up, and the 'goy' didn't come. I said to my brother, "Let's go to the 'Chabad' synagogue (the Chabadski shul). We arrived there, and the synagogue there was also closed. Not even I could go to another synagogue. My brother clasped me with both his hands, shaking...I took him and brought him under the bench by the door and I sat next to him awaiting the sunrise. I don't know how much time passed, because I also fell asleep. All of a sudden, I felt a touch, I opened my eyes, and I saw the shames who was showering me with questions. I couldn't answer and I just said, "I am Itzikl Yehudah Moyshe's"...(after my grandfather Moyshe).

I woke up my brother, and we both entered the synagogue; the shames started massaging my hands and face. I pointed to my brother, I also started to take care of him - - finally daytime came, and in the synagogue they finished saying Tehilim but I couldn't say Kaddish, not me or my brother. We returned home, we did not go to Shakharit prayer. Our sister Leia, may she rest in peace, when she saw us coming in, imagined what had happened. She took us and put us both in bed, she stood by us, she didn't raise her voice, she patted our heads, her eyes tearing on and on...

Now, when I remember those days, my heart tells me that the merciful God probably carried enough tears in his pouch for her that day.

The next day I got up but my brother stayed in bed for over two weeks. A doctor was not called for him but my sister herself took care of him after she consulted with the neighboring women.

In the House of My Grandfather Yehudah Moyshe, of blessed memory

While my mother was still alive, I moved to Grandpa Yehudah Moyshe's house and I was brought up in his house for a few years. Therefore I carry the nickname "Itzikl Yehudah Moyshe's."

While I was at Grandpa's house, I started to learn at the "yeshiva" and in those days my grandfather was one of the gabbaim (ed. note: synagogue treasurer or trustee) from the yeshiva, and when it came time to hire one of the teachers, they would consult with him, too. Once two gabbaim came to him and asked him for his opinion regarding a certain tutor. Is he suitable to serve as a tutor in Gemara (ed. note: Talmud Commentary) in one of the classes? His answer was - out of the question: do not accept him and he shouldn't have any involvement in our yeshiva. On the question of what wrong he found in him, he told them that on the previous Saturday morning he saw him walking to the synagogue and he took out a white handkerchief from a pants pocket to wipe his nose.

"And I'm asking you, couldn't he use the red handkerchief and put it in the back pocket of the "kaputeh" (ed. note: long coat worn by orthodox Jews), as every kosher Jew does, and not do like the "Poritz" (Polish squire)...

My cousin Avraham ben Yoel Tzvi lived in the village Orgineshty and he's one of the few intellectuals of that generation. In his house there were Tenach books with interpretations of "Malbeem" (Meir Leibush ben Yechiel Michal, a famous genius of his time). At his place you could also find the book "Akhiasof" or "Tushia" (ed. note: Resourcefulness). He also then received a Hebrew newspaper (I do not remember if it was "Hamelitz" or "Hatzfirah") and once in awhile he would pass on some of the copies for me to read. I used to treat the copies like something holy; I would spread them on the table and read them like the traditional Gemara "negun" (ed. note: tune) with the same rocking movements. My grandfather wasn't happy with this style of reading but he did not resist listening to what was written in those newspapers and I would tell him what I was reading: a story about someone who had the permit to collect customs duty on meat in a certain town who fired the "shoykhet" from his position and he (the shoykhet), because he was so enraged, attacked the permit holder and injured him and this was in the midst of the reading of the Torah. Or the story about the "gabe" in a synagogue that behaved in a way that was very disrespectful and scornful to one of the worshippers, who became very angry and cursed him and this led to a long break in the middle of the prayer and so on and so on. My grandfather listened and listened and said: "One of the two, if all of this is true, what your newspaper writes, it is an act of gossip, and about gossip the Gemara says, 'You shouldn't be like a peddler that is loading up on people's chatter about one another as if it were merchandise.' But in this case it is the things that this one and that one say to each other. 'And if it is a lie, we have therefore a matter of slander and this is worse than gossip. Anybody who talks slander is going against the core of it all (ed. note: Judaism) and he is multiplying his sins and he deserves to be stoned.' So why do you need all of this trouble Itzikl, you'd better take the book "Reshit

Hokhmah" (The Genesis of Wisdom) or "Khinat Olam" (Analysis of the World) and study them and don't waste your time; and the stories in your newspaper are things that have no wisdom in them and no fear of God and you should stay away from them."

I was then about ten years old...

My cousin Avraham (the son of my uncle Yoel Tzvi) was also one of the grandchildren whose education and upbringing my grandfather supervised. Once some information arrived in the village, and our grandfather demanded that Avraham come to him immediately. This seemed peculiar to everyone, and no one understood why he was being told to come to my grandfather at once. Next day he came to the village to my grandfather's house. When he asked what was the matter that he was asked to come urgently, our grandfather answered: I heard a rumor that you go once in a while to Rezina and that you go to the house of Mr. So and So, and they say in his house there is a Mendelssohn's "I.Sh.V.'Interpretation'" (ed. note: I.Sh.V. is a curse) and I suspect that while you are at his home you probably take Mendelssohn's books and maybe you peek and study them and from here it is just one step toward conversion....Got it? Well now you know why I called you to come to me?...

Avraham couldn't deny it and began to apologize that Mendelssohn is not worthy of such a curse (may his name and memory be erased) and in his book there is no heresy and no reason for worry and suspicion. But my grandfather did not allow him to continue, and finished with a scolding that such things will no longer be tolerated in his house. And he got up and left the room. And after that there was a distance between them. One turned aside and issued a reprimand, and the other was irate.

After a while Avraham brought his grandfather a new interpretation of Psalm number 8 in Tehilim: Lord our God how excellent is your name in all the earth, an interpretation by the Malb"eem. So Avraham wisely delivered the interpretation in a very elaborate and exact way, and my grandfather listened with interest, and after that they made up and their meetings returned to normal.

My grandfather used to take me with him when he went to Orgineshty, where my uncle Yoel (his older son) Tzvi lived. We traveled there quite frequently, whether for his business or when he wished to see his older son and his family. My uncle's family was the only Jewish family in this village and my uncle never forgot this special situation for a moment. He did everything to keep good relations with the people of the village, a relationship of friendship and understanding, although he was not always successful at this...

The police officer (Uriadnik) was my uncle's regular guest on their holidays and especially on the Jewish holidays he would come and visit, and he would sit late over a glass of wine or spirits while making conversation about world events.

The Strosta (village elder) and the priest would come and sit at this table over the holidays, and they would enjoy my aunt's baked goods and the bottles of wine offered to them. And they would sit and talk, in conversation with good neighbors.

The people of the village knew that if they did anything to the Jews' property, no one would take action, and at the slightest opportunity would take a beam of wood or a bar of metal from the yard or a basket of grapes from the vineyard, and no one feared being sued…

Even though the visits of these dignitaries at my uncle's house increased their respect for him, and no one in the village dared to hurt him in a vulgar way and to be openly disrespectful to him, when they would get drunk their tongues would loosen and they would spew words of contempt and disgrace and curse blasphemy toward the "kike" and his God. In the days of Krushbahn in Serbia when they started provocation reviling us in the newspaper "The Serbuts" (Krushbahn's newspaper) and these poisonous words penetrated to every village…

Once during Purim I visited my uncle, and suddenly the Uriadnik came in as usual to bless the owner. They gave him delicatessen and pastries and he ate with pleasure and he drank the wine and spirits. He drank, he wiped his mouth, and he drank again. My aunt served him the "strudel" (baking) and he did not refuse. He took a mouthful of drink and gulped it again in high spirits with his head heavy from drink…

When he got up he turned to my uncle with these words in Russian, "Hershku, how sweet is your religion there is nothing like her, so sweet and delicious…such delicatessen you will not find even at our priests! It's very pleasant to spend time at Hershku's house during the holiday." He was just about to leave and was at the threshold. His legs gave way, and he fell and got hurt. They called people from the street and with much effort they picked him up and led him to his home, and my uncle told me later that for months there were investigations ongoing about this issue. How come Uriadnik fell and was injured? And my uncle used the tested method to avoid court…

The Learning Method in Kheder and the Rabbi's Treatment of his Students

I was three and a half years old when I began the burden of education in kheder with a teacher of very young children. My older sister Charna, may she live long, would come along with me and sit with me the whole time I was there. From there I moved to Rabbi Shlomo Zalman, a teacher of "Khumesh" (ed. note: The Five Books of Moses.) In this "kheder" I learned Khumesh with the interpretation of the vocabulary including "Commentary" (explanations), and after a few months a small group (four or five kids including myself) also started to read Rashi's commentary for the first verses of the Portion for the Week, which the tutor would usually interweave with legends and fables, and sometimes also from the learnings from "Midrash Khuzal" (ed. note: our sages, may their memory be blessed). His voice was very pleasant and fatherly and touched me in such a way that I never forgot it.

We were at the portion of Noah. One of us would read the Khumesh, another one the Mikra (ed. note: the Bible) and another one the "Targum" (ed. note: the Septuagint, the Old Testament as translated by 70 Jewish scholars for Ptolemy II): "God liked Noah." The rabbi interrupted in the middle and asked, "Children, what does Kheyn mean? Kheyn is a tiny dot and thanks to the tiny dot in God's eyes, Noah saved the entire world."

And more from this rabbi's doctrine. We learned in the portion of Kitetze, " When a man takes a woman…and if he does not like her, because he finds something defective in her - he would divorce her and send her from his house." The rabbi explained, "and he found something defective in her - she burned the meals, for example, she burned the roast meat or her 'tzimmes' took on a smoky flavor because she was inattentive." And one of the students addressed the rabbi in these words: "So if she burns the roast or burns the 'tzimmes', is that enough reason for a man to divorce his wife?" he said in amazement. And the rabbi answered immediately, "Listen to me, children. The written text says in one place, 'love covers every crime and hatred will incite quarreling.' If because of the effect of the scorched roast and the smoky 'tzimmes', arguments, fights, and quarrels break out between the husband and his wife, it is a sign that there is no love and domestic bliss between them. And therefore it is better to give her the get (ed. note: a divorce) immediately so he will not continue to irritate her with such complaints."

Figure 67 - The writer of these notes next to his sister Charna

We were at the portion of Noah. One of us would read the Khumesh, another one the Mikra (ed. note: the Bible) and another one the "Targum" (ed. note: the Septuagint, the Old Testament as translated by 70 Jewish scholars for Ptolemy II): "God liked Noah." The rabbi interrupted in the middle and asked, "Children, what does Kheyn mean? Kheyn is a tiny dot and thanks to the tiny dot in God's eyes, Noah saved the entire world."

And more from this rabbi's doctrine. We learned in the portion of Kitetze, " When a man takes a woman…and if he does not like her, because he finds something defective in her - he would divorce her and send her from his house." The rabbi explained, "and he found something defective in her - she burned the meals, for example, she burned the roast meat or her 'tzimmes' took on a smoky flavor because she was inattentive." And one of the students addressed the rabbi in these words: "So if she burns the roast or burns the 'tzimmes', is that enough reason for a man to divorce his wife?" he said in amazement. And the rabbi answered immediately, "Listen to me, children. The written text says in one place, 'love covers every crime and hatred will incite quarreling.' If because of the effect of the scorched roast and the smoky 'tzimmes', arguments, fights, and quarrels break out between the husband and his wife, it is a sign that there is no love and domestic bliss between them. And therefore it is better to give her the get (ed. note: a divorce) immediately so he will not continue to irritate her with such complaints."

Another one from the reaction of the same rabbi. There was a custom that on Purim people would pair up to collect donations for charity, and they would teach the young ones to perform this mitzvah. So the rabbi chose me and another child from our classroom, and he informed us of a very respectable family in great distress (the rabbi did not give the family's name) and it was our duty to ease the plight of the family, and he gave us his blessing and we both went out and canvassed the community for donations.

The people donated generously. Many knew us and we collected more than a ruble. We gave all the money to the rabbi. He counted the coins and bundled them in his handkerchief and told us, "Now, children, come and I will buy you 'kvass' (a fermented beverage like malt) and will pay with the money you collected." We were both surprised at this and we looked at him with great astonishment - what does it mean? From the "tzdaka" (ed. note: charity) money?…He probably understood what we were thinking and told us, "Children, I know that you are wondering about everything I told you. Now listen and remember, among the people from whom you collected charity there are undoubtedly those who suspect that maybe you will take some of the donated money and put it in your pocket and if you are innocent of the above then this is a serious sin 'to suspect those who are honest.' Therefore come and enjoy a little bit from the donated money and the sin of the ones who suspected you will not be as great." And the three of us approached one of the owners of the kiosk, and the rabbi told him to give each of us a glass of kvass. The drink was bubbling and overflowing, and in my rush I brought the glass to my mouth and forgot to make the blessing. My friend noticed this and immediately got my attention: "Itzikl - a blessing!" But the rabbi hinted to me that I should heed his warning and drink quickly, and this was also very puzzling to us but we did not analyze it. Another time the rabbi was explaining a different case to us, and in his words he incorporated the verse "performed a blessing, reviling God," and then he turned to me and added: "Do you remember the glass of 'kvass' that you drank? It was better that you not bless it than bless it..."

In the "Yeshiva"

I spent three or four years in the "yeshiva." The yeshiva was then not in one but rather in several rented apartments. The classes were assigned to rooms far away from one other and were not connected except for the connection provided by Rebbe Yosel Duchovny, the chief supervisor of the yeshiva, who would visit the different classes every so often and by doing so would unify them.

My classroom was in the apartment of little Peretz ("Peretzl der Kleyner") and it was an unlit room with one small window, blocked with a small pillow or blanket, looking into the yard, and another one that looked out on the street, and from that window came the light for the entire room. And in the room there was a long table, on one side a sofa with bedding on it, used for the shorter ones among us, and on the other side - a long bench, and on it sat the rest of the students. In the small yard behind the house there was a cow shed, and in the cow shed a cow and calf lay on the manure, which would pile up from one year to the next. For us, this cow shed was a kind of "playground" for those students who received permission to go out after demonstrating their mastery of the lesson for the week.

The customary curriculum in those days in our yeshiva was learning only the Gemara. They went from morning until noon, and then from noon until the evening.

On Sunday the rabbi would read the lesson for us, and we repeated it over and over all week except for one hour, when we would learn the Weekly Portion (ed. note: from Pentateuch - The Five Books of Moses.) On Friday we would go over two Mikra and oneTargum in the same Weekly Portion, as we followed along with the cantillations (ed. note: the symbols showing the tones for chanting.) They did not allow time for learning to write or even for secular studies. In the supervisor's opinion there was no need to cram the children's brains with external wisdom. "So did we and our fathers and our fathers' fathers not engage themselves with it, and we saw life in our world. When they grow up, each one of them will be able to fill in whatever he is missing, and we only have to fill their brains with Torah as if 'stuffing and feeding an ox' " - in the words of Yosef Duchovny, the yeshiva supervisor.

The first tractate we learned in the Talmud was the Kidushim tractate (ed. note: about marriage), first chapter, "The woman is purchased in three ways - money, a promissory note, and by having sexual intercourse." And I was then seven or eight years old. What was the reason we started in this tractate and in this chapter - only the "gabe" of the yeshiva and the rabbi have the answer to that. I probably was considered the best student in the class in the eyes of the rabbi and "gabbaim." I learned this from something that happened.

In those days a rumor spread in our town, that the "baron" (ed note: as used here it denotes a wealthy Jewish landowner) David Ginzburg from Petrograd was about to tour his estate which was near Orheyev, and he was considering coming to our town to visit a few public institutions. And in the town, a big commotion of course. Every public institution, including the yeshiva, prepared to welcome the wealthy man. The rabbi chose me to be the first among those whom the "baron" would examine in the Talmud, and he started preparing me so that I would know the lesson in a very detailed and meticulous way, with the accuracy that you need to draw from the interpreters (Rashi, Tosafot, Maharsha, Maharamshif). They transferred our class to the supervisor's house (Y. Duchovny), better lit, a more spacious house, and in the center of town.

Men and women gathered at the door and windows to view the "baron's" face. "It's a mitzvah to see the face of royalty." And here in a coach came the "baron" accompanied by the secretary, and they immediately whisked him into the house. And when he had taken his place, the rabbi gave me the signal to read the "lesson." I started to recite all that I remembered and my eyes were fixed either on the Gemara or on the "baron's" face. As I was reading the lesson, I noticed a slight smile suggesting amazement on his face, and the smile became a broad grin, a laugh, after which I lost my composure, and I started to cry…

The "baron" rose from his seat, approached me, and stroked my head to calm me down, signaling the "gabe" and the rabbi to approach him. The three of them entered a special room and conversed for a few minutes and then they came out, and the "baron" approached me and asked me: "And Tanakh - do you know it?" I did not know the meaning of the word "Tanakh," and the rabbi, standing next to me, used simple words to explain what it was: "verse, verse," and he opened the Book of Isaiah and I (a Gemara boy) read two or three verses, and I interpreted them, and with this the exam and the visit of the "baron" ended…

Years passed, and I never forgot the "baron's" visit, and it came to mind every so often even though I still could not figure out and explain the smiling expression on his face. Years had gone by, when I met with Yosef Duchovny, the "gabe," and I asked him, why did the "baron" laugh when I was examined before him?

Yeh, he answered laughing, and he told me - that in the tractate I was learning then, the tractate "Ktubot" page 11 the second side (probably after "Kidushim" we moved to "Ktubot," - a logical progression) the topic was : "she says 'I was struck by a tree' and he says: 'no, you were trampled by a man"…and when joined to the previous topic: "he who marries the woman and finds she is not a virgin," the Gemara offers two opposing opinions, and the issue is in dispute - and I was the main actor - a boy of nine or ten …[1]

In the Yeshiva After the "Baron's" Visit

The "baron's" visit had a great impact on public life. The opportunity presented itself to erect a permanent building for the yeshiva. A short time passed when they started to erect a building in the yard of the small synagogue, and after two years our yeshiva moved to the new building, with two floors, and in it study rooms, a small synagogue, and also a place for the "shames" (ed. note: sexton) to live. The furnishings were, as typical in those days: long tables and on both sides benches the length of the tables, the rabbi sitting at the head of the table and the students around him in a "U"; there were no blackboards or writing boards with which to practice writing, and there was no need for them because writing was not in the plan.

There were three classes then in the yeshiva: first grade for beginners - prayer and Khumesh (the first chapter in the Weekly Portion). The study in Khumesh was mainly to practice reading and translating the words into Yiddish with no relevant explanation, but a translation of every single word: and he said "Adonai - Got, El - Tzu, Moshe - Moyshe" (ed. note: "and God said to Moses"). Second grade - Khumesh and Rashi from the Weekly Portion and beginning of Gemara. And it was interesting that when we arrived in Rashi, with its content being a grammatical explanation, the rabbi would begin to explain and would immediately stop with the remark, "This is a matter of grammar and we do not really need it," and he would skip to the next verse. Our impression was that the grammar in certain places in Tanakh, for example the chapters in Joshua 4-20, was in the same category as the community census, where there is no point in reading it for the student.

[1] A book "The Beginning of Life" written by Sh. Berlinski of Amoved (ed. note: "The Workers") fell into my hands and there I read on p. 110 that the writer when he was a " tender lamb" also started on this tractate "Ktubot". Here's more proof. In the book "My Town Motele" written by Kh. Tchemerinski "Dvere Publishers" (p 75) the writer talks of his childhood, and among other things he writes: "And I was a young boy already able to study by myself and everyday I went to the rabbi and studied two or three hours in 'Ktubot' and 'Kidushim'." The study method was practiced the same way throughout the system, cramming the children of Israel in those days with Torah and with fear of God....

Third grade, entirely Gemara. The rabbi read a lesson the first day and he incorporated in his lecture the interpreters Rashi, Tosafot Marsh'a and we (a class of 20-25 students) had to repeat and memorize it for examination on Thursday. And this was the exam: the rabbi chose one of the weakest students and told him to read the lesson, and we had to listen and correct the reader every time he made a mistake. And there were many who would jump and correct, and the more you jumped, the better you were in the eyes of the rabbi...

Besides the rabbi's lesson we would receive independent study "do it alone" that they would assign to one or two of us, a different tractate, a little easier, a marked lesson which the student would have to prepare by himself in a day or two. The test would begin on Wednesday and would sometimes continue into Thursday. Friday was entirely for the Weekly Portion with Rashi's interpretation - "one for Targum - translation, and two for reading with cantillation the Haftorah in the traditional melody.

The learning methods and the relationship between the rabbi and the yeshiva students were not the same, there was no single accepted method in the institution which would be mandatory for everyone teaching there, but each rabbi would do as was his custom. Each rabbi had his method and his special relationship with his flock.

I remember one of them well, Mordechai Litvak, who slapped my face, and that was the first and only time in my life I got slapped, and this is what happened.

One day, at sunset, we were sitting around the table, and we were praying "Minkha," each one reading a paragraph from a chapter. My fate was to read "Ashrey," and when I reached the last verse "and we are going to bless God from now on to eternity, Halleluyah," I read as if there was only one "lamed". The rabbi commanded me: read again! I read again, and again the same thing. The rabbi: "Observe and see what is written in the Sedur." I looked and I repeated my mistake because I did not know that both "lamed's" are pronounced, and the rabbi lost his patience and approached and slapped my cheek until it became swollen and red. I came home, and when I was asked: what and why, I burst into tears. At the same time the rabbi appeared also, and with a smile on his face apologized and said: "Did you ever hear in such a kheder that a Gemara boy doesn't know 'to break the lamed.' "

Another rabbi, whose name I don't remember, had a special teaching style. How? One of the students would fail in his studies, did not know or did not understand what the rabbi said. He was immediately ordered to leave the table and lean over, and another child got the "konchik" (ed. note: the strap) and he was expected to hit the boy who was stretched out for as many strikes as the rabbi wanted. If the child was slipshod in doing the beating, he would be immediately commanded to lean over, and a third child would take the role of beating both of them as the rabbi commanded.

In contrast with them, there were also other kinds of teachers. I remember one whose method was to attract the students' attention by telling fables and stories, especially when we learned Khumesh and the stories of the sages and the miracles that occurred in life. That one was not severe with us when one of the students did not comprehend what he said. Then he would command one of us to sit and review with the slower child until he understood what the rabbi meant. For the child that received a role like that - it was an "aliya" (ed. note: an ascent, like being called to do a Torah reading.) And I would get a task like that every so often.

Changes in the Air

In those days, I was then twelve or thirteen, a student by the name of Steinbach came to our town. A student who comes to the town makes an impact, a student and his uniform - a "Tuzshurkeh" (a short coat) which was buttoned up with shiny buttons, a student hat, and his Russian talk - all of this commanded respect. When he would incorporate Yiddish words in his speech, he would pronounce them like a "goy". And this quality added to the respect for him. He would go among the youth and become acquainted with them. This was the period of "bringing a message to the people," groups of youths and many workers would get together for "Haskolah," which is really education to gain knowledge, or to read a book or newspaper. Along with this they would get lectures concerning questions having to do with society. This of course was done secretly, so that the authorities would not hear or know about it. And Steinbach headed this entire operation.

Once Steinbach appeared in the yeshiva building, dressed up in the student uniform. The gabe, Duchovny, rushed up, and the students began to guess why the student came to us, and they kept guessing but no one knew anything for sure. It had recently become known, that our class would begin to learn Russian and mathematics twice a week at sunset. And they also announced that they would give each student a notebook and a pencil. That was quite a surprise in the life of the yeshiva students, and it was very exciting. Twice a week Steinbach came to us and engaged us in reading a Russian book for beginners and practicing mathematics orally. He never scolded us or rebuked us. On the contrary, he was soft and affectionate. With a little smile, he would correct and guide the child in his reading. Before he would come, there would be a lot of commotion. They would check their clothes to neaten their appearance, and when he would enter, we would welcome him with a "sholem" in Russian - there was a desire to impress him. All of this probably was not welcomed by the "gabbai" and especially our "rabbi". He taught us for almost a month when he stopped, and for a reason that had nothing to do with him.

But he didn't give up. After a few days, he appeared again in the "yeshiva" and he had a new offer: If it's not expedient that he visit the yeshiva once in awhile, he suggested choosing two or three children to come once or twice a week to continue their learning.

The management agreed to that, and I was one of the two who were chosen.

Steinbach's apartment was in the "Street of the Nobles," in the yard of Dr. Rabinovitz's house. They chose the morning hour for us, when he would awaken. I remember, that the rabbi asked us once, if I continued to visit the student's apartment, and how the studying was going. I answered about this and that. Then he bent over and asked me in a whisper, "I beg you, Itzikl, tell me, child, he does not cross himself when he arises?"

For two weeks my friend and I continued to visit the student's house early in the morning before the morning prayer. It was in the fall when the winter rain had started, and my friend and I did not have galoshes. We decided between us to stop our visits until the mud freezes. We did not tell the teacher about it. The teacher asked us the reason, and he sent Menashe Feinsilver (the son of Alter Menashe), who was a regular visitor there, to investigate to find out why we stopped visiting his home. And he learned the reason, he sent a message by messenger to say that we should not pay any attention to that, and we should continue to come, and by the door he prepared an iron scraper on which we could clean the mud from our shoes before we entered his room.

One day he suggested that we remove our hats from our heads while we sit at the table to learn. We unwillingly fulfilled his request. At that time I was God-fearing and observant and I was very strict with every commandment[1]. And when I thought about the fact that I have to sit the whole hour with my head exposed before my bar mitzvah, my conscience bothered me and I saw it as breaking away from the yoke of Jewish law. In my heart I decided that I should not continue---and when I passed this on to my friend, he also agreed to it. But we decided first to consult with other people. First of all we turned to Rebbe Alter Menashe (Alter Feinsilver), one of the leaders of the community and a yeshiva supervisor, a religious man, observant, but not a zealot. The zealots would gossip about him and they were suspicious that sometimes he reads newspapers, and others added that he should be suspected for occasionally reading chapters from "Be-ur" (ed. note: Hebrew commentary on the Bible by Moses Mendelssohn and his disciples) which his son-in-law (Shmuel Gershon Baru) had at home. Despite all that, he was highly respected and accepted. We turned to him and I was the one who started with this question: "Can a man from Israel sit uncovered before his bar mitzvah while he is preoccupied with such and such a thing?" Rebbe Alter listened to me while a little smile floated on his lips and he turned to me with a smile of a merciful father and said: "Itzikl, dear child, if only all Jewish parents were blessed with such children as you...but please do not forget that we live among the "goyim," they rule over us, and we are under their authority. Every person, whoever he is, has to know the language of the country where he lives. Also among our sages, may their memory be blessed, there were many who knew the Greek language and sometimes they learned external wisdom, and despite that, they remained loyal Jews. Here you may receive some kind of paper or document from the authorities, and you do not know what is written in it, and you have to look for a person to translate what is written in it, and that is not so nice. It is not good for a person to be dependent on somebody else's interpretation, so you should therefore not make it graver than it is, and you had better continue in your studies."

[1] One of my childhood friends (Ze'ev Shaposhnik) reminded me of how God-fearing and very strict with myself I was and he also wrote some of his memoirs. Among other things, he relates that once on a Saturday he came to our house, and I offered to go out with him to the steppe. I went out with him, and when we approached the place where the grass grew, I had misgivings, and told him, from here on, because there is grass here, if we step on it, there is the danger of "desecrating the Sabbath." And I went back home…

I could not accept what he said, and I told my friend, "What he says does not make sense to me, let's ask our rabbi, and let's see what he has to say." The rabbi heard our story, my reasoning, and he jumped from his place and called out, "Be blessed, children! that you did not allow "Satan" to control you. You begin with uncovering your head, and you continue with not following the commandments and not being observant, and you finish with forced conversion…In these days when there are more and more people who break the yoke of the commandments, every Jew has to behave in a more restricted way and stay away from committing a sin. Do not continue to visit in this fellow's house…Who knows, it's possible that he is not even circumcised…since his face looks goyish…" and we of course did as he told us.

From the Yeshiva to the "Kloyz" (a study house or small synagogue)

When I left the "yeshiva" I entered the study house along with some of my friends (Binyamin Mishkis, Nachum Alkushi, Hertz Gilishensky, and others) who learned together. During the time I was at the study house, I was once called to the rebbitzin, the wife of one of the righteous people from Tulne. I don't remember her name or her husband's name but the name "Die Tulner rebbitzin" (the rebbitzin from Tulne). She was a beautiful woman nearing old age, and her image is that of a princess, and she happened to be in our city in one of the "Nine Days" of the month of Av. She suffered from some kind of disease and the doctor ordered her to eat chicken soup and I was asked to finish the Tractate. The time of finishing the Tractate is festive, and the custom is to allow eating meat, even in the nine days between the Rosh Khodesh of Av and Tisha B'Av (ed. note: the ninth day of Av).

I remember I was just about to finish the tractate Mokot (ed. note: "Blows"). I came and entered her room holding the Gemara in my hand. She asked my name, I answered her, and she said, "Very nice, like the name of one of the fathers," and she added her blessing, "You should always study Torah, and it will watch over you your whole life."

When I finished and I was about to leave, she stopped me and said to me: "You are going to eat lunch with me," and she caressed my shoulder and patted my face with both hands. And her hands were warm and soft, like velvet. The look in her eyes was happy and heartwarming, and her face lit up with a small, modest smile…and I remember my feeling then, that that was the first affectionate touch (and possibly - the only one) that I had in my gray childhood…

In the study house, we were free to work independently with no supervision or guidance from anybody, and learning - meant Gemara. It did not occur to us to think about other subjects, even though new ideas were stirring in our town, and I don't remember how they also reached me. I approached Fishel Shtern, one of the first teachers in Orheyev to open a "progressive" school with subjects other than Gemara, and his students were from the wealthy, among them the sons of Yisrael Krasner and Shmuel Lipshits, and more. In this room all the students sat facing the teacher, and every hour the bell would ring, and the students would all go outside "for a break." A thing I did not understand; for what and why are they going hourly to the yard? Surely there is in it an "annulment of Torah study" and in my heart I thought: this is what they mean when they say "that the rabbi gets money for nothing." I don't know how it happened that I became close to F. Shtern, and it is possible that one of his daughters, whom I would meet by chance, was the reason. He gave me instruction in the book of Haskalah (ed. note: an 18th-19th century movement among central and eastern European Jews, begun in Germany under the leadership of Moses Mendelssohn, designed to make Jews and Judaism more cosmopolitan in character by promoting knowledge of and contributions to the secular arts and sciences and encouraging the adoption of the dress, customs, and language of the general population - the enlightenment), and once or twice a week he would choose for me a book that he liked. I took the book to the study house also, and when there was no one there, I put it on the Gemara and I read it standing and swaying, nobody noticed, if I read one of the books of Haskalah at that time.

One day as I was standing by the window, a funeral passed by, and I found out that the deceased was one of our neighbors. I rushed out, and I forgot to hide the book which was on top of the Gemara. The funeral was delayed a little bit and when I returned, it was already time for the "Minkhe" (ed. note: evening prayer) when the shames Rebbe Leib would go between the rows (the bookstands) to remove the books and organize them in the cabinet. He found my book on top of the Gemara, he was shocked, and he brought it to the worshippers: "Such a scandal, a desecration of the holy, we should teach him proper behavior…" and he issued the verdict "from on high," that he would not continue to give me a candle every evening, as he does for all the students, and I was forced to approach one of the students to share his light, and I continued my studies by his candle. I was in torment for two or three days until one evening Rebbe Alter Menashe happened to come to the study house, and when he saw me doing this, he asked me, why am I standing like that? I told him with great shame what had happened to me, and he answered me, with a slight smile spreading across his face: "There is a time for everything," and he ordered the gabe Rebbe Leib to stop withholding the candle. And since I again mention Rebbe Alter Menashe (Feinsilver), it is worthwhile to relate that he was handling something special that we did not appreciate appropriately.

The benches that were along the walls in the "kloyz" were made from crates. Some of the crates were filled with "Names" (ed. note: a symbol or vehicle of divinity, in this case pages from the prayer books and Torah) rendered unfit (ed. note: ripped or ruined pages) until they were taken out to be put away, and other crates were full of regular paper that Alter Menashe would take care of. He would go to Yisrael Pagis's printing house or to Henzel Polonsky's bindery and would pay one of the boys five kopeks to fill a sack with their leftover paper to put in the crates in the study house, and the people would use them before the blessing of "The One Who Created"…

In the yard of the study house there was a kind of bathroom, and the people who used it knew very well that the paper in those crates was for their use…and interestingly enough he knew and felt that the wide community of worshippers would look at his deed as if it was "an oddity" and would mock him, but he paid it no attention and continued to take care of it as if it was just one of the needs of the community, and once in a while he would make sure to fill the crates with scraps of paper…

After Grandfather's Death

After my grandfather's death[1] I moved to my father's house. The housekeeper, my sister Leia (may her soul be in heaven) studied sewing, and in time she gained a name as a seamstress (but also "Leyke Yehudah Moyshe's") and was the sole support of the household, a burden that was too heavy for her, and she carried her pain in silence without complaint. She accepted her destiny, as if it were a decree from God which you should not appeal. She did not get any help or assistance. She was the compassionate nurse, the aching mother who took care of every one of us, and the breadwinner. She gave everything she had to her work, and yet our poverty at home was keenly felt…Occasionally she would sneak out of the house when she became really sad, and she would approach the acacia tree in the yard, and she would cry bitterly, without any of the household aware of it…Dad was away from home all the time and he would return only for holidays when he would stay home.

I continued my studies in the study house for two or three years and the learning went on with no excitement. From the four or five friends who started together in the study house, I was the only one left, each of the others went his own way. This one had the answers to his craft in his hands, the other one took on work or commerce and one, Binyamin Mishkis, he was successful and he devoted all his time to Russian literature and to different sciences, and he became famous. And I, my life became empty with no contacts and no direction.

And at home, poverty and shortage, and I a young man fourteen or fifteen "eating and not doing." My father, although he was busy all the time on the tobacco plantation, could never make a profit so that he could help support the household.

In those days I felt that I had become restless. For days I would walk around confused and absent-minded, and some kind of strange emptiness enveloped me and I couldn't figure it out, inside of me bottled-up pain which I could not express. I neglected my studies. I would sit for hours next to the Gemara, my eyes in the book, as if I were reading and analyzing it, but my head and heart - away from it. I did not find rest at night - usually I had nightmares - and when I would awaken, I could not close my eyes again.

One of those nights when I lay in bed, I couldn't sleep and was thinking about the stressful condition at home and my own condition:

[1] I remember that, at the time of my grandfather's death, I joined the funeral and I went to the cemetery. There I entered the purification room (with no one noticing me) when they were taking care of the body. And suddenly I heard one announcing: "His legs are like marble pillars set in fine golden sockets," and the second began to wash the legs of the deceased: "His head is fine as gold" and they washed the head…they turned Psalms into a guidebook for the purification process of the dead. I asked some of my acquaintances if they also had that custom, to accompany the purification of the dead body with verses from Psalms and no one had heard of such a strange habit. The head of Khevrah Kadisha in those days was Itzikl Shadkhen…

How do I accept such a condition, living on the sweat of my sister's brow, she is weak, eaten up by worries and concerns, and her strength is fading…what to do? To whom to turn? Which way should I choose? I was lost and helpless, in my heart a great confusion. When I got up in the morning I decided to go to Polonsky, a store owner who also had a book bindery, and to offer him my help in the store! Polonsky had known me for awhile. He was from the Tailors' Synagogue and once in awhile he would honor me with a "Maftir" (ed. note: reading from Prophets.) At the Tailors' Synagogue I was a "Gemara Yingl" and everyone knew me and treated me with respect.

The following day I went to Polonsky and I asked him to accept my help in the store. In the beginning he hesitated, and wanted to know what led me to this, and embarrassed, I answered his questions and most of the answers faltered. Despite that, after a few minutes we agreed that I would start coming to the store and he immediately told me that I would earn half a ruble a month (50 kopeks). When I brought home my first pay and handed it to my sister, she burst into tears, and I couldn't calm her down for a few minutes, until I promised her that I would continue to study on Saturdays in the kloyz, and then she calmed down.

I was a helper in the store for about two years, and my salary was raised to four rubles per month but the business in the store and the friendship with the helpers in the store did not give my mind rest. I remember that I was invited once to a dance club by a fellow worker. I came and I did not fit in with them, and that night I decided to leave the store and the helpers and I moved to the Polonsky's bookbinding place. There I met Ben-Zion Finkelshteyn and also Ben-Zion Furer, both of them old workers at Polonsky's place. At this job I felt much better than at the store, the company was much more comfortable and pleasant.

I don't remember what inspired us, and we, a young group of people, most of us students, got organized in a club which was called "Clear Language." Binyamin Mishkis was the lively spirit in the club. He was the initiator, its chair, and its writer/secretary. In what were we engaged? Conversations, and B. Mishkis led the conversations. Usually he would be the one to begin them, and would usually also be the lecturer. The subjects were: the question of "the Settlement in Israel" and also the history of our people. After every lecture, the discussion and questions began. It was everyone's duty to participate in the conversation. And if one tried to evade it, they would comment: "You did not say anything yet,"…and he had to express in one or two sentences remarks regarding the discussed topic. Per one of the decisions each one had to make time for Hebrew conversation one hour a day, it had to be in a place where many people would pass by, as for example in the Street of the Nobles (the street of the aristocracy.)

In my second year of being a binder, and my salary already 6 rubles per month, Moshe Korenfeld, one of the famous externalists (ed. note: one who taught non-religious subjects) in Orheyev (he lived in Sloboda) made me an offer to leave work and to travel with him to the town of Dumbrovitsa, where he was to open a modern school. He would be engaged in teaching the general topics, and I in teaching the Hebrew subjects. This offer appealed to me, and after I said goodbye to Polonsky, I left Orheyev and I began teaching.

From then on I got further away from Orheyev, the course of my life had its ups and downs which got me even further away from Orheyev and its people...

Editorial comment:

The people of Orheyev say that Leibel Mundrian, may his memory be blessed, was the first Orheyev teacher for Hebrew and my friend I. Spivak, also an Orheyev native, was the second one.

Chapter 20

The Library
History of the Library

By Emuna Munder

Translated by Rachel Weitz and Marsha Kayser

The Jewish public library was established in 1902. A group of enlightened intellectuals, headed by Moyshe Ravich, appealed to the public and explained the need for a cultural institution where the Jewish reader would find a book he could borrow and a newspaper for his use in the reading room. The public was asked to contribute books and money to open a Russian Jewish library. The public responded nicely and the library opened in 1902. The first attempt to open a library was made in 1866 (see "Hamelitz" - March 9, 1866) by Mr. Savitch, a Christian community activist and a liberal person who believed in facilitating the public's access to knowledge and culture. Most of the readers spoke Russian and a minority read Hebrew.

The institution also supplied Hebrew newspapers like "Hamelitz," "Kol Mevasen," and "Carmel."

The library existed for a long time. From 1902 until the destruction of the city (1940) it experienced a number of crises due to the tumultuous nature of the times.

During the period leading up to World War I the library continued to develop at a good pace. Everyday the library drew many visitors, and those who came enjoyed the pleasant atmosphere of the place. During this time those who served as librarians were: the old man Yosef Kiperchensky (1902-05), then the late Zelig Veinberg (a member in the Association of Hebrew Speakers) and last Pini Gelbrukh. Many of the people who came to learn would volunteer to rotate the task of keeping order and quiet, and this added a special warm spirit to the library.

During that time the members of the executive committee were Moyshe Ravich, Shmuel Pisarevsky, Sara Nayman, Zolman Nayman, Shmuel Lipshin, Velvel Shaposhnik, Rukhel Ravich, and more.

Chapter 21

The Restoration of the Library

By A. Malovatsky

Translated by Rachel Weitz and Marsha Kayser

During World War I (1914-17) the library was closed, hundreds of books were scattered among the readers, and there was a real danger that this important cultural treasure would vanish.

With the outbreak of the Russian Revolution (1917) a small group of academic students decided to take action to open the library. The city was divided into districts and the volunteers visited all the houses and collected hundreds of books in a very short time.

Since they had no means to pay for this big job, the members of the group who had volunteered - Tzevi Guralnik, Yisrael Grobokopatel, and this writer - arranged the catalogues, worked passionately for many days, and fixed up the library. The woman member, Gilishenskaya, was invited to be the paid librarian. New books were purchased and the readership kept growing.

In the year 1918 the Romanians invaded Bessarabia. Their first action was to uproot the communist movement and Russian culture and impose Romanian as the predominant language. The government was suspicious of the library, where most of the books were in Russian. In the year 1921 a few communists who were regular visitors to the library were arrested, and after the secret police searched their apartments, they also searched the library. Although they found nothing suspicious, they still arrested the head of the library M. Rotkov and the librarian Rukhel Keyser. They were investigated and subjected to threats and insults until a very late hour, and only after secretly bribing the officer of the secret police were they released. Even so, the library was closed for a few months, and only after tremendous effort and persuasion was the library reopened to serve the public.

This disturbance caused a financial crisis, and the community activists worked very hard to maintain the library. The purchase of new books was very limited and only through the reorganization of the community board (1924-1925), was a certain amount of money dedicated to the purchase of books, while the income from library members' fees and fund-raising parties covered the day-to-day expenses of running the library.

The Library and its Incorporation of the Culture-League into its Management

In the year 1927-28 Fania and Piatr Rabinovitz received a certain number of Yiddish books through the Culture-League in Chernovits. Since they did not have a way to offer the books to the public they offered to give us the books on the condition that they be involved in the library's council. The offer was accepted, and with the addition of important books the Yiddish readership grew. The league representative, P. Rabinovitz, saw it as a way to spread "Yiddish". He requested an increase in the budget for books, since he held the views of the Culture-League, and he wanted the Yiddish books back-to-back with the Hebrew books. The board members, mostly Zionists, disagreed. The league representative took measures to increase the influence of the league: mass registration for membership in the library was held for league supporters, with the intention that many of its members would be chosen for the management of the library at its regular annual meeting.

Of course the Zionists were stirred up by this action too, and the provocation between the two "movements" was extremely hard, but the outcome was good, and it was for the best. As the result of this provocation the library added hundreds of members who paid membership fees in advance, and this brought financial relief to the management, which had been experiencing difficulties.

Participation was very high at the annual meeting and the room was overcrowded. From the very beginning, the atmosphere of the meeting was highly charged. It became stormy… the commotion grew to such a point that it was impossible to run the meeting. Thanks to the interference of Vaynshtok, the head of the community who was present at the meeting, the meeting was brought to order and (the attendees) followed his suggestion to begin immediately to hold the elections. The members of the "league" saw this as a complete failure, and they left the meeting before the elections proceeded.

The management was chosen, and they immediately applied themselves to their mission with renewed devotion. The books which the "league" had donated were returned, and they opened their own library. Many members joined it, and therefore it hurt the budget of our library. The community committee responded once more to our request and set aside a specified sum of money for purchasing books. This help arrived at just the right time and encouraged the management to continue to advance the institution with renewed enthusiasm.

Chapter 22

The Library and its Struggles

Translated by Rachel Weitz and Marsha Kayser

The library made a very strong impression on my memory from my childhood on. The rooms with their shelves full of books, the spacious reading room, the polished furniture, and the pictures of famous writers - Jewish and Russian - on the walls, all of this evoked in me a feeling of awe. It seems to me that the golden days of its existence were in this period up until World War I. I remember the period of the "affair" of the library in the period after the Romanian occupation very differently. There was constant agitation from the Romanian government, and often they closed the library without cause, resulting in a lot of damage to its property and to the public thirsty for the printed word.

I remember when the librarians Rukhel Keyser and later on Malka Rotkov bore the burden of the difficult financial situation and only because of a few devoted friends did they manage to sustain it. With every political change the library was shaken up and closed - and Rukhel and Malka left the job. The boredom and thirst for books weighed heavily on the young people. So we got up a young group (Mordechai Vinberg, Yeshaya Frank, may their memories be blessed and may they live long, Nachman Genikhovitz and the writer of this list), and we volunteered to begin with renewed vigor to open the library. The main difficulty was obtaining a license from the government. The public figure Liuba Gluzgold came to our rescue. He invested much effort and a substantial amount of his own money, he promised the government that the library management met political "requirements", and finally he got the license. Then we again applied ourselves vigorously to the collection of the scattered books, we rented a suitable apartment, we invited Miryam Frank to be the librarian, and the library began to operate again. In the meeting that was conducted after its opening, the management was chosen (Gluzgold, Yeshaya Frank, Yehoshua Rappaport, Freida Chokla, a few more and this writer). Because of the difficult economic situation in town at that time, we struggled hard to maintain its existence. With tremendous effort we managed to collect membership fees, and we held evening fund-raising parties so that we could purchase books in the Russian, Romanian, Yiddish, and Hebrew languages.

Member Miryam Frank, the manager of the library, tried to meet the demands of the readers of various levels. She made the selection of library books accessible to them in a very organized way and in a discerning manner. She also served the Christians well, and she continued that successfully for a few years until she made aliyah to Israel (1935).

Chapter 23

The Circle of Theater Fans

by Moshe Bik

("Lyubitelskiy Kruzshok")

Translated by Jerrold Landau

It was the winter of 1902-1903. Persecution and oppression were of the signs of the times. The youth was strangled from lack of air to breathe. Nevertheless, the youth did not make peace with the situation that the Czarist police imposed upon them, and searched for ways of filling their life with content and of quenching their youthful thirst for cultural progress and spiritual satisfaction. Various circles sprouted up and were active in various communal arenas. The Circle of "Fans of the Jewish Theater" was also one of the expressions of the youthful longing. The circle was lucky, for Solomon Mironovitz Loshakov, the photographer from our town, who had artistic talent and a high level of culture, took upon himself the brave task of leading the circle and directing it so that it could also take on a theatrical role. Making this a reality was no simple matter. Without experience and means, lacking a repertoire that was fitting for the "finicky" expectations of Solomon Mironovitz, the government ban of performing in Yiddish unless they "mixed it up" and turned it into "Deutschmerish" (corrupted German) – all of these were serious obstacles to the "fans". Nevertheless, the obstacles did not prevent them from attaining their sublime goals that the activists had presented to them: 1) of enabling the restless forces to express what is pressing upon their hearts in movements and in the language of culture; 2) primarily, coming to the aid of those in need and the charitable and benevolent institutions such as the clothing of the poor, the providing for brides, visiting the sick, providing loans, helping impoverished mothers, etc.

The dedication of the members of the circle for their various tasks that they took upon themselves is remembered. Whether preparing for or staging a performance, the fans were dedicated with their full enthusiasm. They dedicated their precious time without thinking about the inconvenience caused to themselves and their families.

As one of those who later joined the fans, I see it as my personal duty to describe those whose role in the circle was significant.

The Early Ones

In truth, there was more than one circle of theatrical fans operated in our city. Many members older than I participated in the aforementioned circle that existed from about 1902-1910 under the direction of Loshakov. I can only list their names without describing anything about them, despite the fact that they were known in our community as people of high intelligence and artistic development. These are their names: Mania the sister of Loshakov, Pini Shaposhnik and his brother Velvel, Hershel Milshteyn, Nissel Krasilschik and his wife Soibel, Milia Branover, Tzeviya Katz, the wife of Binyamin Globman, Sara Nayman, the sister of Rachel Ravich, Berel Dinovitzer, the son of Yonah the cantor, and others. I will dedicate my article to a later period, approximately from 1910 to 1920, in which I was close to the circle and participated in it.

Figure 68 - Pini Ziserov

Pini Ziserov. Pini "Der Roiter" (The Redhead) earned this nickname on account of his reddish brown hair color. He was the son of Nechama and Asher Kalashnik. His father was a repairer of galoshes, a trade from which he was not able to support his family, for only the poorer people required this, and even so only on the rainy days of the autumn. Therefore, when he was still a young child, his parents sent him over to the basement of Leib Stolyar (Leib the tall) to study carpentry. Since Pini was graced with a fine alto voice, he joined the choir of Yonah the Lame, the cantor of the tailor's synagogue, and became known as a pleasant singer. He studied only very little in the cheder. His knowledge was restricted. Through his own initiative and with his musical sense, at a later age he became the director of the choir of singing fans in the city, and created new musical creations that nobody had ever heard or studied previously. He was also a creator of stage performances. He joined the Circle of Theater Fans at a young age. There as well, he exhibited wonderful talent and artistic sense. He enchanted the audience with his appearance. Despite the fact that he had never received any training, he lived for his roles, his manner of speaking was colloquial. He excelled particularly in the roles of: "Uriel Acosta", "Hershele Dobrobner", "Begat", "Man and the Devil" of Yaakov Gordon, and in "Hameturaf". The audience was captivated by him in these roles, and he brought the audience to a level of exultation beyond their day to day lives.

With the progress of economic and cultural life in the city, the accepted custom of calling the residents by various nicknames was abandoned, and official surnames took their place. The economic and communal status of Pini the "Roiter" grew, and his name changed from "Pini der Roiter" to Pini Ziserov. However, a cruel fate awaited him. He died from a malignant disease at a young age. He left behind an unfortunate widow and two orphans.

Reuven the "Ravich" (the Hunchback) Shaposhnik earned his fame in Orheyev from his three traits - the fact that he was a hunchback, his left eye that was larger and opened wider than his right eye, and from his unique theatrical roles at which he excelled. He had other traits, such as his poverty and his large number of children, but he was not unique in our city with these.

He was one of the first in the Circle of Fans. For what good would the best play be from an artistic perspective if the jester were a good for nothing? He was jovial and jocular not only in his theatrical roles, but also in his daily life.

His improvised verses about matters of the day, such as the miserly ruler, the activist who mixes into communal affairs, and even about the straits and hunger of his wife and children – which were spread around from mouth to mouth. He defined his role amongst the fans as "A character comic".

I will never forget Reuven's success in the roles of "Leyzer the jester" in the play "God, Man and the Devil", Shulman in "Mirele Efrat", the servant "Shmaya" in "King Lear", and the undertaker in Goldfaden's "Kabtzanson and Hungerman". Who can remember the great number of characters and roles that he performed with exceptional success.

Figure 69 - Drama Class 1917-1920

Below from right to left: 1. [feh]. Roitkov 2. L. Kleiner 3. Grobokopatel 4. M. Bik
In the middle: 1. S. Shulman 2. C. Abramovitz 3. M. Shtiken 4. H. Vurgaft 5. C. Kovadlo 6. R. Balan
Above: 1. R. (Horovitz) Shaposhnik 2. B. Z. Finkelshteyn 3. [alef]. Katzap 4. P. Ziserov 5. B. Gleybman 6. Z. Rabinovitz

Reuven Shaposhnik died before his time. He left behind in mourning his wife Chava and his young children. She supported her children by baking tasty "Malaies" and squash stuffed knishes, which her children would distribute door to door – so as to not, Heaven forbid, require charity.

His two sons and daughter made aliya to the Land, and settled in the homeland.

Eidel Lerner. He had a clear tenor voice. He joined the choir of Cantor Yonah the Lame, and he was also a member of the Circle of Fans. He was a shoemaker by trade, and he was also called Eidel "Baitsh" (The Whip). In contrast to others in his dirty trade, he was concerned about his dress, and after a day of work, he would dress like the "Cavaliers", the children of the wealthy people, with the addition of colors of an opera singer, so to speak.

As most of his friends in the circle, he was not from among the highly intelligent. He barely knew how to read and write Yiddish. Despite this, when he appeared on the stage in the role of Dr. Almasdo, Bar Kochba, or Absalom in Shulamit, the audience would listen to his pleasant, captivating voice with baited breath. His external appearance added a great deal to the grotesqueness of his performances, for Eidel was handsome with a rare male grace.

I received the news that he survived the Holocaust and returned to Orheyev. Did he find any of his friends? Or does he go about there forlorn, alone and dreaming of his world that once was so pleasant and nice, and is no longer…

Figure 70 - Ben-Zion Finkelshteyn

Ben-Zion Finkelshteyn the thin, skin and bones, almost transparent, as if he was covered in cigarette paper. Nevertheless, he had a refined spirit, he was a dreamer, and he was the "prompter" (the souffleur in the vernacular) of the Circle of Fans. He was graced from heaven with an opaque voice and a whispery speech, which was particularly suited to this role. He was the expert in the "small letters" and knew how to pronounce every Hebrew word appropriately. He loved literature. (Perhaps that is why he chose the trade of bookbinding). He himself wrote dramas and comedies. Each drama was bound in a special cloth binding for "recognition". His name and the name of the drama were etched in gold letters. If you went to his house, he would always be prepared to read to you at least one scene of his creations. Despite the fact that he was always busy and toiling for bread for his family, he would devote time to you and explain the artistic and technical sides of a flowing dialogue or monologue. His plays and dramas were indeed pictures drawn from life, plays of the times, albeit slightly late for the times. They never attained a place for themselves. They remained hidden in the decorated bindings with golden letters as the dead in their graves.

Chapter 24
The Dramatic Circle

by Rivka Milshteyn

(directed by Solomon Loshakov, 1920-1926)

Translated by Jerrold Landau

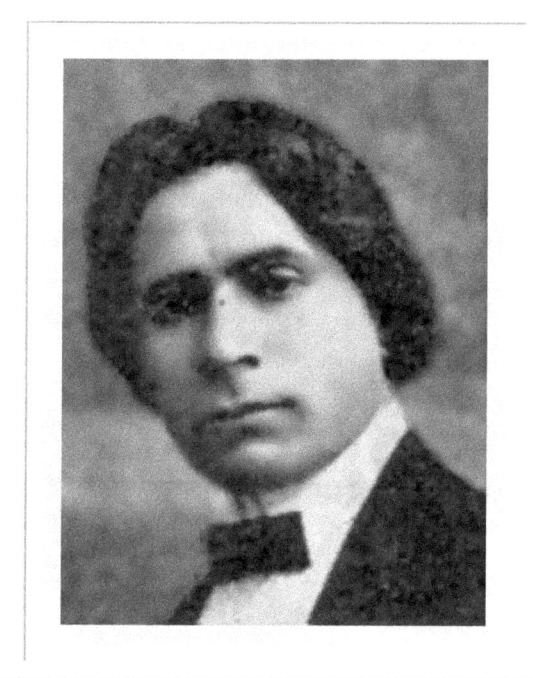

Figure 71 - Solomon Loshakov

There were few cultural institutions in our city. There was a library, whose directors attempted to provide spiritual sustenance to the youth. There was also a movie theater, and at times, artistic troupes on route northward from Kishinev would visit our city. On the other hand, there was a group of progressive youth who longed for self-expression over and above these places of entertainment. The desire for true artistic expression particularly troubled them. To our fortune, the Loshakov family lived in our city with their sons Solomon, Boris and Arkadi and daughter Mania. They were graced with a high level of artistic and cultural talent. We were drawn to this progressive and cultured home for artistic expression. In the company of the family members – Solomon, the actor on the Russian stage; Arkadi the artist and talented exercise instructor; and their talented sister Mania – we found a place for entertainment and discussing the problems of the times. We also arranged literary debates on artistic topics.

Solomon had the idea of operating a dramatic circle that had ceased its performances at the time. We accepted the advice with great joy.

On account of the ban by the Romanian authorities of performing in Russian, we decided to perform a Yiddish repertoire. Solomon, with his good sense, chose plays that would be particularly acceptable to the Jewish community, such as: "Aizik Sheftil", "Der Fremder" ("The Stranger"), "Menshen" ("People"), "Nor a Doctor" ("Only a Doctor") of Shalom Aleichem, and others. He also had the idea of translating "Harechov" ("The Street") of Joskovitz, but for some reason, this did not happen.

Figure 72 - Drama Class taught by Solomon Loshakov 1920-26

Seated from right to left: 1. P. Ziserov 2. Solomon Loshkov 3. Mania Serebrenik 4. …
Standing: 1. R. Milshteyn 2. [feh]. Huberman 3. N. Davidovitz 4. [alef]. Bakovskaya 5. Serebrenik 6. D. Ostrovsky 7. … 8. S. Rapoport

The most successful play that we performed was "Guilty without Blame". The stage-master was of course Solomon. The participants included Yaakov Serebrenik, Dr. Berkovitz of blessed memory, David Bronshteyn, Pini Ziserov of blessed memory, Feivel Rotkov may he live, Dr. Bord, Shaike Rapoport, Mania Loshakov-Serebrenik, Sara Nayman, Rivka Rozenfeld-Milshteyn, Eida Bakovskaya, Polya Adesser, Zenia Kohan and others. Nachum

Davidovitz translated from Russian to Yiddish, and served as Solomon's technical assistant. A significant number of the members of the troupe were blessed with recognizable stage talent.

Experience we did not have, but in all of us there burned a desire and enthusiasm to express our artistic longings. We dedicated ourselves to the roles that we took on with desire and enthusiasm, with the ambition to present the performance to the best of our ability. I recall the enthusiasm and dedication with which we studied our roles for the play "Guilty without Blame". Solomon, Yaakov S. and his wife Mania had the prime roles. The rest of the participants also fulfilled their roles in an exceptional fashion, as was demonstrated by the enthusiasm of the audience and the prolonged applause in the auditorium. Indeed, the troupe was very much loved by the audience. We donated the income to communal institutions such as the Talmud Torah, the Jewish hospital, the library, and at times to individual needy people.

The role of the Loshakov family was very great and important in this cultural enterprise. We would study our lines in their home. There, we would exchange ideas about its educational and cultural value. The opinion of Solomon, with his cultural level and his good sense, always was on top. We drew from this unfailing source for several years. We spent hours and hours in the company of this sublime family. It seemed as if our strong connection to them would never be cut. Then, one fine day, we were informed that Solomon had decided to immigrate to Paris... This saddening news fell upon us like a blow. Without Solomon Loshakov, what were we and what was our essence?

I recall that we arranged a goodbye party in his honor. Each one of us expressed our reverence to Solomon with great enthusiasm. We felt that with his departure, the circle would disband, and we would feel its lack for a great period of time. Indeed, we would still gather in the orphaned Loshakov home for a long time in order to draw from the pleasant atmosphere that still prevailed in the family, to recall our successes that we had with our plays and by spending time in the realm of Solomon. We attempted once more to present a performance, under the direction of Yaakov Serebrenik. Despite the fact that the performance worked out well, the sublimity that pervaded with under the directorship of Solomon was no more.

Time passed, and the members of the circle scattered to the four corners of the world. A few remained alive. Solomon Loshakov was exiled to Siberia, and the only daughter of the Serebrenik family lives in Bessarabia. I succeeded in arriving to the Land with my two children after much suffering and tribulation.

With deep sorrow and an anguished heart I am with you in memory, my murdered and plundered friends.

Translated from Russian by M. R.

Chapter 25

Musicians and Cantors

Translated by Jerrold Landau

"The musical profession was passed on from father to son as an inheritance for many generations" (Stempenyu, Shalom Aleichem)

The folklorist research that delves into Jewish music and its historiography does not contribute much to the question of the status of the musicians in the Jewish Diaspora before the Holocaust. It is known that despite the persecution from the gentile surroundings and the Jewish way of life that refrains from listening to music on days of national and personal mourning – the Jewish towns always had musicians who would make the community happy on days of festivity and birthdays. "A wedding without musicians is like a funeral without lamentation and eulogies," states the popular adage. This soulful need of our people served as the economic base of the musicians who took upon themselves this task. Another popular adage states, "During the days of Sefira, death overtakes the musicians," testifies to how poor the state of those engaged in this occupation was. The musicians, the cantor and the jester – their tunes and laughter were drenched in tears. If the work of the musicians developed and took hold throughout the centuries, this is thanks to the bountiful musical talent that was found within the Jewish masses, who were attracted to this profession.

This and furthermore: throughout many generations, there was not a musical existence, and "general entertainment" was not a Jewish trait at all. The musicians found their expressions by playing their violins at weddings and at events such as Torah scroll dedications in synagogues, Purim feasts, etc.

There were no schools of music on the Jewish street. The profession of musician was a "wonder of nature", a sapling that grew by itself and gave rise to artists and virtuosos who "shook worlds" with their talent.

Despite the fact that most of them did not know how to read music, they created their own repertoire of Jewish content by improvisation or by memory. For names like Podhocer (Aharon Moshe Cholodenko), Stempenyu (Yosele Druker), Michi (Avraham Yitzchak Berezovsky) and others – their names went before them. Others (Yosef Guzikov for example) would travel through countries and play in the courts of royalty. Every town had its own troupe of musicians, and every such troupe in its own right was like Stempenyu in his right. Such a "Caplut" musical troupe existed in Orheyev as well, of which each one in his own right was like Podhocer and Stempenyu.

We do not have any material about the history of musicians in Orheyev. We will begin (in accordance to the sources that are in our hands) with one of them, Reb Chayim, known as Chayim the violinist (at the end of the 19th century) who served as the head of the musical troupe. From him the baton passed to his son-in-law, who was known as Melech (King) of all Musicians. This talented violinist was of his own making. Of course, he aroused wonder with his music. I had the opportunity to record from one of the musicians a "table song" of that "King", who was apparently talented also as a composer of a repertoire for musicians. He excelled not only in Jewish topics, but also in his own uncommon techniques of his own violin music. His talent reached such a level that he was invited to concerts not only in provincial Bessarabia, but also in Kishinev. Nechemya Kovodlo, nicknamed Nechemya the Musician, was also numbered among the prominent musicians in the city. He was an exceptional musician. He learned to read music by himself. He was shoulders above the rest of the musicians. He would compose a tune by ear (something very uncommon among musicians). There was no musical instrument in the orchestra that he did not know how to play. Nevertheless, at a time when the bands divided up into small groups in order to appear simultaneously at weddings or on Purim, he would take the place of the missing musician. He would play the violin, contrabass, and trumpet.

His eldest son Moshe became known as a praiseworthy violinist. (He played in the Blagorodnavaya Sobranaya in Kishinev, and in symphonic ensembles and operas in Poltava. Later, he was a violinist in the United States). His son Binyamin (in his youth he was a singer in the choir in the Great Synagogue) was a talented pianist. He appeared in concerts in Russia, Germany, Romania and Turkey. He composed compositions for bands and also music for operas. He married a violinist, and they appeared together in concerts and on the radio. The couple had a child who excelled in musical talent. Nechemya's daughter Chaika married Shlomo Shpilman, a clarinetist in the Royal Opera of Bucharest. His son Chayim and brother David Shpilman the writer (Tzirolnik) were literally enchanting on their guitars. From the old generation of musicians, we know of Avraham the musician (Leyzer with the bass and his son Chatzkele Barabanchik).

Figure 73 - "Poets" (Religious Choir)

Figure 74 - Choir

* * *

There were two other troupes: "Gypsies" who were headed by gypsies – Monolati the Gypsy and Petru the Gypsy. Both Monolati and Petru, could not read music. Nechemya would compose tunes for dances for them. Most of the musicians in the gypsy troupes were Jews who earned their livelihood from weddings and Jewish celebrations. They maintained a Jewish repertoire. The "Kel Male Rachamim" that Petru the Gypsy composed was played at the weddings of orphans. The writer of these lines recorded the tune from Petru himself. Both of them, Monolati and Petru, spoke Bessarabian Yiddish "like water". He knew how to make the blessings "shehakol", "mezonot", "borei pri haetz", and "hamotzi lechem min haaretz". Petru was also the provider of homemade spices to the women of the town of the old generation. Monolati and Petru did not miss any Jewish festive occasion or funeral, since they were alert to the Jewish community, and they never appeared before the Jews with uncovered heads. We must also not forget the name of Yitzchak Yankel Burla (Rozenfeld) (the seater of the bride) who declared the presents for the lecture, and who directed the bands. He was (who knows if he had these rights from Czarist Russia) the only Jewish policeman ("gorobodoi") in the city. Incidentally, I will tell about the death of "Melech the Musician". A daughter of wealthy landowners fell in love with him and his music. (Albeit he was married and also a very Orthodox Jew.) She took revenge upon him and put poison in his cup in one of her joyous parties in Kishinev. Some say that all of the musicians of Kishinev poisoned him out of jealousy, for his band was often invited to Kishinev, while they were often left without a livelihood. In later years, a jazz band was set up in Orheyev headed by Dashe Vaysman the son of Itzikel the barber, and Froim (Efrayim) Vishkotzan.

Chapter 26

In the Cheder

by Moshe (Morris) Shneider, New York

Translated by Jerrold Landau

Orheyev is my town in which I was born and spent my childhood in the cheder of Reb Hirsh the Melamed (Hirsh the teacher). On that street, not far from there, the cheder of Reb Mendele still existed. To this day, I do not know and do not understand why my father sent me to the cheder when I was still so young.

Thus was the work manner of the Rebbe. He would take six children, seat them on a long bench, and teach them the Hebrew alphabet. He would show the first child the shape of an Alef and the shape of a Beit, and the child would repeat after him "Alef Beit". He would then do this to the second child, the third child, etc. After these six finished, six more would take their place, and repeat the same verses with the same tune. The following days, the Rebbe would add more letters, until they went through all the letters of the alphabet.

The children spent about two or three years in the cheder, and when they reached the level of "Chumash bochur" (a student of Chumash), they would send him to the Talmud Torah or the Yeshiva.

We had a great festivity when one of the mothers of the cheder children gave birth to a male. A male child was a small matter! (ed.note: a play on words since it was really an important matter). That day, we would come to cheder late, and the classes were cancelled. This was the day of the reading of the Shema for the mother who had given birth.

We would go out of the cheder in rows of three and march upright. "Arebersh" (the Rebbe Hirsh) would march alongside as a general (however, a limping general). Just as we entered into the home of the mother, we would all call out: "agitenovent" (good evening), Mazel Tov! Then Arebersh would read out the Shema in a loud voice, and we would repeat it after him word for word. After we finished the reading of the Shema, we once again called out Mazel Tov! Each of us then received a small bag with a small cookie, a candy, nuts and raisins. Those children who had a younger brother or sister at home would receive two portions. Our joy was boundless.

I entered the Yeshiva when I was five years old. I remember that my entrance to the yeshiva was difficult. Moshe Binyamin the Shochet's (Moshe Yonovitz) was one of the trustees of the Yeshiva, and he advised my father to wait one more year until I had become six years old. However, my father advised him to test me, and if I would not pass the test, he would accept the situation, and I would wait one more year. My father's advice was accepted, and I took the test and passed. I was very happy. I had already become a Yeshiva student, and was already able to play with children who were older than me. The games were different than they were in cheder. We prepared a performance for Chanukah, to which we invited the important people of the city, (The "Rabbi Mitaam" Yosef Pagis, Dr. N Berkovitz, and others). The parents of the children also came. The trustees of the Yeshiva delivered lectures about the activities and educational achievements of the Yeshiva. The teachers were Moshe Liva, Ben-Zion from Rybnitsa, and Leib Altman and his son Yonah from Ukraine.

Ben-Zion was the strictest of them. He would enter the class with a leather strap, and hit the strap on the table. Everyone became quiet immediately. All of the children were frightened, and nobody was so brazen as to open his mouth. He issued a reprimand and a punishment for every small transgression. Obviously, the children did not especially like him. My place was next to the teacher, and every time that he wanted to drink, he would honor me with bringing him a cup of water. Once, I had the idea of taking revenge upon him for the gall that he cast upon the students, and I said to myself that when he would send me to bring a cup of water, I would pretend to trip as I brought him the cup, and the cup would spill on his face… However, this did not come to fruition. I was afraid that the wantonness of my heart would become known, and my fate would be bitter. He caught me as I was sitting at the table playing games with paper and not concentrating on my studies. He hit me over the ears once or twice for this transgression. Then I decided that he would receive his recompense the next time. When he sent me to fetch a cup of water, I made sure to bring a full cup. I "tripped" as I approached him, the cup fell from my hands, and the water spilled on his feet. My plan worked, and I did not realize from the outset that it would make it look like he wet his pants. I remained in my place overtaken with fear, and I could not open my mouth. Specifically that time, he did not punish me at all…

* * *

I immigrated to America in 1923. I visited Orheyev in 1929, and found it wallowing in poverty and deprivation. The Jews were downtrodden. Anti-Semitism and the persecution of the Romanian authorities were upon them. I was anguished about my hometown and its people who were in such a sad situation. However, who could imagine that 11 years later it would be destroyed, and most of the Jews would be scattered to the four corners of the earth as they left their loved and dear ones on the fields of murder. Their memory will be preserved forever.

Hebrew: Y. B. A.

Chapter 27

Lag Baomer in the Cheder

by Yechiel Leyderberg

Translated by Jerrold Landau

It was Lag Baomer. It was a lovely day, and hot as a boiling Tammuz day. A cool breeze would blow once in a while and caress the dry parts of the body. On account of the heat, a person would seek shelter under a lone tree near the house or in the shade of the walls. We, the students of the cheder of Rebbe Hirsch the Lame, gathered in the cheder armed with weapons from head to foot, in order to go to "Mount Sinai," that is to say to the mountain that was found outside the city. The Rebbe was not inclined to exercise his failing legs and to climb mountains in this heat, and he advised us to conduct the Lag Baomer events in the yard near his house: "My yard also has vegetation and grass, and it is possible to fulfil the obligations of Lag Baomer". Vegetation and grass did indeed grow in isolated areas of the Rebbe's yard, however it was for the most part nettles watered by kitchen and laundry water, and a rotting smell emanated from them… He concluded his advice with the announcement, "If you do not wish to remain in my yard, I will permit you to go yourselves." This depressing announcement left a serious impression upon us. However, our spirit did not fall. Several of the children, myself included, decided to go without the Rebbe. It is understood that the young children did not want to pass up on their opportunity to celebrate the Lag Baomer holiday on "Mount Sinai" outside the city along with the older children, so they joined us. "I will go with you," he said, "but I warn you, do not act like wild men and madmen on top of the mountains!" A great joy overtook us, the Rebbe was going with us! We arranged ourselves like soldiers, two in a row, and we marched quietly and in an orderly fashion through the streets of the city until we reached "Mount Sinai." There, we spread out on the grass and enjoyed the refreshing smell that came from all sides. As we rested, we took our weapons, toy pistols and other such items, as we enjoyed the explosions and thunder that came from them. After the "first round" ended, we decided to eat. For this purpose, we required water to wash our hands and for drinking. Without giving too much thought, we all jumped from our place and fell upon the well that was nearby. We struggled amongst ourselves as each one pushed his way to be the first to get water from the well, whether with a cup or a bottle. The sounds traveled afar, and when the Rebbe saw what was transpiring, he was not pleased. He was afraid that one of us would fall into the well. He began to shout and warn us that we should keep away from the well, or else he would beat us as usual. Of course, we did not listen, and we continued with our wrestling. Finally, everyone got a portion of water. We returned victoriously to the "camp" and began our meal with joy and mirth. We vigorously chewed everything that we put into our mouths, and our joy was boundless. However, then something happened that dampened our joy. Groups of children from other cheders passed by us along their way to the other side of the mountain, an area that spread out behind the vineyards, to an expansive, green field that was enchanting in its beauty. We pleaded with the Rebbe to accompany us to this place where the students of the other cheders are gathering. However, the Rebbe did not listen. What should we do? My friend and I decided that when other cheders pass by, we would join them. When a cheder passed by in the direction of the wide area, we joined the other children, "and the children of Israel traveled." The young people of our cheder realized this, and they also joined this, without taking heed of the shouts and warnings of the Rebbe. When we reached the desired place, a new world opened up before our eyes! There was a large field, and Jewish children were dancing, jumping like "young goats." Their voices were heard from afar. The teachers also joined in the joy of the children, as they danced and enjoyed themselves with their "flocks". The voices of the children singing the songs of holiday came from afar. It was an earthly Garden of Eden! Who could be equal to us and who could compare to us? However, can a Jew be happy without being sad at the end?! It was sunset. I was sitting at the bank of the river with outer friends, playing "bliafda kada." I was informed that the Rebbe was looking for me. It would be bad and bitter for me. I approached him contritely. The Rebbe scolded me and told me to gather all of the children immediately, for it was time for Mincha, and he was rushing to the synagogue. Sad and embarrassed, we left the "Garden of Eden" and returned home…

From Yiddish by M. R.

B: In The Labor Group

Chapter 28

The Socialist Movement and the Professional Union

By Yonah Shamban

Translated by Jerrold Landau

With the spreading out of the workers' movement throughout the wide expanse of Russia, the first omens that heralded the liberation movement in the country reached our city as well. Emissaries from the centers, activists and propagandists, who organized kernels of groups from among the local intelligentsia and the ranks of progressive activists, appeared in our city from time to time. It was difficult to work under the conditions of oppression and persecution that prevailed at that time throughout Czarist Russia, including our city. Any gathering of workers was strictly forbidden. Nevertheless, the workers were not deterred, and they gathered in groups – some in hidden rooms in a remote home, and others behind the far off vineyards and orchards on Mount Ivanus. There they deliberated and clarified problems of the movement and the direction of local activity.

The workers' movement in our city grew and developed under these underground conditions. In the year 1905, it excelled with stormy and fruitful activism. During that era, members from far off places came to us and developed a wide array of activities among the community of workers. It is worthwhile to make mention of the members Yankel and Avraham the "Kovalies" (blacksmiths). They were workers ingrained with revolutionary enthusiasm and gifted with the power of expression. They were prepared to dedicate themselves to the idea of liberation.

During the time that they lived in our city, they succeeded in organizing the community of workers by profession, such as: tailors, shoemakers, carpenters, bakers, coopers, and others.

From lone, isolated, downtrodden workers, a strong workers' union was established, with an understanding of its status and knowledge of its place in the movement. It watched everything that was before it with vigilant eyes.

With enlightened enthusiasm and dedication, the local workers and socialist intelligentsia stepped toward the revolution.

I remember May 1, 1905. That was the first time we celebrated with great festivity, despite the underground conditions.

From the morning hours, word spread that the workers of the city would gather in the Seleshty Forest, a thick, ancient forest that was 5 kilometers from the city. The workers streamed toward the forest in isolation, excited about the issue of the day. We heard from the members Fania and her brother Yosef Suslik, activists of the local working intelligentsia. We also heard from Menashe Feinsilver and his sister, as well as Amalya Branover (young people with a high level of culture, experts in socialist theory, dedicated and prepared to sacrifice themselves on the altar of revolution). In their speeches, they instilled in the hearts of the gathering the value of the "First" of May for the unity of workers.

The deep impression that this large gathering had upon myself and those gathered is still etched in my memory. A strong spirit of battle was awakened in the hearts of each participant. Indeed, the activists of the movement succeeded in organizing the community of workers for the general strike of all branches of labor in the city. The strike broke out in the middle of the summer of 1905, the time when the need for working hands increased. It encompassed all the workers of the city, even the apprentices in the workshops. The demands for improvement of working conditions were modest:

1) A 10 hour workday (instead of 14-16 hours).
2) Higher wages.

The strike lasted for three days, with general solidarity. The army from Kishinev arrived on the third day. The commander invited a delegation of workers in order to hear their demands. Two young people dedicated to workers' issues were deliberately sent first – myself and Tuviya Nudelman (Yosinkes). The demands were rejected and the commander ordered everyone to return to work immediately.

Indeed, the strike failed, but the spirit of the workers was not harmed. The professional unions continued their efforts and propaganda among their members with increased vigor, to prepare for the time to come.

With the declaration of the "freedom" by the government on October 17, 1905, the movement spread out and grew with greater vigor. Widespread activity took place in the villages of our region. Activists would appear during the days of the fairs. They would issue broadcasts, deliver lectures to the farmers, and explain the value of revolution. However, the Czarist government was not silent for any period of time. It was disgusted by the freedom of the workers from the yoke of oppressive labor, and it reacted by fomenting pogroms in the cities and towns with mixed Christian and Jewish populations.

The reactionary powers also raised their head in our city, and prepared to arrange a slaughter of the Jewish population among us. However, to their ill fortune, they erred in their calculations. "Self Defense" ("Samoborona") was immediately arranged by the Jewish and Christian workers who belonged to all streams of the workers' movement. For many days, joint watches of Jews and Christians guarded the city, and prepared to respond to any blow in a twofold fashion. Thus the Jewish population was saved from a pogrom.

The "Traktir" (teahouse) of Yankel Ukner, that was opened that winter, served as a gathering place for our members. It is fitting to make note of this simple Jew, the carpenter who endangered his family and himself by hosting the workers of the movement, those who came from afar as well as the local members in our city. They would gather in this house on a daily basis and, over a cup of tea, deliberate over questions of the times, establish the ways of the movement, and conduct propaganda activities under the nose of the officials of the secret police. Christian members of the "Iskra" socialist workers' party were also among the visitors of that house.

It is appropriate to note that organizations of workers under the auspices of the Zionist organization Tz"s and Poalei Zion were also founded at that time. There was also an attempt to organize an anarchist group in our city. To finance this activity, they confiscated the home of M. Volovsky, a resident of our city, and fined him 1,000 Rubles for the benefit of their faction. However, this action failed, and as a result of it, Zeidel Bakovsky was arrested. He had spoken at the outset of this action. He was sentenced to ten years of hard labor.

In 1907, the reaction in Russia was in full strength. Despite this, the activities of the movement continued. They produced propaganda by spreading out revolutionary declarations. During one action, I was imprisoned and sentenced to nine months of jail.

The political activity of the movement weakened under the conditions of cruel persecution, and was replaced by cultural activity. Evening classes for the workers and the youth, and presentations on Socialist topics filled the spiritual gap that existed at that time in the city. (There was also no shortage of talks on Zionist topics.) The halls of the Talmud Torah were generally available for this cultural activity. These halls were most appropriate due to their closeness to home, as well as for the purpose of hiding the activity from the eyes of the secret police.

As has been stated, the political activity weakened. Nevertheless, we continued to inject energy into it in order to keep the movement in a state of preparedness until the desired day of revolution would approach. The First World War with all of its tribulations broke out in 1914. Our city was emptied of its youth, including activists of the movement. Activities took a break until the year 1917, when the corrupt army was weakening in Russia.

Indeed, the evil Russian Czarist government fell. The workers' movement was freed from its shackles. All branches of the professional unions, previously enslaved and downtrodden, once again awakened to life. It seemed as if the end came to slavery, and liberty, brotherhood and peace would take its place.

These bright days were very brief. The Romanians invaded Bessarabia in December 1917. They cruelly persecuted anybody who was suspected of belonging to the revolutionary guard. Dozens of Jewish and Christian youth were persecuted, and many were imprisoned. A resident of our town, Bendik Naychin, the son of a well-known Zionist family, was murdered in Kishinev. This murder had an unpleasant effect on all the residents of our city. (1924)

The status of the workers did not weaken. From time to time, when they found it necessary to protect their issues, they stood up to the test. The following story will testify to this.

A tobacco processing and cigarette factory was opened in the spring of 1918. (The region of Orheyev was very rich in tobacco growing.) More than one hundred workers, men and women, Jews and Christians immediately organized the workers to protect their interests. Veterans of the workers' movement, who invested a great deal of effort in organizing activities for the improvement of the conditions of the work in the factory, stood at the helm of this activity. (I had the opportunity to lead it.) More than once, the workers threatened to declare a strike. The members went hand in hand with the organizers of the strike, until the employers were forced to fulfill their demands. During the three years of the existence of this factory, numerous strikes broke out. Most of them ended successfully.

In 1921, the Romanian government decided to take the growing of tobacco under its own supervision. All private tobacco enterprises in the country were closed.

During those years, with the Balfour Declarations, a new era of Zionist activity began. The activity was conducted by the older working youths, with the aim of organizing themselves for pioneering in the Land of Israel. We can see the fruits of this effort now in our Land. Graduates of the working Zionist youth groups from Orheyev can be found on many Kibbutzim and throughout the country.

Chapter 29

From Those Days

Gittel Spivak-Shapin

Translated by Jerrold Landau

Please forgive me, my city of Orheyev, that I did not develop a great love of you in my youth. How could I have loved you, when my soul was given over to something more sublime, beautiful and good?

It was in the days preceding Passover of 1903, and I was not yet 12 years old. In my father's poor home, Baruch Melamed (the teacher) from the village of Chekolteny, everything was shiny. Outside there was mud and mire. Across the courtyard, there were puddles of water covering the "Shes", almost coming to the door of our house. Beggars were making their monthly rounds to collect donations. Among them were women covered with dirty kerchiefs, carrying babies in their arms and wearing tattered rags. The sounds of stifled cries came from the babies. This gloomy picture that appeared before my eyes touched my heart, the heart of a young girl. In my innocence I thought that you, my city, were guilty for all the tribulations that fell into the lot of these poor people.

During those days, news of pogroms against the Jews spread. There were also conversations about Palestine. One night, news reached me that a lecturer was coming to our neighborhood. Men, women and children gathered in the synagogue on the Post Office Street (Postova Gasse) to hear the lecturer. This was my dear Avraham Borsutsky. The lecturer spoke at length, and I only understood the content of his talk with difficulty. His final sentence is etched in my mind. He declared: Jews, "independent defense" is demanded of us!!!

It was close to morning. My father was ill and confined to bed, and I was with him alone in the room. After a sleepless night, I went outside at dawn. I was covered in a sheepskin mantle, and my father's winter hat was on my head. I looked out at the area. Suddenly, from afar I saw three riders on horses, and a group of people marching on foot accompanying them. They were approaching in the direction of our house. Frozen in fear, I clung to the threshold of the house. However, as they approached, I recognized my dear Avraham Borsutsky, Gershon Vaynshtok and other activists of the city. The three horseback riders were students of the agricultural school ("The Ferme"). These were members of the defense that made the rounds to all areas of the city on a nightly basis until the threat passed. Orheyev was saved from the fear of the pogroms that broke out in Bessarabia that spring.

It was after Passover. The spring season in its full splendor spread light and warmth. New winds were blowing... The workers were organizing. Workers and working youth gathered in the "Bulvar" each evening. Police detectives followed us. Great caution was required. We moved our meeting location from place to place on account of the evil eye. What did we speak about? About the improvement of working conditions, first and foremost about shortening the working day to eight hours for workers and apprentices, so that the workers could improve their cultural situation during their free hours. The first signs of revolution reached us. I remember that two students with blond hair appeared suddenly in a large, well-lit room to teach us Russian. These were the Dinin brothers. The members Tuberman and Gilishensky, Bund activists, taught the classes in Yiddish and other elementary subjects. We felt that we were better protected from the police in the framework of classes. However, the agents of the "Czar" did not leave us be. They followed the goings on of the community of workers in the town to the best of their ability. I recall the "Nadziratel" (ed. note: supervisor) Lazinski, who excelled in his diligence and his detective sense. He knew the activists of the movement by name and persecuted them. The Dinin teachers were forced to leave the city. We had to move to a place that was hidden from the eyes of the police. We found a cellar that was filled with mud, into which the rain dripped. We studied in the cold and the dark, as we deliberated about matters of the movement. However, the premises were too small and dangerous for larger meetings. We then had the idea to gather in a field outside the city. Someone advised that the Ivanus would be a wonderful place for meetings. Indeed, that wonderful mountain, with its orchards and vineyards would serve as a most ideal place, and "the eyes of Lazinski will not reach us." We all agreed.

* * *

Every Sabbath, we would gather at twilight behind the vineyards, about three kilometers from the city, under the cover of the heavens. There, we would listen to lectures on events in the world at large, in the workers' movement, and about the approaching revolution. Then the world appeared to me through a new lens. I began to understand that you, my dear Orheyev, were not guilty for all the suffering and oppression that was in your midst. The evil came from deeper, more obscure roots.

One Sabbath, a lecturer from Odessa arrived. Also my brother Avraham, who was there for an extended period, was sent to us for activity by the Socialist movement. The news of the arrival of these guests immediately reached all circles of the community, despite the secrecy. We, workers, students, and ordinary youth gathered on the Ivanus at the set time, in the safest place. The guards took their places and the lecturer from Odessa opened the meeting. He started at first with a low voice, and slowly raised his voice. He broke out with fiery flames against the tyrannical police, the capitalists, and the parasites that suck the blood of the workers. He declared: "Members! If the police appear, do not be cowards. Do not scatter! Gird yourselves with strength!!! Let it be a war of classes. Hurray!" Before the gathering had a chance to cheer, a member of the guard ran up and hinted something with a gesture of his hand, and then continued to run further. (I believe that this was my dear Moshe Bondovitz, one of the activists in our city, today in Philadelphia.) The entire gathering jumped up from their places in confusion and scattered in all directions. Many fled to the side of the Yas, and others to the water mill, to behind the river, etc. My brother, who remained there with the limping Gilishensky, lagged behind the fleeing crowd and was arrested by the police. They remained in prison for one week, and the authorities did not allow us to visit them. Rachel Ravich (Moshe Ravich's wife) who was one of the leaders of the workers in the city, concerned herself with bringing food to the prisoners in jail. Moshe Ravich involved himself with trying to free them, and they were freed at the end of the week. (With deep sorrow and a grieving heart, I hereby recall this noble family who gave so much of their energy to the benefit of the workers, and were killed in such a tragic manner during the Holocaust.)

It was October 17, 1905. This was the day of the Czarist declaration of "Freedom". This included freedom of speech and the printed word. Joy and gladness broke out in Orheyev. The crowds gathered in the courtyard of the large Kloiz (the Kloiz was too small for the gathering). Yaakov Krasner spoke very well from the podium. (He was the son of Yisrael Krasner, one of the wealthy people of the city). He spoke enthusiastically about this great historical event, the freeing of the nations from the shackles of the mighty Romanov kingdom, the liberation of the workers, etc. Suddenly word spread that a telegram arrived from Kishinev that the authorities were conducting pogroms against the workers who were celebrating there. And what about us? There was word that the infantry guards had appeared on Alexandrovskia Street, scattered the workers, and were approaching in the direction of Torgovia. The perplexed and dejected gathering immediately scattered to their houses. This was a hard blow to the movement in general, and to the community of workers of our city in particular. From then on, life was gray, without hope and without purpose. Even the antagonism between the workers and the employers abated. Complete indifference pervaded among everyone. Only after two months did the group of activists of the movement reawaken. They decided to do something to dispel the ennui. The idea was hatched to perform the play "The Zvi Family" of D. Pinsky. They took it upon themselves to broach the subject with the members V. Shaposhnik, Avraham Lipshin, Nachman Krasner, Chava Spivak, and others. The group invested great effort in rehearsals and preparations. However, the authorities forbade performing this play. All of the hard work to obtain a permit was for naught. The winter passed, and left behind gloomy thoughts…

Figure 75 - Torgovia Street

It was the summer of 1906. The summer vacation arrived. The students of our city returned from the universities. They brought a stream of awakening to the community of workers and youth. The meetings on the Ivanus, the splendid mountain, were renewed, each group in accordance with its ideological stream – Young Zion, Poalei Zion, Bund, and general youth – each group with its dreamers, each group with its mottoes, each group with its aspirations. And the individual?… Who would understand his secrets?… Who knows what is transpiring inside his heart?… Suddenly, the humming of a lone melody comes. From the other side, a second voice joins in, a third, and a fourth, until the tune unites them all – Bundists, Zionists from all stripes – into one choir. Everyone is singing, the songs of Bund, the songs of Frug, and the echo bounces back from afar. It seems as if the sky above and the rocks below have joined into the singing, to sing the song of our enlightenment…

Is it possible to forget those wonderful nights, enlightened nights, on the cold rocks of the Ivanus? Whether on an enchanting moonlight night or a night of darkness enveloped with enlightened secrets, to the twinkling light of stars – in the calm silence of night, dreams were knit, and enlightened, bubbly futures were decided... Who will tell me, when and who crowned this mountain with a wonderful view that looks out to the right, left and in front?...

The summer passed. The fall gave forth its signs. The days were short and the nights were long. The workload in all aspects of farming increased as the population prepared for winter. The hired workers were forced to work until a late hour of the night without extra wages. The feeling that after the fall season, the worker and his family would be left without livelihood grates upon you, however... the trade union no longer exists. The reaction in the country increased. The intelligentsia distanced themselves from the workers movement, who were left on their own... Boredom to the point of oppression overtook you... And here was a ray of light! A group of activists stirred up cultural activity. The members Ravich, Pisarevsky, Yisrael Mishkis and others organized literary discussions on various topics of the movement in the hall of the public library. The great participation by all strata of the population testified to the importance of culture to the worker.

I recall the wonderful influence that the community of listeners had upon me. Light in space – the glow from the gas lantern is pasted upon the faces glowing with internal satisfaction. Indeed, in the oppressive environment that pervaded, this cultural activity awakened longings and hopes for the day of social equality, for a time when the workers would be freed from tyranny and exploitation, and would no longer be hungry or limited.

Fifty years passed since then...

How great is the disappointment...

Translated from Yiddish by M. R.

Chapter 30

The Culture League

Rachel Rotinsky-Shaposhnik

Translated by Jerrold Landau

It was 1929 or 1930. The Romanian government in Bessarabia persecuted and oppressed any communal activity that took on a socio-political form. The Bund descended from the communal stage. The Zionist movement was under constant surveillance by the political police. Those activists from Bund and from among the workers whose souls were bound to communal activity found satisfaction with activities in the cultural realm. The only communal institution to which the youth and progressive community gathered was the communal library. However, it was under the influence of the Zionists. The library activists and directors were mainly young people from the strata of householders, people whose economic status enabled them to be supported by their parents. People who were busy with their studies and people who assisted their parents in business were very far from the community of workers. Their aloof attitude to the people of toil, whether in private life or public life, distanced the young worker from their circles. When a worker came to the library, it seemed as if the directors were peering at him from on high. Their relation to him was different than their relation to the children of the householders and the intelligentsia. It was natural for the working youth, male and female to seek and find internal satisfaction among working friends. Even I, who from the time of my youth had already chosen the path of a life of work, found common ground with the community of workers, who were particularly close to my heart.

At the same time, a group of friends with an activist bent arose and organized themselves with the aim of improving the work conditions of the workers and apprentices. A committee of workers was chosen, and they set out to work immediately.

The first two demands that the committee issued to the employers of the city were: a) a shortening of the workday to ten hours; b) a two-hour noontime break during the day, patterned after the customary siesta that was observed by the stores in accordance with the law. The committee conducted a difficult battle until it forced the employers to agree to the demands. However, it became clear very quickly that the employers were ignoring the agreement: a) many of the employers employed members of their family, and therefore, the status of the worker was weaker than that of the workers who were family members; b) fear of the police fell upon many of the workers, lest they be accused of Bolshevism; c) fear of dismissal. In addition, labor-related knowledge was weak among the workers. I recall one member of the hat workers' union who did not observe the directives of the workers' committee. The committee invited her for an inquiry. To our question asking her to explain her actions, she answered that she was afraid of dismissal. With this, she asked the committee to send two representatives to influence the employer to fill the directives of the organization, and free the worker after the set hours. The committee asked me and one other member to undertake this mission. When we came to her employer and explained to him the purpose of our visit, he began to complain about his difficult life and depressed state of economic well-being.

As the discussion was still in progress, the member who had invited us arose, turned to her employer, and said: I beg of you, do not be upset, whatever you will tell me, I will do... It is easy to understand how ridiculous our situation was... We left as we had come...

It is obvious that the weakness in understanding of the situation on the one hand, and the persecution of the government on the other hand, weakened the hands of the workers in the trade union of our city. A few of our members, workers of trades, moved to larger cities in Romania. Their leaving of the city had a bad influence on the few people in our group who remained. The shameful work conditions, the political police who persecuted and oppressed – all of these put so much pressure on our souls that it was hard to bear.

From Professional Activities to Cultural Activities

At that time (1929), there was an invitation to an annual meeting of members of the library. Our group, representing the community of workers, organized itself with the aim of having a majority at the meeting so that we could influence the improvement of the manner of running the library.

However, the camp of directors also did not sit with folded hands. On the evening of the meeting that took place in the Talmud Torah building, we discovered that our efforts to become the majority did not succeed. We could not make peace with the situation as it was, that the library would continue to be run in the future without our active participation. As the proceedings progressed, the representatives of both camps entered into a dispute. Sharp, stormy arguments turned the meeting into a literal battleground. We recognized that we were fighting over whether each member would be able to benefit from the services of the institution without deprivation. This recognition strengthened our hand in the battle. However, we were not able to convince the other side, and the only thing we could do was to leave the meeting. As we were leaving the meeting, we already came upon the idea of founding an independent library through our own power, dedicated to the needs of the community of workers in our city.

The next day, we turned to the activists of the "Culture League," advising them to set up a fund to purchase books and to rent a building for the library. We set out to realize the objective with youthful enthusiasm. Despite the fact that the economic situation in the city was difficult, we gathered many donations from the working class, some of money and others of books. Within a short time, the fund grew to the point where we were able to rent premises and purchase books. A committee to organize the establishment of the library was formed. The following were chosen as directors of the library from among the workers: Chava Nepomnyashcha (the only one who received a meager salary), Yisrael Keyser, myself and others. From the Culture League, there was the teacher Fania Isakovna and her husband Piatr Abramovitz Rabinovitz, and the teacher Yitzchak Sherman. (They were also our teachers in our youth.) We rented a two room premises – a reading room and a room for books and the librarian. We were very happy about the fact that we were able to overcome the birth pangs of our dear endeavor. The assistance that many people extended to us helped us maintain ourselves despite the fact that the financial situation imposed serious pressure. Our desire to expand the collection of books could not be met by the income from reading money alone. Therefore, we conducted various events, including dance night, raffles, etc. We were not helped from the communal coffers. Within a short time, we acquired many new and important books. The circle of readers grew, and many supported the institution. We arranged lectures and literary discussions, in which the activists of the aforementioned Culture League played an active role. Our efforts were not for naught. However, after a year and a half, agents of the sigurnatza (ed. note: security police) started to follow our actions and began to suspect our members of Communism. Even though nothing suspicious was found, an order was issued to close the library. They also confiscated the books. They even imprisoned some of our members and tortured them badly.

We were deeply distressed that all of this property that had cost us so much money fell into the hands of the mortal enemies of the workers. We succeeded in transferring the books to some of our members through a wide variety of means (to Fania Isakovna, Chava Nepomnyashcha, to the home of my parents, and other members), lest they fall into the hands of the sigurnatza. Thus ended the period of communal cultural activity of the workers of Orheyev during the dark days of Romanian reactionism in Bessarabia in the years 1929-1930.

Chapter 31

Took a Chance but…Had Good Luck

By G. Shafin

Translated by Marsha Kayser

In the year 1908 I received information from my friend from Kishinev that two comrades, political prisoners, had been transported from their local prison to the Orheyev jail, and no one was permitted near them. He beseeched me to do everything I could so that we should be able to visit them. I did not see a way to take on this dangerous duty by myself. The risk was especially great; therefore Hertz Gilishensky and another comrade stored two boxes containing illegal literature and Siberian addresses under the bed in my room. My visiting the prisoners would have served as a clear demonstration of political connection with them, and then we should be doomed…after a brief hesitation I and my comrades decided to go to the prison alone to request permission to visit them. After our persistent follow-up and pestering of the prison "authorities," we at last got the permission to visit them. Our shock (at the sight of two naïve 16 year-old girls) was indescribable but, when we encountered the joyous looks from the two young people, we felt at once how significant our feat was in their eyes. How happy they were, after long months of seeing no friendly face, hearing no warm word, that they had obviously found someone who would take an interest in them. (Although we had to talk in the presence of the overseer.)

We visited them almost a year's time, twice a week, with good things: fruit, meat, fish, cigarettes, and ordinary snacks. In the end my dear David Feinman (the uncle of Moyshe Feinman, a resident of Nezhia here in the country) also participated in the action and made it easier for us. I still remember the nice challah and nice meals with a little shnaps to boot, that David would deliver for them on Shabbos or a holiday.

Our joy was indescribable when within a year's time they were freed and said good-bye, showering us with heart-felt and passionate thanks. On behalf of their parents (one Shpirberg from Kiev and one from Poltava) they also conveyed very warm regards and wishes.

I and my friends felt proud that our shtetl, because of us, will be reminded of good deeds, between big cities, from the oppressed Russian proletariat.

Chapter 32

First Workers' Ball

Translated by Marsha Kayser

On one boring winter evening, the young and older workers in our group were sitting and shmoozing, about what to do to drive away the "shtetl" boredom and at the same time benefit the community.

One of us called out - a ball! A workers' ball! - Let us do it. Yes, a ball! Others took up the suggestion with enthusiasm. Said and done. On the spot we quickly gathered a committee, which took upon itself the preparation of a work plan; we, the young people, took upon ourselves the gathering of items for a lottery and the decoration of the hall.

With youthful passion we threw ourselves into the work. From the bridge up to the hospital and back we (I, Rivka Shaposhnik and others) went from house to house and to the credit of our "small town" obtained pretty sewn and embroidered things: towels, table cloths and cushions - wonderful handwork. We also got nice things from the shops for the lottery. Encouraged by the supportive attitude from the town, we threw ourselves into the work with even more intensity and although the time to the "New-Year" was soon too short, we completed all work necessary to start the ball on time.

But now something happened which caused a serious disagreement among us. The proletariat from that time did not have a lot of the city "intelligentsia" except for two families: Ravich, Nayman, and a couple of students, who were close to the worker circles. Suddenly one of those actively involved issues a warning, that we should not allow the intelligentsia to take part in the ball, just because they accompanied friends from the committee. The idea caused a lot of agitation among us. People immediately took sides in the dispute. Each side had strong arguments; the one side, for allowing everyone who wants to, to participate in the ball; the second side the opposite, proposing that in no case should they be admitted. There was much excitement and it threatened the ball.

At last good judgment won out and the "fateful sentence" was revoked on the eve of the ball. The Stolyars, Avrum Iddel and Yankel rush to complete the kiosks, others put up curtains on the windows, others decorate the hall for a dance and the others arrange the buffet. "Runners," "hikers" rush to collect donated and purchased products, and we experience a warm holiday spirit.

Eight o'clock in the evening. The Klezmer musician, with his band, gives the signal to start the ball with a gay march. The crowd streams in, the halls of Talmud-Torah become overcrowded. The bright light from the "luxurious" lamp (there was not yet electric) beams on the festively dressed guests, the music elevates the spirits and after a whole dreary year of being overworked, the workers are seized with ecstasy, swayed by the intoxicating music - sounds from Melech with his band. Our hearts are filled to overflowing with sweet joy, as we receive expressions of gratitude from the guests, especially from the intelligentsia; we are uplifted by the proud feeling, that the intelligentsia also recognized the ability of the workers to carry out such a tasteful and responsible undertaking.

During darker times, what predominated on the workers-street was the memory of what turned out well, bringing together the downhearted workers and craftsmen, lifting them up from sadness and boredom in order to make possible a well-intentioned event to restore their spirits, indeed at the right time and with the right result. For a long time the Orheyev workers inhaled the enthusiasm from the Workers' Ball in the year 1909.

Figure 76 - Group of friends at a ball -- "Babylon" Feast

C: The Cooperative Group

Chapter 33

The Influence of the Workers in our City

M. Rotkov

Translated by Jerrold Landau

The workers in our city were alert to all communal matters. They gave of their energy to the communal institutions and were members of the various parties. They gave the best of their thought to the Cooperative movement.

What was the character of the worker who came to this social status?

At the end of the 19th century, The Jewish community included wealthy householders, merchants, and clergymen, who were considered to be the "well connected." On the other hand, the workers and poor people were considered to be the "lower class."

The disparity in status caused disunity among the Jewish community. Contact between the "well connected" and the "lower class" was considered an infringement of honor to the former. On the other hand, the workers suffered from a feeling of inferiority, and they took a low profile even among those of the same status.

The reason for this economic disparity was based upon the depressed economic conditions that the workers had found themselves in for generations. The reason for the depression and the lot of the worker was – backbreaking work. There was relief when work could be found and poverty and hunger when work could not be found. Here, one trods about without education, and without the ability to read and write. In the spirit of the low cultural situation, time was wasted, and at times, they even became literally drunk.

From that depressed situation, workers came to the Workers' Union. Only the children of the poor were sent to learn a trade. The son of a poor person was sent to work at the age of 9 or 10 under shameful, exploitative conditions. They worked 12-14 hours a day for a tiny salary, or even for no salary. The apprentice youth served the family of the owners for two years, and his knowledge of labor was meager. When he got older and became an expert in his field, he was burdened with the support of the family, without any time for self-betterment. He was a boor in a community of boors, similar to himself. The youth grew up without a purpose.

Thus did the worker live for generations. On the other hand, it is worthy to point out that the community of tailors established their own synagogue and engaged the renown cantor, Yonah the Lame, who served them for many years, accompanied by a choir made up of members of our community. Similarly, the community of shoemakers established their own synagogue in the year 1904.

Relief and salvation came to the workers from the circle of young activists, Yisrael Milshteyn, Ben Zion Furer and Itzel Mishkis, who made strong efforts to establish clubs for reading of Yiddish literature. Other young people (Pinchas Shaposhnik, Hershel Krasilschik, Reuven Shaposhnik) established a dramatic troupe along with young people of the intelligentsia, under the direction of Solomon Loshakov (a photographer), that existed for many years. At a later time, another drama group functioned, in which the workers participated. It was directed by Moshe Shtikon (a cigarette maker).

From that time on, our people attained important positions in communal institutions, factions, cooperatives and local government. Some of our representatives were elected to the city council (the writer of these lines in 1924, Y. Shamban in 1929). Shamban was also elected as the vice-mayor, and proved his worth in the position of chairman of the technical division and social assistance division, through which the poor people were helped. In performing his duties, he also assisted many pioneers as they made aliyah to the Land.

Shamban also did a great thing in helping to establish an ORT trade school. He even served as the director of carpentry for it. Many of his students made aliyah and were employed in that field.

Yitzchak Fasir (a tailor) represented the workers in the directorship of the union of cooperatives in Bessarabia, from the time of its founding through the following two decades. David Belfer (a shoemaker) was the chairman of the "Loan and Savings Fund." Itzik David Cheriyan (a tailor) was the chairman of the "Organization for the Assistance of the Poor." The following people served in other capacities: Aizak Shander (a smith), Zerach Mordkovitz (a tailor), Moshe Perlov (a carpenter), David Hersh Shapanik (a baker), Zalmina Chinkis (a shoemaker), and dozens of other dedicated members, who each fulfilled their tasks, shared in the burden, and dedicated their time and energy for the benefit of the workers of our city.

Those activists, such as Milshteyn and his friends, took upon themselves the goal of awakening the workers to take an interest in helping their fellows by the establishment of a fund.

In 1902, the "Loan and Savings Fund" was founded in Kishinev, the first in Bessarabia, under the direction of the director N. M. Roitman. Roitman answered the request of Yisrael Milshteyn to assist in the establishment of a fund for the workers of our city. After great efforts, a permit was obtained, and in October 1906, a festive proclamation was made about the opening of the "Loan and Savings Fund for Workers." 56 members were registered at that meeting. 160 rubles of membership dues were collected. Directors and an advisory committee were elected, and the official opening date was set for the 19th of the month.

The directors dedicated themselves to their work with enthusiasm. Some of the members loaned significant sums in order to form a capital base for loans. Natan Zubritsky, a member of the committee of directors, excelled. He was ready to assist at any time.

Figure 77 - **Nachman Zubritsky**

Already from its inception, the fund established its credentials among those who were in need of it. A loan of 5,000 rubles from I. C. A. (ed. note: Jewish Colonial Association) enabled it to give out larger loans. Milshteyn offered advice about broadening the cooperative activity by obtaining materials for members from primary sources, and by organizing manufacturing groups. First was the group of coopers. They were granted a loan to obtain materials under the supervision of the directors of the fund with the following conditions: a) the members will receive a salary in accordance with the customary tariff of the workshop; b) the manufactured products would be collected in a joint warehouse. After the sale of the products, the loan would be paid back to the fund, and the profits would be divided among the members in accordance with their agreement. This experiment worked well, and the directors earned the recognition of the members of the group.

At the end of the fifth year of the fund, it grew from all aspects:

Year	Number of Members	Membership Dues	Pledges	Loan from I.C.A.	Loans to Members
1907	202	1527	1694	0	2322
1912	557	7360	20393	8460	35512

Along with the growth, there was a greater need for more comfortable premises. At that time, a comfortable house on Torgovia Street was purchased, that served as a headquarters for the organization, and increased its esteem. The faith of the members in it increased. The faith in the effectiveness of the credit cooperative grew, and the field became open for other cooperative ventures. A member of the audit committee of the fund, Moshe Ravich, proposed the idea of a savings venture. In accordance with his advice, the directors decided to place a small metal box in the house of every member, signed by the organization. There was a dual purpose to this: the family members would become used to saving, and the money accumulated would serve to increase the loans. Results were not long in coming. Significant sums were added to the circulating capital of the fund, and the families of the members found relief from their straits. However, the First of August 1914 came like a thief, and a general conscription was announced. The First World War broke out with all of its horrors, and all the plans were thwarted.

The draft of many members of the fund to the army caused a dwindling of its activity. The depositors demanded their deposits, and the number of those late in their payments increased. Those who were in need of loans were not granted them on account of the shortage of capital. The income decreased, and the audit of January 1, 1915 ended with a deficit of 1,556 rubles. The spirit of the directors and members declined. However, there was one bright ray of light – the dedication of the building, which was conducted with energy and brought encouragement. The workers felt that they had a basis for their dear institution.

Yisrael Milshteyn, who left the institution for a period of time due to family reasons, appeared at the annual meeting in 1915 and encouraged the members to band together at the time of depression in order to take advantage of the opportunities that presented themselves in the cooperative for the benefit of the members. "Especially now, it is necessary to provide the materials for the workers in an organized, cooperative manner. In order to thwart the plans of the black marketers, who hide merchandise and strip the skin of the workers;

to organize, it is necessary to organize a manufacturing group, to provide items for the needs of the army; to establish a warehouse for food provisions."

On the heels of the decisions of the meeting, a group of 24 shoemakers was organized. In their cooperative workshop, they manufactured 100 pairs of boots each week for the army. Similarly, a group of 10 harness makers was organized. Thanks to these enterprises, that deposited a portion of their income into the fund, the capital increased, and the year ended with only a small deficit of 845 rubles. In 1916, a central warehouse for food provisions was established in affiliation with the fund. This warehouse also included wood for fuel, flour, and other such items. The war, the Russian Revolution in 1917, and the conquest of Bessarabia by the Romanians all had a negative influence upon the status of the fund. It is important to point that, despite this, our members gained a great deal of experience in the realm of the cooperative. The young activists also joined in the effort with self-confidence. A new page was opened in the history of the institution.

* * *

In the summer of 1920, a new chapter opened in the Jewish cooperative movement of Bessarabia. At a meeting of the lending fund of that year, in which representatives of the Joint cooperative also participated, it was decided to organize the assistance that was to be given by the Joint to the founding of each cooperative. To this end, the union of Jewish cooperatives in Bessarabia was founded, the "Farband" (ed. note: Yiddish for "union"). The members of our fund decided to join the Farband in July 1920.

From that time on, the influence of the Farband in the development of our fund was noticeable. The capital of the fund continued to grow. The loans were paid in an orderly fashion, and the situation strengthened.

In 1926, festivities were arranged for the 20th anniversary of our fund. It was the only one of the 30 funds affiliated with the Farband that was founded by workers alone. (footnote: to mark the milestone, the advisory committee of the fund published a printed pamphlet called: The Twentieth Anniversary of the Loan and Savings Fund for Workers in Orheyev).

Figure 78 - ORT School – 20th Anniversary Year

The festivities took place in the ORT building (owned by the fund). All of the members of the fund participated. Yosef Pagis was the representative of the Farband, Y. Milshteyn was the representative of the Joint. Present were representatives of the institutions of the city and representatives of the Loan Fund for Small Merchants. We will suffice ourselves with giving over the essence of the blessing of Pagis: "… It is a multiple joy for me to be present at the jubilee celebration of one of the first branches of the Farband. More importantly, the cooperative whose members come from the community of workers and artisans in your city is unique within the network of Jewish cooperatives in Bessarabia. The Jewish cooperative embodies socio-economic contradictions. Since the motto of the cooperative is 'from the manufacturer to the consumer, and banding together to obviate the need for middlemen,' the Jewish credit cooperative encompasses a community that mainly belongs to the petite bourgeois, merchants, etc. At times the interests of these people run counter to those of the class below them that belongs to the same era. Not so with you. As artisans, your interests are in mutual benefit and cooperation. Your future depends on the existence of cooperative institutions. In your activities, and with your members, we hope to see a seed of cooperation that will yet bear fruit, and will serve as an example for the community of workers throughout Bessarabia."

In this spirit, the rest of the speakers at the celebration expressed the feelings of their hearts toward our activities. Indeed, the experience of twenty years of activities in cooperation and achievement encouraged the activists of the younger generation to work with greater energy to consolidate our cooperative and direct it toward broader cooperative provisions, such as the acquiring of raw materials, and cooperative manufacturing and marketing.

As a first step toward this broader plan, the committee of the cooperative started to organize partnership groups for the marketing of the wares of the hat makers, the carpenters, the coopers and the cobblers. A committee was chosen whose tasks included concerning themselves with matters of the partnership, directing it, ensuring credit, and mediating between partners in the case of a dispute. The committee saved more than one partnership from disbanding. This new idea proved its worth, and from it, we learned how to establish and develop various areas of cooperation in the running of the Farband – which placed its financial and organizational power at the disposal of those interested, and assisted them in overcoming social and financial crises.

The Convention of the Workers

The Farband saw the spreading of the cooperative idea among the workers as one of its prime tasks. In January 1927, a convention of representatives of the workers in Bessarabia was arranged through the efforts of our representatives, for the purposes of clarifications of the paths of the cooperative. 57 delegates from 34 cooperatives participated. Our members (Y. Shamban, the writer of these lines, and Fasir) made presentations about the problems of partnerships in labor enterprises, and discussed the difference in interests between this paradigm, and other economic paradigms in Jewish cooperatives. They advised: a) to establish special cooperatives for workers in those places where the objective conditions are appropriate for such; b) if this cannot be realized, a division for labor matters should be set up within every cooperative; c) an office should be setup in affiliation with the Farband to direct the matters of labor. These suggestions were brought to the directors of the Farband for deliberation; however the matter only came to actualization in the year 1930. In September of that year, the writer of these lines was invited to serve as an advisor and consultant for matters of labor under the auspices of the Farband.

Figure 79 - Cooperative of Coopers, 1930

For a period of four months, the advisor visited most of the cooperatives and learned about their conditions. At the tenth convention of the Farband, that took place in January 1931, an accounting was presented on the state of labor, and the means that should be taken to improve the status of those who work. The following were the resolutions: a) Provide cheap materials to the laborers. This could be accomplished by joint purchases for a group with a specific interest, or by establishing a supply warehouse next to the local cooperative. b) Ensure that the benefit that accrues from the centralized purchases is not offset by a loss that might accrue through normal competition in the circles of laborers. Therefore, marketing partnerships must be organized. c) Broaden the limit of credit for acquiring raw materials, under the condition that it be returned at the set time. To this end, multi-purpose warehouses should be established where the workers would exchange their wares for raw materials. Through this manner, they would be able to increase their inventory for the next time, without requiring loans at exorbitant rates of interest. d) Broadly disseminate information to the workers about the value and methods of the cooperatives. Wide ranging cultural activity is extremely valuable in the towns where few people have faith in cooperatives. These suggestions inspired many delegates to express their opinions on the matters under deliberation. The resolutions were accepted. A committee was struck from among the representatives of the workers who would be responsible for the plan of actualization, until the 11th convention that would take place the following year.

Figure 80 - Cooperative of hat-makers in Orheyev, 1924-1928

Below from right to left: 1. M. Fruchtman 2. S. Bobrik 3. M. Roitkov 4. V. Nudelman 5. Y. Spivak 6. Yechezkal …
In the middle: 1. [alef]. Grinberg 2. V. Vaysman 3. C. Vaksman 4. N. Sapozhnik 5. Kopelnikov 6. Y. Shaposhnik
Standing: 1. M. Udis 2. [feh]. Shaposhnik 3. [alef]. Grinshteyn 4. [feh]. Roitkov 5. [feh]. Oberman
6. Yosef Chusid 7. G. Vaysman 8. Ben-Zion …

This achievement found an echo in the "Das Cooperative Vort" newspaper, number 3, (1931), which published the statements of various delegates of the convention (Moshe Ravich and Karpel Shpiller) under the title "Members of the Laborers, Unite"… They discussed the difficult economic situation that pervaded in the land, and progressive impoverishment that was plaguing the workers in particular. They preached the path of cooperative partnership as the only means of salvation from the economic recession and social degeneration. The achievements of the groups of workers in Ryshkany, Orheyev, Teleneshti, Ataki, and Lipkany. "In Ryshkany, the carpenters organized themselves, and their situation improved greatly within the span of a few months. Aside from the material benefit, friendliness pervaded among the carpenters who had been used to competition among themselves which often led to open disputes," wrote Shpiller. Ravich writes in a similar matter in his article. He points out the outstanding accomplishment that was achieved by the workers at the annual convention of the Farband. "The fact that the chosen advisor is a person who is close to you proves the interest displayed by the directors of the Farband. One the one hand, his words found a positive echo among the representatives of the convention, mostly merchants, whose interests are opposite those of the cooperative from an economic standpoint. On the other hand, this matter testifies about the importance of the enterprise. You must demonstrate your positive attitude to the cooperative idea. Therefore, I too join the call of the member Shpiller: Members of the Laborers, Unite!!"

Figure 81 - Council of the Labor Bank

Encouraged by this broad communal support, the advisor worked for nearly a year and a half. The idea of opening areas of the cooperatives deepened and struck roots. That year (1931) the general worldwide depression broke out, that wreaked havoc on millions of unemployed people, and also sent its signs upon our area. Our enterprise was liquidated. In summary, it should be pointed out that, despite the brief life span of this wonderful enterprise, the community of workers and activists in Orheyev were the force that urged the Farband to establish the leadership office for workers in Bessarabia. Through their knowledge of the conditions of life of the workers of Bessarabia, these activists worked to the best of their ability to impart knowledge and faith in the cooperatives, with the aim of improving both the economic and social status of the workers. Furthermore, through the general social development in the first quarter of the 20th century, a progressive and active social force was crystallized, which assisted the advancement of the status of the workers of our city.

Figure 82 - The Craftsman Bank - The last council before the Holocaust

Seated from right to left: 1. Z. Chinkis 2. Y. Malkovitz 3. D. Shaposhnik 4. M. Perlov 5. [alef]. Stravitz
Standing right to left: 1. Y. Filmus 2. N. Belfer 3. A. Gondelman 4. V. Bilmosh 5. M. Grinberg
6. M. Hoichman 7. B. Portnoy

Chapter 33A

Workers in Public Life

Yonah Shamban

Translated by Jerrold Landau

In the first years of the 20th century, an assistance fund, called Krozok, existed among the circles of workers. Every needy worker was able to obtain assistance from it in their time of need.

This fund was organized and sustained by the workers themselves, who contributed 5-10 Kopecks to it per week. After a set period of contributions, every contributor was eligible to obtain a loan of the sum of 5-10 Rubles.

Thus were matters conducted through the first years of the 20th century, until a mutual benefit movement for workers arose in our city, as in other cities, whose purpose was to improve their economic and cultural status.

At the beginning of 1906, the group of progressive members, headed by Yisrael Milshteyn, Natan Zubritsky and Yitzchak Fridman, with the active assistance of M. Ravich, took it upon themselves to found the first "Loan and Savings Fund" in our city.

After much intercession at the windows of high people in Kishinev, the members succeeded in obtaining the required permit.

One winter night, several dozen people gathered for the festive opening of the fund. That evening, a board of directors was chosen, headed by the member Yisrael Milshteyn. Each one of the registrants paid membership dues, and received a savings ledger in which his deposits were recorded.

I remember the degree of seriousness with which people brought their deposits to the fund on a monthly basis.

That time, the fund began to distribute loans to the needy. At first, loans were given to the sum of 10-20 Rubles, with the signature of the borrower and one of his family members who acted as a guarantor. Larger loans were also granted with indentured merchandise as a guarantee. At the beginning of the war, the state of the fund reached a crisis due to the draft of many of the members. With the outbreak of the Soviet Revolution in Russia and the ending of the war, many members returned home. Other young people had come of age and entered the circle. The activities and the fund sprung back to life.

In the year 1919, when one of the founders of the fund the member Yisrael Milshteyn, prepared to immigrate to America, a general meeting of the membership was called. A new board of directors was elected, with the participation of members of the younger generation. It was headed by Chayim Wachsman, Yitzchak-David Cheriyan, Yonah Shamban, Mordechai Rotkov, Yitzchak Fasir, and others.

With the entry of the younger people, the activity of founding manufacturing cooperatives broadened. With the effective assistance of the representative of the Joint, members Yitzchak Milshteyn of blessed memory, the movement took on an organized format. (See the article of M. Rotkov.)

Manufacturing cooperatives were formed for hat makers, coopers, carpenters, cobblers, and others, which were exemplary. The movement flourished in the cities and towns of Bessarabia. At the general convention of the funds of Bessarabia that took place in Kishinev in 1929, it was decided to engage a special advisor to oversee this cooperation. This was M. Rotkov of our city.

The activity of our members also influenced the cultural side of our lives. At the general meeting in 1923, a resolution was accepted to start a trade school, and to duplicate the private house in which the fund was headquartered. When trade schools affiliated with ORT were established in 1923-24, our fund was invited to take part in the activity.

Through a special agreement with the ORT organization, our members entered into a partnership for directing it. With the physical assistance of the Joint through the representation of the member Yitzchak Milshteyn of blessed memory, a building was purchased. More than 100,000 Lei was paid for this. From then, the school bore the name: The Trade School of the "Loan and Savings" Fund of the Workers of Orheyev and the ORT Organization.

There were two divisions of this school, one for girls who studied sewing and the other for boys who studied carpentry. Studies in this school went on for three hours. The rest of the time was dedicated to work. Many of the youth of our city graduated from this school and thereby obtained a trade. One can meet many of them in the Land. These are people who earn their livelihood in an honorable fashion in the trade that they learned at that time. The serious and dedicated efforts of our young members from among the workers had a great influence even on the communal and political life of our city. Our honor rose in the eyes of all strata of the population.

In 1929, with the ascension of the Nationalists to government, we were invited for the first time to send a delegate to the new directorship of the city council.

This representative was this author, who after some time, at the time of the elections to the city council, was chosen to serve as vice mayor of the city, and took over the directing of the technology and social assistance departments of the city council.

I made aliyah in 1933, and later I brought over my family members.

Figure 83 - City Council

Chapter 34
The Situation of The Loan and Savings

B. Z. Furer

Translated by Jerrold Landau

The windfall of 200,000 Rubles for lending and saving

A deep economic recession afflicted Bessarabia prior to the First World War. Obviously, Orheyev was also hit hard. The Jews in particular suffered, for their livelihood was derived mainly from small business and labor. An important factor in the struggle for livelihood of the Jewish community was the small, cheap credit granted by the "Loan and Savings Fund" to its members. The difficult economic situation caused serious delays in repayments to the fund. Therefore, sources of credit dried up. Most of the members could no longer be helped by the fund. The only ones who could be helped were those who were able to guarantee the loan by a pledge of their property. The number of such people was very limited. The situation of those without property was very desperate. Then a miracle occurred. The fund won a 200,000 Ruble government lottery! It is impossible to describe the enthusiasm and joy that overtook the members of the fund and their families when they learned of this windfall. 200,000 silver Rubles amounts to close to 200 silver Rubles for each member (the number of members was close to 1,000). There were very few who had investments in their business close to such a large sum. It is no wonder that the matter of the "windfall" raised the spirit, and the whole town was astir.

The members of the fund stood on the streets of the city day and night to discuss, debate, and make plans. Many who did not have shares in the fund joined them. Both groups started to hatch plans regarding how to arrange the affairs of the fund so as to ensure a division of the windfall in accordance with each person's share. After several days, the directors of the fund met to arrange a plan to ensure that this "miracle" would be for the benefit of the members, and would simultaneously strengthen the basis of the fund. Two opinions came to the fore: One, in accordance with the view of Yaakov Levinson, the director of the fund, was that the money of the windfall would belong completely to the fund, and the members would benefit through the broadening of credit. This would be a case where "this one gains, and the other one does not lose." The second opinion, in accordance with the view of Ben-Zion Furer and others, was that a half of the sum would be divided among the members, and the other half would remain with the fund. The intention was that it was appropriate for the members of the fund to benefit in a personal manner from the once in a lifetime "miracle", while on the other hand, the fund would have a large enough capital basis to conduct its business. Both opinions were based on communal responsibility. There was another extreme view, to divide the entire sum of 200,000 silver Rubles among the members equally. Those holding to that view claimed that the matter fell into the hands of each member, and each member has the right to share in the windfall.

Each opinion was based on its own logic. Groups were organized, with each one attempting to sway matters toward their opinion. The deliberations resulted in disputes in the homes and the street, and even outside the bounds of the city. The "Bessarabskia Novosti" newspaper sent a special reporter to us to obtain locally based information. The meetings of the members that were convened to decide this question became so stormy that a decision could not be reached. Finally, it was decided to select a committee of 36 people who would have the responsibility to make the decision and ensure order. This committee decided that the fund should be the sole beneficiary of the windfall. It would utilize the windfall for the benefit of all of its members. The city calmed down.

Unfortunately, that year, the lack of inventory in the market resulted in a reduction of the standard of living. The value of money declined at a time when the lack of necessities of life grew. In order to provide provisions of food to the members of the fund, the directors decide to establish a cooperative shop. However, after some time, it became clear that the cooperative shop was not supporting itself, so it was liquidated with significant loss. The decline in the value of money and the losses incurred by the cooperative shop once again disrupted the members of the fund. The fund was liquidated without any recourse...

The dream about the miracle... it was hidden away, it evaporated.

D: In Agriculture

Chapter 35

The Agricultural Farm
(the Ferme)

M. Rotkov

Translated by Jerrold Landau

The Attempt to Establish an Institution for Agricultural Education

The Jews of Bessarabia in general, and the residents of our city in particular, always desired to free themselves from the unstable livelihood of business and sales. Their desire was to work the land and to labor.

Numerous attempts were made by the directors and supervisors of the Talmud Torah to teach the children a trade in addition to the regular course of study. The parents and the activists especially desired agriculture, which they regarded as a firm economic base. Therefore, the joy in our city was great when the agronomist Zusman, the supervisor of the "Yugavim" (Farming) school in Odessa, accompanied by the vice-director of "Mitaam" of Kishinev, Mr. Feinbaron, came up with the idea of setting up an agricultural farm near the city. Thus wrote D. K. in Hamelitz, number 96, in 1895: "…The honorable guests visited the local Talmud Torah, and advised the supervisor and directors of the Talmud Torah to establish an agricultural school, to teach farming to the children of the poor people. The directors of the Talmud Torah, Mr. Vaynberg and Mr. Tomaspolski, headed by Mr. David Trachtenberg, accepted the advice willingly, and took it upon themselves to bring the matter to fruition. The next day, they left the city along with Mr. Zusman and chose a large plot whose price was not too high. Thus, they lay the foundations for this great enterprise. Many of the residents of the city expressed their desire to assist in this lofty enterprise, and to provide the needed funds, such as: paying a Jewish farmer who would teach the youths and train them in this work, purchasing implements, and providing food, clothing and shoes for the fifteen youths who would be chosen to go out to this field to work. The local director of Mitaam, Dr. Rabinovitz and his honorable wife took it upon themselves to provide food for the children as they went out to their daily work. The young people who were employees of the 'Chesed Neurim' organization, which had the goal of clothing and providing shoes for the children of the poor, promised to give preference to the children who were studying farming over those who went around idle, without work. The head of Chovevei Zion, Aharon Fikhman and Mr. Brosutsky promised to give ten Rubles every month if this enterprise were to succeed. The Maskil Mr. Temkin, the Hebrew teacher of the Talmud Torah, to whom work of this nature was very close to his heart, was chosen to oversee the work. The local representative Mr. A. Brosutsky was the first to donate ten silver Rubles in memory of his grandmother, Miryam Averbukh, who died on the day of the founding of the enterprise (12th of Iyar). With this money, they purchased all of the needed implements."

After a brief time, we read the following in Hamelitz number 126 of that year: "I am pleased to announce that the visit of the agronomist Zusman bore fruit. We see the students of the Talmud Torah go out of the city on a daily basis, with their spades over their shoulders, to work and cultivate the plot of land that the directors leased for them. How sublime and lofty is the sight of seeing Jewish children standing and plowing the fields, as children of the land!" (Signed by B. Sh. Naychin.)

The Founding of the Agricultural Farm

In the "Vaschad" newspaper of July 6, 1898, a copy of an article that appeared in the newspaper "Bessarabetz" was published. It was published by M. Ravich, as follows: "In a joint effort with the head of Mitaam, Dr. Y. Rabinovitz, the enterprise for agricultural labor was founded in our city. We rented a small house at the edge of the city. Immediately (in the month of March) we were informed of the list of children. Despite the doubt regarding whether we would find parents who would agree to send their children to work the land, 30 children were registered, of which 13 were accepted. These were the first students of the Ferme."

There is a contradiction between the report (of D. K., above), and this copy. D. K. writes that, "Fifteen students of the Talmud Torah go out of the city on a daily basis with their spades on their shoulders." whereas here it relates about uncertainty. We can surmise that the first attempt did not succeed, and only three years later did activists again make efforts to establish an agricultural farm.

In the same article, M. R. continues to relate: "… It touched the heart to see the children with their mothers, widows from among the poor of the people, urging us to accept their hungry children, who would otherwise be relegated to idleness and mischief."

The First Who Offered help

It is worthwhile to point out the positive attitude of liberal Christians. The first sum, relatively quite large, was donated by H. Yanoshovich, the owner of the lands. He gave over for the purpose of the establishment of the institution the sum of 500 Rubles that he had received as arbitration fees from two merchants of our city. Other donations were also collected, amounting to

200 Rubles. These sums served as the foundation to begin the work, albeit in too modest a fashion.

A second Christian, Mr. Zhivkovich (a flight adjutant) donated 4 desaytins (44 dunams) (ed. note: 1 desaytin = 2.7 acres and 1 dunam = 1000 square meters or .247 acres) of his land north of the city for this purpose.

At first the children walked the 3-kilometer distance to work by foot early in the morning, and they returned to their homes at night. A child was chosen on a rotational basis to bring food to them. Later, two tents were set up in the field, which remained all summer.

The students worked diligently and with dedication. They performed all of the tasks, except for plowing, which was done by hired labor. The dedication of the students to work encouraged the founders to improve the living conditions. They obtained building materials and set out to build a house.

To this end, the powers of the I.C.A. (Jewish Colonization Association) were invited. The status of the institution was described to them. They allocated 50 Rubles for the building of the building and 500 rubles for annual support of the institution.

The founders turned to Baron Ginzberg, the owner of large plots of land in the region of Orheyev, requesting him to give over 30 desaytins (about 330 dunams) of land from his estate. He answered positively.

In the summer of 1898, the agronomist Zusman from Odessa visited. He took interest in the details of the work and in the state of the students. He offered suggestions that led to significant improvements in the manner of functioning of the institution.

The Cornerstone Laying Celebration

The cornerstone laying celebration of the "Ferme" agricultural school, built with money from the I. C. A., took place on May 13, 1898.

The celebration opened with the singing of "El Melech Netzor" and the prayer for "Rain" by the student choir. The rabbinical judge Rabbi Mordechai Gelfer was the first to lay the cornerstone. The founders of the institution and invited guests followed him. Moshe Ravich, one of the founders, read an accounting of the activities and achievements of the school during its first year of existence. The number of students reached 21. The area in our hands was now 34 desaytins (340 dunams). We planted 400 fruit trees that blossomed well. (The heirs of Motel Fikhman donated 200 Rubles to the benefit of the garden). All of the work in the garden, preparing the land and planting the trees was done by the students themselves.

An appropriate curriculum of study was designed with the assistance of the "Organization for the Dissemination of Knowledge." The principal was Mr. Turk. Similarly, the "Committee of Farming Communities and Labor" in Petersburg helped us to establish a workshop for agricultural carpentry and wagons.

The guests, the leaders of various organizations, such as I.C.A. and others, toured the institutions of the farm, the warehouse, the pen, the chicken coop, the corn warehouse, and the cellar for preserving vegetables – all made by the students.

At the end of the celebration, the guests lauded the dedication of the founders of the enterprise M. Ravich and the head of Mitaam Dr. Yitzchak Rabinovitz, who were astute enough to be able to establish such an important institution with such modest means. Thanks were expressed to the land donors Mr. Zhivkovich and Baron Ginzberg, to the I.C.A. organization, and to the first donor Yanoshovich ("Vaschad" Number 25, 1899).

Thus, the good will of individuals, visionary activists, to change the gloomy reality on the Jewish street, to educate a generation of workers in labor and agriculture, bore fruit. The cornerstone of the vocational educational institution, in which the activists and students placed great hopes, was laid. However, after two or three years, a difficult recession fell upon agriculture. The parents who were disappointed with the lack of opportunities for their children to earn their livelihoods from agriculture, began to take their children out of the school. At the beginning of the 1900s, the directors discussed the issue of enlisting students from outside the city. Indeed, students were brought from the orphanage in Kishinev. In the meantime, the loss increased, and the school was on the threshold of closing in 1905. The activists, headed by Ravich, requested help from the I.C.A. in Petersburg. The issue was also deliberated upon at the general regional agricultural convention.

"Vashchad" number 41, 1905. Signed by P.

At the regional agricultural convention that took place on October 1 of that year, the delegate Groso (the vice-director of the communal bank in Kishinev) raised the question of the tragic situation of the "Ferme". It was appropriate to consider this institution, which had the potential of becoming a very important educational institution with time: "With our difficult financial situation, it is not possible for us to offer monetary assistance. However, it is impossible to be oblivious to the dire situation of this dear institution." He advised the gathering to present the question to the powers directly involved, asking them to utilize all effective means to consolidate and continue the existence of the school.

After hearing the words of the participants it was decided: to express the sorrow of the convention regarding the dire situation of the "Ferme", an agricultural school for Jewish children, and to urge the directors of the "Ferme" to utilize all means to reorganize in a satisfactory manner, with the purpose of protecting this institution that is precious in the region.

As agreed, Mr. Yanovich, the head of the owners of the estates presented the above decision, with his own words of agreement and appreciation for the institution, to the central committee of I.C.A. in Paris. Minister Heflech also included his opinion on this matter. Nevertheless, after all of the efforts, the institution closed.

Figure 84 - The "Ferme"
The apprentices working down in the
"Avraham Spivak" center, owner of this photo

Chapter 36
The Tobacco Plantations in the Region of Orheyev

By Agronom H. Feigin, Hebrew by M.R.

Translated by Tamar Rachevsky Milner

Figure 85 - The agronom Chayim Feigin

Tobacco was the most important agricultural sector in Bessarabia. The Jewish tobacco growers lived mostly in two regions: Soroki and Orgieev.

Before WW1 there were a few thousand Jewish families in Bessarabia involved in tobacco farming. In Weshood, 1911, the Agronom A. Etinger wrote that in the village of Chinsheutsy, Orgieev District, there were 60-70 tobacco plots owned by Jews. Before the Romanian occupation (ed. note: 1918) each tobacco plantation owner could sell his crops in a free market, to any tobacco trader or factory that gave him the best price. Romanian occupation changed this situation: the Romanian government monopolized the tobacco market – the tobacco plant owner had to sell his tobacco only to the monopoly's warehouse. The prices were determined by a manager in that monopoly and were not negotiable, so sometimes one had to sell at a loss. This, and other conditions, led tobacco growing to reach a crisis stage in the beginning of the 1930's.

Every plantation owner (and his family) were busy all year round growing the tobacco, thus leaving little time for other agricultural pursuits. But the farmer could not know, until the last moment, if he would profit, lose or at least break even for his and his family's work. The final outcome depended both on having a successful crop and on the arbitrary prices determined by the manager (of the monopoly).

One hectare of high quality tobacco demanded a lot of expensive work, costing up to 33-35 thousand Lei. If the farmer (and the members of his household) did the work themselves it could save up to 10 thousand Lei.

The following table shows how much the crops and prices differed from one place to another. One might get a crop of 1000 kg per hectare and a high price for his crop, while another had a small and low quality crop, so his income did not even cover his and his family's yearly labor.

Tobacco crops in several villages in Orgeyev district, 1929/1930:

Village Name	#Families	Hectares of tobacco	Crop/Hectare (kg)	Value/Hectare (Lei)
Koyzovka	14	45	800-1120	11200-21400
Raspopeny	11	14	620-1240	6400-14400
Ignatsey	4	6	560- 960	17120-20800
Kobylka	8	13	400- 880	6400-17600
Izbeshty	8	5	450- 800	6400-12800
Putsintey	6	7	480- 800	5600- 9600
Skortseny	9	8	400- 800	2400-11200
Total	**60**	**98**		

Another difficulty was caused by the lack of financial resources. The cost per one hectare was between 20-23 thousand Lei if the plantation owner did the work himself. This was quite a lot of money for a small farmer. Before the "monopoly" was established, the farmer could receive loans from private sources at reasonable interest rates, since he was able to estimate in advance the minimal market prices for his tobacco. But when the tobacco trade was monopolized, the prices depended upon the decision of a government clerk, who usually acted in an arbitrary manner. Thus, it is important to mention the help that was given by the cooperatives association (with JCA, ed. note: Jewish Colonization Association), by lending funds to tobacco plantation owners, and other farmers. In 1930 only 2,300,000 Lei were placed as low interest loans to tobacco plantation owners, giving great relief through the year, until the government purchased the tobacco.

Following is an article from the monthly journal *Das Cooperative Wart* (ed. note: The Cooperative Word) titled "The Cry of the Tobacco Workers," written by Shmuel Leib Gordon from Dumbroveni, about the hardships that the tobacco growers had to go through in order to make a living for their families.

"The work in the field keeps the tobacco worker busy around the year – first seeding, then planting, watering, hoeing several times in the course of growing, flowering, picking, threading and drying the leaves. All those works are usually done while the worker's back is bent, and are very exhausting. Then, there is the packing of the dry leaves, which is also very hard work. Only if one looked at the workers, working at least 16 to 18 hours a day, inhaling the smell of the tobacco all day, their feet swollen, their faces pale and tired, could one understand how hard this work was. Still, the tobacco workers worked with vigor and devotion, since this work was their only way to make a living."

Selling the tobacco to the government servants was also very sad. The farmer and his family waited for the day that was determined by the examination committee of the government. The examiner acted arbitrarily, sometimes giving a high price, sometimes completely disqualifying the tobacco. That day was a day of enormous anxiety, because it was a day when the fate of the year's work was decided by the government clerks in an unfair and arbitrary manner.

If part of the tobacco, or sometimes the whole crop, was disqualified, it was burnt before the farmer's eyes. The sight was extremely painful. In some cases the farmer did not have enough money to pay for the costs of delivering the tobacco to the government warehouse, where it was later burnt. Even the "fortunate" farmer, whose crop was successful, and was examined fairly, got lower prices than in previous years.

Chapter 37

Second Generation of Farmers

Translated by Tamar Rachevsky Milner

Figure 86 - Zvi Rabinovitz

Reb Hershel Rabinovitz, or as he was named in Yiddish "Hershel Von Der Sloboda," was a simple Jew, a husband and a father of four. He was the third generation in Orheyev and the second generation of farmers. His father, Reb Moshe, was born in Orheyev, and owned a land of about 7 desaytins (ed. note: about 19 acres), mostly planted with grapes, nuts, plums and other fruits.

As long as Reb Moshe's children were single, they all worked and helped in his vineyard. (It is recalled that his youngest sons, Elik and Shmuel, as well as his daughter used to cross the town by foot, on their way to the vineyard at the north-east side of the Ibanus mountain, a distance of about 5 km, with their working tools on their backs). When his children got married, Reb Moshe divided the vineyard equally between them. Reb Hershel got a part in the vineyard too. He and his wife, Melia, were both diligent and vigorous, and devoted to the vineyard. In the autumn, they picked the grapes and prepared wine in a winery that they built. Occasionally, they would buy additional grapes for producing wine in order to sell it in their winery.

With the expansion of their family, the vineyard and the winery were not enough to make a living, and so they opened a small grocery store in their narrow apartment, located on the road in the midst of the city's outskirts, and hoped the store would provide the supplement income that they needed. An uneasy life was always the family's fate: the clients they served, the "gentiles", used to get drunk in their wine house, sometimes becoming wild and aggressive, and causing much disheartening. The peak of the family's suffering was when the Russian "liberated " soldiers (1917) came to town, stayed for a couple of days, and aroused the fear that they would break into the wineries, and then become drunk and wild. Due to that fear, the city commander ordered that all the wine barrels in the wineries be broken, and of course, this order did not skip the Rabinovitz winery. The barrels were broken, and the wine poured like water, thus completing the economical ruin of the family…

With the annexation of Bessarabia to Romania (ed. note: 1918) the hardships of living in our town grew: the tyranny of the Romanian governance, more restrictions on wine selling, more taxes, fewer ways to earn a living, and especially the vague future with no glimpse of hope. All of these caused many of our town's people to wish to escape from this bitter reality to just anywhere else in the world…

At the same time (1918) the news about the Balfour declaration came, and with it many hopes for our people…(ed. note – Balfour declaration: "His Majesty's Government view with favour the establishment in Palestine of a national home for the Jewish people, and will use their best endeavours to facilitate the achievement of this object, it being clearly understood that nothing shall be done which may prejudice the civil and religious rights of existing non-Jewish communities in Palestine, or the rights and political status enjoyed by Jews in any other country.")

Now was the time to leave the damned country and emigrate to the land of Israel, which was reviving. With the initiative of the enthusiastic Zionist, our aquaintance the late Ben-Zion Furer, a group of well off people from our town was organized, with the purpose of emigrating to the land of Israel and establishing an agricultural settlement. Reb Zvi was part of this group. Unfortunately, the British government withdrew from its promise to relieve it's restrictions set on the emigration, and thus the group fell apart. Only 6 or 7 families did not change their decision to emigrate to the land of Israel, and in 1920 emigrated in an unorganized way, on their own responsibility. These families were: Ben Zion Furer's family, Michael Nadel, Yisaschar Rapoport,

Binyamin Duchovny, Berel Lupatner and more. Several months later the
family of Hershel Rabinovitz emigrated to the land of Israel, and he lived to
grow and educate his sons and daughters to be labor people in the free
homeland.

M. R.

Chapter 38

The Hardship Coming to the Land of Israel

Translated by Tamar Rachevsky Milner

We left for Palestine with no certificates and without any preorganization. When we arrived at Kushta, we approached the "Israeli council " and asked for certificates. We were refused since we left without the permission from their representative in Kishinev.

One can easily assume how desperate we were, on foreign land, with no acquaintance, no money and especially no chance to get to the land of Israel. My father sought a solution for 3 weeks and then, to our great relief, he unexpectedly met with Mrs. Fania Borsutsky, a well known public activist, formerly a resident of Odessa, who had much influence on the "Israeli counci " in Kushta, and who herself emigrated (with her daughters) to the land of Israel.

Mrs. Borsutsky persuaded the committee to allow us to continue to the land of Israel. We arrived just a few days before Passover, in 1921. Our arrival in Jaffa started a new episode of mishaps… We were not received at the Emigrants Home in Jaffa, since we told them at the emigration office that we have a relative in the land of Israel, Mr. Ben Zion Furer.

We ran out of money. Finally, after intensive searching, we found an apartment in an Arab house. Then, there was an episode of searching for ways to make a living. At that time, Mr. Ben Zion Furer and Mr. Nissan Duchovny, who were acquaintances from Orheyev, owned a bakery, and they gave my father some bread to sell. The profit was little, and did not suffice to pay the rent. We were forced to leave the apartment and thus built a tent on Carmel St., on the border of Jaffa.

My father approached the Jewish Agency, asking for help to settle in an agricultural settlement, since he was a farmer abroad, but he was refused because of his old age. Father had no choice but to lean upon urban ways of earning a living, which he disliked in Orheyev, and from which he was trying to escape. My parents tried many different labors in the first 20 years in the land of Israel, and supported their family with great difficulties. They experienced suffering and distress most of their lives in Bessarbia as well as in the land of Israel, but did not show it. They went through the incidents of 1921, 1929 and 1936-39** in a tent and in a shack. Only when their sons and daughters grew up and began to work was their suffering relieved. Then they enjoyed the comforts of a one and a half room apartment, built of bricks, on

Kalisher St. My father did not live to see the liberation from the British mandate and the establishment of the State of Israel, which he prayed for all his life. He died on the 1 Sivan 5705 (ed. note: 13 May 1945).

Shabtai, Genosar (ed. note: Shabtai is Zvi Rabinovitz's son and Genosar is a kibbutz on the coast of the sea of Galilee)

**[ed. note: 1921 – after Mr. Churchill's visit to Israel, the Arabs demanded the abolishment of Zionism. They were answered by his call to lead peaceful life with the Jews. Their reaction was to attack the Jews of Jaffa followed by attacks on other towns. 11 Jews were killed.

1929 – a chain of attacks by Arabs that started in Jerusalem, then spread to Hebron (killing 66 Jews) and Safed. What "initiated" the attacks was the Jewish plans to place benches and lanterns at the western wall, for the comfort of the Jews praying there.

1936-1939 – the first wave was a general strike by the Arab population, whose purpose was to press the British authorities to stop Jewish immigration to the land of Israel. When the Arabs realized the British authorities would not change their policies, they started a series of attacks on Jews and on the British army. 80 Jews were killed. The second wave started in 1937, after the conclusions of the Peel committee, to divide the land of Israel between the Arabs and the Jews. The Arabs did not accept that conclusion, and another wave of terror by Arab gangs began.]

Chapter 39

The Rebellious Son

By G. Shafin, from Yiddish by M.R.

Translated by Tamar Rachevsky Milner

When "the farm" was established in Orheyev, most of the pupils were from the lower class. A well-off Jew would not send his son to work the land – this work was intended for "gentiles"! It was proposed to my father (by Baruch Melamud, who was deported from Taschkelmani(?) during the 1890's) that he register my eleven year old brother, who was his only son. My father strongly objected: 1) the child is too thin and small to stand hard labor; 2) how could it be that his son, who is an excellent grammar student in the classroom, and writes sentences himself, and is his source of pride, should leave his studies to work the land, like a "common gentile"? There was no way my father could agree. My brother was attracted to the idea, although he had no clear idea what it meant, and he pleaded with my father to register him in "the farm" school, and get him a doctor's document regarding his health. My father refused to help him but my brother was not deterred. He went by himself to the doctor, got the document and registered for the school. A couple of months later, my brother came home for a visit. All of us, and especially my father, were happy because he did not look like a "common gentile" at all. He remained gentle and handsome as he was before, yet he was more lively and independent. The heavy pair of boots he wore made a harsh impression on my father. It was the only change to his gentle look.

When my father laid his eyes on his feet, in those heavy boots, there were tears sparkling in his eyes. Could it be tears for an only son, whose old father's hopes are all with him, but who has been taken out of his father's home by an unexpected cause? He was losing his only old age support. There was a mixture of joy and sorrow in our father's heart. My brother did graduate from school, acquired knowledge in agriculture, and got a glimpse at the world outside of Orheyev. The workers movement attracted my brother. Finally he immigrated to America, devoted himself to growing flowers and gained much experience in that profession, and my father was left broken for the rest of his short life... Once, during the summer time we (the four sisters) went to visit my brother at school. It was a long unpaved way. We were attacked by dogs whose owners, the "unclean creatures," laughed at our fright and we ran all the way to the school. When we arrived we were received by Reb Mendel, the farm manager. He gave us golden fresh carrots that were cracking under our teeth making sounds like snow and frost under feet. We were so jealous of the boys, who were working, and competing gathering wheat stems to sheaves after harvest. It made a marvelous picture, and it was a pleasure to look at. Still, sad thoughts stuck in our minds: why are the boys taken care of, and the girls are being neglected? A 4-5 year old boy is sent to a classroom, a boy is taught a profession, while the girls are neglected! The girls have a constant role: to serve the husband and the family.

We left "the farm" with this jealousy and returned home. To our great anger, we found our neighbor, father's good friend, at home and he was discussing that same subject, child education, and stating his opinion that for a girl, some knowledge of reading and writing in Yiddish, and writing in the state's language, is enough.

The neighbor left, and I went after him to visit his daughter, who was my best friend. When we entered his home, he noticed she was reading the novel "The Little Black Young Man", by the writer Shmuel R., who was popular in those days. He immediately became enraged, and without saying a word grabbed a weight that he found, threw it towards her, and almost injured her. "Could it be," he shouted, "that you are reading novels, you insolent girl?!" I was frightened, and I ran away.

Figure 87 - Holiday place in the Celeshty forest
The quiet agricultural environment, the forests, the fruit trees
and the magnificent views brought many vacationers here from the city

The agrarian reform and the Jewish farmer

In our district villages, many Jews made a living from agriculture. However, most of them did not have private land, and depended on estate owners who lent them land or on partnerships with non-Jewish landowners. The reform performed by the Romanian government in 1923 made a good change.

Every Jew who proved he was engaged in agriculture could appeal to the agriculture ministry and get 4 1/2 hectares, providing he would work the land himself, with the assistance of his family. We, residents of Putsintey, got our share too, and started working our land. Still, we had difficulties we could not overcome ourselves, although we had agricultural experience and knowledge. We lacked tools and the needed animals' to develop a profitable farm that would support a family. The ORT company, which was involved in developing agriculture among the Jews in Bessarabia, gave us help by placing long term loans, and by guidance, through its representative, the agronom Chayim Feigin.

I can recall Mr. Feigin's first visit (1925). He explained to us that in order to gain more efficiency, we must organize a cooperative. As an organized unit, we would get credit more easily. He also explained that we should base our farm on profitable branches like vineyards, orchards etc. Indeed, after several years of work under his devoted guidance we enjoyed the fruits of our labor. We liked the work, and so did our sons, and the productivity of our farms exceeded that of our non-Jewish neighbors. We hoped our sons would follow us. But, political turnovers in Romania had a bad influence on the economy in general, and on the Jews in particular. The ORT company reduced its activities in Romania, and Mr. Feigin immigrated to the land of Israel in 1934. With the outbreak of WWII we left everything and ran for our lives to Russia, and all our work was lost.

(These details were given by Mr. Guitnik, a farmer from Putsintey, who immigrated to Israel in 1956. His son is an agronom – Mr. Gat in Rehovot, Israel).

Chapter 40

Berel the Greengrocer

By M.R.

Translated by Tamar Rachevsky Milner

Many of the Jewish inhabitants of Orheyev and its surroundings made their living from agriculture. The Jews were involved mainly in: flocks, vineyards, orchards (apples, nuts, pears, plums). Tobacco was also an important sector. Orheyev's Jews were not involved in growing vegetables. The reasons for not growing vegetables were: 1) the farmers from Orheyev's outskirts and nearby villages sold their crops of vegetables cheaply in town; 2) lack of knowledge needed to develop the vegetables sector.

Berel Kruglyak, son of Efrayim and Ester "the Polish", was the first among the district's Jews to be attracted to the vegetables sector. His father was a vegetables merchant, and would occasionally go to a farmer's vegetable field. Berel accompanied him from time to time, saw the type of work and joined to help.

When Berel grew up, the Romanian government distributed 4 1/2 hectares of land to each farmer, non-Jewish and Jewish, who would work it himself. Berel got a plot too and worked it with his own hands, and his diligence and assiduousness brought him a good crop and the best produce.

The famous greengrocer in northern Bessarabia

During this time, Berel leased a big area near his territory, and also a lake nearby it. For several years he transferred the water from the lake to the fields in the primitive way that was used by the farmers: A big wooden wheel was stuck in the lake, and a trough near it. As a worker would turn the wheel with his hand, the water came up and poured to the trough, and from the trough it was transferred to the fields by canals. This method was not efficient and not suitable for a large field. Even 4 mules would not bring up enough water, so Berel wanted to mechanize the system and thus lower the price of his produce. He placed a motor to bring up the water, and he put a set of pipes in the field. He also developed select varieties. It did not take much time for the fruits of his work to come: His vegetables were of special quality and were in demand far beyond Berel's region.

He was especially successful in bringing the first fruits of spring: tomatoes, carrots, green peppers, green onions, onions for seeding, etc., and in the autumn cabbage and more. These products enabled him to get good prices and new markets – in Beltsy, Orheyev, and Kishinev. He was famous as the most accomplished vegetable grower in the vicinity.

His wife, Sorke – from Kalarash

Berel was helped by his wife Sorke, who was beautiful and good-hearted. She treated his 50 workers in an agreeable manner, and gave them presents for the holidays. Although anti-Semitism was very common at those times, the workers liked Berel's family and served it loyally. Many of them were connected to the family as members of the house.

Sorke was active in the farm, especially during the summer, although the family's economic situation was good. She loved animals and took care of many different kinds of fowl and also the cowshed and milking. Most of the summer months, the workers would eat and sleep in the farm and Sorke had to take care of their food. Thanks to her diligence and love of the work, it was not a burden to her, and she did it wisely in a manner that pleased everyone.

E: Self Defense

Chapter 41

The Weapons that were Hidden in our House

Chava Vardi-Yoelit

Translated by Jerrold Landau

(Three episodes from the days of self defense in the city, from 1903 to 1905)

A. The dangerous bayonet in the hands of my young brother

My brother Zvi, who now lives across the ocean, was stubborn in his youth. He decided to study a trade and earn his livelihood through his own efforts. If only he had chosen a refined trade such as watch making or photography, he would certainly have remained at home and studied with the famous photographer in our city of Lukashevka, as did our older brothers Elkana and Yitzchak, who also studied with him during their youth. However his heart was drawn specifically toward "coarser" trades such as auto mechanics and locksmithing – trades that dirty the hands and the clothes. Therefore, he did not receive the agreement of our father, who saw this as a complete rejection of books. Mother, on the other hand, encouraged him and agreed to his plans.

One day my brother arose and traveled to Kishinev to study and work. On account of his work, he joined the ranks of the "self defense," despite his young age. He was injured during the disturbances that broke out in Russia in 1905 with the abrogation of the constitution that was issued by the Czarist government. He returned home one day with his right hand wrapped in a sling, all feverish. We lay him to bed and gave him over to the care of Dr. Bilinski, a Polish doctor who was a friend of the Jews.

He returned to Kishinev after he recovered. After a brief period he returned and brought with him a large trunk, of at least a square meter in size. We brought the trunk into the room of our house that was called the office (Kontura).

My brother spent many hours each day alone in the office.

He invited me into the office one day, and from the trunk containing various "implements" he brought out a large revolver, black and flat, with a magazine that could take several bullets. It was called a Browning. He explained to me that he had mastered the art of not making a sound at the time of shooting. He showed me several other revolvers of various sizes: some were broken in the middle and resealed, and others were presented to me in parts. He showed me how to load and seal the gun before it is put in its case. My brother then gave me some sandpaper and showed me how to clean off the rust.

I was a young girl at the time, and I knew how to polish silver and brass objects with a cream. Now I learned something new, which is to polish steel objects with black paper. I had great pleasure when I saw the "implements" leaving my hands shiny and sparkling. While I was working, my brother was busy with the "implements" that were cleaned. He smeared them with oil and put them aside. After some time, I realized that these "implements" were being hidden, some in the wooden ceiling that was above the space between the double doors.

When father returned on the eve of the Sabbath from the estate in the village of Vorotets, where he served as the farm superintendent and accountant, there was no trace of the "implements" in the office.

That Sabbath afternoon, my parents took a nap as they usually did every Sabbath. The young children went out for a walk, and I left the house as well. When I returned from the walk toward the evening, I was surprised and astonished at the sight that I saw: my young brother Asher Zelig, the son of my parents' old age, was holding a bayonet in his hands and boasting to his friends outside about the weapons of the Cossack that fell into his hands. I advised him to go into the house, but he did not pay attention. I threatened him that I would tell father. However, he did as he pleased. I had no choice. I ran into the house and told my father about the matter. He was also astonished, and ordered my brother to come into the house immediately with his bayonet. The trickster entered the house, all excited from the game and surprised, and stood before father. Father ordered him to immediately place the bayonet on the table. Then he took his dear son over his left knee, and spanked him soundly over the soft place with his left hand.

Our house was astir after the Sabbath. The emotions ran very high. Finding the bayonet made it clear to my father that weapons were hidden in our house.

Fear of the police always pervaded every Jewish home in Czarist Russia. This was especially the case in our home, for my eldest brother did not present himself to the army exam, but rather fled to the United States. From that time, the police would visit us on occasion in order to collect the fine of 300 Rubles that was owing to the state treasury in accordance with the law. At every such visit, they would search and inspect all of the household utensils.

They would record all of our possessions in a complete list, and place an insignia upon them. Thus, one can understand my father's fear. Such a lone bayonet, which was left exposed by chance, was liable to expose our secret and bring a great disaster upon the entire family.

I recall how I hid myself in a crevice at the door of the oven in that room and how my heart ached as I wailed along with my brother out of pity for the thrashing that he endured. Nevertheless, I did not regret that I had exposed the secret. My conscience was clear. I was certain at the time that I could not have done otherwise. The cleaning of the "implements" that I had done, and my knowledge of the secret made me a partner in responsibility for the safety of the hidden weapons.

B. The Cache in the Cellar

The sign of the weapons that were hidden in our house is etched on the middle section of the left forearm of my brother Avraham Moshe, as a memorial of those days. Thus was the story: Our house was built upon a large vaulted cellar, a remnant from the time of Turkish rule of Bessarabia. There was a legend in our house that a treasure was hidden in our cellar. I remember how they came to destroy one of the stone walls of the cellar to excavate it. They dug and dug until another arch was exposed. They continued to dig, and yet another arch was exposed. As I think back now about that excavation, I understand that the entire matter of the treasure was only a pretext, for they went down there as if to excavate, and in the interim, they practiced shooting down there. I only found this out by chance after some time.

One day in the afternoon, my brother Avraham Moshe broke into the house wailing, as he was holding his bleeding left hand with his right hand. He was asked to explain the situation. He explained between sobs that his hand was injured as he closed the heavy iron lock of the door. He was too young to have been included among the ranks of the self-defense, but he would diligently follow what was going on in the mysterious cellar. He decided himself that he should also practice with weapons. He secretly went into the cellar, and started to practice without any training. To his surprise, the bullet that was shot did not reach its intended mark. Rather, it reached an entirely unintended target. He also received his punishment for following after those who were older than he.

Dr. Bilinski also tended to him. He was also registered in the city hospital as having been wounded by accident.

My brother, who received his first "immersion in fire," came to the Land during the Second Aliyah and was active in the Hagana.

C. The Blond Boy

Sometime that summer, when my mother was busy boiling the preserves for the winter, and we, the young children, were running around the boiling tubs in the yard, waiting for a rosy portion of froth that would be removed from the boiling jam at times, the wagon of one of the local wagon drivers stopped before the gate of the yard. My brother Zvi got off, along with a handsome, blond lad, tall and wearing fine clothing. The wagon driver loosened two baskets that were tied with ropes behind the wagon. The two lads raised them with a large swing, carried them and placed them inside the yard.

My brother introduced the lad: "My friend Mesha."

At dinner, my brother described the journey. Among everything, he pointed out that the wagon driver was surprised about the weight of the baskets. However after he explained that they contained presents for Mother, beef tallow and sheep's tails, he was satisfied. The elders broke out in laughter, and I did not understand the meaning of that laughter.

The next morning, when I entered the parlor, I saw the two lads sitting at the large round table that stood in the center of the room. A cloth was spread over the table, on top of which was piled some white, shiny powder. My brother rolled a rolling pin over the powder to break up the clumps, and his friend filled up the empty bottles.

What is this powder?," I asked. "This is Bretolite Salt that is used as treatment for scabies," my brother explained to me. He added, "I suffer very badly from this illness, and I have decided to take baths with this salt."

That evening, the two lads went out for a walk. Mesha, who was a jovial lad, wore a small straw hat with a narrow brim, which was tilted at an angle toward the right side. For some reason, he also took with him a bright, colorful woman's umbrella, in accordance with the style of those times. We were all astonished. However, since my brother had come from Odessa this time, and Mesha was from Odessa, we said to ourselves, "This must be the style of Odessa."

The two lads would go out on their walk every evening, and return home at dusk. The umbrella would be with them on every walk. At times it was closed, and Mesha swung it around in his hand like a stick, and at other times it was open, hanging over his shoulder shielding his back, as Mesha went around with youthful naughtiness.

One day, I walked on the road of the nobility (Dvorianskia, later Alexandrovskia), and waited by the steps that led to the foot of Mount Ivanus. This was a regular weekday. It was late, and there were few people out strolling. Suddenly, my eyes noticed the two friends sliding down the mountain to the creek that led to the yards of the noblemen. Then, I heard the sound of a dull explosion. Fear engulfed me. With a pounding heart, I impatiently awaited for the boys to appear on the steps, so that they could accompany me home. Along the way, my brother asked me if I waited for a long time near the steps, and if I had heard the explosion. I answered affirmatively. The friends exchanged glanced that were laden with innuendoes, and they stopped talking about it. I understood that they were involved with the explosion.

When we came home, my brother informed mother that he intended to return to Odessa as soon as possible. After dinner, he went to the wagon driver. He returned with the news that he was promised two places, for him and for Mesha, on the wagon that was setting out early in the morning for Kishinev. As added security, he took a Ruble from the wagon driver as a pledge that he would not travel without them.

In the morning, the two friends took their two baskets, that now were very light, for they included only a few sets of linen that my mother had time to prepare, and the traditional cake that she would bake when someone would set out on a journey. Mesha took leave of us with great warmth, literally like a member of the family. The wagon set out, and we stared at it until it disappeared behind the corner of the road that led to the long bridge over the Reat River, the route that leads to Kishinev.

They set out on Friday morning. On Sunday evening, we were surprised to see my brother return home, all emotional and agitated. Great preparations immediately started in the home and the yard. My brother and my mother were involved particularly with them. At a late hour in the evening, mother came in and asked me to pour water on her hands that were dirty with clay.

In the outer wall of our yard next to the cowshed, there was a box next to the ground that was called the milk box. In this box were stored the butter churn, the milking tools, the filter, the clay pitchers, and other milking utensils. The next day, I found out that the door of the milk box was sealed and plastered with clay. That day, my brother took great care to plaster the entire tall wall. When the plaster dried, it was impossible to discern the place of the box.

During dinner, as we all sat around the table, my brother told us the following:

My friend Mesha, our dear friend who so endeared himself to all of you, was exposed as a despised provocateur. When we arrived in Kishinev, before we set out for Odessa, I was urgently called to an unscheduled meeting of the central committee. At that meeting, I was informed that Mesha was sentenced to death. The plan was as follows: Mesha does not know the member who was to carry out the sentence. He would be travelling with us to Odessa, in the same train but in a different coach. At a certain stop that was agreed upon from the outset, the train stopped for a certain period of time. Mesha and I went out to attend to our needs. The member waited for us in the bathroom, and there he shot Mesha with a bullet from a Browning. I and the member who executed the operation then returned to our places in the train and continued on until the next stop. From there we returned to Kishinev in a train that was leaving that station in the opposite direction.

Thus was our family saved from a great misfortune that might have awaited us.

Figure 88 - Flooding of the town
Many families were left with no home. There was damage to property and animals were swept away in the streaming water. There were also human casualties.

F. Miscellaneous
Chapter 42

Memories from Orheyev

By Velvel Shafin-Shaposhnik

Translated by Marsha Kayser

My life in Orheyev, where I was born in 1885, goes no further than 1923. Then I traveled to America from Kishinev, where I had directed a school for young children and at the same time was a teacher in a professional school. And although it is over thirty years, memories from that place are still fresh in my mind, the mountain Ivanus on one side of the Reat River with the Shes opposite. I still remember when you could hear the springtime "shushing" of the water from the "Yas" channel in the stream, past the Ivanus valley, and how one would have to skip across stones to the other side to play. Quite often, slippery rocks were stumbling blocks from which I would fall, with new boots, into the noisy water, afraid that my parents would be angry with me for ruining my Passover clothes. I pause now and turn my thoughts to other dear memories of "joyous suffering." To this day I still have a desire to climb up the mountain, the way our gang used to do from Ivanus Peak, from which I was sure, looking up, that one could reach and touch the sky.

Today the wide "Reat" which I used to swim across until the transverse …. "Good friends" wailed to me about my parents, and they warned me, "Be careful! Be careful!" but I forgot, pushed it out of my mind, and embracing life, made a point with my feet up or entirely face-up on my back.

To that end, the winter repaid me when instead of sitting with a seyfer (ed. note: religious book) in school, I was skating on the frozen river. My father, trailing me to Khovodski Shul, where I had come from my "crime" with telltale evidence - a pair of flaming red cheeks, "honored" me with a slap, and I immediately got an old book…as my "dessert".

I remember another obstacle to childhood pleasures associated with the "Shes". Studying in "Yeshivah", which was in the same place as the younger children's schoolhouse, I went one Shabbos to my friend Itzel Yehudah-Moyshe's (Yitzchak Spivak), and we went out on the Shes to carry on, picking up a stork which had been rummaging in the swamp for food - going into a garden after fruit, and now had come along until "The Chapel" on the hill behind Matya Malmud, but to go further? No! because: on Shabbos one must not go on the grass, one could crush sticks or a blade of grass and with the transgressor violate a Torah prohibition. The strict piety had the opposite effect on me. What kind of service to God from good deeds and worship is this, I thought, which does not allow partaking of life?!

But were those notions, resulting in about six dozen strikes and maybe a spanking, obsolete? I will tell about a related matter - how I became a "jargonist" [ed. note: a contemptuous term used by detractors of the Yiddish language.]

Yes, what happened followed private Hebrew reading lessons and then in our Talmud-Torah (ed. note: Jewish school), not long after joining the local "Safa Brura" ("Clear Language") group (see Stirrings of Redemption by A. Zenzifer) [ed. note Tel Aviv, 1952]. During the time that I was writing an article called "This is My Name (Zeh Shmi)" based on the first letters of the name Zev Shaposhnik, at the meeting of the local library, I suddenly proposed buying more Yiddish books before buying Hebrew books and was crowned with the name "jargonist". How come? For what? Running a china shop in those days, my father ordered items along with his furrier materials, half and half, in the first place as a protection against poverty, secondly, so that I should not also have to become like him and my brother Pini (or Fini), may his memory be for a blessing, no craftsman, God forbid. I used to watch how my father struggled to talk to a Russian "fool" and could not. His face would redden and the veins in his neck would throb. I would then take pity on him and run to call my mother, who was a full "Rusashke" [ed. note: Russian woman]. She grew up in Kishinev near "Katzapes", (Russian merchant who sold pigs and pork) and had therefore spoken Russian fluently. Neighbors and relatives would be envious and when they had to speak to a "fool", they would come to her for help. But until my mother came to help, I saw how he suffered, unfortunately, from his not "knowing how to talk." The sad picture of my father's helplessness made an impression on me, particularly when the "tax collector" (not the man from Yampol but the official one) in the company of two "garadavoyen" (policemen) would come to collect the taxes, usually when there was no money in our pockets - and he ordered the "saboteurs" to remove the samovar, the Shabbos candlesticks, and the like. My father, bless his memory, wanted to avoid the humiliation and took to pleading with the chump, as times were hard, no livelihood, not here etc. But go talk, with the tongue in Exile. My father would stand with his hat half in his hand and half on his head because of his head being uncovered, with his tongue floundering between half "goyish" (Kokhlotsky [ed. note: local dialect around Khokhol in S. Russia - also offensive ref. to Ukrainians]) and half Volechish [ed. note: lang. spoken around Walachia, Romania] (which he spoke quite well. But how to use such common talk for the "official"?) At the same time, I would think, is it not enough, that you rip us apart with your taxes when there is not even subsistence here, tormenting us in a foreign ignoble tongue. How easy it would have been, I thought, to argue things out in Yiddish, all the more so concerning such matters as subsistence, struggling, etc. - and the Yiddish language came to mind. Because of this, Yiddish, our mother-tongue, the language of our people, became dear to me, and I saw in it a partial solution, a help in social and public relations, in real life. From there a step further, that education for young and old is necessary for communication of a nation, for us in Yiddish, and for other people in their minority languages.

Later, when the Romanians had taken Bessarabia and began implementing language autonomy for minorities, I was delegated, with the Kishinev Culture-League and with one Ukrainian teacher, to go to Bucharest to demand from the education minister what was due to keep the promise of minority languages in the schools.

Today I acknowledge my sins: after graduating from the educational courses in Grodna, I came to the city of Elizavetgrad to a girls' school, where they taught half in Hebrew and half in Yiddish. I had the support of teachers' counsel and a somewhat more progressive liberal administration, as opposed to the chief assembly and rabbi, Vladimir Tyomkin, to replace the Hebrew classes with Yiddish. Successes mounted from the Yiddish opposition. The children's compositions in Yiddish developed quite a reputation, and the same V. Tyomkin, may his memory be blessed, subsequently advised the teachers from "cheder" (Jewish religious school) to take the example of their Yiddishist colleagues and make changes.

But forgive me, respected reader, I was getting off the path...from Orheyev, therefore:

After my finishing the graduate teachers' courses at the first - Hebrew-Russian - ethnic teachers' institute, where I had, incidentally, together with a small group of Yiddishists led an intense fight for Yiddish, I was appointed as teacher in the Orheyev Talmud-Torah, where they taught boys and girls in separate classes. I finished morning lectures around 2 o'clock in the afternoon. Then the young men would have Pentateuch study classes, where Mendel Naychin, of blessed memory, and I held forth, from which I derived no particular pleasure, and I taught Yiddish and Hebrew with a first class of almost eighty children!

Dear Avrum Barsutsky, may he rest in peace, worked in the school's management.

Although today I am very far from the ideological ties that connected us, (Hershel Chayim Maier - the furrier's son, thinking of the aforementioned Zionist matters) it brings back those pleasant memories of my visits to the 'relatively' wealthy home of dear Avrum Barsutsky and his wife Fania, both devoted Zionists and Hebrew speakers.

Their attractive house had a porch with chairs in front. The big rooms were nicely furnished. In the front room stood a big brown table with a glass cabinet of the same color and a couch, which had also served as a bed for the charming boy with dark hair, the famous Zionist Chayim Grinberg, of blessed memory, during his visits to Orheyev. Off the parlor hall, in the adjacent room, young people from Zionist and also from opposite Bundist camps would crowd in to devour Zionist theories of Sheynkin, Mosenzan, etc. and the opposing arguments from debaters like Yosel Suslik, etc.

The Barsutsky house was therefore a real Jewish meeting place (with no police interference) from which I, like the other members of the Safa Brura Society, derived intellectual satisfaction.

I also now remember with gratitude that home of my then spirituality. Holiday festivities, where one could really - around Simhath Torah - have a small glass from dear Avrum's delicious old wine, served with a generous hand, not only for worldly reasons.

Regrettably, the Jewish "assistant" Barsutsky, whose farm businesses fell into a miserable state, was crushed in Odessa by the people speaking about the awakening new way of life.

I should add, to keep things straight, that our Orheyev also had a small part in this new World Order. When I again enjoyed the hospitality of the aforementioned Zionist circles, as a frequent visitor I would, not without envy, observe what was happening on the other side by the "Bund".

The young workers and employees, whom I had very much wanted to see on "our" side and did not know how to reach - I even tried to get them at least as Labor Zionists - used to gather by Yankel Stolyar in The Teahouse down from Talner Shul. Their director was my yeshivah-mate, Hertz Gilishensky, the crooked "Governor," as the city bosses had crowned him, to fit his physical imperfections. I would sometimes drop into the so-called "inn" where the air was thick with cigar smoke and steam, sounding like a boiling kettle. Sometimes a "celebrity" from Kishinev would come, like the very charming brunette "Susi" Fikhman or "Nechame", a strong speaker and skillful debater. Also a guest from time to time was the "Masavik" Yankel Kavval from Rezina (a Yiskravitz [ed. note: member of the Iskra communist org]).

One time this Yankel, in a Zionist assembly in the Shnayders' Shul, grabbed the Torah-reading platform and began hammering about class struggle on the Jewish street, which the Zionists, according to him, had disrupted. Through the window of the women's shul, someone had scattered proclamations against Zionism and self-rule. The crowd began to run and jump through the window. This Bundist "chutzpah" had been brewing for some time, to hold a meeting which had been called for the Zionists.

On the other hand, in October 1905 they held off capture. The street belonged to the people. The shaken czarist regime was forced to make concessions to the revolutionary movement, which they had quickly suppressed while at the same time fomenting the revolutionary tide. A demonstration with the Red flag had marched through the Lithuanian street to the small synagogue. Doors and gates of the tailors' and shoemakers' small Hasidic houses of prayer stood wide open. Young people, in holiday clothes, hurried into the line, adults following at a slower pace. They were so crowded into the synagogue's wide court that you couldn't get through. On their shoulders the demonstrators had thrown Yankel Krasner - then a Bundist, who would come holidays or as a delegate from his hometown - and when he made a fiery speech, I began to understand the praise I had heard about him as a burning agitator.

The ongoing tragic events and pogroms against Jews, when the czarist dynasty incited the Black Hundreds against the Jewish workers, had slowed the revolutionary movement and called for defense and self-protection.

Orheyev had also raised defense forces, in which there could also be counted non-Jewish workers who understood the cause. And "Kastia Cossack," who was said to be the organizer of the Orheyev-Kishinev gang, was left holding the bag. As after the terrible Kishinev pogroms of 1903, and thus also in 1905 in our town, thanks to the combat-readiness of the Freedom-Force, we were protected from becoming, God forbid, a copy of the Kishinev massacre of Jews.

The czarist regime had made of Russia a "prison of people" and had conducted pogroms but could not withstand the struggle for freedom on the part of all people, when in 1917 they acquired the power of weapons. The czarist regime was destroyed, and the power from capitalism proceeded to crash.

In that summer my wife and our tiny child left for Orheyev from my workplace in Elizavetgrad in the country, and I stayed over vacation with the remaining teachers and intellectuals - conducting political education, I read in "Odeskaya Novosti" (Odessa News) that in Orheyev a pogrom was already in its second day. I left everything and everyone and traveled to Orheyev. I was sure, that I would not find a thing standing with a two-day pogrom. But driving over the bridge, I saw all the houses were untouched. I mean: the "Jew killing" had not yet reached here. But also the higher streets were not damaged. Reading the "news" in the respectable and trustworthy newspaper, I learned as follows: in the town were soldiers, households and families who had left the front and were on their way home. Among them were influential people with Menshevik [ed. note: Bolshevik adversaries] and Bolshevik aspirations. The last, more conscientious and responsible, were afraid that the local wine source, from which the soldiers would indulge, would cause total drunkenness, and so that unrest would not break out, they decreed - using influence and force - to let out the wine from the wine cellars, in order to prevent a pogrom. That was how the reactionary divisions from revolutionary Russia would spread incendiary information with the purpose of exploiting the sinister views of the ignorant masses.

Actually it is appropriate to record the heroic deeds and fathers of the progressive worker-youth in Orheyev. This was in the fateful struggle between the revolutionary and capitalist divisions from Bessarabia. Our Orheyev Fisia (or Pisia), a son of Yankel and Rivka Levinson - the eminent community leader, particularly for children's institutions - took a job at the top of the revolutionary army. A second, Moyshe Gilishensky, was condemned, in his refusal, by the reactionary Romanian-Bessarabian might - to a death sentence. Although he offered his services, incognito, between the borders of Romanian Bessarabia and revolutionary Russia. We need also to be reminded of Yosel Fleshler - Shprintza's - dear Moyshe Fleshler, Chana Abramovitz, and also, those having with youthful ardor thrown themselves into the arms of the liberating revolution and heroically bearing the torture rack of the ruling clique.

Under the fiery speech of the struggle for a better order you were destroyed, my shtetl, and beyond that were destroyed our dear brothers.

Chapter 43

Behind the Small Synagogue of the Market

Mendel Kruglyak-Karol

Translated by Jerrold Landau

There was a row of three or four huts behind the Small Synagogue of the Market ("Mark Shulchl"). Two families lived in one of them, with two four-by-four rooms, two kitchens and a small anteroom: my grandparents and my parents. Everyone who entered this house had to lower his head and bend over a bit so that he would not hit the low ceiling.

The street and the "house" had no attractive scenery. However, they did possess warmth and childhood joy. Eight children grew up and were educated in this warmth, four sons, two daughters, and two of our cousins who were orphaned.

My father, of blessed memory, worked in agriculture and business. He leased a plot of land in a village near the city. The villagers would work the field for a low salary. He himself would supervise the workers to ensure that they did not steal vegetables. However, only rarely did agriculture provide a sufficient livelihood for the ten-person family. He also did business with "Arbshike" (fishing rods), but this business was also only rarely successful.

His partner in supporting the family was my mother of blessed memory. She would get up at dawn to prepare the meal for the children. She sent them to cheder, and immediately went down to the cellar. She purchased all types of vegetables and fruits from the farmers and sold them to anyone who wanted. Aside from this, she would obtain fine, kosher butter, white cheese, Katshkobel and Kash (types of cheese) from the Jews who were dairymen and keepers of sheep. Everyone who wanted such things would turn to the cellar that was known as "the bashke of Esther the Pole," and would enjoy tasty food.

My first visit to the cheder of Reb Leibele is an experience that is never erased from my mind. One bright morning, Zalman Tekel the "belfer" (cheder assistant) came to us, took me on his back and brought me to the cheder on Litvisher Street. The street was covered with puddles and mud for most of the year, and at times it was impossible to cross the road by foot, but rather only by wagon. What did Tekel do? He took two or three children on his shoulders and brought them to the cheder.

When I was brought to the cheder of Reb Leibele, I saw children by the long table, of my age or older. The Rebbe was waving a strap at them and issuing threats through the cheder. Sounds that I did not understand traveled through the air. Everything was boring and strange to me. One day, he started teaching me the Alef Beit (ed. note: the alphabet).

The students were mainly from poor, working families. Some were also of the middle class. It was easy to discern the class differences from the meals that the students brought with them, or that their parents sent them at noontime. The children of the poor would bring dry bread with the head or tail of a salted fish, and at times a bit of halvah. The children of the more wealthy families would bring a warm meal and two Kopecks with which to purchase some sweets. Despite these differences, the relationship between the children in the cheder was friendly.

We had a great festivity on the day of the march for "Kriat Shma." On that day, the Rebbe and Zalman the Belfer wore their Sabbath clothing. They asked us to organize ourselves in rows of five, with both of them beside us. We marched through the streets toward the house of the midwife, proud and happy. I recall how Baba "grandmother" Tzeviya the midwife gave us sweets with such happiness. The day of the march and the image of Baba Tzeviya are deeply etched in my memory.

Figure 89 - The Bureau of Land Registration

I reached the age of six years, and came to the level of studying Chumash. Then my parents transferred me to the modern cheder of my uncle Matityahu the teacher. There, the students were mainly from among the wealthy. My uncle Reb Matityahu set a goal for himself of introducing innovations in teaching in accordance with the spirit of the times. Aside from traditional learning, he invited teachers for general studies. Many of his students who took government exams continued on in the public school. About 1908-1912 he set up a modern school in partnership with Baruch Shalom Naychin, Yosef Pagis and Pini Gelbrukh. This was on Alexander Street, in a large dwelling of four classes. Many of the students later continued their studies at the university.

Figure 90 - House of District Administration

In the years before the First World War, there was an improvement in the development of Orheyev. New buildings were built for civic and regional institutions on Alexander and Gogol streets. Two Gymnasiums (ed. note: high schools) were set up for girls and boys. The main roads and sidewalks were paved. A movie theater was opened. The road to Kishinev was paved. Many people tore down the original walls of their stores on Torgovia Street, and set up fine display walls and large viewing windows in their place, as befits a large city. All of these attracted the residents of the area to the central city. Its business expanded and economic institutions were founded that benefited the city.

The world war broke out in August of 1914. The army draft frightened the community. Many families were left without means of livelihood. The anti-Semitic persecutions in the army added to the suffering of the families of the draftees. I remember a characteristic episode of that spirit: Reb Meir Kira visited his estate one day. One of his Christian workers asked him what is being heard from the front. Reb Meir answered him "Partea noastra câ°tigã" (It seems to be that we are winning). The worker reported on Reb Meir to the chief policeman of the village, claiming that Reb Meir said "Porcul nostru câ°tigã" (Our pig is winning). Reb Meir was immediately arrested and turned over to the heads of the gendarmes. There, they tortured him for a long period of time. Finally, the chief of the gendarmes received a large bribe, and Reb Meir was freed, broken and crushed from embarrassment and suffering. He died shortly thereafter.

Figure 91 - National Bank

In February 1917, the Russian revolution proclaimed: freedom, brotherhood and equality for everyone. Our city as well arose from its lowliness. The Jewish population began to set up communal organization on democratic foundations. The left wing parties, mainly the Bund, saw themselves as most appropriate to conduct the matters of the workers. However, nationalistic feelings and tendencies also took over the community. Inflammatory activities could be seen in all factions. The elections for the "Utshereditielnia Soborania" ("The Founding Meeting") approached. There were meetings and debates. Life was turbulent. At that time, the well-known lawyer from Peterburg, and a fine speaker, Alexander Goldstein, came to us to conduct publicity for Zionist List number 9. The meeting took place in the "Zemskaya Operava" hall. Representatives from all sections filled up the large hall. Goldstein enchanted the audience with his fine abilities. When he finished, the shoemaker Chayim Gildin, who was sent to organize the workers and employees for the elections, ascended the podium. With cutting, fiery words, he advocated for national autonomy in the motherland of Russia, and against the Zionist option. Both of them left a deep impression upon the large audience. They both described the rising "sun" with great ability, one in the Land of Israel and the other in Russia that was freed from the yoke of Czarism – "freedom, brotherhood, and equality" would pervade in wide Russia and our portion will be equal with that of the other nationalities in the country. However, the new reality contradicted the vision very quickly. The dark days of October 1917 arrived. Army battalions returning from the front passed through, causing disturbances in our city along with others, and cast a pall of fear upon the Jews.

At the end of December 1917, the Romanian army invaded Bessarabia, including Orheyev. The appearance of the invaders instilled fear upon the city, particularly upon the youth. Many fled across the Dneister. However, in Russia there was a great chaos, and a civil war. Those who fled returned to Orheyev, and once again fell upon persecution and tribulation from the Romanians. Imprisonment and bloody beatings were regular occurrences during those days. Many of the youth left the city and immigrated to America. With hopes for a free life, I myself also joined the stream of immigrants.

From Yiddish by M. R.

Chapter 44

The Machinations of the Sigurnatza
(The Security Police)

Alec Goldshtern

Translated by Jerrold Landau

Mr. Popesko, the head of the secret police in Orheyev, sat peacefully in his office, peering through the window at the soft snow that fell the previous night and covered the ground. Mr. Popesko thought: Christmas is approaching, the holiday that is honored and beloved by all Christians. How good is it for a person on the days of the holiday! He sat peacefully and enjoyed the pleasantness, surrounded by his family. Nobody would bother him. The telephone won't bother him, neither from the Sigurnatza center nor from anywhere else. He has no duty now to deliver an accounting to the center about his deeds -- to those who disturb him and his officials without any results. He was also free now from listening to the cries of the prisoners with whom his officials fight, and they are not able to utter a confession about their crimes against the security of the state. In short, he was enjoying the joy of the holiday....

However, a worry crossed his mind. From where would he be able to provide his wife with the sums necessary for preparing for the holiday? Indeed, he has lots of friends. They would certainly honor him with visits. If his salary is not sufficient to meet the regular expenditures, how much more so would it be deficient for entertaining guests? It is indeed impossible to arrange even one party with such a dismal salary. "To all the spirits!," he uttered, "There are people born to fortune!..." For example, there was his old friend Mr. Mishkov, the head of the civic police. How fortunate of a person was he. In addition to his regular salary, other sums of money flow into his pocket without effort. As the guardian of order in the city, he was responsible also to ensure that the Jewish workers or shopkeepers would not Heaven forbid violate the Sunday or holiday rest. Apparently, on every day of rest or holiday, Mr. Mishkov had to go through the streets and the marketplace to ensure the observance of the day of rest. However, the head of the police did not behave thus. Due to his great "courtesy", he restrained himself from bothering the merchants of the city. They, as a token of thanks to the "benefactor", would give Mr. Mishkov all of his heart's desire. They would give him presents for himself, his wife and his children, such as textiles and shoes throughout the year. When the holiday arrived, they would surely give him everything that he needed for his house:

food, fine wines, etc. Mr. Mishkov certainly has no worries for the holiday! Not so I, said Mr. Popesko in his heart. I have to find an additional source of income no matter what!. He recalled something. Yoska his faithful friend, visited him and advised him something… indeed certainly a bright idea! You will get benefit from this… without hesitation, he pressed the button. "Panush", the head of the detectives, entered. Mr. Popesko got worked up, and turned to Panush angrily: "Listen, lad! Matters between us are not okay! I have received word that secret groups of criminal Yids are conducting Communist activities by mouth and in print. They are issuing proclamations and interfering with the security of the state. You and your officials are not standing on your guard. You are not imprisoning the criminals. The matter will reach the ears of the central government, and I will be punished because of your negligence." Panush attempted to prove that all of the suspects had already been in jail for some time. However, Mr. Popesko was not assuaged. He demanded immediate serious activities to expose all of the Yid Communists to the Sigurnatza, whatever will be. Of course, Panush had no choice but to listen to the commands of the chief and go out on the hunt… The task was carried out with simplicity. Panush and his people went out at night like hungry wolves searching for prey, and snatched any young man who returned home late at night. They conducted inquisitions until they finally decided to turn him over the secret police for additional deeper questioning.

Woe unto any person who was snatched and turned over to the "care" of the Sigurnatza. On the first night, he was beaten indiscriminately. On the second night they used more convincing methods: scorching the feet, and other cruel tortures until the prisoner fainted. This cruel treatment lasted for at least three nights. All efforts by the parents to save the prisoner from torture did not succeed, until Yoska the "friend" appeared at the parents' house and offered his "assistance". It was known in the city that Yoska, was able to influence the "Poretz" with a sum of money. Woe to the parents who were lacking in means. They went into debt in order to pay Yoska the required sum. The sums that Yoska received from several "incidents" were sufficient to convince the head of the secret police about the innocence of those under inquisition. After due protocol, the prisoners were sent home, downtrodden and oppressed in body and soul. And the head of the secret police and his family had a merry Christmas…

Prepared for print by M. R.

Chapter 45

Orgaver Ladies Committee In New York

By G. Shafin-Spivak

Translated by Marsha Kayser

Whoever emigrates to America, "the Golden Land," finds out that, no sooner does he get off the boat, than he can start to worry immediately about the unfortunate and suffering people exhausted by hunger and hardship, who were left behind in the old home, and thinks he will come to their aid as soon as possible. You are sure about this, that in the Golden Land, everyone rakes in dollars with shovels, and you will not encounter any hungry children, children who have no education or whose upbringing suffers...it seems to you that, after you get a roof over your head, you will immediately immerse yourself in the effort and manage to get money somehow, in order to help out the miserable people left behind in the old home.

But the reality is entirely different. The rosy pictures described before leaving for the Golden Land are transformed into dark clouds. Your own friends, on whom you have built your golden fantasies, are themselves pressed in the struggle for a living...and you look around, totally forlorn, in a foreign environment, without the language, no friendly glance, a stranger among thousands of strangers. Pained, you must refuse to think about those left behind on the other side of the ocean. And even during sleepless nights, in a morbid mood filled with longing and tormented by certain drudgery, the pale images emerge of the old home, and you must, despite the pain and awareness, stifle your feelings because your situation is also wretched and helpless.

Years went by...in 1929, an economic crisis occurred worldwide, especially in Bessarabia. And a cry of desperation reached us from the honorable community leader Moyshe Ravich, regarding the tough situation with which the leaders of the Ladies Committee in Orheyev struggled. The community leaders, Mrs. Rachel Ravich and Mrs. Rivka Levinson, were literally desperate due to the critical economic crisis in which the Ladies Committee found themselves, unable to provide a warm bit of cooked food for the hungry suffering children from Talmud-Torah or Yeshivah.

Stirred by the outcry, I turned to my close friends and we went out to our Orheyev compatriots for help. Our first step was very difficult. For entire days we climbed up the hilly streets in the Bronx and Brooklyn. We returned tired and disappointed by evening with meager donations. But the image of suffering and hungry children in Orheyev stood before our eyes and would not permit failure. We prevailed upon more Orheyev women to dedicate themselves to the important campaign. With their help we achieved gratifying results. At that time my brother Avrum returned from a search in Bessarabia. When we had an opportunity we called together an assembly of Orheyev compatriots to whom he gave a moving and eloquent greeting and described the horrible situation in Orheyev. Moved to tears by the harsh news, we doubled our efforts for the relief campaign. In a short time we sent the collected funds. Our fervent wish, to establish frequent contact with Orheyev, unfortunately failed because the administration of Romanian postal officials was in disarray.

Twenty-five years passed from that time and from the time of the influenza epidemic. The active people, pictured on the previous page in "Orgaver Ladies Committee in New York," now worked not for Orheyev but for the State of Israel.

Figure 92 - Board of Orheyev spouses
From right to left the fifth one sitting is Miss Ravich

Figure 93 - Orgaver Ladies Committee in New York

Figure 94 - Child care, founded by Board of Orheyev spouses

Footnote regarding the writings of Gitel Shafin-Spivak

Mrs. G. Shafin-Spivak was the first to respond to our message, to participate in the book and sent us her memoirs, which show her noble responses to various community organization activities in which she served as a leader. Raised an orphan (without a mother) and with the father a sick man, she relied on her own abilities and earned everyone's respect. What a rarity - like no one else, she showed concern and valued the importance of the Yizkor book, thinking it the least possible expression of our duty to those murdered. Also, in the middle of everything else, she got out the picture of the farm from her brother's archive (a picture that went back sixty years – ed. note: see Figure 84) and sent many letters promoting the distribution of the book and wished to live to see the fruits of the writing. As in her childhood, she had a bitter fate at the end of her life. After three hard sick years confined to bed, her soul soared.

Chapter 46

Rachel the Mourner

Yehoyachin Stotzavsky

Translated by Jerrold Landau

… In days of old, Jews had professional male and female mourners, whose job was to eulogize the deceased, to lament, and to arouse weeping among those accompanying the decease to the final resting place. The eulogizer was an inseparable part of the funeral and burial.

Even though there are very few documents regarding this, many of us remember this custom in our communities. Since the dirges are not preserved in literature, such a document, with text and the tune, is very dear to us when saved from the abyss of oblivion. This document was the first that came to us from Moshe Bik, the composer and conductor of a known choir. He himself wrote down the text and tune of the dirge from the mount of his aunt, "Rachel the weeper." The following is what M. Bik writes about his aunt the eulogizer.

"She was the wife of my uncle, Yosef Velvel Teitelbaum, my mother's brother. She and her husband owned the bathhouse of the community of Orheyev. Most of the work was done by her, but the appellation was for him: Reb Velvel Beder (ed. note: Reb Velvel the Bath Man). She was called Rachel Dei Baveinerin (Rachel the Weeper)." She would not miss any funeral in the city. She would come; bang her head against the wall, cover her face with both hands, and break out with the well-known lament: "Such a young tree." She would repeat her dirge countless times, until her face got white and she fainted. After she regained her spirit and opened her eyes, she would resume her lament. The women near her would accompany her with great weeping and wailing. Her lamenting was "for a purpose," and of course, she also fed the sense of humor of the town. For example they told: It once happened that Rachel was standing, preparing fish for the Sabbath, when all of a sudden, she found out about a funeral. She dropped everything and stood by the coffin. She started, "Such a young tree," and she immediately realized that the deceased was 90 years old. From that time on, whenever someone in town died at an old age, they would joke and say, "Such a young tree." Rachel, who was childless, took upon herself the burden of support and tuition for several orphans. She would send gifts to orphans and to ordinary poor people. She would send firewood in the winter to the houses of the poor, along with a warm cereal of grits in the evening. When I went to the Land of Israel, she asked me to go to the grave of Rachel our mother and pray on behalf of the Jewish daughters who were getting older and were not married, that they should merit finding proper matches. As she was making this request, her eyes filled with tears, for she recalled a child, who was cut off in his prime, and she broke out in her dirge. When I told her that I wrote down the dirge, with its words and melody, for a keepsake, she at first got a bit angry. She immediately forgave me, for I was aspiring to go to the Land of Israel. She learned this dirge from her grandmother. According to her, her grandmother's voice would tear open the heavens and open the gates of the Garden of Eden to every deceased person, may G-d protect us.

Rachel used to wear fine embroidered clothes of silk and velvet. She also enjoyed jewelry and colored kerchiefs. Her Sabbath robes were spiced with perfumes that she purchased from Petru Zigeiner, the chief musician of the town, who knew how to play "Kel Maleh Rachamim" (ed. note: a memorial prayer for the deceased) at the weddings of orphans, as well as haunting melodies, especially the "Avinu Malkeinu" (ed. note: Our Father, Our King) of Reb Yonah the Blind, the cantor of the Tailor's Synagogue. He also would play the Mitzvah Dance (ed. note: a family dance at wedding celebrations), and ancient dances. He certainly also knew "Kalah Badekenes" (ed. note: beckoning the bride), and the Bride-Groom "Dovronotsh" (ed. note: Good night). However, Rachel would come to funerals with worn out, torn clothes, tattered shoes, and covered with a shabby Turkish sheet. She would have copper coins in her pocket for the charity box "Charity saves from death" for the poor. Here eyes were black, exuding the grief of a broad heart that was open to take in the sighs of orphans and widows.

She was strong with her hands. Every Sabbath and festival eve, she would send to the "Bagadelnia" (old age home) horseradish prepared for the meal, which was famous for its sharpness. (People would say that it had the power to quicken the dead and wake the slumbering.) Once she prepared the horseradish with a grater, and injured her finger. Its end was cut off, and her right hand was amputated. She died in her suffering. She was above the age of seventy.

The song is as follows: "Such a young tree, young in years, short of days, woe to me, woe to me. Woe, what is man, and what is his value on the sinful earth. He is like a dish, behold it is whole, and then it is like shattered earthenware. Woe to me, good-hearted and faithful father!"

Chapter 47

Miscellaneous

Avraham Richolsky

Translated by Jerrold Landau

Service in the Romanian Army

The Romanian garrison "The Seventh Hunting Garrison" was stationed in the suburb of Sloboda. Among the Jewish soldiers, who could be counted on one hand, were two students of the army school for captains in the city, I and the engineer Nisenboim (the son of Tzalel the textile merchant).

At that time (1929), Captain Kodryanu, of the reserve (Sub-lieutenant), came to the garrison - from one of the well known anti-Semitic families in Romania. He mocked us at any occasion. It was the custom that a soldier could present his complaints at a certain time during role call. I issued a complaint about Kodryanu, and asked: are we not wearing the clothing of His Highness the King of Romania? The complaint was accepted. That night, Kodryanu went to the city and took care of the daughter of a captain (ed. note: had illicit sexual relations). The daughter complained about him to her father, and he was imprisoned after an inquiry. The soldiers who did not know the reason of the punishment said: See the power of the Jews. Yesterday they issued a complaint about him, and he already received his punishment.

"The Oath of Allegiance"

The day of the Oath of Allegiance arrived. The garrison was dressed up festively. The soldiers wore robes atop their shining weapons, and the mules were carrying polished artillery. They were marching toward the "Soborol" square to the rhythms of a band.

The garrison arranged itself in the courtyard of the church. The captains and the soldiers were at the front. The priests recited their prayers in the church. After that, the garrison again arranged itself for the "kissing" ceremony, with a cross and flag. I, Nisenboim, and two rabbis, the rabbi of Mitaam Yosef Pagis and the Admor Zilberfarb may he live long), who were to administer the oath accompanied by a number of captains, went over to the Great Synagogue. The rabbis wrapped themselves with tallises (prayer shawls) and recited a brief prayer. We then returned to the church, where the official ceremony was taking place. The rabbi recited the "Kol Nidre" prayer from the Machzor (festival prayer book), and presented us our weapons. We kissed the flag and the Machzor, and the ceremony ended. When I had the opportunity to ask Rabbi Yosef Pagis the reason that he chose Kol Nidre in particular, he answered me, "It is written there, 'and our oaths are not oaths'."

I was Appointed "Censor"

The commander of the day informed me that I was appointed as a censor, and I had to appear before Captain Konstantinescu. I was not happy, since my relations with Konstantinescu were quite shaky. I explained to my captain that I cannot accept this task, since it will be difficult for me to get used to the orders of Konstantinescu, who was liable to cause me "difficulties". That evening, I took council with Yagolnitzer of blessed memory, who advised me to accept the task, giving the reason that there has not been a censor for several months, and this was causing delays in the distribution of mail. I was convinced by the words of Yagolnitzer, and the next day, I signed the form that I would be "faithful to the state." I went to the postmaster and took control of the matters. I made my acquaintance with the staff, and we agreed on the methods of work. I asked that the censoring work be done only in my presence. This was important, since there were complaints in the city about lack of order and the loss of mail. Furthermore, it would happen that the secret police with the assistance of the officials of the censor would libel a specific person with the pretext that something suspicious was found in his letter. They would extract money of "silence" from him.

I was very careful that such things would not happen, and thereby, I prevented discomfort among the Jewish population.

Once Captain Konstantinescu came across a letter that was suspicious to him. He summoned me for a clarification. He became angry and warned me: "We will meet further in the military court." I told my captain what Konstantinescu said to me, and I reminded him of my initial conversation with him, and my reluctance to take the task. The captain went outside with me. He calmed me and told me that there would be no court case.

"The Colonel is Sorry"…

A few days later, I received an order to appear before the Colonel in Kishinev. When I presented myself before him, he gave me a scrutinizing glance and said: "Here is a map and binoculars. Spy over the Russian border and bring me daily news." I would generally sign the surveys A. Rasko. One day, I signed my full name Avraham Rechulsky. Within 24 hours, I was summoned to the Colonel in Kishinev. The old man met me with a smile and said: "I am sorry… As a Jew, you cannot fulfill this mission." I returned the map and said to myself: "You are sorry, but I am happy…"

Recognition Accompanied by a "Purpose"

A group was organized from among the studying youth of our city which visited the villages in the area on occasion. They arranged parties for the benefit of the Keren Kayemet (Jewish National Fund), for other social purposes, or for the synagogue. Since I was a native of Mashkovtsy, I was able to receive assistance from the local powers and to succeed. Therefore, we arranged a dancing party or a performance almost every summer.

The large hall that was in its time used for a tobacco factory was given over to us. Our visits to the village turned into an experience for the Jews of the village and also of the region, who would come to the party. The local authorities also related to us in a friendly manner and helped us. For example, the tax supervisor would provide us with wine for a low price. Obviously, the wine brought joy, and added to the exalted spirit and the success of the party.

In the winter of 1925, we arranged a literary party on the topic of "the child in the village." Avraham Malovatsky, Pinchas Zadonaisky, Shrayberman, Miryam Beznos and I participated. Apparently, we were very successful, for the "wealthy man" of the village arranged a party for us in his home and gave us praise and compliments. The goodness of his heart left an impression with us, for there was an accounting of a "match" here.

I Made the Rounds and… was Arrested

On a Sabbath afternoon during the fall of 1930, I went out to the village to give a presentation to an audience of women. However, they had not prepared a permit. The chief of the village gendarmes suddenly appeared during the presentation and got angry about the crime of arranging a meeting without a permit. He conducted a search of the implements, and found a map of the region with a long letter in Romanian. (It was a private letter that was written in the style of love and "acceptance", which would require a great deal of patience to read)… The chief of the gendarmes ordered me to appear in his office the next day. (This incident was arranged, apparently, with the intention of receiving an appropriate "bribe".) When I appeared at his office, he questioned me for hours, and finally sent me on a "convoy" by foot, accompanied by two gendarmes, to the station of the gendarmes in Orheyev. On the way to the station, a young woman saw me, who informed Yagolnitzer about my imprisonment. I was brought to the station, and the policeman who was guarding me told me that Yagolnitzer had sent me food, and was making efforts to have me freed. In the morning, I was interrogated and transferred to the police. Gershon Vaynshtok, the head of the community, was already present, to work on freeing me. The captain invited me, and when I stood before him at that moment, the well-known detective "Costica" (who knew that

I was a Zionist) said to the captain: This is what I often claim, that we always arrest those who are "proper", whereas we do not catch up to the "suspects"....
(As I remember, this Costica used to visit the meetings and greet us in Hebrew, Shalom Shalom.)

The captain who was already prepared to free me was not able to explain for himself the matter of the "map" and to interpret the "secret" letter. He accepted my explanation that I used the map in my lecture about the Land of Israel, and the letter was from that young girl, a friend of mine, who helped the Sigurnatza interpret handwriting on occasion. It appears that the presence of Vaynshtok influenced the captain, who freed me.

Prepared for print by M. R.

Chapter 48

The Rampage of the Soldiers…

Mina Kohan

Translated by Jerrold Landau

It was August, 1917. The garrisons of the Russian army returned from the German front through Bessarabia and arrived also in Orheyev. The commander of the battalion immediately turned to the city council and asked them to prepare places for the captains and soldiers to be put up. The mayor of the city at that time, Pavlov, who did not particularly like his Jewish citizens, forced my father Baruch Kohan of blessed memory, who served as "Starosta" (an official village representative), to billet the soldiers in the homes of the Jews. This was very difficult, for the houses in Orheyev were not particularly large. As well, the sanitary conditions were sub-optimal, and if the soldiers were lacking in hygienic or sanitary habits, they would endanger the health of the population.

Having no choice, my father arranged places for the soldiers to sleep. However, they were not satisfied with this, and issued other demands, that they be given wine and other things… To my father, it was clear that giving wine to these men who had thrust off the yoke and do not control themselves is a danger to the peace of the city, so he tried to avoid fulfilling their demand. However the soldiers did not wait for the assistance of my father. Within moments, they broke into the wine cellars on the main streets, drank until they were drunk, and went on a rampage, breaking the barrels. Puddles of wine flowed onto Torgovia Street. The first "victim" of this disturbance was the cellar of Sander Pagis, whose storehouse was on David Brandis Alley that leads to the street of the Yeshiva. When my father heard about the happenings, he immediately ran to Pavlov and asked him to take control. He displayed criminal apathy, and further demanded that my father fulfill all the demands of the army. He directed my father to the commander of the army. However the commander, rather than taking action, demanded that the Jews provide daughters of the city to his troops, "heroes of the motherland"… Of course my father responded to this brazenness of the commander with a firm refusal. On account of this "brazenness", he suffered a beating in the head that dimmed his eyes. He was brought home accompanied by two soldiers. My father informed us of the demands of the commander, and ordered our four daughters to quickly leave the house and advise the girls of the neighborhood to find a hiding place. A Christian woman named Irina on Dimitri Street took us into her home, but we had to leave the next day since her son, who was also stricken with anti-Semitism, threatened that he would turn us over to the army if we did not immediately leave the house. When we returned home, we found father lying paralyzed. He did not recover from the illness, and he died in July 1918.

Shocked by the events that we experienced, I no longer felt a place for myself in my native city. I left Orheyev in 1920.

Chapter 49

The Jews of Lalova

Yosef Shaiovitz

Translated by Jerrold Landau

The village of Lalova was approximately 25 kilometers from Orheyev, and served as a port of trade for the residents of the Dniester and our city. Boats anchored in Lalova that were making their way from Mohilev, Soroki, Rashkov, Rezina in the direction of Koshernitsa and Heliman, whose waters flow from the Dniester to the Black Sea. Most of the travelers from Orheyev would go in wagons in the direction of Lalova, and from there they would make their way by boat on the Dniester. One would also travel through Lalova to get to Rybnitsa, the closest train station. The riverfront of Lalova served as a beach, and people from Orheyev would go there in the summer to bathe. The trip by boat on the peaceful Dniester in the summer was very pleasant. Traveling by boat was also a form of relaxation, and many were attracted to this diversion. Several Jewish families lived in Lalova. However these families later moved to Orheyev when the Dniester became the border between Romania and Russia.

The boats would arrive at the port of Lalova in the morning, in the direction of Rezina, Soroki, etc., and would set out from there in the evening in the direction of Dubossary. Since there were no hotels or inns there, the local Jews would take in guests. They were happy to receive guests also on the Sabbath if for some reason people could not continue on their journey on Friday.

Each Sabbath, the Jews of Lalova would worship in the home of one of the residents. They also had a Torah scroll. On the High Holy Days, they would hire a cantor for the Musaf service, whereas one of the local people would be honored to lead the Shacharit service.

There were three Jewish families in Stodolna, the nearby village. They would also come to Lalova to worship.

In 1920, where there were battles in Ukraine between the men of Dennikin and the Communists, Jewish refugees streamed to Lalova from across the Dniester.

The Jews of Lalova offered them assistance, and helped them continue on their route to Orheyev.

After 1922, most of the Jews of Lalova moved to Orheyev. The Jews of Lalova played an honorable role in the life of this community. Lemel Brezner served as the Gabbai (trustee) of the Marketplace Synagogue, and Moshe Shaiovitz served as treasurer of the Kapstra Synagogue.

Yom Kippur in Lalova

At the end of the summer, the port of Lalova was full of merchandise and grain, weighing several tons. Hundreds of workers from the village and area worked day and night at loading and unloading.

Boats of all types, including ferries and barges, docked in the port. After unloading, they continued on to the Black Sea.

Heaps and heaps of grain were piled upon the banks of the Dniester.

The owners were afraid of wasting time, and they were also afraid that the rain might ruin the grain. Despite this, work in the port stopped from the Eve of Yom Kippur until the following night. In the large vineyard of the Cush the "Poretz", workers worked at harvesting grapes that day, but that was only when the director of work was a gentile.

Ferries laden with wood from Bukovina, boards, beams, etc. arrived from the mountains of Bukovina to Lalova, from where the loads would be sent to Orheyev and environs.

The holiday spirit of Yom Kippur pervaded the place.

The Jews of Stodolna, Bachushka, the workers of the port, and guests who happened to be there also worshiped in the synagogue that was located in the home of one of the residents of Lalova.

Each of them was honored with an aliyah to the Torah. The guests in particular were honored. The young people proved their abilities in the reading of the Haftorah. This provided an opportunity for them to demonstrate in public what they had learned at Cheder. This served as a test of the teacher, who was most often a Lithuanian.

When the time of the Shofar sounding arrived, the women hurried home, while the men continued on very quickly with the weekday Maariv service.

Chapter 50

Thoughts

Moshe Duchovny

Translated by Jerrold Landau

There are times when I say to myself that my town is like any town in the Diaspora. Many before me have splendidly offered their reminiscences, and what power do I have to add something about the landscape of our town and recesses of its past…

I will confess. I was deeply affected by the enthusiastic atmosphere of the two meetings of our townsfolk.

Feelings of grief are intermingled with the joy of meeting friends, with whom memories of days of yore and forgotten experiences come up during conversations.

However, that which was lost forever will not be returned… Nevertheless, at times, my town floats before my eyes, and many are the visions that I see…

I see the large synagogue in the eyes of my spirit. There the rabbi Mitaam, Yosef Pagis, stood on the podium, discussing a historical event that was being celebrated in the country of Romania – and we school children were listening to his discussion in an appropriate manner.

There was the large Kloiz where the important people of the city worshiped. On the High Holy Days, I loved to listen to the sweet voice of Reb Motia Goldshtern, who led the Shacharit service. How pleasant was the singing of the leader of the Musaf service, and the sounds of the worshippers repeating after him.

By the eastern wall, sat the old man Rabbi Avigdor Rekis, the son of the rabbi of Orheyev. He sat, enwrapped in his tallis, diligently overseeing the opening and closing of the Holy Ark during the time of the "avoda" service of Yom Kippur.

I remember the traditional procession to the Hakafot service of the eve of Simchat Torah. A festive crowd of members of the community accompanied the Gabbai to the Kloiz, after enjoying a reception in the home of the Gabbai. Children accompanied them on the street, carrying multi-colored flags adorned with lit candles. The procession proceeded toward the Kloiz with singing and dancing. How enchanting was this atmosphere of the festival.

The Shtibel stood at the side of the Kloiz. There, the Tehillim (Psalms) recitors gathered on winter nights. Snow and ice did not deter them in their arising for the "service of the Creator."

The Kloiz was too small to accommodate all of those would come, thirsty to hear news from the emissaries of Zion.

The streets of the city come to my memory, each street with its scenery. Alexandrovski and Gogolivski were the most honorable. The communal institutions on those streets were housed in splendid buildings, surrounded by beautiful gardens. The cream of the crop lived there, both Christians and Jews.

On the other hand, there were Torgova and Bessarabski streets. These were centers of business, and the crowded fairs. There was the Synvia market, where there were taverns in which the drunken farmers wallowed. The desolate alley, "Di Poste Lik" was enveloped in mystery. It aroused curiosity and feelings of fear in the souls of the young people who passed through it. Now I can see the Vadafravad (a primitive well) next to the Nicholievsky Church, from which the water-drawers drew their water. The scene around the well during the winter was very pleasant. Children were skating and enjoying themselves on the ice, their faces red from the cold.

From there, we move to the courtyard of the Talmud Torah, next to it. In one of the wings, the Tarbut School and the Hebrew Gymnasium were discretely housed. A small group of teachers were struggling for their existence, holding their stand against the machinations of the authorities, until their strength gave way…

Thus do visions of the scenery of my town pass before the eyes of my spirit. A deep sigh breaks forth from the depths of my heart as I see the frightful reality, for the town of my cradle was destroyed, and is no more. The pleasant and beloved, the hand of the enemy caught up with them.

The heart is overtaken with grief and cries breaks forth: Remember, remember what Hitler and the Amalekite (ed. note: first tribe that attacked the Israelites after the Exodus from Egypt) did to you.

Chapter 51

A Visit of a Sabra

Bogoslavsky

Translated by Jerrold Landau

In 1938, I set out with my father to visit our relatives who remained in Orheyev.

We sailed by ship to Konstanta. From there we traveled by train to Kishinev, and arrived by car in Orheyev on the same day.

This was my first contact with Diaspora Jewry. I came across two youths, roughly my age, who were conversing in Hebrew. This was a very pleasant surprise for me. I strolled in the public gardens. There, I also met Hebrew speakers, who were members of a youth group. We sat together, and I told them about the Land and life therein. From the questions that they asked me, I could see that they were very interested in everything that was taking place in the Land.

Figure 95 - "Boulevard" – in the city garden

From among the few people that I knew, I met one friend, Chaya Mundrian, who enchanted me with her Hebrew. I never thought I would hear such wonderful Hebrew from a girl of the Diaspora. Indeed, she was a Zionist in heart and soul. During all of our meetings, she never stopped talking about the fact that she was preparing to make aliyah, and about her desire to live in one of the Kibbutzim in the Land.

She indeed did make aliyah, after she suffered the tribulations of the war.

We did not have a common language with my uncle, who owned much property. I tried to speak to him several times about investing some of his fortune in the Land, but I got nowhere. I advised him to concern himself with his family and promise them a "place of refuge" when the tribulation would come, but it was for naught. He mocked us and looked upon us as dreamers…

To my great sorrow, I found out that after one year, and perhaps even less, he and his family perished, and their property was pillaged or confiscated.

Chapter 52

Meditations of a Hebrew Intellectual

D. B. Berkovitz

Translated by Jerrold Landau

(From the Book of Memoirs of Yisrael the Intellectual)

I am jealous of you honorable writers and publishers, for you are happy in the Land, and you are able to express the feelings of your soul on every question that comes to your minds relating to Jews. In my eyes, Yisraelik the Intellectual, and in the eyes of people like me, you writers and publishers are not human beings, but rather angels fulfilling a Divine mission. It appears to me that only you have acquired two worlds, the life of this world and the life of the world to come.

But what am I in comparison to you? Dust and ashes! I am only a reader, and not an "honorable reader" who pays good money for each word that comes forth from your heart. Honor flees from me as it chases you, and therefore it is bitter for me!

My desire and objective is to also be an honorable writer as the honorable writers of the Land. But in what manner? Can I write poems or tell stories? But hey! Torah, wisdom and ability, from where do they come?

At times, a serious idea comes to my heart: If only I would come to the house of great writers who write a great deal, I would put a small book in a container and call it by my name. Then I would be happy and joyous. However I am very much afraid lest the true author come and contradicts the living, the pretending author, and what would I do then? How could I raise my head? Would I not be embarrassed and mortified before the people and the community?

At times I think: I will write news from my city and send it to publishers of manuscripts, asking that it be printed as a leading headline or at least a feuilliton (ed. note: as an installment or as entertainment). I imagine in my heart: Is the hand of the publisher too short to do this, if he has a generous spirit and a good heart?

It was the middle of the night. All of the people of the house are sleeping and dreaming. I am not sleeping, and my heat is awake, for I attempted to write news about the synagogue, its Gabbaim, the Talmud Torah, its directors, and other such things – matters of extreme importance. I obtained a new iron pen, and started my article with awe and trepidation. I made efforts to write with clear language and without errors, as the good L-rd was gracious to me. I also wrote a special letter to the publisher, in which I praised him and his publication, which is pleasant to the readers, including every small matter that the writer sends to him. I also promised him to distribute his publications broadly through my efforts, etc., on the condition that he prints my articles in accordance with my will. If not, I would obviously always be on the side against him. I did not say to inform my friends of my future happiness. In my heart, I said that they, in their jealousy, are able to write all the news that I wrote the publisher – behold this is a lie and a falsehood, and the publisher would erect a pillar of disgrace before me until I succeed in demonstrating my correctness. Wait, I imagined, a day would come and you will see with your own eyes that I accomplished great things. The L-rd G-d knows how many drops of sweat dripped from my forehead as I was writing my article for the first time. And I did not try as these ones did. I did not even forget to write the date at the top of my letter, lest the publisher complain that I did not act properly. Of course, I sent my letter insured, as was fitting and proper.

I waited impatiently for a few days to see my name and article printed in square letters, as was my desire. However, I expended my energy for naught! After I searched thoroughly through all of the pages, from beginning to end, I saw the following answer in "an open letter:" "To Yisraelik the Intellectual of the city of Orheyev… Words such as this I cannot publish." A shudder overtook me as I read these words! Is such a thing possible? My reading made my heart groan. I, Yisraelik the Intellectual, worked so hard with the writer's pen for the benefit of the public and not Heaven forbid for my own benefit, and I also spent money on postage from my own pocket, and after all this the publisher answers me in the negative?

After the initial shock passed, and after I thought about and enumerated each word of the "open letter," I thought in my heart that the publisher would relent and publish my article. Without doubt, the editor would not publish something from a simple person such as me. When he wrote: "Words such as this we cannot publish," he meant to say: my words are not fitting in his eyes because of their lack of rhetorical, clear and pleasant language in accordance with his custom and style, and therefore the editor would clean and polish them, to make them fitting for publication. However my hope was for naught! All of my thoughts came to nothing! My letter fell, by accident or on purpose, to the ground or the waste basket.

* This was copied from Hanitzanim (The Buds) – an anthology of literature (published by Hanetz), volume 1, Warsaw 5655, 1894.

Chapter 53

Leyb Stolyar

Translated by Marsha Kayser

Once upon a time, many years back, my Orheyev friends and I shared a very moving story about one of their people, a Stolyar, very short-sighted on the "fine points," who one time in 1905 came to Bet-Hamidrash and stood to say Kaddish together with all the mourners. When the Bet-Hamidrash people found out that no one from their own had died, they naturally confronted him, asking him to explain to them the reason for his saying Kaddish, only Stolyar …became obstinate and did not want to share his secret. He shyly lowered his eyes and stood his ground, so that we would not force him to explain. Only the rabbi succeeded in finding out. Stolyar thought to himself that among the hundred Jews who had been murdered in the pogroms, there were also undoubtedly unknown and solitary people for whom no one would say Kaddish; he had therefore vowed every eleven months to say Kaddish for these nameless individuals. He was very sorry that he could not honor the souls of the individuals with a chapter from Mishnah - (he said) who was he, that he should be allowed to struggle over the Hebrew spots in Mishnah - and so he recited only the Kaddish, piously and quietly, every eleven months.

Figure 96 - Leyb Stolyar

Five years back when I was in Orheyev for several days and met Leyb Stolyar, I immediately realized that this is the same person who had at one time so modestly and passionately blessed the memory of solitary pogrom martyrs.

When I went from Russia to Bucharest, I immediately met with my old friends - Vladimir Tyomkin and Dr. Shvartsman - who had very recently traveled from London "as the first match was struck" for "Keren Ha Yesod" (ed. note: Foundation Fund of the Zionist Organization) and they urged me to join with them and leave, as skittish gangs were "canvassing" Bessarabians. In that region Orheyev was considered to be an old Zionist fortress and we had, on that score, selected it as our first objective.

Well, a fortress… the Jews, who had not wanted to give any money, were quite resolute about the Zionist "fortress," but we obviously did succeed. I do not want to distort history, which would, as you know, get only further and further from the truth. For the sake of "Godly" truth, I have to tell you the secret of the earthly truth: as for the success, we must not credit ourselves, but Leyb Stolyar.

In the former modest Kaddish reciter, suddenly, like a miracle, a community leader was awakened as if by "God's grace." What do I call a "community leader?" A "dictator" who orders and commands, and is obeyed by everyone.

His "dictator-career" began when Orheyev started to receive a large influx of pogrom-refugees. Fleeing from death for being Jews, they crossed the Dniester River from their blessed land of Romania. Everyone knew that two ships always stood ready, the one on the right bound for Eretz-Yisroel, the one on the left bound for America, but until that time came, we had to find a place somewhere for the refugees with their wives, children, and the remnants of their possessions. Orheyev, though, is not prepared to take in such an unexpected immigration. The "committee" sits until 3 o'clock in the morning, we plan, we make speeches, we yell, we become hoarse. The refugees are scattered in the girls schools, in the streets, and we can not find any houses where they could rest their weary bones. Here Leyb Stolyar springs up with a "declaration" to the "committee", tells us that he is not asking for anyone's opinion, and establishes a second "committee" which would work with him and him alone in order to solve this difficult issue immediately.

He does this in a simple way. He raps on the door of a proprietor:

-- "Mister Ghost, today I bring you four guests. Be so good as to prepare a good supper, turn the heat up on the stove, and put them to bed, and tomorrow I will come to see if you treated them well."

-- "Mr. Moyshe, you may lie down, begging your pardon, on the couch, and the bed, forgive me, you will give to the guests which I will soon bring you."

-- "What do you say, Mr. Happiness? You have our guests from across the Dniester? I will therefore deliver one small orphan, and in a pinch, you can put him to bed on your daughter's piano."

-- "Mr. Berl, the Kurilovitser Hasidic Rabbi once stayed with you. A rabbi must have facilities for at least ten people, and he was very comfortable with us. Today, since I bring you only six visitors - it is surely bearable… what's wrong, Mr. Berl? When the Romanian officials stayed with you, you took pride, begging your pardon, now (I'm asking you) to take in the grandchildren of our Patriarch Abraham (Avrum Ovinu)."

In several short days, without an office, without money, without propaganda, without meetings, with only his visits, he solved the housing problem with a profound sense of duty to the refugees. The old "committee" allowed only "patented" community leaders who approached everything with a method, with facts, and with well-defined plans. The refugees saw that with a little audacity and a little levity, one could easily accomplish a lot more. Leyb Stolyar took on "anarchist" methods in order to provide the refugees with clothes and other emergency needs. The border area "does not doze," always new "guests" arrive.

When we arrived in Orheyev he was in the very heat of his Zionist activity. He was very helpful to us in his customary "dictatorial" way. We decided to spend every evening in the Zionist office and there receive by special invitation the well-to-do Jews, one by one and according to a prepared list. But the well-to-do Jews did not come. If it weren't for the "dictator," most of the Jews would have sent us packing without even a "zay gezunt' (ed. note: "stay well" said on parting). The "dictator" came up with an idea and instituted "repressive management." Over several days he became a Zionist enforcer of Torah prohibitions and began to deliver evasive Jews by raising a cry. Every half hour he would go out on his "searches" (for prohibition infractions) and would take "captive" a half dozen and once in a while an entire dozen for Keren Ha Yesod. "Look here, I have brought you 'prisoners'. So good brother, atone! Pay the prisoner's ransom. If not, you will spend the night and your wife will think that they hanged you from a white goat." And the "captives" pay up…They haggle a bit, a ducat lower, a ducat higher, we come to terms. The "dictator" stands during the negotiations and assumes a provocative part. A Jew, a kulak (ed. note: prosperous and stingy), asks us to reduce his ransom by 60%, because he has to pay for a wedding this year for his daughter, so the "dictator" immediately advises him to sell the bird in his stone house on the landowners' street. A second Jew wails like a woman that this year he would have to put up thousands of pots of wine and plums; the "dictator" acknowledges this, only at the same time he gives a distinct wink and reminds him of an important principle. "But my dear Reb Moyshe, why do you not say how much you earned in lambskins?" With one word, Leyb Stolyar gets such accurate information about every single person, that the tax-inspector would want to have it for the city - as the holy gospel says, "big trouble, big headache."

No one could turn away from the "dictator". One time, weak himself, he carried a wealthy Jew into the Zionist office. (Where did he get such strength?) "Here - I have brought you a deserter." The "deserter" was a bit indignant - "We are haunted by Cossacks! Even if it's for Eretz-Yisroel, one still should not carry out pogroms against Jews." Only the end result was that they extracted from him the maximum that they could milk from someone so obstinate that he would fight over a penny. In such a manner the Orheyever landlords and proprietors "sweated it out" for one week, and they probably were as thankful (for no longer being responsible) as a father at his son's bar mitzvah, when the "dictator" sent word that our automobile was already far, far away on the other side of the bridge…

"Yes, I want you to decide the question of ritual purity. Our friends are very good people, but I see that on the fine points - in Jewish matters, I mean - you expect more from them. I am ashamed to go to our rabbi, you will have to make the effort now and tell me the religious law. Just tell me: according to religious law, must a Jew pray?" I am anxious. The "dictator", I think, has discovered that not one of the three Zionist Nationalists "davens" or puts on tefillin (ed. note: frontlets worn on the head and left hand by Orthodox Jews when praying), and now he wants to edify us somewhat. I try to dodge this and give him to understand that a devout Jew must pray, but for a freethinker (I almost never spoke heresy) it is enough that he fulfills the "Seven Commandments of the Sons of Noah."

The "dictator" starts (to pray) but - no. A shopkeeper he knows appears and - good-bye praying! We are excused from afternoon prayers, and we only have to observe the "Maariv" (evening prayer). So do you want to hear something? It happens on occasion that I don't sleep the whole night, and I have visions of tefillin. But sometimes I think - what foolishness! The Almighty is not a bandit, and he loves you no less than he loves Leyb Stolyar… We will soon enough be called to account on the day of reckoning …what do you think! Just yesterday I thought to myself that God himself guides me down the path, he himself leads me to the "guests", to the pioneers, to the Jews ignorant of Jewish tradition.

When the first group of pioneers had already decided to go down to Kinneret (ed. note: Lake Kinneret on the Sea of Galilee) the "dictator" did "quite a job," for which, his wife believed, "death and destruction" would come to him. In those years he was not a great breadwinner. Who had time to work, as you had to provide, with any luck, for so many "guests", driving them over the bridge and finding work for pioneers from obstinate employers. In the evening just to sit in Bet Hakholutz (the Pioneer House), with a tin "teapot" of hot water, which everyone had started to call "tea", and sing with friends happily but not entirely intelligibly, the strangely passionate words of "God Will Build the Galilee." The "dictator" took a break in his unrelenting hard work and spent barely one and a half hours a day in order to keep body and soul together, his as well as those of his household. Quite often there were days when there was no bread in the house, not even some coal to put up the samovar (ed. note: a metal urn for heating water). When the "missus" would sometimes throw open the cupboards of her "poorhouse" and demand what anyone could see was obviously needed, the "dictator" would not, God forbid, lose heart. In reply, he would sometimes begin to sing the Chabadish "Basyanke" song, which he had learned from several Lithuanian pioneers.

> "The poorer the man - the more reveling
> The richer the man - the more pompous
> Oh, what do I hear you
> Oh, what do I need you."

And at that he would snap his big fingers and do a jig - so, for the small gang, it was a clever maneuver: the father goes dancing, let us go to his aid. And all at once the hungry bunch would dance in a circle. His wife would scold and scold - a house full of madmen, "like the father, like the children" - only the scolding turned eventually to laughter, and she was then angry only with herself and informed the dancing "audience", that they had just made her crazy too, and - she went on laughing.

The "dictator" was soon totally "out of the hole," and on a better day, when the pioneers had already started to pack their things, he was overjoyed and went to the photographer and paid what he had as a deposit for fourteen individual photographs of each of the pioneers, who were already standing ready to leave for Kinneret. His wife found out and tore her hair out - "he is possessed by a pioneer dybbuk (ed. note: a sinful soul that has taken 'possession' of another living body)" - and this was his one reproach: "I will obviously not be in Eretz-Yisroel, you will not let me go there, at least let my picture stand in Kinneret, a remnant of Leyb Stolyar..."

You have to wonder what he embraced as managing "dictator" of Keren Ha Yesod. When we arrived in Orheyev, he was fervent in his

"Kineret"-patriotism. In the several days that we spent there, he displayed so much energy and so much power, that it seemed he himself started to wonder and ask what kind of demon had lodged inside him. The hardest question in the entire "campaign" was: how to get hold of the people? With assemblies, you can't get money from the crowd. The "dear brothers" and "dear sisters" evade the appeal. He knows that Eretz-Yisroel consists of two parts: Jerusalem and Kinneret (in the sea of Galilee). To Jerusalem, old Jews travel to die. To Kinneret, young pioneers travel to work. Both have a hold on him, but the young pioneers have a special place in his heart. Why, he does not know. He knows only that he himself would have liked to leave with the pioneers to Kinneret, but his wife won't hear of it. She knows that either the tsadiks (pious Jews) or the pioneers go to Jerusalem. And since she is sure that her husband is no tsadik, he would remain a "libertine" there - it makes more sense for him to stay here, where people know him. The "dictator" provided the pioneers with work. And he posed a question: do you want to present yourselves as brutes? It won't succeed. The town won't believe you. These days there are no brutes here. And he did not know why, only he himself started to believe that his "cruelty" was nothing more than a "performance". He took into his house two speaking Jewish women, who had with them a mute simpleton whom they had "adopted" along the way.

As from a sealed well the refugees uncovered in Leyb Stolyar a "talent" that everyone had to recognize, and there was no one who could not understand in what these talents lay and why they had to obey. During that time his "talent" embraced even the "Tatar-ish" hearts of the Romanian gendarmes. Then the refugees had to travel to Kishinev, where it was "nearer to America." But the Almighty had created a wooden bridge on the way to Kishinev. On the bridge stood "overfed" Romanian gendarmes, whose duty it was to stop the refugees from passing through to the "capital", and when someone tried to sneak through, they were allowed to shoot in place and after the shots - to give warning three times that they would shoot him, if he did not turn back…Leyb Stolyar made a "suggestion" to the gendarmes and won them over. So how? With the same persistence he practiced to win over the Jews: with "a light touch." He took a "Beshenets" (ed. note: probably residents of Beshen') by the hand and led him right onto the bridge. The gendarme demanded their papers; no papers, so the gendarme told them both to "go to the devil." Leyb Stolyar tells him that his "protégé" has already been to the devil. The gendarme shouts "shoot", putting the fear of God into Leyb Stolyar. The gendarme takes out his revolver, Leyb Stolyar proceeds to move forward with the "Beshenets" behind him, he tears open his shirt, gets closer to the gendarme, smiles into his bandit eyes and says cold-blooded: "So shoot! Let us just see if you will shoot. In fact, I wish I were God so that I could see just how you carry it out." The gendarme laughs to himself, acting tough and spitting in the water as he pushes the

"Beshenets" in the back: "Quick - run over the bridge, don't let me see your face again." And such a scene was repeated every day, and Jews traveled to Kishinev, "nearer to America."

There were other important things. Leyb Stolyar was not on that committee, but as a matter of fact, without revolt and without "bloodshed" he was crowned by everyone as the "director" of the town. The border does not "doze", all the time new "guests" arrive. And people pretend not to know that the supposed "guests" are refugees. Everyone wonders - where did he find the words. For such a silent, shy person, who all his years barely smiled to himself and now Leyb Stolyar commands and everyone obeys him. On the other hand, they rebel against Leyb Stolyar's "dictator", and he smiles at being so pegged.

An especially touching moment was when Leyb Stolyar came to say good-bye to us. He asked forgiveness from my old friends and took me away into a separate room "for a private discussion."

"I want you to decide a question for me. According to religious law, must a Jew pray?

"I mean it, actually, in regard to myself. I consider myself, I as stand before you, a devout Jew. Until this year, I never missed "Minhah" (ed. note: afternoon prayer), no saintliness on my part, but this year, it shouldn't happen to you, I cheated a little. Please understand me. I wronged the Almighty a little. Sometimes in the morning I have to see what's going on in town, to discuss with a few gentiles what work there is for the pioneers, to fix up a bed for the Pioneer House, to get a mattress, and the missus - she should live for 120 years - does not let me out of the house. She says - you have someone to take care of right here, better to sit at home and do your work. So, what can I do? Really, a half-truth emerges, as I go to Bet-Hamidrash to pray. I actually take with me a tallit (ed. note: prayer shawl) and tefillen. Only along comes a shopkeeper acquaintance and – good-bye praying!… "I don't know if I was dreaming that "Reboyne She Loylem" (ed.note: God, ruler of the Universe) came to me: so dear Leyb, don't keep it under your hat. Don't worry about me so much. People are a higher priority. I will insist upon it in my own shtetl. I can do without your prayers, but the "guests" are hungry and tired, and the pioneers have to have mattresses. Such thoughts always come to me in my dreams…Say something? The "Reboyne She Loylem" will hold me to account for my sins? What, he does not understand what is going on here? He should go learn wisdom from Leyb Stolyar?"

It is hardly necessary to describe what I felt at that moment, and with a very raw sense of morality, I passed judgment.

"I believe that according to the law you are exempt from prayers."

"And if rabbis, who know the Book of Law better than I, will call me for the purposes of a more thorough investigation and will demonstrate, as two times two is four, that the Book of Law says otherwise, and that Leyb Stolyar is a sinful Jew, I will say that two times two is not four, and that the Book of Law does not know Halokhah (ed. note: the practical implementation of the principle) as Leyb Stolyar does."

Chapter 54

Memories of the Talmud Torah

Miller-Zeitz

Translated by Jerrold Landau

When I reached the age of five and a half, my father took me to register in the Talmud Torah. Already from my first glance, I was impressed with the large courtyard and spacious buildings. On the other hand, I was slightly afraid of the principal, whose facial wrinkles testified to his old age, and who distances everyone who meets him.

The principal refused to take me to the school on account of my young age. I returned from whence I came with a broken heart and tears in my eyes… My father, who saw my anguish, comforted me by telling me that he would invite a teacher who would prepare me for grade 2 for the next year. Thus did he do.

Throughout the year, I took lessons in accordance with the curriculum of the Talmud Torah from the daughter of the Hebrew teacher Michael Groyser. When the time for registration approached, I was accepted to grade 2.

It is impossible to describe with words my great feelings of joy. It was a wonderful thing to spend hours in the company of boys and girls, happy in their boisterousness, or to sit on a bench with many people, in a large room with large windows that let in a great deal of light and fresh air… For some time, we were cramped, for the large building was occupied by the Russian army (1915), and we were forced to study in two rotations. However, when the building was vacated, we once again enjoyed the comfortable space, and I felt myself fortunate.

When I graduated to Grade 3, the teacher Yitzchak Sherman served as principal instead of Krips who retired. There was also a change of teaching staff. With these changes, the children felt a warm atmosphere, closer to their hearts. We literally breathed easier.

The impression that each of the teachers had upon me is still etched in my memory. Before my eyes I can see the image of the principal Y. Sh. Adam, who had a serious face, a self-assured, deep voice, and a pleasant smile for the students. I see the image of the elder member of this group, Reb Mendel Naychin, who was weak in body and strong in spirit. How pleasant to us were his classes in history and Yiddish. There was the Hebrew teacher Michael Groyser, alert and jaunty; and Velvel Shaposhnik, the teacher of nature, who had soft, bright black eyes and was pleasantly disposed to us. His clear Yiddish accent, free of any mixture of Russian words – as many were wont to spice their spoken language – made a strong impression upon me.

His lively "A gut morgen" ("Good morning") greeting in Yiddish instead of "zdravstvuite" that was used by the rest of the teachers, had a special character. His classes brought me special pleasure. V. Sh. had a sense for the dramatic arts. In his time, he participated in the dramatic circle of our city. He organized a drama club for the graduates of the school, who performed with great success when they finished their final year of studies. I remember the teacher Piatr Abramovitz and his wife Fania Isakovna Rabinovitz. The former always looked serious, however he always smiled at the students, and had a sense of humor. He taught us math. She, Fania Isakovna, had an erect stature, was pretty, with golden hair and blue, caressing eyes. She had a good heart and was dedicated to her job. She taught us Russian language and geography. She also guided us in the reading of children's books, which she herself chose and gave to us. We took pride in this.

We had great enjoyment on our excursions, accompanied by our teachers. I still remember an excursion on splendid Mount Ivanus on a sunny winter's day. Blinding, frozen snow covered the ground. We climbed and slipped, fell and got up, and continued to climb, happy and singing from great joy…

Bilah Grigorovna Rabinovitz was our teacher for handcrafts. She was a pleasant woman who conducted herself with simplicity. She wore simple, albeit tasteful dresses. She implanted a great love of labor. We usually gathered around her at recess, and she taught us working songs.

Indeed, this precious institution, with its staff of dedicated teachers, raised and educated hundreds of poor children, who lived in substandard living conditions, were lacking food and clothing – which darkened their childhood years in their parents' home. Their lot at home was bitterness, agitation, sadness and spiritual oppression. Here in the Talmud Torah, when we found ourselves in large, bright rooms, with warm, enthusiastic relationships with the teachers, we were happy.

From Yiddish by M. R.

Chapter 55

Characters And Episodes From The Shtetl

By Golda Zeylikovich-Katsap

Translated by Marsha Kayser

A couple of characters from the place where my cradle once stood. Not from "Aleksandrovski," but characters from below the Market-Shul, below the bathhouse, from "Senoya" and the bridge. Characters toiling, extremely busy, but endowed with an immense wealth of humor...there they hover in my memory with a very infectious smile.

1

Under the "Mark-Shilekhel" (ed. note: small synagogue in the market), against the outside stone wall of the "koshered" church, half sunken in the ground, stood Reuven Maler's "shtibl" (ed. note: small house.) In that "shtibl" Reuven, the comedian from "Lyubitelskiy Kruzshok," lived in constant hardship with his family and his many children. From there Reuven drew his lively jokes and sense of humor.

"Do you hear, Eli," - he says to my father with a broad smile - "look at me, am I not a great 'beauty' Ha?! Yet I doubt if the women run after you, the way they run after me... if only one time before Pesach, to 'rendezvous' in their palaces"...

Reuven does not need special "make-up" in order to get a big laugh from theater audiences. A kaftan, a kerchief, a peculiar ticklish look, a joke from a "shadkhen" (ed. note: marriage broker) or "Batkhen" (ed. note: Jewish improvisational entertainer), and the entire auditorium erupts with laughter.

2

Leyzer "Bass" - the name "Bass" for Leyzer was justly earned. Because what would he have been without the "bass', with which he gambled on life.... Only Leyzer possessed the peculiar means to transform the city's rich men into new-born "paupers". There was a Jewish custom over hundreds of years, to help guarantee that someone's memory would be kept alive, of giving the name of the dead person immediately to a new-born child for a certain sum of money. Leyzer "Bass" would promptly follow in the shadows when an illness lingered longer in a wealthy house... "a long illness is, as you know, a certain death"...and, barely waiting until thirty days after the death, he would generously bring to the orphaned family his expectant wife's preparations for a "bris" ...the rich man's name was "restored" and ...Leyzer with his "wife" fulfilled the religious commandment (ed. note: to bear children) not only for the next world but for this world also...that is how Leyzer gathered to himself several "important men" and relieved their worries during lengthy and chronic illnesses.

3

Moyshe Magich - a hearse-owner, just like a youngster. He had burning black eyes and did not entirely hate "raising a glass"...a Jew like Moyshe was required to make "Kiddush" quite often. But, to tell the truth, he made spirited "Kiddush" with his hearse "associates" after the day's work. And when Moyshe left Yankel Vaserman's "high-class" tavern on the "Senoya," he whistled and danced enthusiastically and filled the air and everyone around with his robust happiness, even the careworn Jews permitted themselves a smile... Moyshe is not drunk ...only happy...a Jew should let himself go.

4

Shmuel "Emes" (truth). They used to call him Emes - as Shmuel himself testified - his whole life long, he had not strayed from "Truth"...For many years Shmuel was a delivery man for matzahs. Tidy, with an ironical grin, beloved by his fellow workers for his practical jokes...for example, Shmuel enjoyed "kibbitzing" with "pretty landladies" and with community leaders.

When Moyshe Klamanovich came into the matzah bakery, Shmuel would welcome him with a melody in rhyme:

I want bread
And a piece of meat as well - eh
And Moyshe Klamanovichn
A colic in the belly.

His coworkers were amused by the last pair of rhymes, and in the noise from scraping floors, the whirling of the machines, his friends chanted the last two lines so long that Moyshe, bewildered, escaped outside...Shmuel was a hit.

Shmuel with his helper delivered matzahs to Pesi Reznik. In the kitchen, unpacking the matzahs, his sharp eyes spied something that could cheer his buddies. Without thinking he tossed the "bargain" into the basket. Rushing back to the bakery... "a whole pastrami, stuffed ducks, gizzards - I bring!" - Shmuel said beaming, "pickles and wine, goodies that Pesi sent you"…

5

Tuviya "Loksh" (noodle) - so why a noodle? Who knows. Maybe a "blind" linguist. Tuviya was not long like a noodle. The opposite - a broad, burly boy, ready to pull every difficult load for a couple of kopecks. Tuviya circles the market and Gitele Volovsky comes around to buy fresh dairy that the farmers from nearby put out at the market. Gitele spots Tuviya and she orders him to carry back to her home the cheese, butter, sour cream, eggs and more that she has purchased …a couple of "chaps" notice Gitele and Tuviya and a devilish idea comes to them: They say something fast to Tuviya. Gitele hands him all her baskets and tells him: "faster, faster, the children are waiting for the food." Bent under the load, Tuviya strides quickly and, panting, barely reaches the door. The "chaps" spy from a distance, and…crash! Everything falls out from Tuviya's tired hands. "Oy, vey", and the "madam" curses. People passing by smile, and dejected, he is remorseful. How could he dare to carry such a heavy load?! Embarrassed, he paces and then he notices his "protector"…a big grin breaks out on his frightened face.

A couple of days later - Tuviya is dressed in a new hat and new trousers. "You really earned this, comrade Tuviya…you're 'really something!'"

6

We young people, thirsty for intellectual stimulation, were very excited about a visit from Yaakov Shternberg with his famous fine arts studio. Shternberg "hit the mark" for us.

The production of the theatre piece "Nighttime in the Old Market" by I. L. Peretz was risky but successful. The young people were unbelievably ecstatic during the scene "We Strike," when a sea of withered hands reached out from under the iron gate on the stage. The scene aroused pain and fury, a youthful yearning for revenge, and the desire to seek out and destroy the exploiter.

7

In ecstasy from revolution.

Mass meetings, gatherings in all parts of the city. In the small synagogue the non-Orthodox Rabbi Pagis speaks about Zionism. The synagogue is packed with more Jews than come in a whole year - the bourgeoisie, middle-income groups and the like. We see a youthful crowd in "Kosovorotkes" (ed. note: Russian shirts that button on the side) shouting hurrah. Above everyone's heads we see someone wearing a black cape with a black coil of hair on her head. Zeydl! Dear Zeydl Bakovsky brings a hush over the crowd and…a mighty silence rolls like thunder and words like sparks fall over the gathering: "Now, when the chains of enslavement are broken, when all the roads of Russia spill with blood for the liberation of all people - do you creep with your reactionary Zionism?! Down with the bourgeoisie, down with capitalism!!!" - shouts the "cape". "Hurrah!!!" thunder the "Kosovorotkes". And dear Zeydl filled with fire…

8

Our "Novi"(Prophet)

From his Pranks

"Novi" (Prophet) we called him because he was an extraordinary "fortuneteller". If the city was surprised by an amazing stunt during the night, we did not need "Scotland Yard." Our prophet Sholem-Shakhna divined it clearly.

One of his homey practical jokes:

One time when all the members of the family are sitting at the table, Sholem-Shakhna comes to our house to sell us a "brand-new" hammer. My father pays him his asking price, with the idea that, should someone from the neighborhood recognize it, he would return it. It looks just like our hammer, someone from our group remarked. A couple of hours later, we turn around and we look for our old hammer - a dark day! Sholem-Shakhna has sold my father our own goods!

During one dreary winter evening at dusk, Sholem-Shakhna walks quietly into Moyshe Klister's courtyard, drives the horses from their stalls and lets them loose, a landlord's story.

A few hours later the building superintendent notices that the horses are gone. He reports the theft to Klister. Klister does not get excited and says to the superintendent: "Go to Sholem-Shakhna and say that I want to see him."

Sholem-Shakhna, knowing what Klister wants, is not impressed and is not in a great hurry to go. The next morning Sholem-Shakhna brings back the horses and gets a "gift" for the "favor"…

Characters, episodes from our shtetl. There they hover with their infectious smiles…..

Revised M.R. (Mordechai Rotkov)

Part IV - The Holocaust

Chapter 56

Yizkor

Translated by Jerrold Landau

Remember the Holocaust of the Jewish people
Remember the loss and the insurgence,
May it be for you a sign and a lesson
To give over from generation to generation
Let this memory
Be always with you
When you lie down and wake up.
Let it be before your eyes
The memory of brothers that are no longer
May the memory be on your flesh, your blood, and your bones
Gnash your teeth and remember,
When you eat your bread remember,
When you drink your water remember,
When you hear a song remember,
When the sun shines remember
When night comes remember
On holidays and festivals remember!

Dr. Dvorzhetsky

Chapter 57
My Hometown

by Dov Sinai

Translated by Jerrold Landau

Figure 97 - The "Scala" on the Ibanus River

My hometown of Orheyev stands before my eyes, with many memories, joyous and sad, arising and floating through the heart.

You now pass over the wooden bridges. The water flowing below is used for washing and bathing, and also for Tashlich on Rosh Hashanah. This is the Reat River, which serves the people of the town for holy and mundane uses.

You continue on, and now you are in the city. At the top of the path, around, the large Christian Church, the Sobor, towers over. You now turn left, and a street is before you. You are at the edge of Torgovia Street, the street of the pure Jews.

You continue on your path and you arrive at Bessarabkaya, the center of economic life. It contains the marketplace with the stalls, selling all kinds of merchandise. There are stalls for vegetables, textiles, household utensils, and a general store. Next to it is the Bulvar Garden. At the edge of the street there is a large, glittery building surrounded by a garden – this is the city hospital.

You continue along the alleys and reach the area of the water well and the bathhouse, having passed over some fields – the Shes.

During the evenings and the Sabbaths, people walk along the Street of the Noblemen (Di Poritzishe Gasse), which is Alexandrovskaya. This is a beautiful, wide street, where there are Gymnasium buildings and government cultural institutions. From here, you go to the well-tended Civic Gardens, with a small river flowing through the center, and boats floating along. There are small tables at the edge of the river. Here, the Jews of the town taste of the fruit of the garden – fine grapes – this is the Gorodskvi Sad (Civic Garden).

You do not find the youth next to the tables. They ascend and climb above the vineyards, as they try to taste a cluster of grapes, stolen and sweet – the joyous mischief that accompanies the thoughts of the youth. He goes up and ascends above the grapevines – dreams are woven between its rocks.

Here is a tall mountain, the Ivanus, which is attractive in its charm. In its center is an ancient rock. The youth of all ages and strata wander around in its shade. Every native of Orheyev has memories of the Skala.

You can see afar from its peak – large gardens with large and small white houses in their midst, scattered around by the dozens. These are the rest of the houses of the town.

I have taken you, oh dear Orheyev native, on a short tour of the town as it was – through its roads and houses in which wondrous life was conducted each day. You will remember in this corner that vibrant Jewish life thrived in the town. It was peaceful.

This was my town of Orheyev, which is no longer…

Chapter 58

The Nation of the Holocaust

by Chaya Mundrian

Translated by Jerrold Landau

It was June 1940. Rumors spread through the city that the Russians had issued an ultimatum to the Romanian authorities to vacate Bessarabia. The Jewish population received this news with mixed feelings. There was satisfaction over the departure of the anti-Semitic government that was an impediment to the Jewish community, and there were doubts and concerns with regard to the new authorities, and fear of the disturbances that were liable to come with the change of government.

Groups of youth organized into self-defense units in an instinctive manner, without any idea of what the community would be facing over the next several days.

At midnight on Thursday night, June 27, the sounds of infantry, wagons and busses were heard. They were laden with military equipment and the property of the Romanian government. They were passing in a state of panic though Bessarabkaya and Torgovia streets, on their way to Kishinev. The light of a large bonfire lit up the darkness of the night. This was the fire of the gendarme building, which the Romanians set on fire along with the archives and office books as they were fleeing for their lives.

That night was a night of confusion for those Jews who lived in Christian neighborhoods. The latter were permeated with hatred of the Jews. The Jews set up barricades in those houses. The next morning, the community breathed a sigh of relief.

The Russian Authorities Arrive

Immediately after the Romanians vacated the city, the representatives of the Communist Party took over the city hall and other communal institutions.

On Saturday morning, June 29, masses of Jews and Christians, dressed in festive clothing, in an exalted spirit, but also with fear of the unknown, went forth in a parade, singing the "International" song. They arranged themselves into rows in a spontaneous manner, the elderly, youth and children, as they followed behind the bearers of the red flags in the direction of the post office, where a delegation of the government was set to appear. The sound of Russian airplanes was heard at 11:00 a.m., and notes of greeting rained down upon the celebrating masses.

When the delegation reached the post office, they were taken to the prefectory building. From there, members of the delegation delivered enthusiastic speeches, promising effusively that the new guard would bring peace and relief to all strata of the population, without difference between religion and language.

Indeed, there was the desire to hope and believe that a new era, bringing with it national and social liberation, was before us. However, already at the beginning of the first week after the reception of the authorities by the delegates of the Communist Party and its supporters, citizens disappeared and were arrested. Some of them were wealthy people whose status did not please the new party, and others were activists, communal heads and Zionists. They were sent to remote Siberia.

The owners of many homes were evicted, and police officials took their place. During the year of Russian rule in our city, dozens of people were exiled to Siberia, leaving their families without protection, susceptible to hunger and cold. Most of the Jewish population was left without a livelihood, since the business was transferred to the hands of the authorities. Bitter suffering was their lot during the time of the rule of the new guard. However, nobody felt this, for across the border of Bessarabia, a great conflagration was running rampant and consuming all of the choicest parts of Europe. The fire was spreading and approaching this remote corner, and would eventually bring with it destruction, ruin and murder. The disaster was approaching like a thief, like a destructive earthquake…

At the end of the month of June 1941, at the conclusion of one year since the Soviet conquest of Bessarabia, the German armies invaded Russia and advanced through Bessarabia to the wide expanses of Russia with almost no resistance. Immediately, an army draft was declared for anyone up to the age of 50, and they were sent to the interior of Russia. The rest of the Jewish population that remained after the "purifications" conducted by the Russian authorities was left without a shepherd and without a leader, and found itself without resources. Before any plan of action could be devised, the German airplanes arrived and dropped a number of bombs that damaged the flour mill that was next to the cemetery. Perplexed and in panic, they waited for the development of the disaster without grasping the full extent of what was to be their bitter fate. A few days later, at the beginning of July, the city was once again attacked from the air, and the news spread that the enemy was stalking near our city without impediment. Caravans of refugees began to arrive in the city from the north, toward the direction of the Dniester. Many people of our city joined these caravans, however many did not make peace with the idea that they had to leave their home of many generations and become helpless wanderers. The situation worsened from hour to hour. The Red Army urged them, encouraged them and helped them flee.

On July 7, at 8:00 p.m., almost all of the Jewish residents of Orheyev, including the women and children, reached Kriulyany on the Dniester. A bridge was immediately erected over the river. The men were directed to cross the bridge first, followed by the families. The men had just succeeded in reaching the other side when German airplanes arrived and bombarded those who remained next to the bank. Many people of our city fell. A significant number remained in Kriulyany completely destitute. Suddenly, news spread that the Germans left the city, and it was possible to return home. A significant number returned to the city, but they found that most of it had been burnt by the Red Army. They returned again to Kriulyany, and from there continued their panicked flight, without knowing where they were going.

As has been stated, the men crossed the Dniester themselves and the families waited by the river. In the interim, contact was lost between them and their husbands. The families wandered throughout the expanses of southern Russia for many months under unbearable conditions, in wagons and trains with indescribable crowding, naked and barefoot in the cold and the rain, under the buzzing of enemy airplanes, in one long nightmare without a shred of hope, as they attempted to reach points of settlement outside the battlefield. Epidemics spread, and countless victims fell. Fathers fell victim in front of their children, and babies in front of their mothers. Those who remained alive were nauseated from the filth and stench in which they found themselves. It was bitter to see the death of the father, mother, baby or child, but it was sevenfold heartrending to see the suffering of loved ones as they withered away from hunger and as their wounds were infested by lice and insects, without any ability to help, due to the lack of a drop of clean water. However, man is stronger than iron! Many fell along the way, and their graves are not known. However, many persevered and arrived in Stalingrad and its environs, which was far from the front. The government dispersed the refugees in kolkhozes (collective farms), and they were finally able to rest from the tribulations of the long journey.

However, this respite did not last long. The enemy armies advanced forward and reached the gates of Stalingrad after some time. The refugees once again had to pick up the wandering staff and wander thousands of kilometers to unknown places. The refugees were divided into two directions by order of the Red Army. Some went in the direction of the Ural Mountains and others went to Central Asia and Uzbekistan. A large concentration of refugees, including some from our city, was in Tashkent and its environs. Many were absorbed into kolkhozes, and many earned their meager livelihoods as hired day workers and peddlers. Many of the women worked at cotton picking and at other agricultural work, primarily on the kolkhozes. The wages were very meager – about 300 grams of barley for a day's work. Throughout five years, many people from our city lived their lives filled with hunger, diseases, and despair without a shred of hope, without any content or purpose, cut off from any cultural or recreational activities. They were immersed day and night in agony and fear of the shadow of death that stalked them at every step.

1945 came. Hitler and his armies fell. News of peace arrived. Hope sprung that the day was near when it would be possible to return to the native town and rebuild a nest for the survivors.

Here and there, individuals obtain permission to return to their native city. Fragments of families, broken and mourning over the lost ones, returned to Orheyev. The ground was burnt, and most of its central streets were turned into heaps of rubble. Here and there, an abandoned house stood out, that was also half destroyed. The few that returned, orphaned and bereaved, pining for a warm corner, found a cold strangeness, a frightening desolation. Of the thirteen synagogues, only the Kapestarov Synagogue remained. Of the communal heads, only the chairman Dr. Nirenberg and the shochet and communal council member Reb Moshe Yonovitz survived. Most of the survivors left Orheyev in agony and moved to Kishinev, where they found a larger concentration of Jews despite it being emptied of Jewish content and a warm national atmosphere.

Fate laughed. The cemetery in Orheyev was not damaged in the least.

Written by D. S.

Chapter 59

The Last Days of Our Community

Ben-Zion Chaimovitz

Translated by Jerrold Landau

In the morning of June 29, 1940, Radio Moscow broadcast an edict that the Romanians must leave Bessarabia. The Romanian population, as well as civilian and military officials, had to leave the region. When the announcement was broadcast, an army force was already ready for invasion. The next day, Saturday, Soviet airplanes flew over the Bessarabian skies and distributed propaganda flyers calling on the population to return to "Mother Russia" and to be freed from the thievery of Romanian taxes, etc. That day at noon, automobiles filled with army personnel arrived at the outskirts of Orheyev. In direct contradiction to the propaganda flyers that promised the "Garden of Eden," I heard from groups of soldiers who were talking among themselves in the barber shop that "now you bless us, but soon enough you will curse the day that we arrived." To my dismay, these words proved true. Within a few days, they ruled over all areas of life; they harmed private business and imposed heavy taxes. Persecutions and expulsions to Siberia began. The first expulsion consisted of 42 men, including Dr. Nachum Berkovitz, Chayim Yassky, Lemel Kupchik, Leyzer Shvartsman, Efrayim Pagis, Moshe Frant, Yaakov Vlobsky, Motel Reznik, Gluzgold, and others. The Jewish population subsisted mainly from its former economy. Work was available. The Russians divided up the land and organized groups of Jews to work in the vineyards. (I as well received a vineyard on the Ivanus.) It seemed that life was slowly entering into its normal path. On July 7, 1941, an announcement was issued that permitted any resident to leave the area and move to regions in the interior of Russia. (The train transport would be covered by the government.) The Jewish population began to make feverish efforts to leave the city, for they were afraid that the Germans and Romanians would invade Bessarabia. People began to flee to the border, some by foot, some by train, some by wagons hitched to horses and oxen. Some of those that fled set out for Kriulyany and others for Rezina. Within two days, the city was emptied of its Jewish population, with the exception of the few who did not have sufficient means to flee.

With the invasion of the Germans and Romanians to the city, a delegation appeared before the new authorities and greeted them with bread and salt. Reb Moshe Boks and Reb Moshe Rishtant, both honorable elders, headed the delegation. Apparently, they thought that no harm would befall them. However the evil hand did not pass over them, and they were murdered along with the rest of the Jews.

One day, news spread that the Germans retreated, and whoever wished could return to Orheyev. However, it was verified that this was a false rumor, and many who were caught in the trap met their deaths on their way home.

The action of the deportation from the city to Kishinev was carried out with cruelty, and there were a number of victims. When they reached the lime kilns of Sloboda, they were shot by soldiers that accompanied them. At that time, the soldiers ordered Reb Shmuel Roitman (who was the undertaker of the Chevra Kadisha burial society) to dig a grave for the victims. When he finished the task, they threw him in alive.

In the town of Isacova, the Jews of that village and nearby villages were gathered into the house of Kolichman. A few days later, they were murdered by machine gun. The survivors were sent to labor camps in Balta and Zherinka.

The judge from Orheyev, Reb Avraham Yosef Elkin, met his death in the Rybnitsa Ghetto. As he was walking to the synagogue, he veered from the route by mistake and was shot. The fate of those who remained alive in Orheyev was bitter. The Romanian government libeled them and oppressed them. For example, they ordered the dentist Dr. Averbukh to clean the latrines, and they forced 75 year old Reb Avraham Goldenberg to work at backbreaking work. When he was brazen enough to ask that he be treated as a Romanian citizen and a senior citizen, he was beaten with deathblows. Many of those who succeeded in fleeing were lost on the remote ways to the interior of Russia. Many were separated from their families and did not meet again. Only a portion of them succeeded in persevering the tribulation of their wanderings and returned to Orheyev in the fall of 1944, at the end of the war, and after the Russians once again took over Bessarabia. However, they found the city destroyed and desolate. A few remained in Orheyev. Most of the returnees went to Kishinev and somehow organized themselves there…

Chapter 60

Wanderings

by the lawyer Yosef Shaiovitz

Translated by Jerrold Landau

In May 1941, the Jews of Orheyev began to leave their houses. Many people of the region joined them – some by car, some by carriage, and some by foot. The people moved in the direction of the train station or the Dniester with one desire, to flee for their lives from the Nazi and Romanian murderers.

Already during the first days of the Second World War, the residents of Kishinev and Orheyev were shrouded in fear because of the German air raids. The Jewish residents remained in fear even after the bombardments passed. They knew that death and annihilation awaited them if the Germans or Romanians would take control, Heaven forbid. This fact urged them to flee for their lives and to leave their property and belongings to the hands of thieves. The train cars were too narrow to contain the masses of Jews and Christians. They went by foot to Kriulyany on the Dniester. Only the children and the sick rode on wagons.

When the German and Romanian pilots recognized the refugees going along the way, they lowered their airplanes, fired at them, and thereby killed hundreds and thousands of people. The refugees of Orheyev went to the villages of Lalova, Stodolna, Zhura and Molovata. They were treated nicely, as guests, in these places. Thus did they wander from village to village until they reached their objective – the train station. After days of walking on foot, signs of hunger could already be seen in their faces. Their energy dwindled, and they became afflicted with serious illnesses.

The wandering and tribulations of the journey took their toll, and after two or three weeks, many of the refugees disappeared. The members of their families did not know to where they disappeared. Some members of the Shaiovitz family fled from Orheyev and others fled from Kishinev. After several months, they met each other at Rostov-on-Don. They passed through Odessa along their journey. Their eleven year old Siuma got separated from her parents and went to bathe in the sea. When the father realized that the son had disappeared, he jumped off the train and ran to the train station. To his good fortune, he found his son at the seashore. He grabbed the boy in his arms and returned to the wagon.

The train was shot at each night. It was necessary to leave behind the destroyed wagons, as the train continued along its way.

Hunger and disease afflicted the refugees in the train. Some of them got out at one of the stations to search for water or bread, and they did not succeed in returning. At times, the train moved along different tracks, and members of the family lost track of each other. The train continued along its way mainly at night, in the dark, thereby attempting to escape the eyes of the Nazi pilots who were pursuing it.

After a month of tribulation, some of the Shaiovitz family arrived in Morozovskaya in the region of Rostov-on-Don, and the rest to a kolkhoz near Rostov.

They found out each other's location by chance. Thus they were reunited once again and lived in Morozovskaya, a town near the Rostov-Stalingrad intersection. In the meantime, we heard of the approach of the Germans, and the family decided to continue wandering to central Asia.

It was impossible to obtain travel tickets. The family remained in the train station for seven days and seven nights, until they were able to go on a train to Rostov, and from Rostov to Liski. Their objective was central Asia.

The train ride with the entire family was under impossible conditions. The women and children were set up first in the train, which set out in the direction of Ponza. Food for the journey consisted of one sack of bread and five kilograms of sugar. However the bread was stolen on the first night of the journey. A portion of warm water and a bit of the remaining sugar saved the people from death.

The harsh winter greeted us when we arrived in Ponza. The people were forced to sleep outside. As a result of the cold and hunger, the child Siuma became ill with the serious illness of scurvy. It was impossible to obtain appropriate food for the sick person there. Therefore, the only choice was to continue on with the journey to central Asia.

Three months passed before we arrived in Tashkent. There was a small garden near the train station. There, the refugees found some rest to the light of electric lanterns that remained on all night. There, they were safe from the German airplanes that dropped bombs. The entire family found themselves a place between the trees. There, they set out their belongings. Someone always remained there to guard the belongings. The rest were able to go about their business. Despite the protection, acts of theft were very common. The thieves did not pay any attention to the guards, and were not afraid of them. They stole anything that they could. There was no point in complaining about acts of theft.

Certainly, nobody would pay attention to such a complaint. The refugees lived in this garden until they found another place to live.

On occasion, government officials came, took the refugees out of the garden and transferred them to one of the kolkhozes or to another place. Only those who receive a special permit from the government were permitted to live in Tashkent.

It was difficult to obtain bread-cards. The allotment was only 300 grams per person. The children were always sick and the adults always hungry.

The ride in a transport train from Tashkent to Odessa lasted for a month. We arrived in Kishinev on Passover. At the time, of course, it was difficult to find a place to live. One of us went to Orheyev with the hope that we would find a place to live there, but after he saw the terrible destruction, he retraced his steps. Only two rooms remained of the house in which the family of Moshe Yonovitz lived. Later we moved to Chernovits and from there to Romania. We arrived in the Land at the end of 1950.

Chapter 61

Rescue Missions

(From the archives of the lawyer Shaiovitz)

Translated by Jerrold Landau

Much has been written about the murder that was carried out against the Jews of Bessarabia and Romania on their way from Orheyev and other communities to Transnistria. Much time has passed since then, and many things have been forgotten. However, the terrifying impression obtained from one news article that I read at the time in a Romanian-Jewish newspaper still remains etched in my mind.

The following is a summary of the words of that article about the task of the lawyer A. Shapira. (The lawyer A. Shapira was a native of Chinisheutsy in the region of Orheyev.)

You my brothers, please turn your attention for a moment from your private worries about your property that was pillaged, about your homes that were destroyed, about your money that was lost, about your status that has moved out of the world. Turn your ears to the following words:

One morning in November 1941, the well-known lawyer Avraham Shapira came to me, perplexed and emotional. He started telling the following gloomy story.

"I have just arrived from Kishinev (I dressed up in captain's clothing to make it here, for civilians were forbidden to move along the roads), with the purpose of alerting Dr. Filderman about the dangerous situation in which the Jews of Bessarabia find themselves. Every day, the danger hovers about that they might be transported across the Dniester. The Jewish leaders in Bucharest are duty bound to take action immediately in order to avert this terrible decree. Some have already been expelled, and the rest await their fate within the coming days. To our ill fortune, the weather is also bad, with rain, cold and mud. What can we do? Gloomy despair consumes our essence. We await your answer."

Pale and emotional, he awaits our answer, and we have no words in our mouth. With us is also Dr. Shafran, the chief rabbi. With weak voices we utter half words. We have already tried to prevent them, but to no avail... The authorities do not answer our requests.

We attempt to comfort him by stating that Dr. Filderman continues to deal with the matter, and perhaps he might succeed at the last moment in averting the harsh decree. "Perhaps a miracle will take place! Let us wait another 2-3 days…" Shapira is shaken. G-d forbid, my masters! It will be late, too late for any good! He adds – "I intend to return to Kishinev immediately. I promised to return to the ghetto tomorrow." "We gaze into the pale face of Shapira and tears choke his throat. Finally, Dr. Filderman arrives. To our dismay, he also repeated the stubborn refusal of the authorities to change their decision regarding the Jews of Kishinev. "There is no hope at all for salvation.", he states in agony. One of us advised that Shapira should save himself and remain in Bucharest, however he refused. "I am the acting chairman of the community of Kishinev, and I cannot leave it in a time of distress to save my flesh. I must return to them, come what may. Wherever it is decreed that they should go, I will also go."

I met a Jew from Kishinev in 1944, one of the survivors of Transnistria. With trembling, I asked about the fate of the lawyer Shapira. He related thus: Two days after Shapira returned from his mission for the benefit of the Jews of Kishinev, the decree of expulsion of the Jewish population was issued. They were sent in three transports. Shapira went in the first transport. Eyewitnesses relate that, 15-20 kilometers from Kishinev, the deportees were commanded to remove their clothes and shoes, and to give over their money. Those who did not comply were shot on the spot.

Shapira also was among those that fell. The person who risked his life to save the Jews of Bessarabia at the last minute before the deportation perished along with them. May his memory be blessed!

Edited by Y. Sh.

Chapter 62

Where Does One Run To ?!

By Riva Milshteyn-Rozenfeld

Translated by Marsha Kayser

In memory of my husband, a precious and noble person,
Yitzchak son of Avrum Milshteyn

How difficult it is to dig up memories from that accursed time of such savage cruelty in 1940. What befell me, with my two tiny children? What did we have to go through in order to be affected so powerfully by those deep memories? It is too painful: even in the rare event when life brings you something - a happy event - to enjoy, a smile spreads instinctively across your face, and you want to let go of the sadness from your crying heart - the rare smile is only on the outside. But the pain remains - incurable.

Yes, hard to remember that dark chapter, which one wants to forget. Still, I will try to recall only those things that lay so heavy on my heart.

Bright summer 1941: the overblown friendship between the Soviets and Germans had collapsed. The political situation brought on the German assault. Everyone trembled for tomorrow. But the survival instinct kept terrifying thoughts at bay, as the rapid assault approached…"Maybe, maybe the storm will pass over us and not touch us…"

In those dark days, after sending off my unforgettable husband and best friend Isaak Abramovich Milshteyn to Siberia, my boys and I were supported by my uncle Itzel Rozenfeld in Orheyev. With us there were his daughter - dentist Liza Naydelman, Gerisha Rozenfeld his wife, and Veva and Chasya their children. With trembling and terror we waited out the charge but no one's wildest fantasy could imagine to what extent the czars would blow up…

In the clear early morning I went out in the street and saw many shocked and shaken people fleeing. Many had heavy packs on their backs. Petrified, I remained glued to the spot, looking at the terrifying picture, not absorbing it, too dazed by what was happening.

Suddenly, I spotted Udel Snitkovsky-Shistik. I went up to her and asked what was happening. She stared at me in amazement. "What, you don't know that Hitler's air force is approaching Kishinev and their population is fleeing?"

I immediately returned to the house and told everyone about the calamity that was coming.

Shaken by the unexpected announcement, the household debated various proposals. "We should pack up now and flee," others - "we should wait." "Where can one run. From death, one cannot hide." "Maybe the calamity won't happen. And if we are destined to die, could it at least happen in our own beds." Frightened, I ran to my brother-in-law Yosel Milshteyn for a piece of advice. Where we waited and thought, we heard a faint noise from an enemy plane. Frightened, we ran to find a hiding place…For two whole days we pondered, run or not. In time there were widespread rumors that the Soviets would let Bessarabia go, setting fire to everything. There was great panic. There was no time to think…but with what does one flee, and where does one go?

With the Current

I went to my brother-in-law again. He had looked for a truck (this was not at all simple, as all equipment had been mobilized), and I and my children with my brother-in-law and his family moved with the current of evacuees. Not only was it heart-breaking and tragic to have to escape into unknown territory, but for me it was the separation from all my relatives and friends, with whom I had spent the saddest and most difficult days of my life, after sending off the dearest love of my life to Siberia. I found with them a warm welcome and much earnest consolation and had now to desert them, not knowing what the unhappy morning would bring them (they actually were killed).

The major tributary flowed straight to the Dniester River and from there over to Soviet territory. For the first time I understood the substance of eminent artists' paintings of "The Eternal Wanderer," which I had never seen for what it really was, having seen only the imaginary artistic concepts. And now here I was with my children, one among many sad thousands, taking themselves to faraway and unfamiliar places and delivering themselves to oblivion and fate, terrified of the enemy planes shooting from high in the bright skies with death and devastation…

In Kriulyany we had to halt a few days, because the bombing raids had damaged the ferry. There I encountered many acquaintances from Orheyev and Kishinev (the Raviches, Yosel Munder and wife, Mineylov and family, the doctor Vaynshtok and wife, Ita and Veva Rozenfeld etc.)

Not expecting to be able to cross the Dniester to the town of Kriulyany, we moved, with many others, to Vada-Luy-Voda. But there we could not cross either. All this time the German planes pursued us and continued the bombing. Where the bombs were falling, we sought protection under the thicket of trees near the border forest. Meanwhile we soon ran short of the meager provisions we had prepared, and our hungry stomachs, especially the children's, were empty.

Driven Off the Enemy?

Germans 60 kilometers and whoever wants to could turn around and go home. I, among many others, also decided to return to Kishinev. As it was, we looked for a peasant, who drove us to the station building in Kishinev and threw us out with our few bags. Not finding someone to drive us into the city, I had to leave the children with my brother-in-law's family and look for someone who would take us into the city.

Tired and weak, I reached Favlovski Street and was terrified to find the place empty, everything locked, no living soul to be seen. Although it was a light summer day, everything looked misty and sad. Suddenly I heard an explosion and a racket from an invisible airplane. Instinctively, I fell to the ground and very quickly thereafter came a second explosion from the direction of the terminal. Shaking with fear for my children, I ran around looking for anyone, to get the children from the station. Finally I met the Brillman family. Mr. Brillman seemed like an angel to me, when he looked for a wheelbarrow and went with me to the station. We found the children unharmed and we returned to the Brillmans.

It's Burning

Late on the third night Brillman awakened me. I looked out the window. Fire! Shocked, we rushed outdoors…The skies were ablaze. Huge sparks fell on our heads. Thick black smoke filled the air in the houses. Frightened, people ran gasping from the smoke. We looked for a hiding place for ourselves. We went into a house by a church, where there were thick trees, and we caught our breath. There we spent the night. In the morning I left to look for a means to leave the city. But the search was futile; there was no way out, except to walk. I went to Tiabashevski Street to my friends, the Goldenberg family, to say good-bye. There I captured an image that pierced my heart and which I cannot forget. When I entered their house and met the old man, sick and weak, begging for mercy from their only daughter Basya, I saw that she wanted to save herself and flee with everyone. But she said categorically that to leave her parents behind would be dangerous. I used all my tricks to persuade her that she should save her young life, because her parents could not flee. With many tears, I said farewell to them, taking my growing silent pain for the parents, and for Basya's self-sacrifice, in order to bear their dire fate with her parents.

Weak, with not an ounce of strength left, I returned to the children, we took some food and a basket of small things for them, and we ran to the station.

During that time the bombing had intensified, and crowds of people were running back and away from the station, holding us up, warning us not to proceed to the station, because the entire region was under attack. How I wanted to turn around, but my older son grabbed my hand and shouted, "Mama! I want to run further. If we choose now not to flee, we will never see our father again. Whatever happens, happens" and he started to run ahead.

Alone on the Empty Field

The child's determined words and bold action were intense. I thought no more, and we ran after him under the fire and smoke, avoiding the station. We looked around, finding ourselves in an empty field outside the city and all alone. No living creature except us. Tired and weak, we fell on the bare ground under the burning sun. I looked around and spotted a military transport approaching. I went up to an older officer and with tears in my eyes said to him "Tovarisch [ed. note: Comrade], you are probably a father with children and you can sympathize with me, help me, save my children." He looked at the children and at my elderly mother and immediately called over a driver and ordered him to drive us to the entrance of the nearby train station where there was supposedly a troop train for transporting refugees.

We got right into the car. But the joy did not last long. After riding several kilometers, a military man stopped us and ordered us out of the car, because he was requisitioning it to go to the front. Tears and begging were of no help. We were out of the car and were left again alone in the field. Where are we and where do we have to go? Circumstances forced us on further. Looking for a miracle… and we again realized there were marching military divisions. But not so much as one of them wanted to look over at us, avoiding our desperate shouting and pleading. Finally one of them took pity and took us up in a wagon and brought us within reach of the train station at Bykovetz. There we met transports waiting for the homeless, our Jewish brethren, to send deep into Russia. We went where they were jamming people into the train and immediately were thrown onto the filthy bare floor, not having something to spread underneath us. In a couple of minutes the locomotive gave a wild fearful whistle and blew steam, pulling out of the station and further away from the enemy's air attacks.

The fast tearing away from the place, the dizzying, disappearing hundred kilometers under the sound of the train, carrying us through strange places far from home - I realized quickly how it would break my heart…Now the best and the richest pages from my life story were torn away…and a new leaf, a leaf with inhuman humiliation, from indescribable bitter hunger, hardship and mental anguish and rivers of tears…the page from…homelessness taking shape in my heart.

Only those who have experienced the loss of home still feel the taste of what would have been. Whoever has not experienced the suffering can in no way comprehend it. Consider all the misery, what happened to us early on in the first days after leaving Kishinev behind; it was like a background to which we had to become accustomed on the way to anywhere in far-off Russia and to anywhere in the areas where we were cast away. The second day out of Bykovetz we came to Tiraspol. There we had to change to a second transport that would take us further into Russia. The cars of the train were soon overcrowded. With much effort, we got ourselves into a car. There to our delight we met people we knew from Kishinev. I had been on my own and had not known to buy food, which was soon hard to come by as a matter of course. Finding ourselves among people from home, certainly for me, lightened the misery, with a good word and a chat and essentials that they shared from their limited provisions with me and also with my children. But how to say, they were themselves alone and limited in what they had, so my shy children endured more hunger.

From time to time, they struggled with each other, wanting to still the hunger. Fear came over me seeing them suffer and possibly, God forbid, dying from hunger. At least from time to time, as we came across military transports on the way, they would share a piece of bread or a little soup, but it wasn't enough to stop the hunger. In every train station, we would throw ourselves at the water-cranes and drink up to silence the hunger. On the third day my older child fainted. Fear for the children's fate forced me, at the first opportunity, to remain in a settlement, maybe there I would take something to eat. In the first station where our train stopped, I left our good friends and got off in order to find a little food.

In the Hands of Destiny

With a very heavy mood, I left the friendly people, who had been so kind to my children and who had lightened our suffering and loneliness. I thought that the evacuation would surely proceed in a certain direction and we would meet again. But what happened was otherwise, a nod to the indiscriminate hand of fate. I with my children and mother were saved from certain violent death. The transport, which we had left, went away in the direction of Piatigorsk, where the Hitlerites savagely attacked, killing the entire transport. Because of a miracle, we again survived. After long torment, we came to Krasnodar neighborhood (in Karinovka village.) There we encountered many people from Orheyev and were especially gladdened to see our former beloved teacher Mikhael Groyser, who had already lived there (in Krasnodar) a long time with his children. This again demonstrated how the person is at the mercy of blind fate. I still shudder now, when I am reminded. In Krasnodar I encountered Avrum Lipshin and family. Our shared happiness was indescribable. He related how, as he had a 'good arrangement' in a nearby settlement, Masyedovka, is a bookkeeper in a plant there, and that his wife Tzilia works at her profession (dentist), he suggested that we come to them. I was delighted to accept the proposal. Only my Tsevika happened to become sick from scarlet fever and I could not travel to them then. Meanwhile the Hitlerites approached Krasnodar. I called out for Lipshin to rescue us. My view was that we must, based on newspaper reports, leave the neighborhood as many transports had already done. I could not prevail upon Lipshin. He returned to Masyedovka and I went away with the evacuation. We were saved, Avrum, Tzilia and also others there died tragically.

Chapter 63

Orheyev in 1957

by M. Frayman

Translated by Jerrold Landau

We hereby bring the description of Y. Frayman of Orheyev after the Holocaust and destruction passed over it. Y. Frayman arrived in the Land from Orheyev in 1957. There, he was in the center of Jewish life. Therefore, it is possible to relate to his story as a historical document of the town and the Jews who live there presently.

In his description, he brings to us a picture of life in the town from the era after the Second World War, when the Holocaust survivors began to return to the towns of Bessarabia from their exile.

His story completes the picture of the events of the Jews of Orheyev after the Holocaust. It is the most detailed and clearest greeting that has come to us from Russia of the most recent era, and I believe that it is also the final one, which will conclude the book of Orheyev.

We will not dwell on that part of his story that is known to us from before, and on those things about which others have already written in the book. We will not detail the terrible personal tragedy, the tribulations and suffering that were the lot of Y. Frayman from the time he fled the city until he returned to its ruins at the end of the war. Over the years – Y. Frayman relates – my family and I wandered along a route that was not a route with an endless stream of refugees – thousands of Jews, women, men, and children who were fleeing from fear of the battalions. However, their flight did not prevent the cruel fate that awaited them. The enemy airplanes cut them down along the roads and in the open fields, felling many victims. Only very few escaped. A few succeeded in returning to the town. Frayman and his family were among those.

When he returned to Orheyev, he did not find the town or its Jews. No remnant remained of his house and of the entire street upon which he lived for many years. Only a small area in the east of the city remained complete. The entire area that was populated by Jews was turned into a ruin. Few people, half shadows and half men, walked on the dirt of these ruins, digging through the mounds of ruins as they searched for a spark of their lives of yesterday. These were people who returned from the expulsion, were without hope, consumed with despair, and afflicted with hunger. A few were from Orheyev, and the rest were from the towns and villages of the area.

In this gloomy atmosphere where people walked about as mourners, the life force continued to strengthen. These Jews along with Y. Frayman began everything from scratch. The ruins were re-erected and improved. Some of the ruins of Orheyev were rebuilt.

At first, they wished to reconstruct some sort of synagogue. To this end, they rented the Kapestary Shtibel, the only synagogue that was designated to serve as a gathering place for the Jews in a place where they could pour out their hearts to each other. Of course, officially, this was a house of prayer.

At the end of this holy task, they started to restore the cemetery. There were two aspects to this restoration: the entire eastern fence, and many of the monuments that had been destroyed. Many of them were taken by the local non-Jewish population for their personal needs. Stolen monuments were also used for communal buildings.

Once a storm broke out, and strong thunder damaged the mill that once had belonged to Gluzgold. The building fell, and 28 corpses were removed from under the ruins, including 7 Jews. Monuments from the Jewish cemetery were exposed among the stones of the ruin. After this incident, the thieves began to return the stones to the cemetery.

Slowly but surely, Jewish life began to grow there. A Jewish community council was established, headed by Y. Frayman. Of course, these activities were dependent on a permit from the local Soviet authorities, with the exception of the appointment of the chairman, which was delegated by the local authorities and required a permit from the "Rispulkum" in Kishinev. (The Rispulkum presented a document which noted the name of the candidate, and which had the signature of 20 Soviet-Jewish citizens from that city.) According the law, each community had to have a rabbi in addition to a chairman. A similar procedure took place with regard to the selection of a communal rabbi, with the addition of the need for letters of recommendation from two rabbis from two large cities of the U.S.S.R. Officially, there was no contact between one community and another, and between one rabbi and another. The connection between them was through the intermediary of the Ministry of Cults and Culture. In accordance with that law, Y. Frayman was selected as the chairman of the communal council. Later, he was authorized by the authorities to serve as the rabbi of the community. He served in these roles until he made aliyah to the Land.

Approximately 450 Jewish families live in Orheyev today. Most are old timers of the city who returned. Some of them are Jews from the villages of the region. Jews did not return at all to the villages, and therefore, one cannot find Jews in the nearby villages. These Jews earn their livelihood primarily from trades, official positions, and free professions. Some of them are organized into cooperatives: shoemakers, tailors, carpenters, locksmiths, and others. There are no Jews working in building and street paving, other than Jewish engineers. There are Jewish doctors and teachers. There are no Jewish schools. Until the age of 11-12, children do not receive nationalistic education at home. However, when they get older, the desire to know more about Jews is awakened in them. Longings for Jewish life are awakened. Of course, as they get older, a longing for Israel is awakened. Most of the children are circumcised at birth, except for the children whose parents hold high government positions. Most speak Yiddish to their children. However, at school and on the street, Russian and Moldavian are used.

Jews go to the synagogue to pray every day of the week. However, on Sabbaths and Jewish holidays, the synagogue is too small to accommodate all of those who come. The courtyard and entryways are also filled to capacity. The non-Jewish population also is restricted in religious affairs, but not to the same degree as the Jewish population.

The synagogues that were not destroyed serve other purposes. The large Kloiz is an institution for the handicapped. The Shister Shul (Shoemaker's Synagogue) has turned into a cooperative carpentry shop. The Yeshiva has turned into a dormitory. The Jewish youth desire higher education in university. Of course, this is not always possible. They know what is going on in Israel. (From letters, every detail is spread around from mouth to ear.) Jews have no role at all in the civic leadership and the police. The relationship between the Jews and the general population that numbers approximately 25,000 souls is not good. In the most recent period, several industrial enterprises have opened, primarily based upon local raw materials that service the agricultural sector. There are two flourmills, and a canning factory that employs 50-60 people and produces juice and jam from local produce. There is a beer factory that exports its products to Kishinev. There are limekilns, and a factory for tiles and pipes. There is a textile factory that also produces blankets. There is a large winepress that produces wine from the grapes of the kolkhozes in the area.

Thus, the city has arisen and continues anew upon its old ruins. It is possible to surmise that the city will develop better than it was previously. However, we Jews have no part in it.

We only have sad memories that are tied with the old cemetery and the chilling, gloomy reality. Its Jews have only one hope – Israel.

Transcribed by M. Frank

Chapter 64

Hertz Barinboym of blessed memory

Translated by Jerrold Landau

Figure 98 - Hertz Barinboym

Hertz was educated in the traditional spirit. Hertz made aliya to the Land together with his mother at the age of 13. His mother decided to return to Orheyev due to difficulties in absorption, and she pressed Hertz to return along with her and not abandon her in her old age. Therefore, he returned to the city. Nevertheless, Hertz remained committed to the Zionist idea and was active in the movement. He donated generously to the funds and the community. He was a member of the directorship of the library, and throughout his days, he attempted to obtain an inheritance in the Land. He educated his only daughter Naomi in the national spirit.

When Bessarabia was captured by the Russians, he was exiled to Siberia where he perished. His wife Fuga and 20 year old daughter Naomi also perished in the wastelands of Russia during the Holocaust.

Chapter 65

Elka Bronshteyn of blessed memory

Translated by Jerrold Landau

Figure 99 - Elka Bronshteyn

The children of the family were Shmuel-Zelig, Yosef and Moshe Bronshteyn.

This was a well rooted family going back many generations in Orheyev, Bessarabia. They perished and were destroyed at the hand of the enemy.

Chapter 66

Dr. Berkovitz of blessed memory

Translated by Jerrold Landau

Dr. Berkovitz, the son of Berel and the grandson of Rabbi Nachumche (the Orheyever Rabbi) received a Torah education in his youth, and later completed his general studies privately. Despite the difficulties imposed by the Czarist government in preventing the Jews from studying medicine, Nachum succeeded on account of his talents in being accepted to the faculty of medicine in Odessa, in completing it and receiving the degree of Doctor of Medicine. Dr. Berkovitz was drafted to the army at the outbreak of the First World War. He obtained great experience in the army in internal medicine and surgery.

When he returned to the city, he was immediately accepted to the Jewish Hospital, where he worked together with the physicians Dr. Warshavsky and Dr. Lashko for many years. Within a short period of time, he endeared himself to the ill people whom he tended, both in the hospital and in his private practice. In addition to his professional expertise, Dr. Berkovitz excelled in his popular character traits, through which he earned his place in the community. He tended to the sick out of humanitarian feelings, without concern about their status. In cases of need, he would forego monetary compensation and continue to take interest in the state of the sick person even though he was not summoned a second time.

His livelihood was constricted even though he was an expert physician. As has been stated, he was not particular about compensation, and he devoted the majority of his time to communal affairs. He was the vice chairman of the credit cooperative for the middle class. He was a permanent delegate and a chief spokesman of the "Union of Jewish Cooperatives in Bessarabia." He was a member of the city council and the first on the regional Jewish List for the Romanian parliament in 1922.

Dr. Berkovitz contributed greatly to the cultural realm. He was a man who was raised and educated as one of the "folk," and he was fluent in spoken Yiddish. Large crowds came to hear his readings of the works of Sholom Aleichem. The writer of these lines had the opportunity to participate with him in the performance of Shalom Aleichem's "Only a Doctor." I recall the enthusiasm with which the community received the appearance of Berkovitz. Laughter mixed with tears and endless applause accompanied him. Whomever came in company with him, whether as he hastened to visit a sick person, in a meeting of a communal institution, or in his modest home, enjoyed full hearted words of humor.

Dr. Berkovitz worked greatly in many areas of our community, but he paid special attention to Zionist activity. He worked in the movement in Odessa from his earliest youth. During the time of his university studies and later, he dedicated his time to the funds (the Keren Kayemet and Keren Hayesod). He appeared with great success in public gatherings of the movement.

Even though he belonged to the general Zionists, the Zionist-Pioneering-Socialist youth and others were attracted to his home for conversation and exchange of ideas. His home was a gathering place for all the Zionists in the city, and was open to everyone. There, literary celebrations, Zionist debates, and even holiday and festival celebrations were arranged.

His very lovely wife Marika assisted him in arranging the celebrations and receiving the crowds. Those who came to his home enjoyed great spiritual satisfaction – he with his jovial attitude and unique sense of humor, and she with her pleasant voice, charming smile and love of life. The two of them imparted a sublime spirit upon anyone who came into their shadow. Thus did the years go by until the Russians conquered Bessarabia in 1940. Dr. Berkovitz's house was destroyed and ruined, and the family was exiled to afar.

He was exiled for close to 15 years for the crime of Zionism. He lost his human form. When he was liberated, he did not return to his hometown that had been emptied of its friendly residents, but he lived near his sister Fania in Beltsy. Mordechai Gitnik of Putsuntey described his final days.

"I met Dr. Berkovitz often in the home of his sister (the widow of Yaakov Globman). He left an oppressive impression upon me already from our first meeting. This was not the alert, enthusiastic man who once was, whom I knew from my visits to the Credit Cooperative in Orheyev. He was lost within himself, downtrodden, his clothing was sloppy, and his body was emaciated. To my advice that he should arrange himself in a human form, strengthen himself, and also pay more attention to his dress, he answered negatively: "Life is not worthwhile. I can no longer bring benefit. My time to leave this accursed world is already at hand." Indeed not long passed until the news arrived that Dr. Berkovitz, the jovial and alert, left his barren and lonely life in the strange city. May his memory be blessed!"

R. Milshteyn

From Russian by R.

Chapter 67

The Family of Matityahu Globman

Translated by Jerrold Landau

About the home of my parents that is no longer.

Figure 100 - Matityahu and Frayba Globman

Figure 101 - Melech, Chaika and Perl (Polonsky)

Figure 102 - Binyamin and Yocheved Globman

A memorial to my dear mother Frayba, to my brother Binyamin, Tzeviya his wife, Yocheved their daughter who was a student, and Chaika their child, Perl my sister, Melech her husband and their daughter who perished in the Holocaust. May G-d avenge their blood.

We were six sons and daughters in my parents' home, all of us working. My mother labored and toiled to provide our needs. When we got older, our home became a meeting place for the youth without differentiation between stream or factional direction. My brother Binyamin had "weapons" of "defense" hidden in the chimney. Once, the news arrived that the police were conducting searches in the neighborhood. Binyamin of blessed memory took out his revolver and bayonet, covered them and gave them to me to transfer to Aunt Susia, on the Post office Street. I was nine years old at the time.

Each of us had our own friends, and the meetings took place primarily in our home. There, we arranged literary parties on Sabbaths. Sometimes the friends of my brother and of my sister of blessed memory met at the same time, and took over all the rooms in the house. My good natured mother smiled and enjoyed this greatly. When we met on the Sabbath, my mother appeared with a plate of steaming potatoes in one hand, and salted fish and home made challas in her other hand. The group enjoyed the food with great relish, and my mother's face beamed with joy. These were the few moments of happiness that gave us strength to bear the life of tribulation during the dark days.

My father of blessed memory died in the month of Elul 5696 (1936) at the age of 80, and my mother had to suffer the great suffering during her latter days as we fled from the persecutors along with the family. There, everyone fell at the hands of the murderers.

May their memory be a blessing.

Zipora

Chapter 68

Yaakov Globman of blessed memory

Translated by Jerrold Landau

Yaakov the son of Matityahu and Frayba was born in Orheyev in 1890. He received a traditional education from his father the teacher, and began to study externally from the age of 12. Because of the difficult situation of his father, he had to start giving private lessons at the age of 16. He displayed great pedagogic talent, and became well known among the youth who were studying externally. He was drafted into the army in 1911, and participated in WWI from 1914-1915. He was wounded in his right hand. He registered in the university in Odessa after he was freed from the army. About two years later, he was invited to the Hebrew gymnasium in Akkerman as a mathematics teacher, and from there he transferred to the Hebrew gymnasium in Beltsy, where he lived with his family until the time of the Holocaust in 1941. His former student Zvi Pinkenzon writes the following of this era.

The Beloved Teacher

Hundreds and thousands of all ages studied arithmetic from Yaakov. He searched for and found the means of teaching and educating each one, so that nobody would be left without the requisite level of knowledge... "Sit down and listen, perhaps you too will understand something" -- said this man who taught with love. He remembered everyone who had been his student.

Indeed, teaching was the source of his livelihood, but nobody suspected that he was using this as a means of getting wealthy. Yaakov was strict with those students who tried to evade rigor in their studies and engage in "guesswork" in the fields of exact science. However, beneath the veneer of strictness beat a sensitive and loving heart, which would draw one close and offer explanations immediately after the dose of "strictness" that was meted out, until the point where you would understand, despite yourself, that which a few moments earlier was far from your understanding and ability to grasp.

His faithfulness to the Hebrew language was great and deep. He spared no efforts in filling his classes with comprehensive content by teaching arithmetic and mathematics in the Hebrew language, even before he had appropriate textbooks for such. When the Hebrew arithmetic books arrived from the Land, he was very happy. Yaakov was the first among our teachers to put the theory of modern teaching methodology into practice.

These were unforgettable periods of sublimity and connection between teacher and student. He earned the trust and love of his students, and all of them sought means to meet him and to find themselves in his domain as much as possible, even outside the hours of study.

As I bring forth these sections of memory for Yaakov the distinguished teacher, I am convinced that I do not exaggerate when I state that hundreds and thousands of his students remember him with love, reverence, and appreciation.

Tz. Pinkenzon

Chapter 69

Michael Groyser of blessed memory

Translated by Jerrold Landau

Figure 103 - Michael and Rivka (wife) Groyser

He was a popular personality in Orheyev. He was a Hebrew teacher with a progressive outlook, an enthusiastic Zionist and an orator when needed. He was active in the Zionist funds and communal life for decades.

At the beginning of WWI, the youth of our town were drafted to the war, and many families were lacking their sustainer. Elderly Jews were snatched up to work on the fortifications surrounding the city. Columns of tired and broken soldiers passed through our city, including many Jews. The living spirit in the assistance organization for these crushed wayfarers was Michael Groyser. Thanks to his influence in the community and his dedication to this good deed, many answered his call and offered their assistance.

In teaching, he excelled in his battle for new methodologies. His clear explanations and sharp humor with which he was graced endeared him to his students and anyone who knew him. He was also well received by the

Christian residents and the teachers of the two Christian gymnasiums in our city.

Despite his advanced age, Michael Groyser was young in spirit. On May 1, 1917, the first of the Russian revolution, he arranged a large public parade. Young Zion marched at the head of the Hebrew contingent under blue and white flags. Michael marched along with them and enthralled the masses of Jews with his declarations and nationalistic slogans.

During WWII, large areas were cleared of their population. Michael arrived in the city of Krasnodar in the north Caucasus. There he met up with many refugees from Bessarabia, including also some from Orheyev. Due to his old age (he was approximately 70), he was unable to continue with his wanderings, and he remained there.

Michael met his death along with the murder of hundreds of Jews by the German soldiers.

Many of his students and friends will bear his memory in their hearts.

Chapter 70

The Dyukman House

Translated by Jerrold Landau

Figure 104 - Shaul and Sima Dyukman (parents of Yonah and Hertz)

During the years 1920-1925, the home of Sima and Shaul Dyukman served as a meeting place for the Zionist youth in our city. The circles of youth who were dedicated to the national movement gathered in this house while they were still students of the gymnasium. With the passage of time, both the circles and the house turned into an important local center of Zionist activities.

Shaul, the head of the family was only marginally involved in communal affairs. He had a different honorable task: to sustain and raise eight sons and daughters to Torah and good deeds. The man was quite occupied with his business – the sheep and cattle trade. He educated his children in the spirit of the times: He gave the children a combined traditional and general education and the girls a general education.

The mother of the household Sima, the daughter of Reb Yosel Mundrian, an honorable Jew well liked by his fellowman, was a valiant and good hearted woman who opened her home wide to all in need. She even extended a faithful hand to the youth who would come to her house.

Figure 105 - Yonah Dyukman, son of Shaul and Sima

The Dyukman house stood in the center of the city opposite the market square, in a large yard. It had large rooms and a porch that extended the entire length. There was noise and commotion in the house and yard throughout most of the hours of the day and the night. Various groups of young people gathered there, some studying books and debating matters of the movement.

When a representative of the movement came to town, he would head to the Dyukman house. This house was the locale for gatherings of youth and the organization and execution of Zionist activities.

I remember that their son Yaakov prepared to make aliya to the Land with a group of chalutzim. The group came to town, and of course where should they head? To the Dyukman house. Sima the mother solved the problems of accommodations in her usual fashion. Doors were removed from their hinges to serve as stools. She spread out mattresses, and behold, there was the place for the chalutzim to sleep. She also provided food with her good heart.

This house was bustling day and night for 5-6 years. The faces of Shaul and Sima radiated with pleasure. The tumult caused by the youth did not burden them for their hearts were alert to their wishes.

Figure 106 - Hertz Dyukman, son of Shaul and Sima

Indeed, this was the meeting place for those thirsty for Zionist activities during those days. When the turn came for the rest of the family members to make aliya, the situation changed, and the father walked around sad and crushed: "It is too quiet in our house," he told me as I took leave of him as he left the house. The father Shaul longed for those days when the group of youths was attracted to his home in their masses, on their way to the desired Land. Now the house was quiet and sad.

Dov S.

* * *

I arrived in Orheyev on 5 Tevet 5681 (1921). I had given over the balance of my money as ransom to the gendarme who captured me on the route. I was left without anything, and I still had a long journey to the Land of Israel. Without any options, I wandered through the city. I turned to the Young Zion and asked that they help me get to Kishinev, since I had heard that in

Kishinev groups of chalutzim organize themselves to make aliya to the Land. The members of Young Zion sent me to the Dyukman family, whose son Yaakov was also preparing to make aliya. When I turned to him and told him the story, he introduced me to his mother. The "mother" Sima, even though she was busy with caring for her children, did not find that the place was too small. She fed me immediately, and I felt her soulful warmth. When I wanted to leave, she stopped me and said I should stay with them in their house until I could arrange my trip to the Land.

I remained in their home for five weeks. This was a brief but lovely period. During those days I felt as if I was among family. All the members of the family starting with the father who was constantly busy with his business, to the youngest of the children Sara, all drew me close and bestowed upon me the goodness of their heart and the warmth of their soul.

When the chalutz group was finally organized and was set up in the synagogue of Leib Reznik, I, as one of the organizers, decided of course to move and live with the members. Then, the mother urged me not to leave their house. "How will you be able to sleep on boards and on straw filled mattresses? Will the food cooked by inexperienced women be good for your palate? Are you fitting to be a woodchopper?" I felt that the words were coming from the heart of a merciful mother who was honestly concerned about me. The difficult living conditions that I was willingly taking upon myself especially concerned her.

Then, destruction came upon them. They were burnt at the stake along with the rest of the House of Israel, the father who exuded strength and trust, the good hearted mother, the children Yona and the pleasant Sarahle... May their memories be a blessing!

Moshe Arazi

Chapter 71

Gedalyahu and Rivka Veitzman of blessed memory

Translated by Jerrold Landau

Figure 107 - Gedalyahu and Rivka Veitzman

He was a farmer. They were among the honorable residents of the village of Mashkauts (Orheyev region).

His prime livelihood came from the growing and working of tobacco. With the agricultural reforms in Bessarabia, he received a plot of land as did most of the veteran farmers. He also received a plot that was planted with grapes on the land that Y. K. A. organization obtained from the Sirbu estate in the village. For various periods, Gedalya was the head of the Jewish farmers of the village, and served as the liaison between the group and the farmers.

Gedalya had a sense of community, and he concerned himself with communal affairs. His first activity was to establish, along with his friend Avraham, a synagogue in the place. He served as the gabbai until the end of his days. He concerned himself with educational matters in the village, engaged teachers and assured them fitting recompense.

He educated his only son Leib in the national spirit, and helped him reach a high level of education as an agricultural engineer.

(Leib and his family made aliya after WWII, and he serves today as the head of the division of manufacturing produce – cotton, sugar beets and tobacco – in the ministry of agriculture.)

Gedalya and Rivka were of good temperament, and provided food to all in need or any guest. Their fate was like the fate of the millions. It is not known if they were brought to a Jewish burial.

Chapter 72

Leib Ziserman of blessed memory

Translated by Jerrold Landau

He was a man of generous qualities and traits. He was from among the simple folk, and was brimming with warmth and love of his fellowman. He was a father of sons and daughters, and he made great efforts to educate them in the spirit of the times. He gave them all higher education, a matter which was exceptional in those days. He earned an honorable living in the textile business, but he did not find satisfaction solely with proper economic status.

His heart was attracted to doing good for his fellow, and he dedicated himself to communal affairs with his whole heart. He was a member of various committees in the community. He was one of the most active of the builders of the new hospital, in the Ezrat Aniim (Assistance for the Poor) committee, etc.

He did not merit in enjoying the fruits of his labor. The communal institutions to which he dedicated the best of his time were destroyed. He fell as a victim of the Holocaust.

Chapter 73

Itzik David Cheriyan of blessed memory

Translated by Jerrold Landau

He was a tailor by profession. He was one of the most prominent people in the community and among the tradesmen. He was a dedicated and active activist both for the benefit of his profession and the community in general. He was scholarly, and would study the ancient literature. He was the chairman of the Ezrat Aniim organization, and vice chairman of the loan and credit committee for tradesmen. He educated his children according to the tradition and with love of work.

May his memory be a blessing.

Chapter 74

Avraham David and Faya Katz of blessed memory

Translated by Jerrold Landau

Figure 108 - Avraham David and Faya Katz

He was one of the progressive members of the group of tradesman. He was a dealer in fine furniture. He was one of the leaders in this realm, and his products were in demand by those who appreciated modern style. He earned his livelihood for his eight member family in an honorable fashion, and he educated his children in a progressive national spirit. During his time, he was appointed as an "adjured judge" in the regional court. When he saw a group forming to make aliya to the land, he joined the group, but for various reasons, he was not among the actualizers. He responded to any national or local appeal in a generous fashion.

His children prepared to make aliya when they grew up.

His oldest son Itzik did not succeed in obtaining a certificate for aliya, so he immigrated to Argentina.

Figure 109 - Rivka Katz (daughter of Avraham and Faya)

Later, three of the children made aliya. The parents made aliya in 1935, and the family was reunited in Hadera (except for their daughter Rivka who got married to a young man from Akkerman and established her family there.)

On account of the difficulties of absorption and the weak state of health of the head of the family, they had to go back.

They wished to establish themselves and live near their daughter Rivka, who gave birth to their first grandchild. However, fate was cruel to them, and Rivka and her family fell at the outset of the Holocaust, before they were able to escape from the enemy. The old and weary parents found out about this tragedy after they returned to Kishinev from their wanderings in the expanse of Russia. The disaster weighed heavily on them and they were not able to recover from it.

They died in Kishinev in 1945.

Chapter 75

Avraham and Zila Lipshin of blessed memory

Translated by Jerrold Landau

Avraham's father Shmuel was a Zionist activist during the time of Chibat Zion. He was a delegate to the national convention of the movement along with Avraham Borsutsky, and one of the founders of the "Bessarabia Palestine" organization, whose purpose was to serve as a bridge between the Jews of Bessarabia and the settlement in the Land of Israel. He was a scholarly Jew, quiet and measured, who knew how to express his opinions appropriately.

His son Avraham was graced with a similar sharp grasp and talent. He was educated in the national tradition, faithful to the nation. Avraham joined the Bund socialist movement in our city, and even served as its head. Avraham dedicated himself to this movement with all his energy and youthful enthusiasm. At times, the Jewish youth were lost in their way and were given over to the ideological confusion that pervaded the Jewish street at that time. Avraham knew how to guard the national values, and everything that took place in the Jewish community was dear to him. When he was once invited by the activists in our city to become involved in communal affairs, and was even asked to be in second place on the list for the elections of the town council, he responded positively. He displayed great dedication and ability in protecting the affairs of the Jewish community through a strong struggle with the Zionist reactionary forces in the Jewish community and the general community. Through his activities he was able to realize his error (regarding solving the Jewish national problem through autonomy in their places of exile), and he recanted. One day we found out in our city that Avraham was going to scope out the Land (in 1929). He toured its length and breadth for an entire month. His wonder knew no bounds. When he returned, he found various opportunities to tell about its social and economic achievements, and from that time forward he joined the ranks of the activists of the Zionist movement with his typical enthusiasm.

His home was a meeting place for anyone who entered. I recall the pleasant evenings that I spent in his home, the politeness, and his various statements that won him renown. I will always recall this fine spirit. It is unfortunate that all of this disappeared, and he is no longer – Avraham and his noble family have been cut off.

May these lines serve as a discrete monument to these fine souls!

Y. Torkanovsky

Chapter 76

Arkadi Loshkov of blessed memory

Translated by Jerrold Landau

Arkadi was born in Orheyev in 1892. He received a Russian education. He studied in the arts academy in Odessa for two years. He also loved sports. When the Maccabee organization arose in our city, Arkadi volunteered to lead the members of the organization, and he dedicated a great deal of his time and energy to this. The public appearances of the Maccabee members are remembered. These appearances were enchanting.

He was drafted into the Russian army at the outbreak of WWI. He was at the front. He excelled and received high recognition. Later, he finished the school for captains.

He went to Paris in 1920 where he was active in the "Meeting Place of the Independents." Among other things, he drew the portrait of the Romanian "professor" Yorga and of the poet from his hometown David Knott. The portrait of the latter was displayed in the "Autumn Meeting place" in Paris with great success.

He arranged an exhibition of his portraits (80 in total) in the Osman gallery in 1932. He also exhibited at the large international exhibition in Paris in 1937. About a year later, his creations were displayed in the international exhibition in Chicago.

He gave some of his creations as a gift to one of the museums in Paris.

Arkadi was a faithful artist, but he kept separate from the group. He even refused to meet with his good friends, so as not to impose himself on them. Arkadi lived in poverty and straits, and did not want to arouse the pity of his friends. He did not want them to help him as he did not want to become a burden on them.

Arkadi, the splendid dresser, lived the life of an ascetic. He did not smoke, ate little and spoke little. He was refined and he kept to himself. He died alone and was buried on October 9, 1941 in Paris.

From Yiddish by M. R.
From the book: "Our Fine Artists", published by Hirsch Fenster in Paris, 5711 (1951).

Chapter 77

Yechiel Leyderberg of blessed memory

Translated by Jerrold Landau

Figure 110 - Yechiel Leyderberg

Yechiel was orphaned at a young age. Nevertheless, he studied diligently and obtained wide knowledge in literature, especially in Yiddish. He even took to writing poems, and served as a writer in the Jewish newspaper in Bessarabia (Unzer Zeit).

Yechiel, full of suffering and orphaned in his youth, felt for the suffering of his fellowman and did the best to help anyone. When he was still in the fourth year in gymnasium, he volunteered to guide the working youth in reading and even to actually teach them. He had an open heart, understanding of the situation of impoverished students.

This fine and noble soul bore the burden of his orphan hood even in his adulthood. "If only my mother were alive and I had grown up in her bosom and had benefited from her care, I would have been stronger physically and I would have been able to join the chalutz movement like many of my friends, and be among the builders of the Land" – he said. Yechiel was not a Zionist in the common sense of the term, but he was faithful to the nation, and aliya to the Land was in his opinion a good solution for the masses of Jews. Whenever he accompanied a group of friends on their way to make aliya to the Land, his eyes filled with tears and he parted from them with deep anguish. I did not merit being among those making aliya…

He expressed his longing for the Land of Israel in his poems.

His weak body and refined soul were swept away in the storm of the Holocaust.

May his memory be guarded in our heart.

Chapter 78

The Family of Moshe Lemberg

Translated by Jerrold Landau

Figure 111 - Moshe and Perl Lemberg (parents of Motel)

My father Moshe the son of Mordechai Lemberg was born in Yampol in 1867. He lived in Orheyev from 1890. He served as the prayer leader for many years in the Great Synagogue and also in the Tolner Synagogue. He was one of the scholars of our town. He remained in Orheyev at the time that the rest of the family fled. He trusted that G-d would save him and the house of Israel. He was murdered along with all the residents in 1941.

My mother Perl the daughter of Leib and Leah Korenfeld (nee Ribokoli) was born in Rybnitsa in 1876. She lived in Orheyev from 1897.

During the time of the Holocaust, she fled with my brother Motel and my sisters Ester and Rachel. They reached Uzbekistan. She lost her son Motel during the war, and returned after the war to Orheyev with her sister, broken and crushed. She died and was buried in Orheyev on 24 Tammuz 5716 (July 25, 1954).

Figure 112 - Motel Lemberg (son of Moshe and Perl)

Chapter 79

Yitzchak the son of Avraham Milshteyn of blessed memory

Translated by Jerrold Landau

His personality and life activities

He was born in Orheyev in July 1890, and perished in Siberia in 1942.

When he was still young, his parents moved to a village in the area of Orheyev, where his father accepted a job as an accounting director in a liquor factory. His father had to sustain and educate the family on a very meager salary. Itzele displayed his talents while still a schoolboy. His father later moved to the city, where Itzele completed the public school and was accepted as an apprentice in the office of the lawyer Gozshteyn at the age of 14. The refined, handsome boy with dark, brilliant eyes attracted the heart of anyone who came into contact with him. After some time, he moved to the home of the lawyer Moshe Ravich. Itzel endeared himself to the Ravich family and those who came into their home. He simultaneously continued to study in a private fashion. When the loan and credit fund for small scale merchants was created at the end of 1906, he transferred to work there. Milshteyn saw in this communal enterprise the seed of an important social institution and a wide field of activity for him, therefore he forewent the good conditions in the Ravich household and satisfied himself with little, so that he could study and understand from close up the field of communal work that was dear to his heart.

His first job in the loan fund was as the assistant to the accounting director. However, after several months, he entered into the depths of the matters of the loan fund, and when the director of accounting left the loan fund, Milshteyn was asked to fill the role of chief accountant. He displayed exceptional initiative and diligence, like a veteran and experienced professional. He maintained the accounting ledgers of the loan fund, and created interest tables that were used as templates by many loan funds in their work. His name became known publicly and he earned great public acclaim.

In 1909, fate offered him an experience that seemingly became a decisive factor in his life. The "New York" international insurance agency set up branches throughout all areas of Russia. Milshteyn took it upon himself to direct the branch in our city, and put in the best of his abilities and initiative. At that time, the company conducted a competition to study more effective organizational practices in the matters of insurance in Russia, and promised eight prizes for excellent work. 19 year old Milshteyn participated in the competition and won first prize.

Figure 113 - Yitzchak ben Avraham Milshteyn

He was drafted to the army during WWI in 1914, and received a medal of excellence.

In 1916, Milshteyn was invited to the city of Yekatrinoslav by the committee for the assistance of refugees in Russia in order to organize the assistance for the refugees of the war. Simultaneously, he arranged cooperative shops for the needs of the Jewish communities in the region of Yekatrinoslav, and also stores for the sale of wheat to the Russian army. He also fulfilled the role of director of the loan funds in those settlements through the agencies of the Y. K. A.

In 1917, the committee for the assistance of refugees organized a committee whose job it was to organize assistance through credit and productive work for a number of areas outside the Pale of Settlement. Milshteyn was invited to Moscow to direct this important activity.

Milshteyn returned to Bessarabia in 1920 and joined the active committee that was headed by Nachum Roitman of blessed memory, a particularly prominent personality in the Jewish communities of Bessarabia, to organize a union of Jewish cooperatives in Bessarabia. Milshteyn researched and examined every loan fund that was still functioning, searched and gathered material from remote forgotten archives, met with past and present activists, and organized and reestablished the destroyed loan funds.

The communal work in the Jewish communities of the center and south of Romania was conducted primarily by philanthropic organizations. With his leadership talents and persuasive abilities, he succeeded in transferring the assistance which was fundamentally philanthropic to the realm of independent and mutual assistance. He gathered the best of the activists around the idea of cooperation. Through his leadership, loan funds were set up in the cities of Bucharest, Iasi, Botosani, Harlau, and others. He also played a significant role in the founding of loan funds in the cities of Cluj and Sighet in Transylvania.

Thanks to his initiative, the active organization of national loan funds and the accounting division were organized, and independent loan funds in various localities were established. He conducted a comprehensive census among the Jewish farmers and artisans. Toward the end, he conducted successful work in improving the status of the loan funds that had endured the difficult depression of 1929-1932.

Milshteyn excelled in his ability to express himself clearly and persuade people – both orally and in writing. While he was still young, he published articles on various economic and cooperative topics at the invitation of the editors of the Russian economic publication "Vestnik Znani." He also published many articles and feuillitons (ed. note: short stories that are published as serials) in the Yiddish "Dos Cooperative Vort."

Despite his prime activities in his responsible role as director of the "foundation," the Joint asked him to direct its social institutions in Bessarabia and Romania. He dedicated a great deal of his time to the ORT and Azeh trade schools in Kishinev, and summer institutions for children and teachers. He worked at all of these without expectation of remuneration. He did not desist from assisting charitable organizations and individual needy people. He extended goodhearted and generous assistance to them.

Indeed, our city merited to have a sublime person who was born into a family of workers, and grew up and became a man who forged paths as he directed cooperatives for Jewish workers throughout Romania.

He was a refined, goodhearted man who dedicated all of his days to the improvement of the society, the society of workers and the oppressed. He was uprooted from his family and from the society to which he dedicated his entire essence and sent to Siberia, where he died…

May these lines serve as a monument to a dear man, a man of great action, whose wonderful and honorable name will be guarded in the hearts of Orheyev natives forever…

M. Rotkov

* * *

In Memory of a Friend

It is not easy for me to write my memories of Yitzchak Milshteyn. This will not be about Yitzchak Milshteyn himself, for who knew Yitzchak Milshteyn? Isaak Abramovitz was the name by which he was known to everyone. He was accepted, honored and loved by all circles in Jewish Bessarabia and all circles outside of that with whom he came into contact.

Approximately 14 years have passed since I last saw him. I came to Kishinev in response to his urgent request for consultations on matters of the central bank and cooperative institutions in Romania – institutions of the "Foundation" in Kishinev that was directed by both of us. These were the days of WWII, and the atmosphere was tense. Nazi vassals ruled Romania, and in Bessarabia, they waited each minute for the entry of the Russians. At the end of our meeting, Milshteyn expressed his regret that I must return to Bucharest, where trials and tribulations under the anti-Semitic government that is drawing close to Nazism await me; whereas he will remain in Bessarabia where the Russians will come and everyone will be free…

First and foremost, Milshteyn offered his own contribution generously. His great experience, his outstanding intelligence, his understanding of how to deal with people, his work ethic and talents – everything that was within him he dedicated to the needs of the Jewish community. People heeded his words, paid attention to his reasoning and his conclusions were often accepted even by his opponents, and of course by his followers and admirers. He knew how to break down matters to their fundamentals and to place matters in their proper perspective. He knew how to convince those assembled, if not by straight logic then by brief targeted parables, if not by proofs then by single-sentence sharp witticisms. A compromise down the middle, a speech of a disputant, a light witticism that elicited general laughter would weaken all effects of opposition and often decide the status of a dispute. He was quick in both his decisions and actions. He knew how to forge a compromise in difficult circumstances. He knew how to assist those in need at the time of difficulty both in deed and with advice. The masses paid attention to his advice which was full of wisdom, insight and foresight. When he stood at the crossroads of life, when his fate and the fate of his family required quick and decisive action, the wise and experienced Isaak Abramovitz who was full of foresight did not know what was forthcoming. He remained in Kishinev full of hope, certain of his future.

Milshteyn engaged in the activity of reviving the Jewish cooperatives in Bessarabia after WWI with great dedication and diligence. He ran from city to city in his search for human and physical material to establish the cooperatives. He brought out activists from their alleyways, camps and workplaces, forced them to forget their own daily worries, and appointed them to head the cooperatives – the centers of general concern. He brought out books, documents and papers from cellars and storehouses, dusted off the cobwebs, cleaned the dust of years from them, and restored them to new life. He was one of the first and the most active of the people who renewed the cooperative movement of Bessarabian Jewry after WWI.

He was one of the founders and chief activists of the supervisory committee of the Jewish cooperatives of Bessarabia that became with the passage of time an example for other parts of Romania, as well as for other countries such as Poland, Lithuania, Czechoslovakia, etc.

While he was still busy with his work of strengthening the supervisory committee in Bessarabia, the Foundation and the Joint appointed him as their delegate. He became the delegate for the assistance money for the Jewish community that was arriving from America and England. However, he never ceased being the spokesman for the Jewish community and its institutions to the worldwide assistance and productive help organizations.

As a representative of the Foundation, the role of Milshteyn was great in the organization of the cooperative movement in other parts of Romania. As in Bessarabia, he did not know what difficulties and obstacles were, and did not begrudge his time and energy to attain the goal. Similarly, at a later time, he dedicated himself to repairing the cooperative in Czechoslovakia. We saw him act with the same dedication in organizing assistance to the victims of floods and droughts – organizing assistance for the refugees and supervising the day to day activities of the communal institutions and populist endeavors of all forms.

The Russians entered Bessarabia a few days after our parting. Isaak Abramovitz was imprisoned a day or two later. He endured a long journey from Bessarabian Kishinev to far off Siberia, where he passed away alone and forlorn, far from his family, friends and acquaintances, far from the cities and towns of Bessarabia and their residents to whom he dedicated most of the days of his life and a significant part of himself.

In far away, cold Siberia, without a warm environment, without friends and acquaintances, isolated from society, this man of life and society Isaak Abramovitz Milshteyn spent his last days and months. Who knows what his final journey was that ended his life and who accompanied him. However, his memory remains alive among Bessarabian Jewry. Every historian, every chronicler of days gone by who tells about life in Jewish Bessarabia during the first half of the 20th century must give an honorable place to Isaak Abramovitz Milshteyn, who lived his life in such a manner and participated in no small manner in forging that life.

To his wife and two children in Israel, to his friends and admirers in Israel and the Diaspora, may the knowledge that the man did not live, act and suffer for nothing serve as a comfort.

Moshe Asuskin

Jerusalem, Tishrei 5615 (October 1954)

Chapter 80

Mendel and Leah Naychin of blessed memory

Translated by Jerrold Landau

Figure 114 - Mendel and Leah Naychin (parents of Bendik)

Mendel Naychin was a teacher of bible and Hebrew language for many years. He taught in the Talmud Torah of Orheyev for many years, and gave private lessons as well. Despite his weak body, he bore a heavy yoke of work to sustain his eight person family, and to provide his children with education according to the spirit of the times.

Hundreds of children from our city received their education from this illustrious teacher and educator. I also had the merit of being one of his students, and I see it as my duty to dedicate these lines to his memory.

Reb Mendel was short in stature, thin and sickly in his body, but healthy of spirit. He was full to the brim with the fundamentals of both the written and oral Torah, expert in Hebrew and Yiddish literature, and his command of grammar was great.

Figure 115 - Bendik Naychin

His pleasant mode of explanation, and his flowery language filled with natural humor attracted the hearts of his audience, and a strong bond was quickly formed between them and their teacher. During the class, he felt the obligation to present the material in a fashion that the student would be able to understand thoroughly, without being satisfied with a mechanical understanding. Therefore, the students loved the studies and we thirsted for his lessons. The time that we spent with Reb Mendel of blessed memory gave us great spiritual enjoyment. He knew how to instill his love of bible to his students. I recall his enthusiasm during the studying of the Book of Isaiah. His teaching of that book always aroused in us a deep feeling and a unique experience. We learned entire chapters by heart, and it was not too difficult for us. His stories about the poet Yehudah Halevi and his longing for the return to Zion ignited in us the first spark of love of Zion. The pleasant voice of Reb Mendel as he read sections of the poems of Yehudah Halevi still rings in my ears. Our enthusiasm grew when he reached the following stanza: "To weep for you I am a jackal, and when I dream about the return to you, I am like a harp for your songs."

It is difficult to describe the soulful enthusiasm and special love of Reb Mendel for the poems of Ch. N. Bialik of blessed memory. As one of the enthusiastic fans of this poet, he dedicated the best of his strength to impart his poems to his students. It is no surprised that we also studied diligently and knew many of the poems by heart.

The educational style, the refinement of the soul and the unceasing dedication of the education ensured the maintenance of the bond between him and us even after the conclusion of the time of study. His home was always open to us, and we would visit his home willingly. We asked for his advice in private matters, and pleasantly discussed topics of sports and matters relating to the Zionist movement. All of the members of his household had a Zionist consciousness. To our dismay, not one of them succeeded in making it to the Land. The cruel Holocaust cut off the fate of this precious family: From the two sons and two daughters, only one (Sara and her family) survived. The youngest son Bendik worked in the offices of the Keren Kayemet in Kishinev. He dedicated himself completely to the Zionist movement (in "Hanoar Hachalutzi"), and prepared to make aliya. However the cruel fate ambushed him, and he was murdered by a Romanian policeman on May 1, 1924.

The tragic event completely destroyed the weak health of Reb Mendel, and it was difficult for him to overcome this until his last day.

The bitter fate also overtook the older son of Reb Mendel, Nissan Naychin and his noble family. The hand of the murderers reached him as well during the tragic circumstances of World War II.

Figure 116 - Sara and Nissan Naychin

A. Malovchki

Chapter 81

Yosef and Yehudit Naychin-Geler of blessed memory

Translated by Jerrold Landau

Figure 117 - Yosef and Yehudit Naychin Geler

Yehudit was born in Orheyev. She was attracted to the activities of the Zionist movement from a young age. She married Yosef Geler, an intelligent and handsome man. Yehudit's heart strove for greatness, and she did not find satisfaction with the provincial life in the four ells (ed. note: in the minutiae of Jewish Law) of her family. Communal work was a necessity for her soul. Her talents and character spurred her on to action. With the little money she saved, she moved on to study in the Faculty of Law at the University of Iasi. When she finished, she received her permit to serve as an attorney. The family moved to Kishinev. There, their home became a meeting place for activists of the movement. Yehudit and Yosef, with their joy and pleasantness, attracted the hearts of anyone who thirsted for vigorous conversation and pleasant company. The "stormy" Yehudit played an important role in the Zionist center, the Young Zion center, and the Aliya center, and became the president of Young WIZO (Women's International Zionist Organization). This task suited her the most. She won over many with her pleasant countenance and nobility of spirit…

*

…Yehudit Geler of blessed memory was a woman with Jewish-Hebrew cultural inclinations that she inherited in the home of her erudite father. She enchanted the audience in her appearances with her deep knowledge, her polished oratory, her fine, flowery language, and her soft, pleasant voice.

Even though she was well accepted in the circles of lawyers in Kishinev and had the opportunity to forge for herself a stable economic status, she abandoned the work and spent most of her time on communal affairs, especially with WIZO and the Keren Kayemet. She was willing to fulfill her duty at all times that she was needed. Her visits to cities and towns were always crowned with great success. More than one city awaited her visit impatiently. The time that she remained in such a city was like festival days for the Jewish population. With all this, Yehudit dreamed of a new life in the Land of Israel. However… fate did not desire that this dream be actualized.

The Red Army invaded Bessarabia in July 1940. All of the dreams of Yehudit Geler were hidden away…

When the Red Army camped in Bessarabia, Yehudit maintained the hope that she would be able to extricate herself and make aliya to the land. She did not exhibit depression like the others. On the contrary, when she met her friends and acquaintances, she exuded optimism and encouraged others. She waited to meet them in Israel, for despair and doubt were foreign to her spirit. This was the manifestation of her high character.

*

When the Red Army left Bessarabia, Yehudit remained in Kishinev. She had her own reasons for this. To her, going to the depths of Russia meant parting forever from the idea of making aliya to the Land. In Bessarabia, there was hope that she might make her way there.

In time, when she lived in the closed ghetto of Kishinev and her husband was dragged from there to death (she did not know of this), she continued to believe in a miracle, that she would be able to arrive in the Land from the ghetto… this time she placed her hope in the activists of Bucharest, hoping that they might redeem the active Zionists. However, the Zionists of Romania did not succeed in their efforts, and nobody made aliya.

All of the afflicted people were deported to death camps in October, 1941. She walked on foot along with thousands of orphaned deportees on the long, difficult route to Transnistria, in rain and cold. Broken and crushed, ill with typhus, with swollen feet, dripping with blood, the refined Yehudit was dragged along with her last strength on the long route to death, and she still hoped for a miracle…

Yehudit Geler was shot in Transnistria along with many others by the Fascist beasts. She suffered a cruel and painful death…

May her memory be a blessing!

Y. Shildkroit: "On the Ruins of Bessarabia"

Chapter 82

Dr. R. Nirenberg of blessed memory

Translated by Jerrold Landau

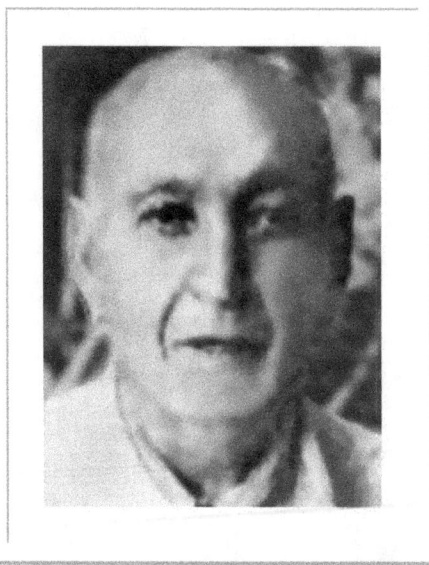

Figure 118 - Dr. R. Nirenberg

Dr. Nirenberg was his name as known to everybody, young and old. This name encompassed his essence – love and honor.

I do not know from where Dr. Nirenberg came. One clear day, he appeared on the streets of the city. He had a solid body, broad shoulders, with the uniform of a high army captain, an army cap with an insignia (kokarada in the vernacular) sprouting from his head. He was splendid of countenance, and won the hearts of all who saw him. As he passed through the streets, people whispered to each other: This is the new doctor who has just now (1904) returned from the war (between Russia and Japan).

Within a brief period, he became the most popular person in the city, both as a doctor and as a man of the community.

However, his nobility and splendid countenance with which he was blessed separated him to a large degree from the wide community. He was even somewhat strict with his fellowman. Nevertheless, everyone loved him and revered him.

On account of the spirit of reverence that surrounded him and his fine relations with all strata of the community, the communal activists crowned him as head of the community. They imposed difficult and even unpleasant tasks upon him, as the times required. Dr. Nirenberg has the power of forging compromise and straightening out the obstacles that came up within the community in our city.

For example, when a dispute broke out among the activists of the loan fund of the small scale merchants, Dr. Nirenberg was invited to make peace between the disputants.

He was once again drafted into the army during WWI. At the end of the war, he returned to Orheyev and once again was asked to stand at the head of communal affairs.

At times one would ask oneself why did men of greater experience and influence than Dr. Nirenberg, more active than him, such as M. Ravich, Yosef Yoelich Pagis, Moshe Kalmanovitz, Aharon Gluzgold, Gershon Weinstock and others, activists with great communal vision – why were they not called to the helm of the community despite their important and effective activities in many communal areas of our city, and only Dr. Nirenberg was given the mantle of head of the community?

This is what we answered: His splendid countenance, his combined internal and external nobility, his boundless integrity, his level headedness and even his insistence on the truth – all of these positive characteristics caused the leadership of communal affairs in our city to be given to him.

At the outbreak of WWII (1940) he was again drafted by the Russians as a physician. He was close to 70. He overcame all of the difficulties that faced an army doctor during wartime. He returned to Orheyev filled with suffering and weakened, widowed from his refined and noble wife who perished on the way. He returned to the place where he dedicated the vast majority of his life – to both the sick and the healthy… However, he found emptiness and nothingness… Orheyev was destroyed, abandoned, desolate and ruined… There was nobody, no friend or acquaintance…

A few months before his death, he answered the writer of these lines with a letter written in Russian, as follows:

"23 February, 1955.

Dear M. Rotkov!

I received your letter on the 10th of this month. I was very glad to hear the news that old acquaintances are alive and well, and take interest in me. I am already very old and severely ill. I am 83 years old. The Yonovitz family is well. I gave them your regards and told them of your wish to correspond with them. The elder Yonovitz and his daughter live in Kishinev. Both of them work. To those in whose house you saw a picture of my granddaughter and from whom you received the news about us and about the death of my wife, please give them our best regards. I wish you health, long life, and all good things.

Dr. Nirenberg"

Fate was favorable, and his words will be perpetuated in the book of the community to which he dedicated the best of his efforts.

Chapter 83

Avraham and Charna Spivak of blessed memory

Translated by Jerrold Landau

Figure 119 - Avraham and Charna Spivak

One of the activists about whom is said "those who faithfully work for the welfare of the community." One of the few maskilim in our city, and the only one in the city who subscribed to the Hamelitz newspaper. He also possessed Sifrei Agora which was published by Tushia, and he generously lent them to whomever wanted them. He viewed this as a national duty, that he was able to benefit the public.

He was a native of Chinisheutsy, a large village in the region of Orheyev. Later, during the 1930s, it became a town. Then, the Jewish population grew to 100 families. A Jewish community was formed that established a synagogue and set aside a place for the cemetery. Avraham was the gabbai of the synagogue and the head of the Chevra Kadisha (burial society).

His large home stood in the center of the town. Anyone passing through the town would stop at his home, whether for conversation, for rest, or to obtain news about what was going on in town. Whenever there was a dispute between residents of the town, they would turn to him, and whatever he decided would stand. This was not only for his community, but also for the gentile community, who also related to him with honor and trust and regarded him as an expert not only in monetary matters, but also in religious matters. On one occasion there was a dispute in their church about the setting of the date of one of the holidays (at that time, they transferred from the Julian calendar to the Gregorian calendar). The dispute was growing stronger. One of them advised turning the question over to Avraham. They all agreed (including the priest). His advice was accepted by all of them, and the storm in the church abated.

Another incident took place at the time of the change of regime. A Romanian official arrived in town and set up residence in his home. Obviously, the relations between him and the official were very friendly. It happened that a certain Jew was caught smuggling sugar across the Dniester from Rybnitsa to Rezina. The smuggler was brought to the police, where they treated him as a guilty prisoner. The relatives immediately turned to Avraham, who went to the official and explained to him that the captured man was about to get married, and the sugar was brought for the wedding celebration. The official accepted this, ordered that the prisoner be freed and that the confiscated sugar be returned, on condition that he too is invited to the wedding. They did this…

During the years of 1918-1920, when the refugees were streaming in, his home was open to every refugee who came through the town. There they received assistance and support as was needed, whether with food, clothing or lodging, as well as legal advice relating to the preparing of the documents that they needed to continue along their route.

In the interim, the family prepared to make aliya to the Land. They decided to send the children first (three daughters and two sons). Two daughters remained at home and waited their turn…

When the Holocaust arrived in 1940, the lot of this family was the lot of all of their exiled brethren. Their lot included hunger, want, and all the tribulations of the journey that afflicted the rest of the exiles. Avraham died of hunger and tribulations of hell on 25 Elul 5702 (1942) enroute to Astrakhan. His wife Charna died a few months later (23 Iyar 5703).

May their souls be bound in the bonds of eternal life.

Chapter 84

Efrayim Pagis of blessed memory

Translated by Jerrold Landau

He was the brother of Yosef the son of Yisrael Pagis. Like Yosef his brother, he was educated in the new spirit of the times, placing precedence on general studies over religious studies.

However, he did not display any special inclination to his studies, and his father brought him to work in the printing press while he was still a youth. With time, he became fully involved in the work and mastered all matters of printing.

He was in contact with the national movement from the time of his youth, and he remained faithful and dedicated to it until the end of his days. He moved to Chernovitz after he married Sara Muchnik (from Kishinev). After a brief period of time, he returned to Orheyev and took over the printing press. The printing press took up all of his time. Nevertheless he dedicated some of his time to the movement, and participated in almost any activity that was arranged by the Zionist movement.

Like Idel Yagolnitzer, he did not like to appear at lectures and in the community, preferring to dedicate his power and his will to actual activity. He was the secretary of the Keren Kayemet and Keren Hayesod, and he sometimes organized other activities from the movement. He was the instigator and living spirit in them.

Chapter 85

Yosef ben Yoel and Ina Pagis of blessed memory

Translated by Jerrold Landau

Figure 120 - Yosef ben Yoel and Ina Pagis

The anti-Semitic guard ruled Russia during the years 1906-1907. This guard was felt in particular in the public school, whose entire purpose was to prevent the Jews from attaining higher and also middle education. Yosef ben Yoel failed the exams many times. He remained in Orheyev and occupied himself with teaching Russian language and other subjects in the Talmud Torah and in private lessons.

At that same time, around 1907-1908, the office of the government appointed rabbi (Rabbi Mitaam) was open, and Yosef ben Yoel Pagis was chosen to fill that role. From that time on, he showed himself as an active communal force of great value, representing the affairs of the Jewish population to the government with force and national strength. He demanded budgets for Jewish institutions from the korovka (meat tax) and from the regional treasure (zemstova). Despite his official status, he did not disdain smaller things. He continued to work with dedication in the various institutions. He represented the underprivileged strata in the loan fund of the middle class, increased his activities in the Zionist movement, and appeared at every meeting and made his views known. Despite the fact that his command of Yiddish was imperfect, interspersed with entire sentences in Russian and at times grating on the ear, his content was filled with heartfelt enthusiasm and attracted the heart of any listener. The meetings at which Yosef B. Y. appeared were always packed with people.

He was quite involved in communal affairs and participated in many institutions, whether as a delegate or when specially invited to give advice and express his opinion. For him, the communal council was the center of his life, to which he dedicated the best of his time and energy. The council was composed of representatives of most of the communal institutions. Every institution had its worries, problems and affairs, and at times there were complications, obstacles and difficult situations. Yosef ben Yoel bore the yoke and delved into each issue no less than the member who was directly responsible for the particular institution, even though this was not his task. He was a typical communal activist with his integrity, diligence in all matters of the community, with clean hands and a pure heart, honored by both the Jewish and gentile population.

When the Romanians took over Bessarabia, Y. P. felt the lack of the government language, which he was used to using in his role as government appointed rabbi when he appeared before the government. He attended the University of Iasi and studied law despite his advanced age (he was 40 years old then).

After he completed his studies as a lawyer, he did not work in the profession, for this was not in accordance with his spirit.

When Bessarabia was conquered by the Russians in 1940, Yosef ben Yoel was sent to Siberia, where he died of hunger and cold. Throughout his entire life he gave of himself to his fellow, to Zionism and to change the orders of life. All was for the benefit of the public, and he himself was trampled under the stormy wheels of the time…

Chapter 86

Asher and Feiga Fisher of blessed memory

Translated by Jerrold Landau

Figure 121 - Asher and Feiga Fisher

Asher Fisher was modest in his demeanor and pleasant with his fellowman. His integrity and good heart won him the respect of both Jews and non-Jews.

He was active in the Jewish defense (Samo-oborona) in our city, and the cellar of his house served as the storehouse for weapons of defense.

He was captive to the Zionist idea from his youth, and his precious dream was to make aliya to the Land and dedicate himself to agriculture. He was among the first in our city to obtain shares in the "Colonial Bank." He paid his shekel (token of membership to the Zionist movement) and donated regularly and generously to the national funds.

His wife Feiga was an intelligent woman, active in the Zionist movement in our city during her time. She was among the first who took off her jewelry and gave it over to the Keren HaYesod.

Her progressive ideas and Socialism that she drew from Russian and Yiddish literature intermixed well with the Zionist idea, and she raised her two children, Leah and Moshe in this spirit of Socialist Zionism.

She was an enthusiastic supporter of the settlement of workers, and was one of the activists in the Hechalutz movement. Her home was a meeting place for the young Zionist generation.

Both of them were murdered as they fled to Ukraine at the last minute.

May their memories be blessed.

Chapter 87

Leah (Liza) Fisher of blessed memory

Translated by Jerrold Landau

Figure 122 - Leah (Liza) Fisher

She was born in 1896. Her parents' home was filled with the Zionist atmosphere, and Leah absorbed this atmosphere. She studied Hebrew and Bible, and was fluent with the language. She completed the government gymnasium at the age of 15 with a gold medal, and went to Odessa in 1916 where she studied agronomy at the university. She intended to complete her studies and make aliya to the Land.

She was active in the "Hechaver" Zionist student organization in Odessa, and was a member of the local Zionist council of southwestern Russia.

She succeeded in returning to Bessarabia after the revolution and dedicated herself to Zionist activity with her entire soul. As a member of the center of United Young Zion in Bessarabia and a member of the Tarbut Center, she participated in conventions and was elected to high institutions.

When she was in Iasi, she was active in the Jewish student union and fought with all her might against the Communist tendencies within this union. She founded the first chapter of Young Zion in Iasi.

During the later years, she worked as a teacher in the Jewish schools in Beltsy. She was very active in the field of Socialist Zionist education, and even led the pioneering youth in the Gordonia movement. She gave a great deal to the Haoved movement in Romania.

She was murdered by the Nazis in Beltsy.

May her memory be a blessing.

Chapter 88

Yeshayahu Frank of blessed memory

Translated by Jerrold Landau

Figure 123 - Yeshayahu Frank

The son of Asher Anchel and Malka Feiga.

Yeshayahu found his purpose in life in working for the future of the activists of the world. He dedicated himself with youthful enthusiasm to this work, which was conducted clandestinely during the time of Czarist Russia.

In 1916, he left Orheyev and traveled to Odessa. There he found a wide field for his activities in the community of workers in a large weapons factory, where he was accepted for work as a professional.

He returned to Orheyev and continued his activities at the outbreak of the revolution.

He was arrested several times as a revolutionary at the time of the conquest of Bessarabia by the Romanians.

As a result of a mishap at work, he had to leave his professional realm and he moved over to business.

When he reached adulthood, he joined the Zionist movement and wanted to make aliya along with his wife Zila Fikhman.

He did not succeed in obtaining the desired certificate, and in the meantime tragedy stuck. His wife Zila died and he had to fulfill the role of father and mother to his young daughter Niura.

At the outbreak of WWII, he fled along with the rest of the Jews from Orheyev to the Soviet Union, where he was drafted into the Red Army as a professional. The last news from him came from far off Omsk in Siberia.

Like his older brother Moshe-Zalmina, who fell during WWI, he also fell victim in a strange land in a war that was not his…

His daughter Niura remained in Kishinev, where she is studying at the university.

Mordechai (Gan Shmuel)

Chapter 89

Moshe Chalyk of blessed memory

Translated by Jerrold Landau

Figure 124 - Moshe Chalyk

He was one of the first of the union of Hebrew speakers and one of the founders of Young Zion in our city. He educated his children in the national spirit. He was one of the initiators of Hebrew education and a member of the committee of the Tarbut School. He was one of the forces behind the Forer group that prepared to make aliya to the Land. He was a dedicated communal man who was modest in his demeanor, spoke little, and defended his opinions strongly with the aim of arriving at justice and truth.

Due to family reasons, he was not able to join the Forer group and make aliya to the Land. However, his desire for aliya never left him throughout his life. His last hope to join his daughter Penina and her family in Gan Shmuel while he still had strength came to naught. The Holocaust arrived, and he fled to far off Russia where he met his death. Woe on the loss!

Chapter 90

Reb Simcha Kestlicher of blessed memory

Translated by Jerrold Landau

Figure 125 - Simcha Kestlicher

Simcha Kestlicher was a scholar, expert in Talmud and legal decisors (ed. note: renders legal decisions on Jewish Law), and comfortable with the new Hebrew and Yiddish literature. He managed the flourmill and wheat and flour business of the owners of the mills Yisrael Krasner, Aharon Fikhman and his partners. He was an experienced accountant, delving into the details, and a man of sublime personal qualities.

When he came to live in Orheyev, he earned the complete admiration of all who came into contact with him, both with regard to work and communal affairs.

He headed the general Zionists in our city for many years. He was the gabbai of the Chabad Synagogue until the outbreak of WWII. He also excelled with his special capability of forging a compromise between disputants, whether with regard to monetary matters or with issues that related to impinging on the honor of one's fellow. His decision was always just and logical, for he was intelligent and the ways of living were clear to him. He had another fine trait: the splendor of his countenance. With his splendid countenance and enthusiastic smile, he brightened up and added honor to anyone who stood before him.

Another benefit accrued to anyone who heard the utterances of his mouth: his humor, Talmudic statements, and general jokes that were on his tongue at all times.

Reb Simcha was well received by people from all circles. Even though he was not wealthy, and not even well-off for he lived by the toil of his hands, men of industry and business heeded his advice. He even won his acclaim among the craftsmen of our city. There was a case where a harsh dispute broke out in the community of craftsmen. The dispute was about the leadership of the loan fund of the craftsmen, and the disputants were divided into two camps. The more objective camp, dedicated to the matters of the fund, turned to the group of activists of the intelligentsia to ask them to take over the fund and take it out of its crisis. All of the members of the fund agreed to place Sh. Kestlicher at the head of this institution. Thanks to his dedication, the fund was returned to its stature, its success grew, and the credit activities progressed.

Sh. K. lived a modest life in the midst of his family, surrounded by the love and reverence of anyone who turned to him. He served the community faithfully and honorably. He assisted anyone who needed him to the best of his ability. He did whatever he did without any pretences and haughtiness. He was straightforward, upright and honest. At the age of 70, he was murdered with his wife in his home in the autumn of 1941 during the time of the German rule of Orheyev.

Chapter 91

Berel and Sara Kruglyak of blessed memory

Translated by Jerrold Landau

Figure 126 - Berel and Sara Kruglyak

Berel was educated by his uncle Matityahu Globman. He was educated in the spirit of tradition and was connected to it even though he was not observant at all. He would worship with a nice voice and was interested in the cantorate. At a young age, he led the services on the High Holidays as well as the three festivals (Pesach, Shavuot and Sukkot) in the Mark-Shuelchl synagogue. He voluntarily took the place of a hired cantor in that synagogue for many years. When he was offered payment, he would donate it to one of the local charities (the hospital or the old age home).

Berel was a contributing member of all of the Zionist organizations, with generosity and enthusiasm. He wanted to check out the possibilities of aliya for his family, and the opportunities for getting set up in an agricultural role in the Land. However this was in 1936 (July 8) when the disturbances were taking place in full force, and of course, it was difficult for him to make a positive decision.

Sarake was like Berel – both had large hearts, were concerned about their fellowman, related well to people and were well liked. They were of a like mind with regard to the doing of good deeds, supporting those in need, feeding the hungry, and donating generously to all social organizations. Berel and Sarake were beloved and pleasant in their life, and in their death they were not parted…

They were a seven-person family, two boys and three girls. The boys were drafted into the army when the Russians entered Bessarabia. The eldest fell in battle. Berel, Sarake and two of the daughters died when the Germans invaded Bessarabia, and the site of their graves is unknown. Of the seven-person family, only one daughter, Mania made aliya to the Land and set up a fine household. G-d blessed her with four children.

Chapter 92

Moshe and Rachel Ravich of blessed memory

Translated by Jerrold Landau

Figure 127 - Moshe Ravich

The Ravich household was known to all residents of our city, young and old. This was a family full of activity and full of merits. Its praise was not only heard in our city, but also outside of its bounds.

His father Velvel Ravich earned his livelihood by writing letters of petition to the civic offices and government.

Moshe was educated in his father's house with the conditions that were prevalent at that time. At first he went to cheder, and later, privately with his own initiative, he succeeded in obtaining knowledge of the Russian language and of general studies. He assisted his father in his work, also writing petitions and visiting government offices and the justice of the peace. He became known as a talented and intelligent youth.

At the end of the 19th century, Moshe was a leader in the effort to establish an agricultural school. To this end, he established contact with Y. K. A. in Paris. In 1898, he stood at the head of the ceremony for the laying of the cornerstone of "Firma". He stood at the head of this institution that he loved for seven years, and fought valiantly for its existence. At the end, he had to liquidate it.

In 1902, M. R. founded the Jewish Public Library, and organized independent intellectual groups for the youth. At the beginning of his communal work, he dedicated himself to the Zionist idea and participated in Chovevei Zion conventions in Odessa along with Borsutsky. With the spread of the workers movement in Russia, he transferred to the Bund, and stood at the head of that movement for many years. He was elected to the Duma along with A. Borsutsky in 1905.

Ravich did not suffice himself solely with local activity. He always desired to spread his outlook on communal matters publicly, especially to large crowds. At meetings, he would speak in poor Yiddish, spiced with Russian words, as was the custom of Yiddish speakers at that time. Even though he had difficulty expressing himself, he won over the hearts of his audience with his content, and with the clarity of the idea that he was presenting. He contributed to the Bessarabian newspapers. His local articles and essays had great influence upon his readers.

Mr. R. saw the cooperative movement as an important popular social and economic enterprise. He invested a great deal of energy to it, and saw in it the solution to many problems that vexed the workers and those who lacked means. He dedicated himself to it with his whole heart and soul and worked for it until it was destroyed at the beginning of WWII.

He was the first of the founders of the two loan funds, the loan and savings funds, in our city (in 1906). He stood at the head of the committee of the fund for the middle class for many years. He worked for many years on the craftsmen's fund with all his enthusiasm, and he was the force behind and the founder of the Jewish cooperative shop in the city. This was an important matter at that time, for the supply of the market was disrupted in the country in general and in Orheyev in particular, and the workers were assisted in their ability to obtain vital necessities and low prices. The enterprise suffered losses, and closed after two years.

M. R. found a wide field of activity in the cooperative movement with the founding of the Union of Jewish Cooperatives in Bessarabia.

From the first cooperative convention (1921), at which he was elected as a member of the advisory committee, he was constantly active in the headquarters, he participated in all of the conventions, and the delegates heeded his advice and opinions. He especially endeared himself to N. Roitman, his friend from the beginning of the existence of the movement in Bessarabia.

M. R. contributed to the cooperative newspaper "Dos Cooperative Vort." He published many articles to clarify matters of the movement. He struggled against the destructive influence of the masses of members who were influenced by various passing crises, and who were liable to bring serious damage to the cooperative. He always stood on guard for the matter, without veering from the path that he felt appropriate.

M. R.'s partner in life was his wife Rachel Isakovna.

She was an educated woman, beautiful, a daughter of the noble Suslik family, with a good heart that was open to the suffering of the worker and those who met ill fortune. Rachel dedicated the best of her energy to help the individual and the community. She was also a Bundist like her husband Moshe. She gave her entire essence to the organization of the workers; she urged them to revolution, and first and foremost to self understanding and labor uprightness, especially to the improvement of economic conditions. We recall the complaints that the "well off women" of the city had regarding Rachel's speech as the representative of the "maids" to improve their difficult working conditions. Rachel did not lose her resolve even though there was danger of imprisonment with this matter. She conducted the struggle with might and strength.

The role of Rachel along with another educated and active woman, Rivka the wife of Yaakov Levinson, in their concern for children is a story full of activity.

Even before the U. Z. A. (Uvshtshestova Zdarovia Yevreyev) Jewish hygiene organization was founded, a women's committee (Damen Komitet) under their direction was established. Both Rachel and Rivka organized a wide variety of assistance for children and those in need in a personal fashion.

Rachel, with her comprehensive cultural level, knew Russian literature very well, and she appreciated the popular language, Yiddish. She fought for the upper hand of this spoken language in the Jewish street. She was especially able to influence the community of workers in our city during the years of revolutionary unrest in Russia (1903-1905). The Ravich family was a bastion of opposition to "Reactionary Zionism" for many years, however, when the day of "The hoped for Socialism" arrived, they changed their outlook. As well, as the horn of Zionism rose on the Jewish street during the 1930s, they no longer thought with the same "Ravichist" stubbornness against the masses who regarded the Zionist movement as the solution to their national and social struggle. True democratic minds such as Moshe and Rachel took heed of the wishes of the people…

At the end of their days, they were subject to wandering like the rest of the refugees of Orheyev. There they perished.

Chapter 93

Zvi (Gerisha) Rozenfeld of blessed memory

Translated by Jerrold Landau

Zvi Rozenfeld received a traditional education, and worked in the regional pharmacy as assistant to the chief pharmacist. Later he went out on his own, and he opened a shop for medical supplies. However, he earned his livelihood with difficulty in this field.

Along with a group of parents, he established a Hebrew kindergarten and also took upon himself the yoke of heading this organization from the outset.

He was modest, upright, and refined. These traits stood out in the eyes of anyone who came in contact with him. People were attracted to chat and exchange ideas with him. People always took leave of him with a pleasant feeling.

Zvi was an enthusiastic Zionist even though he was not able to dedicate much of his time to the movement on account of his economic status. Nevertheless, he worked a great deal toward the establishing of the Tarbut Hebrew School. He bore the burden and did not stumble with obstacles. His wife Ida helped him and also bore the yoke. Both of them stand before my eyes as alive. It is hard to believe that they are no longer living. They did not succeed in coming to the Land. They perished along with their daughter Chasya and the rest of the Jewish people.

May their memories be bound in the bonds of eternal life.

Riva

Chapter 94

Nachum, Feiga, and Golda Rotinsky of blessed memory

Translated by Jerrold Landau

Figure 128 - Nachum and Feiga Rotinsky

Nachum Rotinsky, his wife Feiga and their daughter Golda died in Ukraine, to where they fled from Bessarabia.

Figure 129 - Golda Rotinsky

Nachum owned a store in the village of Selishte, where he lived with his family. He was known as an upright man who was careful not to disadvantage his fellowman, even a non-Jew.

Jews in need would come to the village, and they would find rest and food in his house, presented generously. He was known as a man who tended to his guests. Aside from this, he would send goods to the poor of Orheyev. He had an abundance of lamb meat during the season of the birthing of sheep. He would send this meat to the poor with his sons, along with a list of to whom it should be distributed.

His sons in the Land of Israel awaited the arrival of their parents to the Land, but this did not happen. They died among the martyrs along with their daughter Golda.

Chapter 95

Yitzchak Shapirin of blessed memory

Translated by Jerrold Landau

Figure 130 - Yitzchak Shapirin

Yitzchak the son of Efrayim Shapirin was born during the 1880s in the village of Chinisheutsy in the region of Orheyev.

He studied privately with a teacher in the village, and was a classmate of the late Meir Dizengof (Dizengof was from the adjacent village of Akimovitchi). He attained a wealth of knowledge in ancient literature. When he got older, he decided to leave the village because of his desire to expand his spiritual and social horizons. He met his wife in Orheyev and established a family with five children, four daughters and one son. He educated them in the spirit of the times.

He became involved in the Zionist group in our city. He was one of the regular visitors to the Borsutsky house. He was active and dedicated, faithfully bearing the yoke of duties to the movement. At the time of need, he took upon himself the role of commissar of the Keren Kayemet in our city. He filled this role tirelessly.

He was sensitive to all that happened on the Jewish street. He rejoiced at the news of the Balfour Declaration, and was upset at the news of the murder of Arlozoroff. He could not be comforted over this tragedy for a long time.

He was the type of activist who did not push himself to the head of the line. He never wished to take an official role, however when the community asked him to do so, he took it upon himself from an internal sense of duty.

When the social and financial crisis took place with the loan fund of the small scale merchants of our city, he took upon himself the leadership of this fund. He held this role for many years, despite the social and financial difficulties and obstacles. He had a unique character trait of being able to listen, to pay attention to and to talk with the bitter of heart and those who had a downturn. Therefore, he was beloved by the people.

He was quiet by nature, but he explained his ideas and opinions in such a fashion that even the few words were able to convince the opposing side. For his words were upright and penetrated the heart. He was asked to mediate any dispute, whether between individuals or with communal affairs.

Yitzchak Shapirin, the quiet and modest man, bore a great tragedy upon his heart for many years. His only son rejected the national Zionist tradition, and transferred to the Communist movement. He estranged himself to everything that was so holy to Yitzchak. He was finally imprisoned and sentenced to ten years of hard labor in the Doftana prison in Romania. After he was freed, he was forced to move to Russia. The last hope of the father that the only son would set up his home alongside the family was destroyed.

Chapter 96

Mania Shulman of blessed memory

Translated by Jerrold Landau

She was a good soul, loved by everyone. She was a constant wellspring of advice and comfort. We, her grandchildren, included her in all our activities. From our first steps in life, she knew how to restrain hasty deeds. On the eve of my aliya to the Land she said to me: Moshele, please fulfill my desire. I wish to make aliya to the Land and to die in the Holy Land. However, I did not fulfill her wish, and I do not know where she met her death.

May her memory be a blessing!

Her grandchild Moshe Ziserman

Chapter 97

The Shaiovitz family of blessed memory

Translated by Jerrold Landau

Figure 131 - Moshe and Rivka Shaiovitz

Figure 132 - Avraham Shaiovitz

Figure 133 - Liebe Shaiovitz

Moshe Shaiovitz and his family moved from Lalova on the banks of the Dniester to Orheyev in 1920.

The home of Moshe Shaiovitz in Lalova was dear to the people of Orheyev, who often visited Lalova.

They not only found a place to sleep, but also to visit at all hours of the day, without expectation of monetary payment. For the commandment of "Hachnasat Orchim" (tending to guests) was the constant wage of this family.

When this family moved to Orheyev they did not desist from the commandment of Hachnasat Orchim. For the Jews of Lalova and Stodolna would often visit Orheyev, and they were their constant guests.

In 1941, when the German and Romanian murderers destroyed Orheyev, the family was forced to flee for their lives along with most of the residents. The family wandered along the way for three months until they reached Tashkent in central Asia. The authorities did not permit them to remain in Tashkent even on a temporary basis, and they were forced to move on to Kokand.

Moshe, the head of the family, died in May 1942 when his energy was spent. His wife Rivka died a short time thereafter in Tashkent. Their son, the lawyer Avraham Shaiovitz died two days before the death of his father. Liebe Shaiovitz, also a lawyer, died in the Red Army in battle against the Nazis.

Four victims of one family, in such a short time!

The lawyer Yosef Shaiovitz, his brother Yitzchak (Izak) and their families, and the sister Miriam (Mania) arrived in the Land along with the refugees. Motel (Mordechai) Shaiovitz , an engineer, remained in the Soviet Union.

The wife of the late Avraham Shaiovitz along with their son Natan also arrived in the Land.

Y. Ben Moshe

Chapter B1

Pictures of Holocaust Victims

Translated by Terry Lasky

Figure 134 - Chayim and Nacha (wife) Bronshteyn

Figure 135 - Lieba Bronshteyn (daughter of Chayim and Nacha)

Figure 136 - Mabashavka Bronshteyn

Figure 137 -Yaakov ben Shimon Bronshteyn

Figure 138 - Zvi and Susia Bronshteyn

Figure 139 - Avraham Gershkovitz

Figure 140 - Moshe Lazar and wife Sharf

Figure 141 - Charna Davidovitz

Figure 142 - Motel and Elka Gleyzer

Figure 143 - Idil Daskal

Figure 144 - David and Batya (wife) Duchovny

Figure 145 - Efrayim and Zorik Noyman Daskal

Figure 146 - Sheindel and Yisrael Gonik

Figure 147 - Motel and Feiga (wife) Taran

Figure 148 - Bracha and Moshe (husband) Yaroga

Figure 149 - Yocheved and Yaakov (husband) Yagolnitzer

Figure 150 - Moshe Yonovitz -
- ritual slaughterer

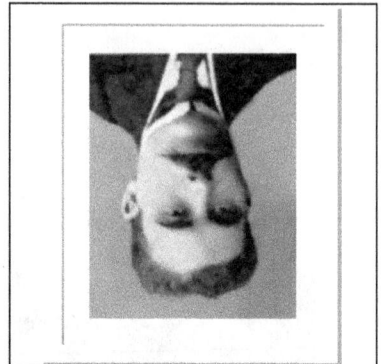

Figure 151 - Mordechai Man

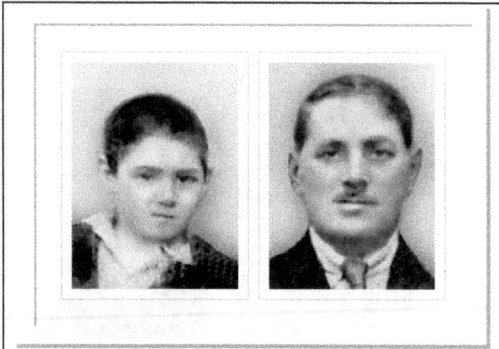

Figure 152 - Menashe and Feivel (son)
Liniveker

Figure 153 - David
Muchnik

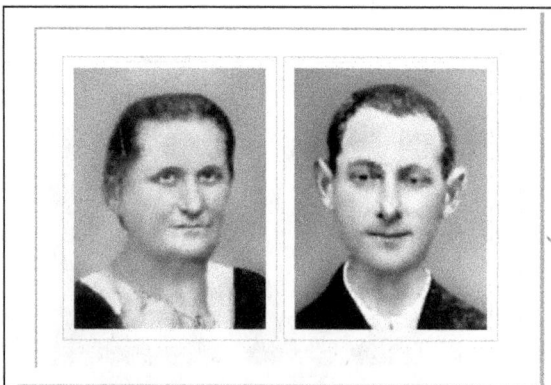

Figure 154 - Zerach and Machla
Mordkovitz (parents of Zvi, Chayim,
Tova and Mania)

Figure 155 - Zvi
Mordkovitz (son of Zerach
and Machla)

Figure 156 – Chayim Mordkovitz

Figure 157 - Tova Mordkovitz

Figure 158 - Mania Mordkovitz

(children of Zerach and Machla)

Figure 159 - Simcha Kulik and Gissa Mishkis

Figure 160 - Malka Mishkis

Figure 161 - Baruch Shalom and wife Naychin

Figure 162 - Raizel Naychin

Figure 163 - Yisrael Naychin (son)

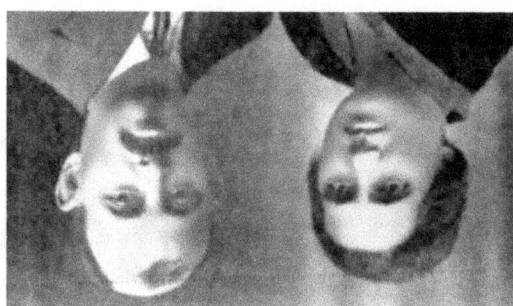

Figure 164 - Bluma and Yisrael (husband) Snitkovsky

Figure 165 - Zorik Noyman-Daskal -- died in Russian Army

Figure 166 - Frimme Sandler

Figure 167 - Miryam and Avraham Strol

Figure 168 - Yaakov Mikelman

Figure 169 - Akiva Simes and (daughter) Hanita Katzap

Figure 170 - Frayda and David (husband) Filarsky

Figure 171 - Mendel (husband) and Chaika Fuchis

Figure 172 - Avraham Finkel

Figure 173 - Leah Ziserov

Figure 174 - Gedalyahu (father) and Motel (son) Zokolov

Figure 175 - Sara Katzap -- family matriarch

Figure 176 - Moshe Katzap

Figure 177 - Silva Katzap

Figure 178 - Eliyahu Katzap

Figure 179 - Reuven Katzap

Figure 180 - Zina Rapoport (mother of Nachman)

Figure 181 - Nachman Rapoport (son of Zina)

Figure 182 - Nechemya and Neche (wife) Kovadlo

Figure 183 - Binyamin Kovaldo family

Figure 184 - Hana Kleinman

Figure 185 - Hanry Simon

Figure 186 - Sima Kleinman

Figure 187 - Gitel Kruglyak

Figure 188 - Avraham Kruglyak

Figure 189 - Bayla Kruglyak

Figure 190 - Rachel Rozenfeld (mother of Moshe and Perl)

Figure 191A - Moshe Rozenfeld (son of Rachel)

Figure 191B - Sara Rozenfeld (wife of Moshe)

Figure 191C - Perl Rozenfeld (daughter of Rachel)

Figure 192 - Solomon Rozenberg

Figure 193 - Yechiel Shichman

Figure 194 - Yaakov and Chaika (daughter) Shaposhnik

Figure 195 - Yosef and wife Shustik

Figure 196 - Bayla Shustik

Figure 197 - Michael Zeitz

Figure 198 - Bileh and Hershel Shinman

Figure 199 - Yechezkal and Peysa Shaposhnik

Figure 200 - Avraham Polinkovsky

Figure 201 - Shpilberg Family

Chapter B2
Names of Holocaust Victims

Translated by Terrry Lasky

Averbukh, Niuma	Mordkovitz, Machla
Averbukh, Lyona	Mordkovitz, Zvi
Barinboym, Hertz	Mordkovitz, Chayim
Barinboym, Feiga	Mordkovitz, Tova
Barinboym, Naami -- daughter	Mordkovitz, Monish
Beker, Shmerel	Mozhelyan, David
Beker, Chaysa Korenfeld	Muchnik, David
Bendersky, Ben-Zion	Muchnik, Sara
Bendersky, Eliezer	Muchnik, Yosef
Berkovitz, Dr. Nachum	Munder, Dov
Beyder, Mendel	Munder, Malka Mishkis
Beyder -- Eltzufin -- Raisel	Munder, Moshe
Beyder, Moshe	Munder, Sara
Boks, Moshe	Munder, Yosef
Bradichansky, Zvi	Nairner, Sara
Bronshteyn, Zvi	Nairner, Brina
Bronshteyn, Susia	Nairner, Binyamin
Bronshteyn, Chayim	Nairner, Arye
Bronshteyn, Nacha	Naychin, Mendel
Bronshteyn, Lieba -- daughter	Naychin, Leah

Bronshteyn (Mabashavka)

Bronshteyn, Shimon

Bronshteyn, Miryam

Bronshteyn, Elka

Bronshteyn, Yaakov

Brosman, Sara

Chalyk, Moshe

Charak, Yisrael

Charak, Feiga

Charak, Yitzchak

Charak, Yehoshua

Cheriyan, Yitzchak David

Cheriyan, Chana

Cheriyan, Sara

Chulsky, Motel

Chulsky, Zlata

Daskal, Efrayim

Daskal, Sara Noyman -- wife

Daskal, Zorik -- son

Daskal, Idil

Davidovitz, Charna

Dizengof, David

Dizengof, Charna

Duchovny, David

Duchovny, Batya

Naychin, Baruch Shalom

Naychin, Rachel

Naychin, Raizel

Naychin, Yisrael

Naychin, Nissan

Naychin, Sara -- wife

Naychin, Yehudit Geler

Nirenberg, Dr. Yitzchak

Nisenblat, Zecharya

Nisenblat, Leib

Pagis, Yosef the rabbi -- lawyer

Pagis, Ina -- wife

Pagis, Efrayim

Pekar, Efrayim and family

Polinkovsky, Avraham

Polonsky, Melech

Polonsky -- Perl Gleybman

Polonsky, Chaika -- daughter of

Polonsky, Yitzchak

Rabinovitz, Tova

Rabinovitz, Chaya-Bayla

Rabinovitz, Moshe Aharon

Rabinovitz, Bayla Gitel

Rabinovitz, Avraham

Rapoport, Chayim Yonah

Duchovny, Baruch -- Buka

Dyukman, Shual

Dyukman, Sima

Dyukman, Yonah -- son

Dyukman, Riva -- wife

Dyukman, Chaika

Dyukman -- and two daughters

Elkin, Yosef -- [daleth-"-nun] of congregation

Eltzufin, Chaika

Filarsky, David

Filarsky, Moshe

Filarsky, Frayda

Finkel, Efrayim

Finkelshteyn, Ben-Zion

Fishelyov, Zvi

Fisher, Asher

Fisher, Feiga

Fisher, Leah

Frank, Yeshaya

Fridman, Moshe -- teacher

Fuchis, Mendel

Fuchis, Chaika

Gertopan, Zina and spouse

Gertopan, Moshe -- son

Geynichovitz, Zlata

Rapoport, Moshe and his daughters

Rapoport, Baruch

Rapoport, Zina

Rapoport, Nachman (Niuka)

Ravich, Moshe -- lawyer

Ravich, Rachel wife

Reznik, Motel

Reznik, Shifra

Roitman, Shalom and wife

Roitman, Avraham and wife

Roitman, Mendel

Romalis, Yekutiel

Rotinsky, Nachum

Rotinsky, Feiga

Rotinsky, Golda -- daughter

Rozen, David -- at Siberia

Rozenberg, Solomon

Rozenfeld, Rachel

Rozenfeld, Moshe

Rozenfeld, Sara

Rozenfeld, Penina

Rozenfeld, Perl

Rozenfeld, Yechiel

Rozenfeld, Itzel

Rozenfeld, Yisrael

Glantz, Leib

Glantz, Chayim

Glantz, Etel

Gleybman, Matityahu

Gleybman, Frayba

Gleybman, Binyamin

Gleybman, Tzeviya

Gleybman, Yocheved

Gleybman, Yosef -- child

Gleybman, Chaika -- girl

Gleybman, Yaakov

Gleyzer, Motel

Gleyzer, Elka

Gluzgold, Liebe

Gluzgold, Rama -- wife

Goldenberg, Avraham

Goldenberg, Moshe -- ben Avraham

Goldenberg, Shabtai

Goldshtern, Motel

Golerkansky, Zecharya

Gondelman, Mordechai

Gondelman, Shimon

Gonik, Getzel

Gonik, Sheindel

Gonik, Yisrael

Rozenfeld, Yenta

Rozenfeld, Zvi

Rozenfeld, Eida

Rozenfeld, Veva

Sandler, Frimme -- France

Savransky, Fishel

Savransky, Gitel

Shaiovitz, Moshe

Shaiovitz, Rivka

Shaiovitz, Avraham -- lawyer

Shaiovitz, Leibe (Arye) -- lawyer

Shaiovitz, Zalmina - agronomist

Shaiovitz, Chana and grandson

Shapirin, Yitzchak

Shaposhnik, Yechezkel

Shaposhnik, Pesya

Shaposhnik, Chaya

Shaposhnik, Yaakov

Sharf, Moshe Lazer

Sharf, Motel -- son

Sharf, Efrayim

Sharf, Mania -- wife

Sharf, Yosef -- son

Sharf, Bracha -- girl

Sharf, Mordechai

Goril, Chaika

Goril, Moshe

Goril, Zippe

Goril, Baruch

Grobokopatel, Yisascher

Grobokopatel, Ben-Zion -- Engineer

Gershkovitz, Avraham

Gershkovitz, Chaya

Gershkovitz, David

Gershkovitz, Leah

Gershkovitz, Sima

Gershkovitz, Mordechai

Gershkovitz, Dina

Grechanik and family

Groyser, Michael

Groyser, Rivka (wife)

Gulkis, Avigdor

Herman, Pinchas

Kandel, Yisrael

Kandel, Raizel

Katz, Avraham David

Katz, Faya -- wife

Katz, Rivka -- daughter

Katzap, Avraham

Katzap, Reuven

Sharf, Rivka

Sharf, Avraham

Sharf, Henikh

Sharf, Leibel

Sharf, Meir

Sharf, Mania -- wife

Sharf, Chava

Sharf, Riva

Sharf, Shoshana

Sharf, Shmuel

Shargorodsky, Yaakov

Shargorodsky, Chava

Shargorodsky, Mordechai

Shargorodsky, Moshe

Sherman, Yitzchak

Shichman, Yechiel

Shinman, Moshe

Shinman, Penina

Shinman, Yosef

Shinman, Hershel

Shinman, Bayla

Shinman, Netanel -- son

Shpilman, Shlomo

Shpilman, Chaika

Shrayberman, Yosef

Katzap, Moshe

Katzap, Eliyahu

Katzap, Silva

Katzap, Sara

Katzov, Ozer

Katzov, Mania

Kestlicher, Simcha and wife

Kiperchensky, Shmuel

Kiperchensky, Naftali

Kiperchensky, Yosef

Kiperchensky, Sara

Kiperchensky, Avraham

Kiperchensky, Mendel

Kiperchensky, Sima

Kleiner, Zelig

Kleinman, Avraham

Kohan, Rachel -- (mother of Shel, Avraham and Chulda)

Korenfeld, Yisrael

Kovadlo, Binyamin

Kovadlo, Nechemya

Kovadlo, Ganya

Kozhushnyan, Moshe

Krauthamer, Leah -- girl

Kruglyak, Berel

Shrayberman, Rivka

Shtern, Fishel

Shteynberg, Moshe

Shteynberg -- Sonia Marinyansky

Shteynberg, daughter

Shulman, Mania

Shustik, Yosef

Shustik, wife

Shustik, Bayla -- daughter

Shustik, Mendel

Shvartzman, Eliezer

Simes, Akiva

Simes -- wife

Simes, Mordechai -- son

Simes, Hania Katzap -- daughter

Simon, Hanry

Simon, Miryam Kleinman

Sirkis, Matityahu

Snitkovsky, Yisrael

Snitkovsky, Bluma

Snitkovsky, Baruch

Spivak, Avraham

Spivak, Charna -- wife

Spivak, Motel

Kruglyak, Sorke

Kruglyak, Ester -- daughter

Kruglyak, Eliezer -- son

Kruglyak, Gitel

Kruglyak, Bayla

Kruglyak, Avraham

Kulik, Simcha

Kulik, Gisya

Kupchik, Chana

Kupchik, Binyamin

Lemberg, Moshe -- the father

Lemberg, Perl -- the mother

Lemberg, Mordechai (Motel) -- the son

Levinson, Yaakov

Levinson, Rivka

Leyderberg, Yitzchak

Leyderberg, Yechiel

Liberovitz, Nachum

Liberovitz, Freiga

Liberovitz, Zila

Liniveker, Menashe

Liniveker, Feivel

Lipshin, Avraham

Lipshin, wife

Lipshin, Feiga -- daughter

Spivak, Sara -- wife

Spivak, Velvel

Strol, Avraham

Strol, Miryam

Strol, Chana

Taran, Mordechai

Taran, Yisrael

Taran, Feiga

Tartakovsky, Velvel

Trostnitsky, Dashe

Tuberman, Niuma

Tuberman, Roza

Tuberman, Yechezkal

Veitzman, Gedalyahu

Veitzman, Rivka -- wife

Vernik, Chayim

Vernik, Malka

Volovsky, Moshe

Yagolnitzer, Yaakov

Yagolnitzer, Yocheved

Yaroga, Moshe

Yaroga, Bracha

Yaroga, Chana

Yaroga, Avraham

Yaroga, Mindel

Lipshin -- son

Loshkov, Solomon

Loshkov, Arkadi -- in Paris

Malovatsky, Reida

Mikelman, Yaakov

Mikelman, Yosela -- child

Milshteyn, Yisrael

Milshteyn, Yitzchak

Minaylov, Yaakov

Moldavsky, Fania

Moldavsky, Zehava Zenia -- girl

Moldavsky, Yosifina -- girl

Mordkovitz, Zerach

Yassky, Chayim

Yonovitz, Yeshaya-Leib

Yonovitz, Itta

Yonovitz, daughter of Sheva

Zeitz, Michael

Zinman, Alter

Ziserman, Leib

Ziserman, Ester-Chaya

Ziserov, Leah (Liza)

Zokolov, Gedalyahu

Zokolov, Motel

Zviebak, Yosef

Zviebak, Tama

This list comprises only a small portion of the victims of the Holocaust.

Chapter B3
Memorial List from the "Hagana" and Israel Defense Forces

Translated by Terry Lasky

Muchnik, Anchil -- Hadera

Spivak, Yehudah

Etziovny, Nachum

Roitman, Moshe -- Haifa

Averbukh, Shaul -- Negba -- general Israel Defense Forces

Rotkov, Menachem -- general Israel Defense Forces

Chapter 98

Yizkor

Translated by Jerrold Landau

May the nation of Israel remember its sons and daughters who fell in the Israel Defense Forces, the faithful and brave ones who gave their lives in the battle for the founding of the State of Israel. May the nation of Israel remember and be blessed through its children, and mourn over the eternal splendor, the beauty of bravery, the holiness of the will and the dedication of those who perished in the terrible battlefield. May the brave ones of the War of Independence and the victory be engraved upon the heart of Israel for all generations.

Sh. Shalom

Chapter 99

Shaul Averbukh of blessed memory

Translated by Jerrold Landau

He was the son of Emanuel and Sara, a family of farmers from the village of Vaskovtsy in the region of Orheyev. He spent his childhood in the vineyards, fields and forests on the banks of the Dniester. He loved agriculture and was expert in all of its manifestations. He pined for agriculture even when he studied the trade of carpentry. "I feel the field," he would say. "The machines are not in accordance with my spirit." He was a member of the Hashomer Hatzair movement in Bessarabia, and he prepared himself to make aliya. He made aliya in 1935. He joined the Shamir Kibbutz (near Ramat Yochanan) and worked toward the conquest, and also worked in the port of Haifa. He was active in Shamir during the disturbances of 5696 (1936). He took part in reconnaissance. He was a member of the Fire Squadron under the command of Wingate. In 1938, he transferred with his squadron from Shamir to add to the strength of Kibbutz Negba. He immediately participated in the local defense and was one of the pillars of the battle of Negba. He had gray eyes, a smile, strength, power, and a good heart. He was quiet and modest like a working man during the time of peace, but the strength of his spirit was especially revealed as a soldier who fought with extreme might, self sacrifice and boundless dedication. He was calm and collected at all times of nature. He willingly accepted every command, but he was not interested in commanding others. He always went out at the head of every activity.

At the beginning of May, 1948, he was active in the region of Negba as the head of an armored force of Palmach. He was the right hand man of the Negba commander Yitzchak Dubno of blessed memory. When the Egyptians invaded, he was a machine gunner in the front lines against Irak A-Syudan guard. At times of need, he was also involved in laying mines. He went out to the minefields each night to gather the weapons and armor that had been left by the enemy. In his final activity, he went out to lay mines around an Egyptian tank that was stationed between Negba and Irak A-Syudan. He fell a few hours after the commencement of the second truce of that period, on 12 Tammuz 5708 (July 19, 1948). He was buried in Negba.

From "Yizkor" of the Defense Office – 5617 / 1957

Chapter 100

Anshel Asher Kamchi of blessed memory

Translated by Jerrold Landau

Figure 202 - Anshel Asher Kamchi

Anshel was born in Orheyev. He received a traditional education during his childhood, and later studied in a gymnasium. He was a veteran of Gordonia, and he always desired to make aliya to the Land. His desire was for a life of agriculture in the land of Israel, and in 1935, his dream was realized and he made aliya. His first steps were in the direction of agricultural work. However, there was unemployment in the Land, and despite this, many of the orchard owners in Hadera did not engage Hebrew labor. This affected him strongly. He was not content, and continued to struggle for his livelihood in agricultural work.

On Friday 27 Tammuz 5696 (July 17, 1936) he was killed by shots from an ambush next to Kfar Kakon, as he was returning to Hadera from his work in the neighboring orchards. He was 22 when he died.

In his diary entry from 4 Nisan 5689 (1929), I found the following written, along with everything else: "I desire to defend my people with my blood and my soul." He was 14 years old at the time. Years passed, and he became fully immersed in the pioneering youth movement. He influenced his friends in the gymnasium to follow after him, and they did so. He had the power of persuasion, and many of his friends respected this appropriately. "With Anshel in Gordonia" was also our place. While he was still a child, just beginning to read books, he would bring friends of his age to the couch near the hot fireplace during winter days and read to them Jewish history, especially the legends of the strength of our nation in ancient days.

Chaim Kamchi

Two weeks before his death, he wrote to his friend Mordechai Ziserman about his work situation and how he became accustomed to it. The following is the content:

"I wandered about for many weeks and was not able to get myself set up with work. I was very worried, for I saw no possibilities before me. I returned to Hadera. After weeks of idleness, I began to work in an orchard for 15 grush a day. I could not continue in that orchard. I found another place where I worked only until the outbreak of the disturbances, for the orchard was located near Kakon, a dangerous Arab village. After two weeks of idleness, I worked once again for 14 days in another orchard. Later I transferred to this orchard where I now work in spurts, for it is also located in a dangerous place. However I hope that I will be able to earn enough to sustain myself, if only I remain healthy. I got used to work quite well. I passed through the most difficult period of getting used to a working life, and now I have no more fear of work, for I participated in the most difficult tasks in the orchard and did not retreat. I work hard and return from work tired. I would be happy if the few hours of rest would be richer in content, but I have not yet found this. I have male and female friends, but I am not sufficiently interested in them so as to be able to spend time in their company and forget the tribulations of the day of work. If only we were together, friends from the past, it would undoubtedly be good for us. Of course now, with the agitated state of life, we cannot think about actualizing our plans."

From "The Disturbances of 5636" page 659, by Mordechai Ziserman

Chapter 101

Yehudah Spivak of blessed memory

Translated by Jerrold Landau

Yehudah Spivak (the grandson of Yudel Spivak) was born in Orheyev. He made aliya to the Land in 1933. He was injured during an ambush on the Netanya – Givat Chaim Road on 14 Elul and died on 19 Elul 5696 (1936) at the age of 23.

He and his three sisters were educated by their elderly grandmother. In the Land he was a driver. He was injured on the road as he was sitting at the steering wheel, and he died.

He was always prepared for this. After the death of his friend Kamchi, he said to his friends: You will see that I will also fall as I am at the wheel on the road. Regarding the question – Why, for what reason, do you drive on the roads during these days? He would answer: Who will drive? It is forbidden to show them that we are cowards and people who give in.

Yaakov Zeevi

Chapter 102

Moshe Roitman of blessed memory

Translated by Jerrold Landau

Figure 203 - Moshe Roitman

He was born in Orheyev in 1899. He assisted his father in the sheep and cattle trade while he was still a lad. However, business was not in his spirit, and he was attracted to the work of the land. Moshe went out in 1917 to work in the fields with his brother and two of their friends.

He joined the Forer group in 1920 and made aliya to the Land. He remained in Haifa, and looked for work already on his first day there. He started in a bakery and moved over to the port. He was among the defenders during the disturbances of 1921.

That year, we arrived in the Land as a group of chalutzim, and Moshe greeted us with words of encouragement. He advised us to join a group of porters who work at the port (the group of Berel Raptor).

Moshe excelled with his diligence and eagerness. After some time, we obtained animals for the work. The competition from the Arab wagon drivers was fierce, however thanks to the connections Moshe had with the Arab merchants, and his talent of being able to forge good relations with whomever he came into contact, we were able to withstand the competition for two years. When the group broke up, Moshe continued to work among the Arabs on his own. Moshe was a strong, fearless youth. One day, he decided to open up a butcher shop in the Arab marketplace in Haifa. He had to pay rent for the store, and he was a Jew among the Arabs. He trusted in himself and in his relations with his Arabic acquaintances that nothing bad would happen to him…

When the disturbances of 1929 broke out, we warned him and begged him not to go to the marketplace. However he laughed and said, "I am not afraid." He went and did not return. He was murdered by one of his neighbors.

Moshe, the fine land, my friend who was loved by his fellowman, was brought to burial without any opportunity to bid him farewell. Only four friends, myself included, were given permission by the British to accompany him to the cemetery in lower Haifa, to be buried among the rest of the victims in Haifa.

May his soul be bound in the bonds of eternal life.

Y. Rapoport

Chapter 103

Menachem Rotkov of blessed memory

Translated by Jerrold Landau

Figure 204 - Menachem Rotkov

Menachem the son of Mordechai and Tzipora Rotkov was born in Orheyev on November 11, 1925. He was educated in the Tarbut School in his city, and he made aliya to the Land with his parents in 1936, and continued his studies. Due to the difficult economic circumstances of the family, he was forced to end his studies at age 13. After a long and difficult job search, he was accepted by the Af"k Bank. He quickly demonstrated his practical talents, diligence, his love of order, dedication to work, and primarily his well-developed sense of responsibility. He endeared himself to his workmates and to his entire surroundings. He joined Hatzofim and Gordonia, and devoted most of his free time to work in the movement. He decided to go to Hachshara (preparation for agricultural work in Israel), but he had to delay this for two years due to the situation with his family, until his father found a job. Only then, at the age of 17, did he go to Degania Alef. About a year later, he transferred to Neve Eitan, and there to his permanent place in the Chermonim group (Chemdia). He was a member of the secretariat of Chemdia, the central

Orheyev Alive and Destroyed

work committee, the organizer of work, and the security forces. He was the first to fill any responsible and dangerous task, without hesitation. He saw service in the Haganah as a personal obligation and found his place at all times, even though by nature he was not one who thirsted for battle. He excelled with his straightforwardness, his external neatness and the pureness of his heart. He was modest in his actions, a lover of peace, a faithful friend to his friends, and a dedicated and beloved child to his parents.

He formed a strong bond with the land and its soil. At the age of 14, he was one of the first of the demonstrators against the While Paper. He was injured during the demonstration. He always bore the idea of national independence and communal life upon his heart. He desired a life of labor and creativity. He gave expression to all of his thoughts and desires in his letters and articles.

As a soldier and a commander, he had great influence upon his men with his appearance, his personality, his persuasive talents and his faith. He bestowed of himself upon his charges. He was drafted in May 1948, and served as a company commander of the 13th squadron of the Golani Brigade. He participated in the defense of the farms in the region of Beit Shean, Gilboa and the Jezreel Valley. At the end of the first ceasefire, on July 9, 1948, the Iraqis opened a large attack and began to advance in the direction of Zarin. Some of their forces turned to the eastern Gilboa in the direction of Sandala-Mizaar. Menachem and his squadron were in the brigade whose task it was to check the advance of the enemy in that direction and to guard the left flank of our forces. A soldier of his squadron was injured during the battle with the enemy on July 10, 1948. Menachem left his fortification and hastened to assist the injured soldier. On his way he was shot in the neck and he fell on the spot. Due to the conditions, his corpse remained on the spot along with the rest of those who fell in the battle. Only after 30 days were the bodies of the martyrs given over to the hands of the Israel Defense Forces, and Menachem was brought to burial in the cemetery of his kibbutz.

May his soul be bound in the bonds of eternal life.

(Parchments of Fire, 572-573)

Chapter C

Orheyev descendants who died in Israel

Translated by Terry Lasky

Alkushi, Nachum

Averbukh, Shmuel

Averbukh, Muvia

Beznos, Yaakov Yehudah

Beznos, wife

Borsutsky. Fania

Charak, David

Feigin, Chayim -- agronomist

Frank, Anchel

Frank, Malka-Feiga -- wife

Furer, Ben-Zion

Furer, Pesya-Batya -- wife

Gershkovitz, Idil ben Meir

Geynichovitz, Yeshaya

Geynichovitz, Edel

Globman, Mordechai

Globman, Udel-Ada

Golani, Avraham Yitzchak

Golani, Yehudah

Goldenberg, Meir

Goldenberg, Mordechai

Goldenberg, Moshe

Goldshtern, Zlata

Gotlieb -- Miryam Svavolsky

Kamchi-Nairner, Tova

Katzap, Mordechai

Kohan, Yosef

Krasner, Nachman

Levinson, Zila

Petrushka, Levi

Portnoy, Peretz

Portnoy, Leah

Rabinovitz, Zvi

Rapoport, Yisaschar

Rapoport, Bluma

Rechulsky, Chana

Rotkov, Zipora

Shamban, Miryam

Shander, Aizik

Shander -- wife

Shpitzberg, Eliyahu -- doctor

Skliar, Leib

Tartakovsky, Velvel

Yechieli, Yisrael

Chapter 104

Tuviya Averbukh of blessed memory

Translated by Jerrold Landau

Figure 205 - Tuviya Averbukh

He was one of the first three of "Bnei Yisrael" and one of the first of any of the youth who went out to Hachsharah in Hechalutz in order to actualize the order of the movement. The journey was difficult, starting from the Hechalutz chapter in Kishinev (Benderskia 20) through Bilicheni to the Hechalutz chapter that was opened in Orheyev. Despite the difficulties, Tuviya remained strong and faithful to his path.

When he made aliya to the land, he pitched his tent in the valley of Ein-Badeh in the region of Nahalel along with the first ones of "Bnei Yisrael." There, they worked on the road. As the son of a large and veteran family of farmers, he also desired agriculture. In his vision, he saw the group sitting on a plot of land and opening an agricultural farm. Luck went his way, and our paths split on account of the division in the Bnei Yisrael group. After some wandering through other groups, Tuviya arrived in Moshav Rashfon, where he established his family and realized his dream of opening a farm.

He was drafted into the guard unit during the disturbances of 1946, and he and his group were the first to go to any place of danger. He survived many battles with Arab gangs. Tuviya died in a work accident during the battles of the War of Independence on the eve of Passover 5708 (1948). Many tragedies befell the Averbukh family, and the tragic death of Tuviya surpassed them all. This family should remember their son and father who inscribed a bright page in the annals of the birth of Israel.

Shlomo Bronshteyn, Gan Shmuel

Chapter 105

Nachum Alkushi of blessed memory

Translated by Jerrold Landau

Figure 206 - Nachum Alkushi

Nachum was one of the members of the Second Aliya, one of those about whom it can be said, "I have seen those who made aliya and they were few." I first met him as I was passing through Egypt, as I recall in the first year that I arrived in the Land (5667 – 1907). He made aliya a short time later. After he made aliya, he called himself Alkushi (in the Diaspora he was Birnbaum). I met him among the first of the workers of Sagara. He was among a small company of agricultural workers. He worked in the field during the day and dedicated himself to communal affairs during rest times and in the evenings. Nachum, who was blessed with administrative talents, centralized the organizational activity of the Poale Zion in the Galilee region.

I met him once again during the convention of Passover 5669 (1909), and from that time, we remained in contact through letters, primarily about matters of the movement. At the time of the founding of the first Hebrew newspaper of Poale Zion "Heachdut," I invited him to Jerusalem to direct the newspaper. He always fulfilled this task with diligence and dedication. During the time he was in Jerusalem, he dedicated all his free time to communal work as a member of the headquarters of the movement. During the time of the persecutions of Gamal Pasha, he went to America, where he was one of the first to answer the call to the organization of the Hechalutz and the Hebrew Brigade. He was one of the first to return with a brigade of 40 people (Kalei Hamelech) and one of the first to assist the united movement that was formed at that time, that is the movement of "Achdut Avoda," which included the Poale Zion, those not a member of any faction, and some members of Hapoel Hatzair (5679 – 1919). He moved to Jerusalem in 5680 (1920), where he organized the first worker's kitchen, and participated in the first group of Haganah. He married his friend Miriam Meshi in 5681 (1921). They settled and set up their household in Jerusalem. Here, Nachum opened a Kupat Cholim branch, which he headed for many years. They moved to Tel Aviv in 5695 (1935). He was active in the movement and in communal life for many years. Toward the end he became seriously ill. For three years he was so ill that he could not move at all. He was forlorn and isolated.

He died in the Ziv House, and was not eulogized appropriately. However his friends from the Second Aliya remember his diligence, his talents and his boundless dedication. His memory will remain in their hearts forever.

Y. Ben Zvi

*

Days of greatness came to Hebrew Jerusalem in the year 5682 (1922) with the outset of the Third Aliya. There was a need to create and develop several institutions to serve the workers whose population was then growing in the city. There was a need to open a worker's kitchen, and Nachum Alkushi was called to do this with the help of several friends, all inexperienced yet full of will, talent and responsibility. There was a need to open the first Kupat Cholim infirmary, and Nachum Alkushi was asked to take care of this institution. Dr. Pruzhinin of blessed memory came at that time from the Galilee.

Nachum Alkushi stood with him as a faithful guard. He fulfilled his duties with his typical exactitude toward himself and others. He guarded every coin, demanded order, exactitude and responsibility from everyone, and even more so from himself. Indeed, thanks to this small group of the doctor, the nurse and Nachum Alkushi, the young, small institution took root, earned an honorable place, and became one of the most important and respected medical institutions in Jerusalem.

Nachum and Miriam moved from Jerusalem to Tel Aviv in 5695 (1935) on account of work in the institution. This move from Jerusalem which was so beloved to him was not simple for him, and it was not easy for him to acclimatize himself to the atmosphere of that city. There too he served the Kupat Cholim with the same dedication, knowledge and deep, true concern toward the matters that were in his hands.

He was a faithful member of the Histadrut, the community of workers, and to all of the activities of the Workers' Movement in the Land. He served Kupat Cholim and its members with true service.

May his memory be blessed.

Al. Feri

Chapter 106

Yaakov Yehudah Beznos of blessed memory

Translated by Jerrold Landau

Figure 207 - Yaakov Yehudah and wife Beznos

He was involved with the community and pleasant to his fellowman, one of those who won his acclaim by his straightforwardness, his faithfulness and his uprightness to his fellowman.

He fulfilled a special role in the preparation of matzos for Passover, and he was the first in our city who brought machines for the baking of matzos. Before this time, all matzo baking was done entirely by hand. When the community decided to centralize the baking of matzos on the eve of Passover in its own hand, so as to increase the collection of Maos Chitin, the community council turned this over to him, and he answered willingly. He agreed to direct the activity to the best of his ability. Thereby, the Ezrat Aniim (Assistance for the Poor) society was able to expand its activities in general, and expand its assistance for the Passover holiday in particular. Yaakov Iddel's role was great in interceding on behalf of those who were particularly needy and who needed greater support. He knew the situation of each person, and his intercession was decisive. A second enterprise worthy of note in which he had first rights was the fishing enterprise in our city. In the Reat and the national pond (Yas) where there were many fisherman, the fishing was concentrated primarily in the hands of gentiles who were not professionally adept. Yaakov Iddel developed this profession for the benefit of the population. He had an additional spiritual benefit from this, in that he provided portions of fish for the needy, for the Sabbath, without any payment.

His children made aliya to the Land when they grew up. He and his wife remained in Orheyev to liquidate their property. He and his wife made aliya in 1934.

The heart of Yaakov Iddel, the working man who was upright in his ways and always concerned about his fellowman, was broken during the War of Independence which took place in the Land.

He died before his time and was brought to burial in Herzlia.

Chapter 107
Fania Borsutsky of blessed memory

Translated by Jerrold Landau

Figure 208 - Fania Borsutsky

Fania B. was born to a wealthy, pedigreed and scholarly family in Heisin (Podolia). She grew up and was educated in Balta, where she received her education with the renowned teacher Reb Baruch Schwartz (the father of the journalist Shalom Schwartz). At that time, Sheynkin was given the position of Rav Mitaam (government appointed rabbi) in Balta, and the city became an important Zionist center in the region. Fania joined the group of those who assisted Sheynkin in his Zionist activities, and dedicated herself fully to the movement, despite the fact that the communal environment was not comfortable with Zionism. The left saw it as a bourgeois movement, and the right related to it with general disdain. She, the "daughter of the bourgeois" did not refrain from dedicating herself to this movement with all of her youthful energy. She worked a great deal in all areas, and dedicated herself especially to the establishment of the Zionist school in Balta, where the students were primarily the children of the poor. Fania B. participated as a delegate to the Zionist convention in Minsk in Elul 5662 (1902) along with her husband Avraham Borsutsky of Orheyev who married her that year. They moved to Orheyev.

She participated along with her husband in the Chovevei Zion convention that took place in Odessa in Cheshvan 5663 (1902).

(From the words of B. Shochtman of blessed memory, published in the Hayom newspaper.}

Chapter 108

Udel and Mordechai Globman of blessed memory

Translated by Jerrold Landau

Rabbi Mordechai and his family (his sons were Akiva and Pinchas Guvrin) arrived in Orheyev with the stream of refugees from Ukraine in the winter of 5680 (1920). Akiva and Pinchas stayed with their uncle Reb Matityahu Globman. Within a short time, Reb Mordechai started teaching in the Yeshiva and became involved in communal affairs as a veteran. He was a man of noble spirit, who quickly endeared himself to the activists of the community and the Zionist movement. His home was open to anyone in need. He had a strong connection with the Land of Israel and the Hebrew Language, and saw Hechalutz as an important means for ensuring the future of the nation. He was saturated with Jewish religious culture, expert in Talmudic literature, and a man of great deeds. He often lectured and had a large audience of listeners and fans.

Figure 209 - Mordechai and Udel Globman

His wife Udel assisted him in his communal endeavors. He took counsel and advice from her intelligent understanding and her alertness to the problems of the day, especially with regard to people who were suffering and required assistance.

Reb Mordechai and his wife Udel made aliya to the Land in the year 5684 (1924), and realized their dream of settling in the holy city of Jerusalem.

They lived there until the end of their days. In Jerusalem their home served as a meeting place for those who had come from Orheyev. Reb Mordechai maintained contact for a long time with his friends in Orheyev, and exchanged correspondence with them. The letters were full of enthusiasm about the issues of the Land.

They passed away at a good old age.

Chapter 109

Idil Yagolnitzer of blessed memory

Translated by Jerrold Landau

Figure 210 - Idil Yagolnitzer

Yagolnitzer was a model veteran of a youth movement whose motto was boundless dedication to the idea and the principle.

I was drawn to him while I was still involved in Gordonia. He had a unique charm that made him look young in spirit while he was old in years. His soul was and always remained young and vibrant.

He was known to all of us as an activist, who preferred the duty to the community over his own affairs. He was faithful to his nation and struggled with dedication for his civic and national rights. He struggled valiantly against any event that had an air of sycophantism, and complained against all those who learned how to bow their heads in deference and get used to being dishonest with their souls.

Even the state authorities recognized his talents and honored him for them.

He was a teacher, guide, and friend for the youth. The youth related to him like a man of vision and understanding. He was a member of the Jewish party during the elections to national institutions. He stood as one of the candidates for the list that was to protect the interests of the Jewish population.

When he appeared as a lecturer or in public gatherings in the city, he always knew how to delve deeply into the Jewish question. He did not hesitate to fight against those who mislead and are misled.

He was faithful to his principles, and served as a personal example to his acquaintances and fans. His aliya to the Land served as an example of this.

His influence was great upon all of the youth, without concern for factional affiliation. He was considered to be one of the primary leaders in the instilling of national consciousness in the youth of Orheyev and in preparing them for the road to Zion…

I loved to listen to Yagolnitzer during a debate. He was very sharp when he arranged a battle against the enemies of Zionism. He knew well how to express the complete truth and the ideological essence of Zionism. His answers were on the mark, clear and convincing. His appearances at gatherings always left a great impression, not only upon those who agreed with his outlook, but also upon his opponents. They too related to him with great honor.

He stood at the helm of the endeavor of arranging self defense. He instilled in the heart of everyone the understanding of the need for defending oneself, and he also took upon himself the distribution of weapons to the members. He was the living spirit in all events and matters where the spirit of Jewish pride and independence was felt.

I met very few Jews with as much spine in communal affairs as had Idil Yagolnitzer. His heart ached so much when he witnessed the communal activism in the Diaspora tend toward ingratiation and sycophantism.

I will always remember him as a teacher, an activist and a friend. Not only I, but all of the youth of Orheyev who were connected to him with all strands of their souls will remember him.

The publication of a book on Orheyev is perhaps the finest floral wreath over the grave of this faithful and dedicated activist who did so much to educate and guide the younger generation.

May his memory be blessed through the mouths of all his friends and fans.

D.   Chaimovitz

Chapter 110

Yosef Kohan of blessed memory

Translated by Jerrold Landau

5660-5718 (1900-1958)

Figure 211 - Yosef Kohan

He was a native of Mashkovtsy in region of Orheyev. His father was a shochet in the town. He spent the better part of his youth in Orheyev, where he came to study and teach. As a teacher, he proved his pedagogical ability worthy of the name. He was one of the activists in Tzeirei Zion.

He made aliya to the Land in 1923. Here as well, he dedicated himself to the worker's movement.

We read the following in Davar from January 3, 1958.

Yosef Kohan, one of the veterans of the Hamekasher Company, died at the age of 58. His friends from work, the secretary of the workers' committee M. Brem, friends from the council, the acting vice mayor M. Ish-Shalom, as well as friends and relatives participated in the funeral.

As a member of Hechalutz, he worked in the development work, stonecutting of Jerusalem stone, and other tasks. From 1931, he worked in the accounting division of Hamekasher.

He was modest, with clean hands and a pure heart. He was prepared to help his fellow in his profession.

Chapter 111

Zila Levinson of blessed memory

Translated by Jerrold Landau

Figure 212 - Zila Levinson

Zila Gondelman finished the ORT sewing school, and immediately went to work with one of the sewing enterprises in the city.

Her father died while she was young, and the responsibility of supporting the nine person family fell upon Zila. She concerned herself with spiritual satisfaction at the same time. She joined the Poale Zion party and started productive activities.

In 1933, she entered Hachsharah in Fokshany, Romania along with her husband Moshe Levinson. There as well, Zila excelled with her diligence and dedication to work. She endeared herself to everyone.

Immediately thereafter, in July 1934, they made aliya to the land. Zila was happy. However, the pains of assimilation came quickly. The search for work and difficulties of settling in were their lot. However, Zila, with her great energy, bore the yoke and supported and strengthened her husband.

They encountered many obstacles and difficulties. Zila overcame them all during her 20 years of living in the Land. However, she did not have the strength to overcome one of them. She took ill with a serious illness. She succeeded in marrying off her daughter, and her refined soul left her a few days later.

People from near and far extended last honors to her. A fine tree was cut down in the midst of its blossoming.

Chapter 112

Eliyahu Ben-Zion Furer and his wife Pesya of blessed memory

Translated by Jerrold Landau

Figure 213 - Eliyahu Ben-Zion and Pesya (wife) Furer

Ben-Zion was born in Akkerman (Bessarabia) in 1880 [2]. He was orphaned from his father at a young age. Nevertheless, he received a traditional education during his childhood, studying Torah and Judaism. He moved with his mother to Beltsy at the age of 12, and they moved to Orheyev about two years later. There he was accepted as an apprentice by Hinzl Polonsky, the owner of a writing materials store and bookbinding workshop. There was also a lending library, primarily for Yiddish books. This was before there was a public library.

Ben-Zion learned about the business of the store through his work in bookbinding. When the lending library was placed under his control, he broadened his knowledge in Yiddish literature. He exhibited talents in all these areas, and with time, he was the de facto manager of the business.

During that time, at the end of the 19th century, it was a brazen act on his part to turn the attention of the readers to the new Yiddish literature. Obtaining such literature was quite expensive, and this was obviously against the interests of the owner of the store who was forced to exchange the old literature with books of Mendele, Shalom Aleichem, Deninzon, Peretz, etc.

At the beginning of the 20th century, the student Steinbach arrived in our city. He made contact with Steinbach and recommended some of his friends to him. He placed a condition that he should teach the friends Bible, literature and Hebrew as well, for Ben-Zion was a Zionist, and he would not have agreed that his friends should receive guidance and education that is foreign to their spirit. For they, like him, were inclined toward the vision of national revival. This group that was composed of tradesmen later established the foundation for the loan and savings fund for tradesmen in our city.

Ben-Zion the Zionist

From his youth, Ben-Zion bore in his heart the vision of the revival of the Jewish nation and the Hebrew language in its land. He was one of the enthusiastic followers of the Zionist activist Avraham Borsutsky, and he frequented his house. He participated in all activities of the movement that took place at that time. When his turn came to set up a Jewish home, he married Pesya of the Hentin family of Orheyev, left his place of work with Polonsky and opened up a store for writing implements. On account of his great diligence, his business acumen and the participation of his wife, he succeeded in developing his small store into a first class business in the region of Orheyev.

Ben-Zion the Actualizing Zionist

In 1904, the year of Herzl's death, Ben-Zion had a son, whom he named Herzl after the leader. He gave the rest of his children Hebrew names. He educated them in the national spirit.

However none of this quenched his thirst for independent national life. His desire to build his permanent home for his family in the Land of Israel was great. In the summer of 1912, Ben-Zion took his oldest son Herzl and went to visit the Land in order to see from close up the conditions of settlement, with the aim of making aliya with his family later. He took his eight year old son Herzl with him in order to set him up in the Herzliya Gymnasium in Tel Aviv. It became clear that this was impossible due to the young age of the child. They returned to Orheyev and prepared immediately for the aliya of the entire family. In the interim, WWI broke out, and the Furer family was forced to delay their aliya.

With the Balfour Declaration, Furer renewed his preparations to actualize his vision. Ben-Zion convened a group of those interested in the idea in Kishinev, and lectured them in a very detailed fashion about the various issues of settling in the Land. In the meantime, he concluded his preparations for aliya.

Ben-Zion Furer and his group arrived in Jaffa on Chanukah of 1920. During those days, before the improvement of the conditions of settlement for members of the middle class, the members of the group did not succeed in obtaining land for settlement despite their efforts. The members began to scatter slowly but surely, with everyone seeking out his own means of livelihood. Ben-Zion also decided to grasp at anything that he could. He opened a book and writing implement store. He was the first to open such a store in Tel Aviv. With time, thanks to his diligence and his fine relations, the name Furer became popular among teachers and students, and he earned an honorable livelihood.

Chapter 113

Batya (Pesya) Furer of blessed memory

Translated by Jerrold Landau

She was a modest woman with a quiet demeanor. Motherly tenderness exuded from his pleasant face. The Furer home was open to all. The place for meeting and parties of the Zionists in the city was in the Furer house, and Pesya, the matron of the home, greeted them all pleasantly.

Pesya followed her husband's Zionist path with her great intelligence. With her full agreement, Furer decided to make aliya to the Land and to liquidate their business for that purpose. The obstacles in their path to settling in the Land were many. Pesia withstood the disturbances of 1921 and all that was related to them with spiritual calmness, without uttering complaints against the Land. On the contrary, she drew near and encouraged the newcomers to the land. She attempted to ease their difficult suffering during the first days of their absorption. A large number of Orheyev natives were guests in their home. Those in need turned to Pesya for help in every difficult situation. On occasions, a sick person outside of the city who required prolonged medical care would find shelter and rest in family style in their home. At the threshold of happiness in her life, fate turned against her and she died in a work accident in her home.

Many of the natives of our town appreciate her and will remember her in their hearts.

Chapter 114

Peretz and Leah Portnoy of blessed memory

Translated by Jerrold Landau

Figure 214 - Peretz and Leah Portnoy

Peretz worked diligently in the transporting business. He was the first to acquire a transport truck to serve the Orheyev-Kishinev route. This was a bold and important step in those days, which later brought additional improvements in communications. Their only son made aliya, and later the entire family followed in 1936. Thanks to their diligence and life experience, they reached a very satisfactory economic situation.

In Israel as in the Diaspora, they answered the call of all who required their help.

In the later years, Leah became seriously ill and died. After a short time, her husband Peretz also died.

Chapter 115

Levi Petrushka of blessed memory

Translated by Jerrold Landau

He was a native of Teleneshti (Orheyev region), an experienced farmer, expert in vineyards. When the Hechalutz emissary D. Chaimovitz asked him to train the members of Hechalutz in the work of the vineyard, Levi answered enthusiastically, and convinced other vineyard keepers in the region to accept chalutzim for work. Hundreds of chalutzim obtained knowledge in this field thanks to Levi's instruction. His home served as a fine inn for any chalutz, delegate, and any passer-by in that town. In this manner, Teleneshti turned into a center of agricultural Hachsharah in those days. There are many chalutzim today in the land who remember the warm treatment that they found in that home.

Figure 215 - Levi Petrushka

His love for his fellowman was great, especially to those who were preparing to make aliya to the land. His love for the Land was great and enthusiastic. His desire was to make aliya to the Land and settle there. When his daughter Etia made aliya to the land, he waited eagerly for the day when he and his family would be able to make aliya.

In the meantime, the war broke out with all its fury. He and his family uprooted themselves from their hometown and wandered to Uzbekistan in far-off Russia. When he returned to Chernovitz after the war, he did not find spiritual rest, and he desired to go to the Land. He succeeded, and made aliya with his wife in 1955. He was so enthusiastic about the landscapes of the Land and its flourishing. He wished to return to the work of the land which was his calling throughout his life. However, he died suddenly, and Levi was removed from his family and friends in an untimely fashion.

Chapter 116

Reb Anchel and Malka Feiga Frank of blessed memory

Translated by Jerrold Landau

Figure 216 - Anchel and Malka Feiga Frank

He related to well to people and was liked by them. He was a member of the loan and savings fund of the small scale merchants. He occupied himself in business throughout his life, and sustained his family in an honorable fashion. He educated his children in the spirit of the times.

He arrived in the Land with his wife in 1934, approximately ten years after the aliya of his son Mordechai. They established their home near their son in Kibbutz Gan Shmuel. Despite their old age, they quickly got used to Kibbutz life. They reorganized their lives and made every effort to not be a burden upon others. Malka Feiga kept their small home orderly and clean. She ran a kosher kitchen and often prepared meals for the other parents in the Kibbutz. Reb Anchel became involved in handiwork. He filled every task in building and agriculture that was given to him by the work office of the Kibbutz. They did not succeed in arranging for the aliya of their son Yeshayahu who remained in the Diaspora.

They died in Gan Shmuel and were buried there.

May their souls be bound in the bonds of eternal life.

Chapter 117

Rivka Dacha Frank of blessed memory

Translated by Jerrold Landau

The daughter of Asher Anchel and Malka Feiga.

Figure 217 - Rivka Dacha Frank

Dear Dacha was taken from us while still young and full of promise.

She decided at a young age that, for a girl, the study of a trade would ensure her independence in life. She studied sewing. In addition to studying a trade, she helped her mother with her housework.

At times that she should have been free, she dedicated herself fully to work in the movement. She worked with great dedication in the activities of the Keren Kayemet, publicity, fundraising, organizing celebrations, etc.

She saw her future in making aliya to the Land along with the entire family. When M. Usishkin visited Kishinev during a harsh winter in the 1920s, she traveled with her friends to a large meeting that was arranged by the Keren Kayemet in Kishinev. During this journey she caught cold, took ill and never arose.

Thus did Dacha leave us, the dear and dedicated soul, the pleasant girl, at the young age of 22.

She did not succeed in realizing her dream of making aliya to the land and dedicating her activity to the upbuilding of the homeland.

Mordechai in Gan Shmuel

Chapter 118

Mordechai Katzap of blessed memory

Translated by Jerrold Landau

(From "Cholmim Velochmim" (Dreamers and Strugglers) by Yaari-Polskin, with minor omissions and changes.)

Mordechai Katzap was born and raised in Orheyev. He received a Hebrew education in cheder during his childhood, and absorbed love and longing for the Land of Israel.

The event took place in 1906. I recall that I saw him for the first time in Petach Tikva. He was a strong youth with broad shoulders. The good and fine fields of Bessarabia were recognizable on his face and in all his action. Might and health exuded from Mordechai's face.

Mordechai Katzap took upon himself a particularly difficult task. He was responsible for cleaning out the abandoned valley, softening the hard roots, clearing the thorns and removing the stones. He worked for many hours during the day and night without tiring.

The group worked at the Kinneret and was full of contentment. The area was full of bogs and some people got a fever. However, the main thing was: not all of them at the same time... The work progressed. Each day before eating they took quinine, which prevented the fevers from recurring at short intervals. Months passed, and life was conducted calmly, until an unexpected accident took place to our friend Mordechai.

The agronomist Berman brought horses and donkeys from Damascus, who had never had a yoke placed upon them. It was difficult to get the horses used to going along the furrow and pulling a plough or wagon. They got them used to this somehow, and the wildest horse was given to the strongest youth among us, Mordechai Katzap. He approached the horse every day and pushed it to drag wagons full of stones from the valley at the banks of the Jordan, to the point where sweat dripped from it and white foam was seen on its skin. Thus did he bring it to a point where it was comfortable walking with a wagon. However one day, the horse got upset, and when Katzap began to harness it, it kicked him in the abdomen. Strong Mordechai did not tell anyone about this, and went out to work again the next day. He hoped that everything would pass safely. Later he told us about this, and some of us took him to the hospital in Safed in a stretcher, for it was forbidden to transport him in a wagon.

His consciousness was not disturbed even a few hours before his death. He did not think about death, and asked endlessly about the details of the work in the farm. As death approached he moved his hands, supplicated and wept. He lifted himself from the bed, spoke some things toward Heaven… fought valiantly against the bitterness of death, and expired.

The news struck us all like thunder…

Chapter 119

Fishel Rozen of blessed memory

Translated by Jerrold Landau

(A section from a story)

(Also known as Fishel Stern)

Figure 218 - Fishel Rozen

Zvi was sent to the modern cheder "Cheder Metukan" of the teacher Fishel Rozen when he was about seven years old. The "teacher" was not called a "melamed" and this was not a "cheder" but rather a school with several classes, benches and desks. Hebrew and Russian were taught, and the teaching style was "Hebrew in Hebrew." However, the greatest innovation was the teacher himself. Fishel was a stout man of splendid stature, with a pleasant face and a well-kept beard. His intelligent eyes exuded nobility and internal calm. He talked calmly and enthusiastically, at times with stifled excitement and convincing self control – everything exuded honor. A new world opened up for Zvi in the home of the teacher Rozen. Zvi attempted to recall the spirit that pervaded that home, and only one word came to mind: love. The teacher gave his entire heart over to instilling into his students a love of Hebrew – the new Hebrew, pleasant, with clear expression and proper intonation, the stories of the scriptures and the images of the Bible; a story in the playground, the material in the Olam Katan and Hechaver children's publications, the national

Hebrew poem in recital and song, and the dream of the revival of Zion. When he was still a child of eight or nine, Zvi started to long for the real Land of Israel, a desire that was not relegated to the far-off Messianic era. Fishel Rozen was an active Zionist. He lectured splendidly in the synagogue and at gatherings. A picture hung in Rozen's school, the picture of the noble, splendid, enchanting Dr. Herzl. Zvi recalls, as if it was only recently, one summer day when Uncle Yisrael came to the home of his grandfather, and fell upon grandfather with bitter weeping, lamenting: Dr. Herzl died! Everyone was enveloped in gloom. Even grandfather, who maintained tradition but also regularly read Hatzefira, Hatzofeh, Hazman and Haolam; even Uncle Efrayim, even Father who had no time for issues of Zionism although it was always in his heart. The entire house of the teacher Rozen was enveloped in mourning.

"The entire house of the teacher" included his wife Gutcha. She was talkative, and imbued with love and friendship. Zvi quickly became at home with her. There was the son, the healthy, strong, diligent son who disappeared from the house one day, and after some time the news reached us that he made aliya to the land of Israel and was working in the orchards on a Moshav. There was the daughter Miryam, a young teacher, with charming beauty, who also expressed great love to Zvi. There was the younger daughter Riva, approximately Zvi's age, a beautiful girl whom he made efforts to look at whenever she was in the classroom or the yard. Later he would think about her also in school during studies as well as at home. There were winter days when frost covered the windows at home. Zvi would run his finger along the glass and without paying attention, he would draw the letters Reish Yod Beit Ha, and would whisper to himself "Riva." The feeling of love that filled the Rozen home warmed the heart. Rozen's home enchanted and pampered Zvi, praised his talents, and treated him as a son. Miriam, his young teacher, would joke and say: I will wait for Zvi to grow up… However Zvi was thinking about Riva. One day the teacher surprised him during Bible class and asked: Where are we? Zvi was lost in his thoughts and did not know where they were, and his world suddenly darkened: He received a slap on the face from his teacher, from Fishel Rozen!

The matter was forgotten with the passage of time. For Zvi, the house of Rozen remained a house of friendship and love. Throughout his life, he still met up with that house – a dear Hebrew house in the Land of Israel.

Ch. Sharer

(A small section from his book)

Chapter 120

Zipora Rotkov of blessed memory

Translated by Jerrold Landau

14 Av 5653 (1893) – 13 Tevet 5618 (1958)

Figure 219 - Zipora Rotkov

She was noble, modest in her manner, a dedicated mother and faithful wife, prepared at all time to help her fellowman from the breadth of her heart.

From her childhood, from an internal sense of duty she bore the burden of helping her children care for the large family.

When she set up her own household, she put herself with a full heart at the right side of all members in the family, with regard to sustaining them and educating them. Her first concern was about national education, in which she herself was educated in her father's home (he was the teacher Matityahu Globman). She extended a hand of assistance to the group of parents in setting up a kindergarten and the Tarbut School, and was a faithful assistant to her husband in his communal work.

She dedicated her entire essence to her family. When the eldest daughter joined the Gordonia movement and Zipora realized that the time for her aliya was drawing near and that the integrity of the family would be impinged upon, she hatched the idea of the entire family making aliya to the Land in order to prevent this split up.

This brazen decision took place at the beginning of the disturbances of 1936 – when the bloodshed in the Land was at its height and the danger was great. Nevertheless, Zipora was not fazed. She accepted everything upon herself with the hope of a future in settling in the land. The family made aliya, and felt the pangs of absorption and all the difficulties involved with it. Even then she bore what fate decreed upon her with calm and love, as she supported and encouraged the members of her family.

It was 1948, in the midst of the War of Independence. The daughters were with their families and the son in the farms (in the Negev and in the valley of Beit Shean), and the list of victims arrived daily. Only Zipora herself knew what she felt during those awesome days... and the terrible news reached her. Her son Menachem was among the victims. Her heart was broken inside, but the family behaved with restraint.

The wise, patient Zipora, to whom complaining was foreign, drunk from the cup of agony to its full extent, with the strong hope and desire to merit a peaceful and contented life among family. She did not merit thus... She died after terrible suffering.

Chapter 121

Yisrael Yechieli of blessed memory

Translated by Jerrold Landau

Figure 220 - Yisrael Yechieli

From his childhood, Yisrael excelled in his diligence and love of work. When he was still a student in the gymnasium, he assisted his father in the store, and did any work that was necessary to help the family. He made aliya to the Land in 1929. He became involved in various tasks to cultivate the Land. He was a member of the Bnei Yisrael group in Nahalel, and he later joined Kibbutz Gan Shmuel. He did not get accustomed to farming life, but rather preferred life in the town. He did not seek out an easy life after he left Gan Shmuel, but rather joined the founders of the town of Brandes (his place of residence until his last day). He set up a small farm with his own hands and the assistance of his family.

He also worked as a builder in Hadera and the region. In his latter years, he worked as a driver in the porting office of the drivers of Hadera, and was also a member of its leadership. He excelled as a Hagana man in the town. He dedicated all of his free time to his family and his fellow. He had now free time for himself, and he even continued to work when the accursed illness overtook him. Only when all of his strength failed him did he lie down and not get up anymore.

Woe over the loss!

Chapter 122

Aizik and Leah Shander

Translated by Jerrold Landau

Figure 221 - Aizik and Leah Shander

Aizik was one of the first activists of the community of craftsmen in our city and one of the founders and members of the loan fund for assisting craftsmen. His son Yosef and daughter Malka were educated in the spirit of the times. After the Balfour Declaration, Yosef decided to make aliya to the Land with the first group of chalutzim.

Aizik and Leah did not hesitate to uproot themselves from their roots, and the entire family made aliya in 1920. Aizik and Leah bore the difficulties of absorption and the Arab disturbances of 1921 with strength and patience. They accepted everything with love, with the hope for better days to come... Although Aizik's spirit was strong, his body was crushed under the suffering. He took ill and died before his time.

Leah died at an old age and was buried in Pardes Chana, where she lived for her last years with her daughter Malka.

Chapter 123

Dr. Eliyahu Shpitzberg

Translated by Jerrold Landau

Figure 222 - Dr. Eliyahu Shpitzberg

Eliyahu (Elik) was born in Orheyev. He chose the path of Zionist actualization, even though the national movement was in decline during that time. When he was a student at the technical school in Kiev, he suffered from the relations with the teachers. This gave him the urge to make aliya to the Land. He spent some time in Beirut on his way to the Land, where he completed the faculty of medicine. From there, he came to live here. He was active in communal affairs in the Land. (As a token of appreciation, his photo was hung in the Kupat Cholim infirmary in the Borochov neighborhood.) He was drafted into the army at the outbreak of the first war, but death pursued him. He became ill with typhus and died in his prime.

Chapter D1

Photographs of Orheyev descendants who died in Israel

Translated by Terry Lasky

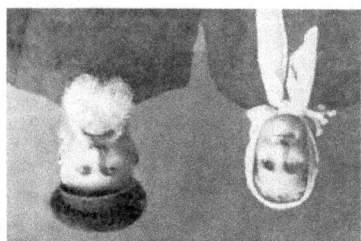

Figure 223 - Eidil and Yeshaya Geynichovitz

Figure 224 - Miryam Shamban

Died 8 Elul in Tel Aviv at 68

Figure 225 – Moshe Goldenberg

Figure 226 – Meir Goldenberg

Figure 227 – Mordechai Goldenberg

Figure 228 - Miryam Gotlieb

Figure 229 - Zlata Goldshtern

Figure 230 - Nachman Krasner

Figure 231 - Radulsky

Figure 232 - Moshe and wife Rabinovitz

Figure 233 - Bluma (wife) and Yisacher Rapoport

Chapter D2

List of Orheyev descendants that died in Israel

Translated by Terry Lasky

Dyukman, Hertz

Vurgaft, Pinchas

Zubritsky, Nachman

Yonovitz, Moshe

Mundrian, Yosef

Naychin, Bendik (Ben-Zion)

Frank, Dacha

Ziserov, Pini

Rabinovitz, Simone Moscyovitz

Chapter 124

Avraham Borsutsky

Translated by Jerrold Landau

We provide an extensive article on him because we regarded him as a founder and leader of the movement in our region, and its living spirit. He was the educator and counselor, and his influence was great upon the following generation who continued to bear aloft the flag of renaissance. The hundreds of people who came to participate in the first and second conventions are witnesses to this. His name was blessed and remembered with feelings of honor and appreciation by all of them.

Figure 234 - Avraham Borsutsky

Something on his Roots

He was a native of Orheyev, born in the year 5630 (1870) to his parents who owned a large estate. He received a traditional education as was customary in those days. However, instead of at cheder, he received his education from private teachers (melamdim). During his childhood he studied secular courses in addition to regular studies. These were also taught to him by private teachers. When he grew up, he earned his livelihood by running the affairs of the estate. The farm primarily grew crops, and was partially a dairy farm. He managed the farm until his last days in Orheyev.

A. B. as the Delegate of Orheyev

None of us knew A. B. as the owner of the estate. We knew that there were days when he was not at home for those who came to seek him – those who came to seek him were solely involved in affairs of our community, primarily of the Zionist movement from its first steps and through the various incarnations that it went through during his days. The exchange of correspondence between him and M. Usishkin began from the year 5654 (1894). In one of the letters, he told of the special celebration that took place in the Zionist organization at its first decade of existence. It is clear that this movement took its first steps at the dawn of the Chibat Zion movement. Throughout all those days he was the living spirit in the movement. He was the initiator, the founder and the energy behind it. He was the one who ensured that the movement would not be swallowed up by the various winds that blew at that time through the Jewish street. He was known by everyone outside the borders of our city as the power and delegate of the Zionist of Orheyev at gatherings and conventions.

A. B. as a Talented Orator

We, the people of Orheyev, knew him as a talented and wonderful orator. He was calm, deep and pleasant to the ear. He was a modern orator in his day. During his time, the Zionist orators were of the type of Yitzchak Nisenboim or Yavzorov, to whom the biblical verse served as the source of their words, which were spiced with statements of the sages or wonderful Midrashim. A. B. was not like this. He always talked about and around the topic. The background and topic of his lectures was always real life with all of its changes and experiences.

He delivered his lectures with deep faith in the justice of his words, with clear enunciation and popular simplicity that always spellbound the audience. The members of his audience were his fans. During my day, almost all the youth and all the people of the city would go once a week to listen to his words. It was also pleasant to listen to him in casual conversation – pleasant and informative simultaneously. There was no need for a public announcement about the appearance of A. B. It was sufficient to paste a note on the western wall of the kloiz, and the news would spread through the community through various channels. People would stream to the kloiz from all corners of the city.

I never saw a case where the entire audience was sitting in their seats. Rather, everyone stood crowded and cramped, listening with great attention, afraid lest they miss even one word of the lecture. It once happened that one of his opponents started to heckle him in the middle of his speech. However, he was smarter than his opponent, and was able to brush it off and continue on unfazed. For the most part, unexpected success came to him after such an incident. Heckling such as that did not take his mind off the topic for even one moment. On the contrary, he gained additional enthusiasm, which was transmitted to his audience as well. It was as if all partitions were removed between him and the community. After he concluded his speech, everyone would breathe comfortably, as if everything became clear and there was no room for doubt and dispute. I recall that on one occasion, a public gathering was convened in the Synagogue of the Tailors (Di Schneiderershe Shul). One of the Bund activists opened the meeting. A. B was supposed to be second to him. He began his speech with the following point: "The words of the previous speaker can be divided into two parts. In the first part, he cursed and riled against the Zionist camp, rendering it dirt and ashes. In the second part, he repeated what he had said in the first part." Great laughter broke out in the audience. This reaction encouraged him further, and he continued on calmly and pleasantly. It is interesting that he rarely talked about the dark things and incorrect spirit of the opposing camp. He was not eager to disprove and contradict the deductions and conclusions of the preceding speaker, but rather he arranged all of his words around the obligation and light that emanates from our renaissance movement. This also draws from the realities of the daily life of the masses of the people, but its roots stem from the splendid past of the nation, and it is our obligation to continue in this direction to greet the future, which is a continuation of our unbroken golden chain… As he concluded his words, the audience applauded him endlessly.

I recall another meeting, also in the aforementioned synagogue. There, A. B. was the opening and main speaker. Hertz Gilishensky also came to the meeting. (He was a school chum of mine from the yeshiva and the kloiz, and later he abandoned his piety. We knew about him and realized that he came to dispute and disrupt the order of the meeting. This came to the attention of A. B., but he did not pay attention to this, and continued his words with the same tone and style with which he started. Gilishensky was apparently waiting for an utterance of the speaker that he could grab hold of. When the chance arose, he jumped onto the bench, cut off the speaker, waved the thick stick that he held in his hand and began to scream and pour out invective against Zionism, etc. The crowd became quite perplexed, and a tumult arose. In the confusion, many began to push for the door and escape through the windows.

In the letter of A. B. to Usishkin from May 2, 1905, he wrote among everything else: "The relationship between the Bundists and the members of Ch. D. to Zionism of late has taken on the form of hooliganism. They use all despicable means to disrupt our assemblies. When we arranged a gathering on the first intermediate day of Passover in one of the synagogues, they also entered and instigated a great tumult. The crowd left through the windows. The synagogue was filled to the brim, and among those gathered were women, including pregnant woman. They perpetrated a scandal in the name of freedom. Miraculously, no human tragedies occurred aside from two pregnant women who miscarried. Others were lightly cut and their clothes were torn... The appearance of the synagogue was like those I saw in Kishinev after the pogrom." Finally, he asked M. Usishkin to send a speaker who would also know how to use the words of Marx and Engels... "It would be good if you could find a member of Poale Zion who is also a Zionist of Zion."

In the exchange of correspondence that we have brought down between A. B. and M. Usishkin, the reader will find material of great interest about the state of the movement a half century ago, along with several themes about the communal persona of Avraham Borsutsky as a Zionist activist. These testify to his faithful dedication, the extent of his understanding, and his various reactions to several tasks and assignments that required his attention. Avraham Borsutsky's heart was alert, and his ear was attentive to everything that took place and every flutter that went through the movement...

The family left Orheyev and moved to Odessa, where he received a job in the office of H. Zaltopolsky. In this position, he traveled to Samarkand and other places. He was imprisoned by the Bolsheviks in 1920 and was murdered by them as a Zionist and a businessman...

Y. S.

Avraham Borsutsky was the founder of the Chovevei Zion organization in Orheyev, and its director throughout its existence. Avrahamel stood at the helm of all communal matters. He was the head of the Haganah (defense) in the years 1902-1905. During the elections of 1905 to the Gasodarstvenya Duma, he was elected in our region along with Moshe Ravich to the assembly of electors who had the duty of electing delegates to the first parliament in Russia. During those days of the Black Reaction, there was a great struggle with respect to establishing the character of the democratic parliament by the representatives of the people. Borsutsky and Ravich had the honorable task of voting for the most progressive Christian delegate (in accordance with the allocation of electoral rights, Jews did not have the right to be represented in parliament). This was a responsible role within the network of relations that existed between the Jews and the Christians.

Avrahamel dedicated his generous talents to the Zionist movement. He dedicated himself to it with his heart and soul, and invested the best of his energy and most of his time and efforts to it. He was an active member of the Odessa Committee from the day of its founding. His entire aim was to draw the masses close to the movement by conducting activities for the people and speaking their language of spoken Yiddish. In one letter to Usishkin from 6 Tammuz 5654 (1894), he strongly presented the case for publicity to the simple folk. "It is extremely necessary now to write a book in Yiddish which will explain the matter of settlement in all of its details. From all that has been published until now, there is not one that can properly explain the rationale of this idea." Avrahamel took up the case of "our simple brethren." "Show us the light of this idea; show us what our brethren have done throughout the 12 years of colonization in the Land of Israel." He added, "It is a great and holy thing that you have taken upon yourselves to love the idea of the settlement for our youth and our maskilim – have mercy also upon those who 'walk in darkness,' give them spiritual sustenance, brighten their path, breathe the breath of life in them, and perhaps... Perhaps they will join our ranks for the settlement of the Land..."

He was involved in the upper echelons of the Zionist movement even though he was hundreds of kilometers away from its epicenter. He was a delegate to the Chovevei Zion conventions in Odessa (1896, 1901, 1902), and also the second convention of Russian Zionists in Minsk in 1902. He was also elected to the third convention of Russian Zionists in Helsinki in 1906. Avrahamel watched and observed the ways of the movements with a deep investigative sense. He exposed omissions and follies, and did not hesitate to describe his fears for the fate of the movement before its leaders.

(From his letters to Usishkin) "At times we read and hear that there are more than 1,000 Chovevei Zion groups in Russia. Is this not a painful joke to refer to that group of people who never did one thing for the benefit of our idea, and who only incidentally joined the ranks of our organization, as a 'movement'? I doubt if we can count even half of them as active members.

"I do not exaggerate if I state that our movement is standing on nothing, and we must begin everything anew.

"The truth is very bitter, but we must state things as they are."

However, Avraham Borsutsky, the vibrant activist and eternal optimist, did not give up. There is a cure to the decline in the movement, and he continued on in that letter. "… In my opinion, it is possible to set our movement on firmer foundations. Only then, if we change our values, and place our stress on the essence rather than the quantity…"

Avrahamel was known as having a good disposition. He honored and believed in his fellowman, and he was especially exacting and demanding in imposing personal responsibility upon all those who took it upon themselves to serve the movement. He set conditions:

"A member of the movement can only be such a person who is prepared to donate his time and money to the degree that the matter demands of him."

"A member of the movement is duty bound to fulfill all demands and obligations that the leaders of the movement place upon him. He must be a person with strong discipline. Heaven forbid that he should turn away even one hairbreadth from all that the leaders of the movement command him."

Avrahamel immediately returned to his fundamental idea, the idea of spreading the movement among "the broad strata" of the people. He continued:

"… We must establish another form of the movement which will be called 'the masses.' The purpose is to attract hundreds of members who will be exempt from the responsibility that is imposed on the members of the type of the first movement. The members of the second type will be required to come to general meetings no less than once every two months, where the leaders of the organization will be given an accounting of what is happening in the Zionist world, so that the members will become associated with the Zionist idea and its appropriate timely development, and they will not be misled by rumors and exaggerations about the footsteps of the Messiah in the immediate future…"

Out of deep fear for the future of the movement, he turned to Usishkin at the end of the aforementioned letter:

"… Here I finish my letter with the request to pay attention to my recommendations. All of my advice came after a great deal of thought and the experience of many years. I feel in my soul that I still have a great deal to state about the methods and techniques of reorganization, but I believe that you will understand more than I have written here…

"I request from you that you remember only one thing, that our organization is very weak and unsteady, and if we do not search for means of repairing and improving it, it will regress from year to year..." (Signed Borsutsky.)

In a later letter, from August 1902, he informed of the development and flourishing of the new organization and Orheyev that had taken place over more than a year.

"It is true that if we make such demands, the number of people who will be prepared to join the organization will be very small. But we must recall that this small number will be those people who will be able to bear the entire burden of the deed. It would be sufficient if three or four members would be found in the entire city who would take these obligations upon themselves. If we indeed lose thousands of inactive organizations in numbers and in locations, and only 100 remain, these would be strong and solid organizations composed of responsible members who truly love Zion and are prepared to make sacrifices to develop the movement. For what good to us are those who pay their dues and purchase shares when they stand far from the ideals of the movement, and their Zionism is restricted to the donation of money to some cause or another, without delving into the depths of the revival of the nation and the redemption of the Land for the nation..."

And once again... Zionism for the broad masses...

As a man of the people and a democrat in the full sense of the term, he did not make peace with the fact that even after the important organizational development that took place after the Zionist Congress, the Zionist movement had not yet turned into a broad national movement based upon and relying upon the masses of the people. In one of his letters to M. Usishkin he wrote: (26 Cheshvan 5662, 1901) "... In the regional assemblies and periodical literature we hear one voice and one statement: The work is lax and the organizations are run heavily. We always find reason to place the blame upon a different scapegoat: Some attribute the decline in our movement to famine, the general recession, etc. I see the reason in the organizations themselves:

"Every large edifice, the Congress, the active committee, the authorizing institution and others stands on a rotting and weak base, and we should not be surprised if they weaken or fall completely. The organization is the kernel from which the Zionism is expressed, and what hope can we have in all of our efforts if the kernel has no life force to propagate and flourish. Why should we deceive ourselves? Why should we delude ourselves with images that we have a large army of Zionists and of organizations, when in reality our power is extremely small and poor? 158 organizations are registered in the region of Bessarabia and Podolia of which 59 have not written one word to the authorizing committee throughout the entire year. Only 39 of these organizations sent their dues (shkalim) to Kiev. We do not have numbers from the other regions, but I am sure that approximately the same situation applies to them as well…"

M. R.

Chapter 125

Avraham Duchovny of blessed memory

Translated by Jerrold Landau

"Avraham Our Forefather"

"Avraham Avinu" (Avraham our Forefather) was the nickname of the grandfather of Nissan Duchovny. Avraham earned his livelihood from baking various pastries and cakes that were sold on the days of the fair. He also was involved in the sale of liquor and tobacco on the black market. After a time he was captured, fined a large sum of money, and was set to be sent to jail. He escaped to Romania, and returned to Orheyev after wandering for five or six years.

He made atonement for his "non-kosher" livelihood. He would give tithes to the poor from his meager earnings. He maintained this custom throughout his life. In his old age when he no longer had the means of earning a livelihood, he sold his remaining moveable goods and set aside the full tithes from the proceeds. He observed the commandments, and was meticulous in matters between man and G-d and between man and man. He was a man of the book, and would immerse himself daily in the mikvah of the Great Synagogue, in which according to tradition the Besht (ed. note: Baal Shem Tov, the founder of Hassidism) had immersed himself. Even during the winter, when there was a layer of ice upon the mikvah waters, he would break the ice and fulfill the mitzvah of immersion.

Indeed, the man was a student of Avraham our Forefather, modest and supportive of the poor.

Chapter 126

Rabbi Getzel Honik of blessed memory

Translated by Jerrold Landau

Figure 235 - Getzel Honik

Reb Getzel was one of the veteran residents. He was from a family of wheat merchants. He himself was not successful in business, and he sustained his family by being a "trusted person" for one of the gentile forest owners near the cities. This work became difficult in his old age, and the economic pressure in the household increased.

Despite all this, Reb Getzel was always content with his lot. He even put aside tithes for the poor, and fulfilled the commandment of entertaining guests each Sabbath eve, even though he did not have everything that was needed for the honor of the Sabbath. With his pure faith, he trusted that the Creator of the World would not leave Getzel to his fate. With the help of G-d, his wife would take care of him, his children, and even the guest that the Holy One Blessed Be He would prepare for him in the synagogue on the Eve of the Sabbath.

During the 1880s, the edict of expulsion was issued to the Jews of Bessarabia, and Reb Getzel had to abandon his place of residence in the village. Even then he did not complain, but rather bore everything with quiet and calm. He took up the wanderer's staff, gathered his entire family and set out for Orheyev. As he was approaching the city, he heard the voice of weeping. He saw a woman standing next to the carcass of her animal. Reb Getzel approached her and asked her why she was weeping. The woman intimated to the tragedy that took place to her with the loss of the cow, her only source of livelihood. Reb Getzel comforted her and said to her: "Here is my cow and wagon, take them, and you will soon be able to give of its milk to your children."

He died in the bosom of his family at a ripe old age.

Chapter 127

Rabbi Alter Menashes of blessed memory

Translated by Jerrold Landau

Reb Alter was of tall stature, both physically and spiritually. His face was adorned with a white beard. He wore a long, wide hemmed cloak, and his tallis katan stuck out from under his cloak, with the tzitzis extended to his knees. He exuded honor. He was learned and observant of the commandments. He was tolerant of the non-observant even though he tried to influence them from his spirit. It was said of him that he was of two minds, the first to keep the Torah and the 613 commandments in their entirety, and the second to be part of the "liberal" world without being affected by it. He was an enthusiastic lover of Zion. His livelihood and that of his family was from a textile store, which was run primarily by his wife. Reb Alter himself dedicated most of his time to various communal endeavors. The study of Torah was primary. Therefore, he supervised the students in the Yeshiva. He went to the Yeshiva every day during the lessons, discussed with the students, and derived pleasure from the student who knew how to answer his questions.

He was involved in the unique activity of obtaining books for the kloiz. What did he do? He would go to the homes of mourners or those observing yahrzeit for a member of the family, and collect both secular and holy books in memory of the departed. He would bring the books to the bookbinder, who would engrave upon the cover or the front page the name of the donor, the name of the deceased, the date of the memorial and the day that the book was received. The letters were in engraved gold, and he added to this: "To strengthen and add might to Torah."

Even though Reb Alter held fast to the Orthodox faith that G-d would send his Messiah to redeem the nation and the Land, he opposed the opinion of the Orthodox that a Jew is forbidden "to bring near the end." He engaged in a fierce debate with the Orthodox people who excommunicated the Chibat Zion movement and its activists. Reb Alter especially angered them by obtaining secular books for the large kloiz, dealing primarily with the Zionist movement and other national problems. He as well was careful about books of apostasy. However, the Orthodox did not tolerate this, and they placed all sorts of obstacles before him. It came to the point where they would destroy books that were not in accordance with their spirit.

Reb Alter had two daughters and one son. The daughters studied in an external manner – for there was not yet a high school in the city. He spent most of his time in educating his only son Menashe. He would accompany him to the cheder and pour over the studies with him. When his son got older, he went to study in university and abandoned religious observance. Of course, this was not pleasing to Reb Alter, but he bore this calmly and wisely. His relationship to his daughter, the wife of Shmuel Gershon Baru was quite different. After her marriage, she refused to wear a wig as befits a proper, modest woman. Reb Alter could not make peace with this, and excommunicated his daughter. He did not visit her home for a long time.

When B. Z. Furer decided in 1912 to travel to the land of Israel along with his 8 year old son Herzl in order to tour the Land, and Reb Alter found out, he hastened to prepare two tallis kattans (ritual fringed undergarments). He gave them to Furer and said: "Take these from me, and I hope that you and your son will use them according to the law and tradition, and if not for G-d, then at least for me, and you should not remove them until you arrive home in peace…"

Chapter 128

Yitzchak Shvartz of blessed memory

Translated by Jerrold Landau

Yitzchak was born in Orheyev. He was educated in the home of his stepfather Reb Baruch – a shochet. He became involved in the Zionist movement and the dissemination of the Hebrew language at a young age. He was the first to gather the working youth around him to draw them near to the Tzeirei Zion movement (1910-1915). As a veteran man of the community, he had a great role in communal life and all of its various problems. He fought based upon the principals of democracy, and demonstrated his nationalism at every citizen's meeting. Issues of the Zionist movement and Hebrew culture were always at the forefront of public and private debates with the representatives of the left leaning and assimilationist streams in our city. In 1912, he realized his dream of making aliya to the Land of his desire, however due to his weak physical state, he did not withstand the difficulties of absorption in the Land. He spent a few months there, and then left to the dismay of his heart.

Figure 236 - Yitzchak Shvartz

During the 1920s, he was invited to the Tzeirei Zion center in Kishinev, and played an honorable role among the central people of the movement.

At the end of the 1930s, he was invited to the Hebrew Gymnasium in Beltsy as a teacher of Hebrew literature for the upper grades. He set up a Tzeirei Zion chapter which he successfully headed until his last day. The students of the gymnasium and members of the chapter revered and honored him greatly.

Yitzchak became ill in 1934, and was transferred to a hospital in Iasi. He underwent an operation, and died after great suffering.

The Teacher and Counselor

There are teachers who impart knowledge to their students, and those who forge the complete character of their charges. Yitzchak Shvartz was graced with a blended talent: of being a teacher and scholar as well as an educator and counselor. He was a teacher of Hebrew language and literature, and educator and counselor for Zionism with his entire essence, and a Socialist who was into the renewal of man and society. All of these were intertwined in a single unity that could not be separated or detracted from. He imparted these characteristics to his students in an enchanting manner. The hours of study were not classes where one studies a chapter in order to be able to repeat it during the following class. The studies were intertwined with broad knowledge, depth of understanding of the nation and the world, and the spirit of man that struggles for justice and righteousness.

Who does not recall his sudden appearances in the Gordonia hall in Beltsy in 1929? Bad tidings were arriving from the Land. These were days of disturbances and crisis. The youth who knew Communism from afar were enchanted by it and went along the path of assimilation. Yitzchak would arrive and explain: the revolt of the workers of Vienna – the fall of the Mivtzar workers movement during those days – the youth in confusion. He would smooth over hills and restore faith through his great power of persuasion.

What was his power in the Tzeirei Zion movement? Did he dedicate his energy solely to organizational activities as the chairman of the movement in Beltsy? He spent his prime energy in educating the generation with the proper values, and in nurturing the faith in the future of the nation in the Land and the working man.

When he was on his sickbed, a short time before his passing, I brought him new books that were printed in the Land as a gift from his charges. How happy was he to know that his students shared common interests with him.

Throughout the Land, in its kibbutzim, moshavim, villages and towns, there live many workers who were sheltered under his protection and the tent of his doctrine. All of them remember him with awe and holiness.

Zvi Pinkenzon.

Figure 237 - Motel Goldshtern

Figure 238 - Yonah Vurgaft

Figure 239 - Pinchas Shaposhnik

Figure 240 - Yosef Mundrian

Figure 241 - Yosef Muchnik

Part V - In Summary

Chapter 129

The First Meeting of Orheyev Natives in Israel

Translated by Jerrold Landau

Figure 242 - Emblem prepared for the first convention – The Bridge

Much was spoken among the natives our city, who came together for various meetings and joyous occasions, about the gatherings of Orheyev natives in Israel – gatherings that took place to unite ourselves with the past for a brief period. The idea crystallized with time, and at a meeting of friends who were natives of Orheyev at a joyous occasion of one of our townsfolk, the idea of a gathering came up again. Efforts were made, and the gathering took place.

Those who began should be blessed, and those who continue should be strengthened.

The gathering left a great impression. The joy was great when the natives of Orheyev arrived in the Chof Movie Theater in Hadera. Those from far and near met with those who were veterans in the Land along with recent arrivals. The gathering was a gathering of brothers.

From the words of the opening:

Brothers and sisters!

Orheyev, one of the many towns in the region of Bessarabia, surrounded by forests and rivers, fields and gardens, existed for hundreds of years, wove its fabric of life faithfully and with constancy in the traditional Jewish way of life from generation to generation. In the latter generation, we saw the people as faithful to the Zionist ideal, which slowly captured the hearts.

The city was somewhat remote. Railway lines or roads did not reach it. However, it was alert to anything that went on in the life of the Jewish community.

Zionist activity began in the town already from the time of Chovevei Zion. After the year 1905, the first immigrants from the town arrived in the land of Israel. There was a break in Zionist activity for some time with the outbreak of the First World War. Then the Russian Revolution came, and its echoes arrived to our corner as well. At first there was valiant activity by the veteran Zionist forces. With the annexation of Bessarabia to Romania, the town became the first stop for the refugees from Petliura's sword, who crossed the Dniester by the thousands. How great and wonderful was the alertness and dedication of the residents of our town toward these refugees. We were children when we set out for the fields at night along a path that was no path, to greet them and house them among our compatriots.

Groups of the best of the Russian Zionist youth reached our town along with these refugees. With their influence and participation, the Zionist and pioneering activity in the town grew. The town became full of life and energy – and the youth began to organize and embark upon Zionist activity, organization for labor, and efforts for the national funds. The mass meetings in the Kloizes are remembered well, as is the generosity of the town.

In 1925, the gymnasium students formed the pioneering youth movement. Hechalutz and a Hebrew youth group called Bnei Yisrael were formed. The activities of Hechalutz were far reaching. It grew and took in hundreds of youth organized for the purpose of aliya to the Land.

Aliya continued from then until the final days before the Holocaust, at times in large groups and at times by individuals. Both types spread through the land.

Then a small group of Orheyev natives hatched the idea of organizing this gathering. Our strong desire is to establish and strengthen it, not only to remember the departed – even though that is indeed a great commandment –

but also so that brothers from far and near can gather together and unite in mutual assistance:

1. To establish a fund for mutual assistance

2. To publish a book that will perpetuate the martyrs of Orheyev and recall the sons and daughters who were murdered by the enemy.

We are aware of the faithfulness and friendship of the natives of Orheyev, who know how to fulfill what they took upon themselves.

Dear natives of Orheyev, in this gathering we will strengthen our bond and brotherhood among us, and fulfill that which our friends, brothers and sisters commanded us in their deaths – to live in the Land a life of labor, a life of building and creativity.

The natives of Orheyev worked and established a great deal in this Land, and we are fortunate that we merited being among the first of the actualizers and builders – among those who laid the cornerstone for numerous enterprises that were instrumental in assisting in the establishment of the state. Dear brothers! Notice that on the lapel of your clothing is a photo of the bridge over the Reat River that linked the town to the outside world. We wish ourselves that the bridge will be renewed in the near future, and our brothers and sisters who remained there will cross it, and we will all merit to gather together under the skies of our Land.

May you all be blessed, those who came and those who were unable to come...

After these words of introduction, the festive program began with the participation of the native of our town, Chava Yoelit-Varda, Yaakov Zeevi and his daughter Galila, Bava and Moshe Bik and the choir he directed, the comrade David Vardi and others.

The following day, friendly discussions took place about the past, that which is distant, and about future activities. The foundations for the publication of a book on Orheyev were laid...

Dov Sinai

Chapter 130

The Second Gathering of Orheyev Natives in Israel

From the Words of Y. Spivak

Translated by Jerrold Landau

It is an ancient custom, a tradition from time immemorial, to recall at set times the names of those who are no longer with us, to unite ourselves with their memory in order to bring merit to their souls. This custom took root in our traditional faith, a faith of the immortality of the soul. We believe that when the end comes to the body, the spirit does not end. It has continuity and the chain is not severed… Continuity exists in our history, a continuity that unites all of the links across the face of the earth and through the depths of the generations into one unity. A continuity that has responsibility for the past and a destiny for the future. "For the spirit is in man," and the spirit is not confined in space, and not restricted to a period of time… If this is true for an individual life, how much more so for the life of a community.

Dear friends! Orheyev, our native city, is no more. It was destroyed, annihilated, and almost wiped off from beneath the G-d's heavens. Its people were murdered by sword and fire, hunger and thirst, and it is not know if they all found their graves… Thus was the fate of all those holy communities over which the German Amalek waved its impure hand with the destructive campaign of the swastika. This was also the fate of Orheyev, our native city.

We are under the obligation to establish a memorial monument so that its name will not be forgotten from our midst, as long as we, the final generation who were born, educated, and raised there, are still alive – its name will be remembered with a blessing. However, we are not the last ones. After us will come the generation of our dear Sabras, who did not know what came before them, and will not feel any connection to the generation from which we were hewn… as if the chain has been severed. Therefore, we are obligated to establish a token of memorial to the crucible that forged us.

We are not the only ones who are occupied with this type of activity. The feeling of the need to establish a memorial to that which preceded us is a national feeling, and it afflicts all of us and demands actualization, for we have not fulfilled our obligation regarding the martyrs who perished during the time of the Holocaust.

Friends! About two months ago, the "Law of the Holocaust and Might – Yad Vashem" was brought before the Knesset. This is a law that has no precedent in any nation or language – for the matter with which it deals is unique. It never occurred before in the history of man on earth.

The name "Shoah" designates the destruction of European Jewry, the annihilation of six and a half million of our Jewish brethren, the destruction of thousands of Jewish communities, myriads of cultural enterprises and institutions, synagogues, study halls, hospitals, old age homes, orphanages, children's homes. The destruction encompassed 21 countries in Europe. These were countries in which there were 8.5 million Jews prior to the war, and in which approximately 1 million survivors remained after the war as refugees from the sword. Our Jewish brethren were not killed in the battlefield, but rather by pre-planned and organized murder and annihilation by governments, by police that were established by force of law so to speak, and that existed with the participation of the German nation. These people perpetrated despicable murderous deeds in the open, before the eyes of the nations in which our brethren dwelled for hundreds of years. These beasts of prey had but one aim – to wipe out the name of Israel from the face of the earth, to destroy its culture, and to annihilate its progeny and memory.

The law came to ensure the establishment of a memorial for every Jewish person in such a manner that we will be able to collect the names of all those who perished though the designs of the evil hands. A ledger will be organized in which the names of each of the martyrs will be registered. This ledger will bring before us the names of our brothers and sisters, fathers and children, grandparents and grandchildren – all of them testifying to the horrific deeds that were perpetrated by the people of the nations of Europe during in the middle of the 20th century... We will certainly guard the memory of the early generations in our hearts, for the Jewish nation keeps faith with its past.

We have been advised that we should establish a central repository in which will be preserved every remnant and picture testifying to the ways of life, the struggles, the youthful energy and talents, the fear of Heaven and piety, the joy of life of the toiling masses. All of this should be gathered into a central storehouse. This storehouse will be here, in the holy city of Jerusalem... This and more. They also discussed there about granting citizenship to all of those of our nation who were murdered during the time of the Holocaust. There is no precedent in the world in granting citizenship to those who are no longer alive, but there is also no precedent to this situation in the world – a precedent to the murder of 1,200,000 children from among the 6,500,000 souls, children and babies... What is the meaning of this concept? I would say that it is an Israelite concept, from way back, the concept of being "gathered unto one's people" (ed. note: the term that the Torah uses for the death of the patriarchs of the Jewish people).

The profane intention of the murderers was to annihilate us and to wipe out the name of Israel from the face of the earth. We, the entire nation, will gather them in as citizens in the roster of citizens of the state. Thus we will gather them to the bosom of the homeland, and from there, they will not be cut off from their people. This memorial citizenship will symbolize the "monument", their place after their deaths.

This book that we intend to publish will free us from the agonies of guilt feelings, for it is more than ten years from when the terrible Holocaust overtook the community of Orheyev, our native town, and we have not rectified the injustice. Each one of us turned to our own worries and concerns. There was a lack of activity from our side, and we completely passed over one of the most tragic and stormy events. This lacuna is felt and stands out now even more so after the Knesset has already decided to deal with the matter of perpetuating the names of the cities and towns.

Our duty is a holy duty as well as a great merit. We who are gathered here are living in the Land, and we are able to think and prepare plans for the establishment of a memorial to the martyrs of the community of Orheyev, as well as to the community itself.

We must surely remember that we are the only ones upon whom this obligation rests. Aside from us, nobody will take upon themselves this task. If we are here – everyone is here. We are the first to this task, we, who are tied to Orheyev with flesh and blood. There, we spent the best of our days, the days of childhood and youth. There, our spiritual and communal spirit was forged. There, we nurtured the longing of our souls. Now, there is no memory to all of this. Who will come to fill the lacuna and correct the injustice, if not us…

Chapter 131

The Celebration of a Friend

Translated by Jerrold Landau

(On the occasion of the 70ᵗʰ birthday of Y. Spivak)

To mark the occasion, D. Sinai arranged a party in his house in Kiryat Chaim. The undersigned were unable to participate due to their state of health, and they sent the following greetings.

To the chairman of our organization, members of the committee, and to you, our dear friends, Yitzchak and Yehudit, we send our heartfelt greetings.

The day of July 22, 1956 will be etched upon the hearts of each of us as the date of an important event, for us, Orheyev natives, have merited to mark the celebration of a faithful and revered friend, our friend Yitzchak Spivak.

A significant number of erudite people stemmed from Orheyev, but few are found among us in the Land, and of those, many are not involved in our community. Now, our member Spivak, you stood ready and prepared for the call, and for the activity in our midst.

Indeed, this festive gathering knows to appreciate your efforts and your dedication for the joint enterprise, the perpetuation of the name of our city, our native town of the past, and its murdered sons. Indeed, you are fortunate that you merited thus, and we are fortunate that we participate in this.

It is a special merit for us that we have merited noting the harvest of the fruit of your labor on this date. You toiled for decades, you dedicated your energies and thoughts to creativity in the fields of education and culture. From the oral doctrine that you imparted during your young age to the school students, you have successfully moved to the written doctrine. With your articles in periodical newspapers, you have expressed heartfelt thoughts to the hearts of the community. However, you have specially searched out a way to the heart of the child and the youth, and you never tired of publishing articles that would light the way for the younger generation.

I recall those long gone days when I was a youth, and I was together with you in the Hebrew Speakers club in our city. Your name already preceded you, and you were only 17 years old – albeit rich in thought and expression. You displayed your diligence, your great ability to learn and teach, to think and create. Now, we have merited to celebrate the celebration of your harvest, and we must recite the Shehecheyanu blessing.

Our blessing to you is that you merit to have many more years of activity for the public with your wife Yehudit as your faithful partner.

From the depths of the heart,
Mordechai and Zipora Rotkov

Figure 243 - Board of Orheyev descendants
Seated from right to left: 1. Aliza Shemovny 2. Mordechai Rotkov 3. Dov Sinai 4. Yitzchak Spivak 5. Mordechai Frank 6. Yonah Shamban 7. Malovatsky
Standing from right to left: 1. Shneur Geynichovitz 2. Aizik Rozenfeld 3. Chayim Lipshin 4. Aharon Filarsky 5. Yaakov Zeevi 6. Yitzchak Rapoport 7. Frayda Zokolov

Chapter 132

From the Committee to the Editorial Board

Translated by Jerrold Landau

In this book that is before us, memories that are close to the hearts of every native of Orheyev are laid out. They place the near and distant past before our eyes.

Many of us thought about the idea of perpetuation that which is dear to us, and we imposed the actualization of this task upon Yitzchak Spivak, Mordechai Rotkov, and Mordechai Frank. They answered us willingly, and succeeded at this…

These friends embarked upon their task without anything prepared before them. They had to search for material that was connected to Orheyev from any source. This material required sifting and reworking until it was in a fitting form.

An extremely great effort was undertaken by these friends, and there is no power in these words to appropriately express our appreciation for their efforts.

Yitzchak Spivak, the teacher and scribe, dedicated himself with great diligence to this enterprise, despite the fact that he left our city when he was still young. His activities are his praise. Mordechai Rotkov, whose task was to collect the greater portion of the material, made his nights like days, as he refined the manuscripts and prepared them for editing.

Finally, our friend Mordechai Frank, who was the life force in the publication of the book, worked in various roles, from the gathering of material, the working of the material, preparing the book in general, and bringing it to print.

We know that the editorial committee was at the threshold of despair on more than one occasion. The doubts and disappointments gnawed at the heart, and in moments of doubt and struggle, the desired objective floated and stood before their eyes – to establish a memorial for our city. That is what encouraged their spirit to continue with the burden until the publication of the book.

It is clear to us that without the dedication and diligence of the members of the editorial board to this holy task, we would not have succeeded in seeing the book being published.

Therefore, we extend to you, our dear friends, thanks and blessings. May your strength continue!

We are certain that this memorial enterprise that you have established for our city will stand as a monument for future generations…

The Committee of Orheyev Natives
23 Iyar 5619
The 11th year of the State of Israel
May 31, 1959

Chapter 133

From the Editorial Board to the Committee

Translated by Jerrold Landau

With the appearance of the book, we see it as our pleasant duty to come before the members of the committee and to express our deep gratitude for the trust that you placed in us in giving us the responsibility of preparing the book and publishing it.

We must apologize for the extreme lateness of its publication, a matter that caused deep disappointment to all those who followed our work closely. Many obstacles obstructed our path and caused many delays.

As we come now to give our blessings to the completed task, we would not fulfil our obligation unless we note the role of our friend Dov Sinai in establishing this memorial enterprise to the community of Orheyev.

Dov stood at the head of the enterprise from its beginning, by establishing the organization of Orheyev natives. In the two gatherings, he encouraged and urged the establishment of a memorial to our city. Today, we, along with him, are able to bless the conclusion of the enterprise.

The book, the fruits of our collective efforts, is presented to the natives of Orheyev and to all of our brethren who take interest in it.

Av 5719 August 10, 1959
The Editors

TABLE OF CONTENTS IN ORIGINAL BOOK

Translated By Boaz Nadler & Marsha Kayser & Terry Lasky

Part III - Memoirs

A: Education and Culture

B: In the labor group

C: The cooperative group

D: In Agriculture

Part IV - The Holocaust

Part V - In Summary

INDEX

A

B

C

D

Index of the Roman Numeral Numbered Pages

www.ingramcontent.com/pod-product-compliance
Lightning Source LLC
Chambersburg PA
CBHW082002150426
42814CB00005BA/197